THE VALUE OF NAMES AND OTHER PLAYS

THE VALUE OF NAMES AND OTHER PLAYS

Jeffrey Sweet

Foreword by Richard Christiansen

NORTHWESTERN UNIVERSITY PRESS
EVANSTON, ILLINOIS

Northwestern University Press
www.nupress.northwestern.edu

Printed in the United States of America

10   9   8   7   6   5   4   3   2   1

Library of Congress Cataloging-in-Publication Data

Sweet, Jeffrey, 1950–
    The value of names and other plays / Jeffrey Sweet.
       p. cm.
    ISBN-13: 978-0-8101-2395-3 (pbk. : alk. paper)
    ISBN-10: 0-8101-2395-9 (pbk. : alk. paper)
    I. Title.
    PS3569.W369V33 2008
    812.54—dc22
                                      2007049759

♾ The paper used in this publication meets the minimum requirements of the
American National Standard for Information Sciences—Permanence of Paper
for Printed Library Materials, ANSI Z39.48-1992.

To the memory of my father,
James Stouder Sweet

CONTENTS

FOREWORD

Richard Christiansen

The plays contained in this collection cover three decades of the work of a man who has remained determinedly and zealously devoted to the theater. Since coming of age as a writer in the late seventies, Jeff Sweet has served at various times as journalist, historian, critic, editor, and teacher, but his central goal and abiding passion through all those years has been to write for the living stage.

He has been influenced in his approach by the improvisational techniques of Chicago theatermakers, whom he chronicled in his pioneering 1978 oral history, *Something Wonderful Right Away*, and some of his scripts indeed have had their start as exercises in improvisation; but in print, and in performance, his plays are carefully plotted, meticulously paced, and, when necessary, exhaustively researched. At the same time, he is a playwright of great surprises, capable of coming up with a knockout curtain line (see *The Value of Names*) and a razor-sharp riposte (see *Stay Till Morning*). He knows how to toss off a stunning zinger as well as how to put together a solid story.

The sweep of action in Sweet's plays (and his ventures into musical theater, which are not included here) is far ranging. Their locale can be a small town (*Porch*) or a big city (*Bluff*), and their time frame can be nineteenth-century Chicago (*American Enterprise*) or post–World War II Germany (*Berlin '45*). Whatever the play's scale, small or large, and whatever its mood, light or dark, its characters are always keenly imagined and truly felt, whether they are dealing with domestic details or global matters. What makes remarkable such works as *Court-Martial at Fort Devens* and especially *The Action Against Sol Schumann* is not so much their historical veracity as their human truths—the way in which the eternal moral issues are embedded in the specific conflicts of vivid, particular characters, all of whom are trying to cope with the crises of life that are confronting them.

This is certainly evident in two key works, both of which concern the devastating aftermath of historic events. *The Value of Names* takes on the large, well-documented topic of blacklisting in America in the 1950s but does so within the framework of a spare, tightly constructed three-character drama set in 1983. The issue here is huge, but it is given its immediate, urgent impact through the intimacy of the story and through the minutely observed actions in the interplay of the characters. The historical background of the Holocaust that surrounds the title character in *The Action Against Sol Schumann* is immense, but the deep emotions and the profound shattering of personal relationships in the play are unleashed many years after World War II—in Ronald Reagan's America.

Like almost all the plays in this anthology, *The Value of Names* and *The Action Against Sol Schumann* have been produced at Sweet's artistic home base, Victory Gardens Theater in Chicago, and it has been my pleasure over the years to see them there as they were faithfully presented. Reading the plays now in this collection, there is a renewed pleasure in encountering and enjoying the work of a versatile and compassionate artist, who is at once a dedicated playwright and a genuine mensch.

ACKNOWLEDGMENTS

I owe particular debts to Dennis Zacek, Marcie McVay, Sandy Shinner, and Joyce Sloane of the Victory Gardens Theater, and to Richard Christiansen, who, as critic for the *Chicago Tribune,* managed the delicate balancing act of both maintaining standards and encouraging the community even when he had to write disappointed reviews. A big thanks, too, to Gary Houston, both for his fine work as an actor in my plays and for suggesting to the folks at Northwestern University Press that this book was worth doing.

INTRODUCTION

My friend was alarmed. She had just read a draft of my play *Flyovers* in which the leading character is the target of a blackmail plot and gets beaten up. "My God, Jeff, when did this happen to you?"

It didn't. It happened to someone I knew many years earlier, though I had changed incidents and invented characters to enhance the plot.

It's a common assumption that playwrights primarily mine the events of their own lives for what they write. Certainly Tennessee Williams, Eugene O'Neill, Neil Simon, Wendy Wasserstein, and Lanford Wilson did, and in the process they produced some of their best works.

I may be an exception. I don't write overtly autobiographic plays. I don't summon up personal experiences, build characters based on me, or write my side of what occurred. I don't pay back old lovers, family, friends, or adversaries by placing them in contests with surrogates for me and then have the surrogates respond with what I should have had the wit to say or do in real life.

Instead, I seem to find myself hooked on other people's situations— something that has happened or could happen to someone I either know or know of, or a speculation on a choice faced by someone in another time or place triggered by an intriguing aspect of a documentary or an item I've read. If I find a character sneaking into the work who threatens to become my mouthpiece, I write him out. Autobiographical characters often too overtly articulate the play's theme or display an off-putting combination of passivity, self-righteousness, and self-pity.

My plays seem to fall into two groups—ones that are extensions of my speculations about people vaguely in my circle of acquaintance and ones with their roots in a political or historical subject that has grabbed my interest. Among the former in this book are *Porch*, *With and Without*, *Bluff*, and *Stay Till Morning*. Among the latter are *American*

Enterprise, The Action Against Sol Schumann, Berlin '45, and *Court-Martial at Fort Devens.*

The interest in history probably came from my father, James. He earned degrees in the subject from Harvard and University of California, Los Angeles, and had hoped for a career teaching at a university. To his dismay, when he was assigned a class, he discovered that he couldn't convey his excitement about the subject to a roomful of undergraduates who were only there to fulfill a course requirement. Instead, he spent most of his career writing in the service of institutions (the Library of Congress, Northwestern University, and the University of Chicago). He claimed particular satisfaction in assisting Chief Justice Earl Warren on two speeches Warren gave in the fifties. One, delivered in St. Louis, was about the erosion of civil liberties. The other, delivered in Madison, Wisconsin, was a tribute to "Fighting Bob" La Follette, the progressive politician who stood in obvious contrast to another figure from that state, Senator Joseph McCarthy. Both speeches were interpreted at the time as being Warren's attack on McCarthyism, though the term wasn't used in either speech. The bulk of the language was Warren's, but my father had the satisfaction of seeing significant elements of his drafts make it to the versions that were delivered and published. Though Dad felt the work he did to be of value, I know that when he was young he had dreamed of writing fiction. He put this aside when he had to support a family, but he was the one who gave me the idea that one could make a life writing. (A life, if not a living.) It gave me a good deal of satisfaction that he viewed my work as an outgrowth of his hopes. He died on May 8, 2007.

My mother, Vivian, brought music and performance to the mix. She studied violin at Juilliard; played duets with pianist William Kapell; worked in orchestras on Broadway, at Radio City Music Hall, and in the USO; and was part of the string section behind Frank Sinatra during his run at New York's Paramount Theater. Later, she organized a quartet that toured the Chicago area and taught a lot of kids what to do with a bow.

My parents introduced me to the theater early. One of the first LPs they gave me was the original cast recording of *Oklahoma!* and the first professional show I saw was a touring production of *The Music Man.* We settled in Evanston, a suburb of Chicago (and home of Northwestern University) mostly because of the reputation of the school system. I was a bookish kid who was inept at sports, wore glasses, and mostly made friends with girls. I found a refuge in acting—taking drama classes in downtown Chicago on Saturdays, attending a summer camp that put up plays, and doing a little professional work on local TV. (My mother was terrified I might actually try to be an actor when I grew up, and after a couple of jobs she called the agent who had gotten me the work and told him not to get me any more. She wanted me to be normal. Ha!)

Guests on Jack Paar's TV show helped define the direction I wanted to explore. Mike Nichols and Elaine May performed their scene about the rocket scientist and his Jewish mother, and I was startled. How could Elaine May possibly be quoting my mom on national TV? In 1963, when I was a freshman in high school, most of the kids around me were waking up to something new via the Beatles, but for me the call came from four other young Brits—Alan Bennett, Peter Cook, Jonathan Miller, and Dudley Moore. On Paar's show, they offered an excerpt from their revue, *Beyond the Fringe*. It didn't escape my attention that Nichols and May and the *Fringe* team had achieved status by mocking authority in material they had created themselves. That looked like fun.

My early efforts were woeful imitations of these satirists. (I discovered later that being a satirist requires something more than an attitude. You actually have to know a little something about what you're mocking.) I was lucky to attend Evanston Township High School. With faculty support, I put up a series of original revues and one acts and started learning something about what the stage demands of a writer.

In those days, Chicago was not a lively theater town. New York producers sent us road companies of Broadway shows, the legendary Alvina Krause taught acting at Northwestern, and The Second City had launched in 1959, but if you were seriously interested in writing for the stage, you had to go to New York. So I did. In 1967, I enrolled at New York University (NYU), eventually getting a bachelor's of fine arts in film. My professors were a starry lot—Martin Scorsese was still there teaching film, Paul Simon ran a seminar in songwriting, and Clive Barnes taught a course in critical writing.

While I was at NYU, I also was admitted to the BMI Lehman Engel Musical Theatre Workshop as a composer-lyricist. Allan Becker, an executive at BMI, had recruited Broadway musical director Lehman Engel to head a program in which Engel trained developing composers and lyricists. I was eighteen when I joined, and my classmates and colleagues during my six years there included Edward Kleban, Maury Yeston, Thomas Newman, Susan Birkenhead, Brooks Morton, Donald Siegal, Howard Marren, and Alan Menken.

At the beginning of the first year of the workshop, Engel gave each of us an anthology of American drama, and over the next several months he asked everyone in the class to write songs for the same moments in some of the plays. The first assignment was the moment in Tennessee Williams's *The Rose Tattoo* when Serafina learns her husband has died. Then we were told to write a song of attempted seduction for the wayward husband in George Axelrod's *The Seven-Year Itch.* Some of the songs the students brought in were glorious; more fell short in one way or another. Drawing on these dozen or so attempts by a roomful of talented people to solve the same problems, Lehman extrapolated theories about how successful songs for the theater are built and what pitfalls can be avoided. It was the first time it occurred to me that such theorizing was possible or that it could be helpful in creating material.

In the meantime, Clive Barnes was kind enough to find something in my critical writing worth encouraging, and he introduced me to Otis L. Guernsey Jr., the editor of the *Best Plays Annual* and *The Dramatists Guild Quarterly.* Otis recruited me to write pieces for the *Quarterly* and eventually made me an associate editor. He also asked me to join him as junior editor of the *Best Plays Annual,* in which capacity each year I chose what I thought were the ten best plays and wrote a long article discussing the season. I found myself applying some of Engel's theories in analyzing what I thought successful and problematic in other people's writing. When I encountered issues that I didn't think his system addressed, I tried to come up with theories of my own.

One night, a couple of years out of college, while scouting for the *Best Plays Annual,* I saw a preview off-off-Broadway of a new work about the residents of a shabby hotel called *Hot L Baltimore.* It floored me. I returned to see it again. In the lobby, I encountered a thin figure radiating nervous energy. I went up to him and guessed, "Lanford Wilson?" He conceded his identity. I wanted the excuse to talk to him, so I asked if he would agree to an interview. He said OK, and a few days later he submitted himself to my curiosity and tape recorder. Shortly thereafter, *Hot L* opened to rousing reviews and moved to a long commercial run off-Broadway. I phoned *Newsday*'s arts editor, Joe Koenenn, and told him I'd written an interview with its author and asked if he'd like to see it. He said yes, read it, published it, and did me the favor of giving me more interview assignments, leading to encounters with Richard Rodgers, Sheldon Harnick, and two of my *Beyond the Fringe* heroes, Peter Cook and Dudley Moore.

Around this time, I had begun to notice that many of the actors, writers, and directors I most admired in theater and film (including Nichols and May) were alumni of Chicago's two pioneering improvisational theaters, the Compass Players and The Second City. I wanted to read a book about this community and find out why so many people whose work spoke to me began their careers with these companies. When it turned out that no such book had been written, I decided to write it myself. The credits from *Newsday* served as credentials to the people I approached for interviews.

When I began work on the book, I thought I was taking a vacation from playwriting. It hadn't occurred to me that a company that creates comic scenes through improvisation would have much to teach a playwright. Then it dawned on me that the audience doesn't care how a scene is generated—whether by a handful of actors on their feet or by someone pounding away at the keyboard. All the audience cares about is whether the action compels its interest. This suggested that the same principles that make improvisation work might be adapted to writing material for the stage.

I had the benefit of several months of workshops with Second City director Sheldon Patinkin. I can't say that at the end of these workshops I could hold my own with the likes of Barbara Harris or Severn Darden, but I understood as I had never understood before what an actor needs to sustain a scene. I spent the next few years running around the country with a cassette recorder asking questions, and mostly the improv community was generous with their time. (I owe a particular debt of thanks to Mike Nichols who, after our interview, passed along word to other potential interviewees that the book was worth supporting.)

Something Wonderful Right Away was published in 1978, and I visited Chicago to publicize it. Joyce Sloane, one of the producers of The Second City, noted that my bio said that I was a playwright. She was on the board of the Victory Gardens Theater and introduced me to artistic director Dennis Zacek. A year later, Victory Gardens presented *Porch* in the first production of one of my plays that actually paid royalties, and that began an association that has endured almost three decades. As I write this, our latest collaboration, *Court-Martial at Fort Devens*, has just completed its premiere run there.

At about the same time I was finishing *Something Wonderful*, I grew frustrated with some of the writers' groups I had encountered. In 1978, I decided to try to put together a group of my own. I took the advice of those who suggested that, instead of limiting the group to writers, I should also get actors and directors into the mix. There were a few whom I knew from the start I wanted to be part of the group. I also invited a few whom I had gotten to know doing interviews for *Something Wonderful*, notably two couples, Mark and Barbara Gordon and Jerry Stiller and Anne Meara, all alumni of branches of Compass Players. Friends made some other recommendations. Julius Novick was convinced of the potential of one of his former students, which is how Donald Margulies joined. David Mamet told me that Jane Anderson struck him as having a particularly sharp mind; she came in as an actor but shifted to writing. Mark and Barbara suggested that their son Keith would be a good addition; he was sixteen when he became part of the group. Others who clocked time with us included Ellen Byron, Matt Witten, Kate Draper, Polly Adams, Winnie Holzman, Michael Wright, and the late Percy Granger. (Alas, we lost Barbara Gordon in 2007, too.)

I wanted to call the group the Negotiating Stage (because I believe successful scenes are negotiations between the characters), but the group voted instead to be called the New York Writers Bloc. We met weekly for ten years, mostly in each other's living rooms. Donald has spoken of the group being a place where we taught one another through example, experiment, and discussion, and I'd certainly agree. (Donald, of course, went on to win the Pulitzer Prize for *Dinner with Friends* and to write several other fine plays, Jane and Keith have become important filmmakers, Matt is active in TV, Michael wrote some very good books on playwriting and teaches, Anne wrote two well-received plays, and Winnie created *My So-Called Life* for TV and wrote the book of the musical *Wicked*.) The group finally broke up when a significant percentage of the membership moved to Los Angeles (and started a bloc there). While it lasted, the group was where I consistently received the most useful comments on works in progress, and I've carried the lessons learned from those friends and colleagues into all my subsequent work.

There is irony in the fact that I left the Chicago area to go to New York to pursue the theater but ultimately found my artistic home back in Chicago. (Though people often assume that I live in Chicago, I'm based in New York but visit my hometown whenever I can manage it.) I became active there toward the end of the first wave of the Chicago theater boom.

Several of the people featured in *Something Wonderful* told me that they had not been aware that they were part of anything special when they were working at the Compass or The Second City in the early days. I think, by contrast, that those of us who started working in Chicago in the seventies and eighties knew we were part of a wave that was significant and going to grow. Given that others knocking around during those years included David Mamet, Joan Allen, John Malkovich, Robert Falls, William Petersen, Frank Galati, Amy Morton, Gary Cole, James Sherman, Gary Sinise, Alan Gross, Del Close, Barbara Gaines, Harry J. Lennix, Mary Zimmerman, Stuart Gordon, Charles Smith, Laurie Metcalf, Austin Pendleton, Jeff Perry, William H. Macy, Roslyn Alexander, Mike Nussbaum, Russ Tutterow, Linda Kimbrough, Kristine Thatcher, Gary Griffin, Byrne Piven, Scott McPherson, Gary Houston, and dozens of stars in training at The Second City, it would be hard to be unaware of an extraordinary community and an extraordinary time. What delights me as I write this is that, more than thirty years since it began, the Chicago theater movement is alive and vital and still produces new talent and new work. It is an honor to keep company with them.

I have made a few adjustments in the texts. I generally have rejected the temptation to update, but I have added a handful of lines to more firmly establish that the action of some of these plays takes place in the specific years when they were premiered (e.g., *The Value of Names* debuted in 1983, and I've included reference to the year in one of Norma's speeches). I have also taken the opportunity to correct what now seem to me to be obvious technical errors, such as shifting the occasional passage from the past tense to the historical present. I will bet that most people who have seen these plays won't notice the emendations.

My comments on the scripts in this collection sometimes precede and sometimes follow the texts (sometimes both), depending on whether I think familiarity with the play in question is necessary for the remarks to register.

Incidentally, I maintain a rudimentary Web site at www.jeffreysweet .com and am happy to hear from readers or people attempting productions of the plays.

THE VALUE OF NAMES AND OTHER PLAYS

THREE SKETCHES

While working on *Something Wonderful Right Away,* I thought I would better understand the work created by The Second City by attempting sketches myself. Two of the following pieces—"The Award" and "Separate Vacations"—were originally written as exercises while I was a member of the New York Writers Bloc. "Cover" began as an outline I wrote that my friends Stephen Johnson, Sandra C. Hastie, and I then used as a basis for improvisations we did together. I finished the piece by rewriting a transcription of these improvs. All these pieces appeared in a revue called *Holding Patterns* that was presented by the Body Politic Theater in Chicago in 1981. The show was directed by Tom Mula and featured a cast that included Andrew Gorman, Tim Halligan, Felicity LaFortune, and Audrie J. Neenan. An off-off-Broadway production directed by John Monteith for the Directors Company included Fran Brill, Colleen Dodson, Bob Higgins, and Lee Wilkof.

The reference to Andros in "Separate Vacations" is a little nod in the direction of my late friend, actor-playwright Anthony Holland, who used to improvise verses at The Second City about a New York poet's obsession with goat-boys. "Cover" anticipated *With and Without,* which also began improvisationally and dealt with the politics of marriage. There is nothing remotely autobiographical about "The Award."

CHARACTERS

THE AWARD	SEPARATE VACATIONS	COVER
Lerner	Charles	Frank
	Nadine	Marty
	Myra	Diane
	Russell	

THE AWARD

[LERNER, *a well-dressed man in his midthirties, is discovered holding an award he has just been given.*]

LERNER: Thank you. This is an honor I never dreamed I'd . . . I mean, the Charles Jensen Briggs Award! There are so many people to thank. Professor Herman Krause, who was the first to encourage me. The Leona Fielding Foundation for the funding, because, let's face it, this does cost money. And, of course, my colleagues in the lab—Ira Crutcher, Fred Jory, Anita Pleshowsky, and Andy Kramer. And, of course, I want to . . . Wait a second, did I say Anita Pleshowsky? I'm sorry. I meant Anita Petrakoff. Petrakoff, Pleshowsky—you can see how I might, uh, confuse . . . [*Trying to remember*] Pleshowsky. Anita Pleshowsky . . . Oh, yes. I remember Anita Pleshow—we were in high school together. That's right. Mr. Champion's homeroom. Oh yes, I used to think that Anita was about the neatest person in the world. I would write her notes in social studies. Also in music, English, math, and hygiene. I would have written her notes in gym, but, of course, boys and girls don't do gym together. Though sometimes I would see her and the other girls in Mr. Champion's class running laps around the playground in their blue shorts and tops.

My feelings for Anita Pleshowsky were . . . Well, I thought about her, I dreamed about her, I followed her home and peeked through the window of Alma Ferret's School for Charm, where she took classes every Saturday at 10:30. She played very hard to get. If she saw me looking at her, she would look away, or make a face, or stick her tongue out.

And then, one day, Mr. Newman, the school counselor, called me into his office. He said to me, "Morris, um, I realize that you are a young man—a growing young person—and young people your age start to develop. And this development is sometimes awkward, sometimes painful. Sometimes we find ourselves attracted to another young person—a young lady, say—and we try to express our feelings. This is normal, this is natural. But sometimes the young lady in question doesn't feel the same way we do. This is something we must learn to accept. You in particular must learn to accept this because you find yourself in this situation. You know the young lady I'm referring to, Morris. Now, I think it would be best for everyone concerned if you cool it, OK? Do you understand what I mean? Good. You may go back to your class."

I think of this now. I think of Mr. Newman and the red wisps of hair on his knuckles. I think of the blush that I could feel suffusing my young cheeks upon learning that my secret yearnings and communications were not as secret as I had hoped. I think of these things, and I laugh.

For I have gotten over you, Anita Pleshowsky. You were once the object of my fantasies and daydreams, but that was fifteen years ago, and a lot of time has passed. Other women—nicer than you, smarter than you, prettier than you—have favored me with their company, and not one of them ever found cause to stick her tongue out at me.

I am beyond the reach of your cruelty. No, your sadism! I am untouched by it. Unmoved. If you were to phone me now, if you were to dial the number here—area code (212) 555-3076—if you were to call and say, "Morris, I am sorry. Morris, I want you. Morris, can you ever forgive me? Morris, please hold me in your arms and let me know the joy of you!" . . . I would hang up. Just try it and see.

That number again is (212) 555-3076.

Thank you for this lovely award.

SEPARATE VACATIONS

[*Two couples*—CHARLES *and* NADINE *and* MYRA *and* RUSSELL—*run into one another in a theater lobby.*]

MYRA: Nadine, Charles!

NADINE: Well, hello, you two!

RUSSELL: You enjoying it?

NADINE: The play?

MYRA: From the reviews I didn't expect too much, but I'm having a good time.

NADINE: I do wish they wouldn't try to do the accents.

RUSSELL: We were just saying how long it's been since we've seen you.

CHARLES: We've been away.

MYRA: Oh?

NADINE: On vacation.

CHARLES: Just returned last night.

RUSSELL: Where from?

CHARLES: Greece.

NADINE: The Hamptons.

MYRA: Greece *and* the Hamptons?

NADINE: Charles went to Greece; I went to East Hampton.

CHARLES: We take separate vacations.

MYRA: I didn't know that.

CHARLES: Oh yes, every year, for years.

RUSSELL: I didn't know that.

CHARLES: Oh yes.

NADINE: Each of us packs up his or her own valise and it's off to our separate pleasures.

RUSSELL: Don't you miss each other?

NADINE: Of course we miss each other, but we find it sort of recharges the batteries.

MYRA: Oh?

CHARLES: Well, we're in different places, having different experiences. When we return, we find we have so much more new to share with each other.

NADINE: Interesting sights, adventures—

CHARLES: Fascinating people.

RUSSELL: Yes, I can see.

NADINE: For instance, do you know about Michael Clement?

MYRA: He's an artist, isn't he?

NADINE: Yes.

MYRA: Landscapes.

NADINE: That's what he's famous for, of course.

MYRA: There was an article in *New York* magazine.

NADINE: Well, he lives in the Hamptons.

RUSSELL: You met him?

NADINE: Mmmmm.

MYRA: What's he like?

NADINE: Very shy, very sweet.

MYRA: Oh?

NADINE: A perfect animal in bed.

CHARLES: Did you sleep with him?

NADINE: Didn't I tell you?

CHARLES: I don't think so.

NADINE: I'm sure I told you.

CHARLES: Did you?

NADINE: You remember. I showed you the picture he gave me.

CHARLES: The one of the bridge? The little red bridge?

NADINE: I showed it to you this morning.

CHARLES: At breakfast.

NADINE: That's right.

CHARLES: Of course. I'm sorry, it must have slipped my mind. I'm not senile, swear to God. You believe me, don't you, Myra?

MYRA [*slightly shocked at this turn in the conversation*]: Uh, yes.

CHARLES: So he was good?

NADINE: Michael? Mmmmm, yes. A great attention to details.

CHARLES: I would have guessed as much from his brushwork.

NADINE: Though he had nothing on you.

CHARLES: Oh, darling, you embarrass me.

NADINE: No, it's true. You're still *ultimo* for me, my dear.

CHARLES: You're too kind.

[*They kiss.*]

By the way, Russell, I have hellos for you.

RUSSELL [*recovering composure*]: Yes?

CHARLES: Harold and Adrienne Lampert.

RUSSELL: Oh, uh, how are they?

CHARLES: Doing splendidly. Harold's based in Rome now, you know. But your name came up, and he asked me if I saw you to say hello. So, hello from Harold. And Adrienne, too, of course.

RUSSELL: Well, thank you.

CHARLES: Ran into them on the boat. Spent a most enjoyable evening. They showed me some very interesting permutations on that Tibetan position. Myra, you know the one I mean.

MYRA: Uh, no.

CHARLES: I gather women find it particularly provocative. Something you might want to look into, Russell.

NADINE: Is it as uncomfortable as it looks?

CHARLES: Initially, yes. But if you learn to relax the proper muscles, penetration is really remarkable.

NADINE: You tried it, did you?

CHARLES: Well, first, of course, Harold and Adrienne demonstrated. And then I tried with Adrienne. I must say I was a bit apprehensive.

NADINE: Why?

CHARLES: I don't like to do that which I cannot do well.

NADINE: That's very true; he doesn't.

CHARLES: But they were most supportive, so it worked out very well indeed.

NADINE: You must show me tonight.

CHARLES: Of course. They made me promise I would.

NADINE: Share the wealth, so to speak.

CHARLES: Yes.

NADINE: They were always terribly generous.

CHARLES: Lovely people.

NADINE: Very dear. Don't you think so, Russell?

RUSSELL: Very friendly.

NADINE [offering to MYRA and RUSSELL]: Raisinets?

MYRA AND RUSSELL [with a start]: No, no, thanks.

CHARLES: Oh, and I didn't tell you—

NADINE: Yes?

CHARLES: I'm sorry, I don't mean to monopolize the conversation—

RUSSELL: No, no, you're not.

CHARLES: It's just that I happened on an exquisite goat-boy.

MYRA: Goat-boy?

NADINE: Oh, I'm so happy. You *did* find one this year.

CHARLES [*to* RUSSELL]: Have you ever had a goat-boy?

RUSSELL: Not that I can remember.

CHARLES: You don't know what you're missing. His name was Andros.

NADINE: What a lovely name.

CHARLES: You know, I think you would have taken to him.

NADINE: Really?

CHARLES: After all these years, I think I know your taste, and, yes, I feel reasonably sure you would have just eaten him up.

NADINE: Well, perhaps next year *I'll* go to Greece—

CHARLES: And *I'll* go to the Hamptons!

[*They laugh together playfully.*]

NADINE: You know, I haven't had a really good goat-boy in years. Or *goat* for that matter.

[*They laugh as* RUSSELL *and* MYRA *attempt smiles.*]

CHARLES: Oh, isn't that Edna and Gilbert Gersheney over there?

RUSSELL: I don't think so.

CHARLES: Why do you say that?

RUSSELL: I'm afraid they're getting a divorce.

NADINE: Oh no.

CHARLES: The Gersheneys?

RUSSELL: I'm afraid so.

NADINE: But they've been married how long?

CHARLES: It must be thirteen—

NADINE: Thirteen years?

CHARLES: What a shame.

NADINE: Tragic.

CHARLES: I'm really quite shocked.

NADINE: Sort of makes you stop and think, doesn't it?

RUSSELL: Yes.

MYRA: Yes, it does.

CHARLES: Why can't people get along?

NADINE: Sad.

CHARLES: Yes.

MYRA: Yes.

NADINE: Oh, it looks as though the second act is going to begin. Meet us afterwards for drinks?

RUSSELL: That sounds like a good—

MYRA [*cutting him off*]: I'm afraid our sitter wants us back by ten thirty.

NADINE: I know how it is.

CHARLES: Well, then, some other time. Dinner perhaps.

RUSSELL: OK.

MYRA: We'll talk.

NADINE: Call you soon.

[CHARLES *and* NADINE *exit. A beat.*]

RUSSELL: You know, honey, I've got two weeks vacation coming—

MYRA: No.

RUSSELL: But maybe it would—

MYRA: Don't even think it.

COVER

[*An office.* FRANK *is working at his desk.* MARTY *enters.*]

MARTY: Work, work, work.

FRANK: Oh, Marty.

MARTY: I'm early.

FRANK: You're early.

MARTY: If I'm interrupting—

FRANK: No, this is nothing. Just odds and ends.

MARTY: Nice office.

FRANK: Oh, that's right—you've never been up here, have you?

MARTY: No, this is the first time.

FRANK: Well, you've got to take a look out this window. I've got a view that will knock your eyes out. My big status symbol.

MARTY: You've got to be good, they give you a window like this. They've got to like you.

FRANK: See Jersey over there?

MARTY: I'll be damned, Jersey.

FRANK: What's great is to watch thunderstorms come over the Hudson. Hell of a show. Lightning and thunder.

MARTY: Always said that was the best thing that could happen to New Jersey.

FRANK: Well, OK.

MARTY: No, I'm impressed. I really am. This is very nice.

FRANK: Yes, I'm very—

MARTY: So, you all set and ready to go?

FRANK: Just let me put this stuff away.

MARTY: Take your time.

FRANK: Where's Diane?

MARTY: Oh, she'll be along in a few minutes. I told her to meet me here. She had an appointment across town, so I figured—

FRANK: Sure.

MARTY: Actually, I'm glad I got here a little earlier. There's a favor I want to ask of you.

FRANK: Ask away.

MARTY: OK. Well, see, as a topic of conversation, it may come up during the evening where I was last night. And it would make it a lot easier if we could decide between us that I was with you.

FRANK: To say that?

MARTY: Not to say necessarily, but to sort of give the impression that we were together. It would make things a lot simpler for me. I mean, if it comes up.

FRANK: You want me to say—

MARTY: Just to say—

FRANK: That you and I—

MARTY: That we were—

FRANK: Together—

MARTY: Together—

FRANK: Last night.

MARTY: Yeah.

FRANK: You want me to lie.

MARTY: Well—

FRANK: Not *well*. You want me to lie.

MARTY: Well—

FRANK: That's what you're asking.

MARTY: I wouldn't—

FRANK: Is that what you're asking?

MARTY: Well, yes.

FRANK: To lie?

MARTY: A little bit. Just to give the impression so that Diane won't worry. To avoid confusion and upset for her.

FRANK: I see. You want me to do a favor for you for her.

MARTY: I couldn't have said it better myself.

FRANK: Where *were* you last night? I mean, I have to know.

MARTY: It doesn't matter.

FRANK: Well, yes, it does. I have to know whether you're wanting me to tell a white lie or a black lie.

MARTY: It's a white lie.

FRANK: How white? I mean, where were you?

MARTY: I was out.

FRANK: Alone? With someone?

MARTY: With someone.

FRANK: Yeah?

MARTY: Diane wouldn't understand.

FRANK: A woman?

MARTY: She'd take it the wrong way.

FRANK: You were out with another woman.

MARTY: Yes, I was out with another woman.

FRANK: I see. And that's a white lie?

MARTY: It's no big deal.

FRANK: I'm sorry; I can't do it.

MARTY: Hey, really, it's no big deal.

FRANK: No, I wouldn't feel good about it.

MARTY: Why not? It's just a little favor.

FRANK: It's not a little—you're asking me to lie to her. You don't understand. She's my friend.

MARTY: Aren't I your friend?

FRANK: You're my friend and she's my friend. But she's not my friend because you're my friend. I mean, it's not that you and I have a primary friendship and she's a secondary friend by extension. You're both primary friends.

MARTY: I understand that.

FRANK: There's trust, and that's part of the relationship. And you don't break that trust.

MARTY: I'm not asking you to break the trust. I'm asking you to spare her confusion and upset.

FRANK: You're asking me to lie to her.

MARTY: To give a different impression of the truth.

FRANK: A false impression, which is a lie.

MARTY: You've never told a lie in your life?

FRANK: That's not the issue.

MARTY: Of course it's the issue. You're saying you don't tell lies.

FRANK: I'm saying I will not tell *this* lie.

MARTY: How do you decide when you will or will not tell a lie?

FRANK: I try not to lie.

MARTY: But what makes you decide if you'll tell a given lie? Say that an opportunity for a lie presents itself—how do you decide if you'll tell it?

FRANK: This is not the issue.

MARTY: You have told lies, haven't you? You've told lies in the past.

FRANK: I have, but that has nothing to do with this.

MARTY: You just won't tell a lie for me.

FRANK: I don't want to tell an active lie, no.

MARTY: Well, are you going to tell her that I was out with another woman last night?

FRANK: No, of course not.

MARTY: Then isn't that creating a false impression? Isn't that, in fact, a lie?

FRANK: That's a passive lie, my not telling something.

MARTY: Ah, that's different.

FRANK: It is.

MARTY: A difference in kind, right? Active versus passive.

FRANK: There *is* a difference, whether you see it or not.

MARTY: Oh, I see it. I do see it. No, very subtle. I like it. Nice.

FRANK: Thank you.

MARTY: Would you care to elaborate?

FRANK: What do you mean?

MARTY: On the distinction. Active, passive.

FRANK: What does this have to do with—

MARTY: I'm trying to determine which lie you will tell and which you won't. If we correlate an active lie as being a lie you won't tell and a passive lie as a lie you will, then perhaps we can find that point in the gray area between where we can come to an understanding.

FRANK: Look, I don't want to lie to her.

MARTY: I'm not asking you to *want* to.

FRANK: You're just asking me to do it.

MARTY: Yes, as a favor to a friend.

FRANK: No, I don't want to.

MARTY: You do lots of things you don't want to do. Everybody does.

FRANK: The things that I sometimes do that I don't want to do are things that I have to do. I don't have to do this. I don't have to break that trust.

MARTY: No, and we don't have to be friends, either.

FRANK: Oh, come on. Are you saying if I won't lie for you we won't be friends anymore?

MARTY: Of course not. I'm just asking you for a favor.

FRANK: I can't do it.

MARTY: Can't means *won't.*

FRANK: Can't means *can't.*

MARTY: Can't means *won't.*

FRANK: Can't means *can't.*

MARTY: No, you could.

FRANK: I couldn't.

MARTY: You *could.*

FRANK: I couldn't.

MARTY: Of course you could. Your mouth could say the words. Physically, your mouth could say the words.

FRANK: I couldn't do it.

MARTY: Of course you could.

FRANK: No, I couldn't.

MARTY: You could, but what you're saying is you won't.

FRANK: I'm saying I can't.

MARTY: You're saying you won't.

FRANK: I'm saying—OK, I'm saying I won't because I can't.

MARTY: But you *could.*

FRANK: I wouldn't if I could, but I can't so I won't. Anyway, you don't want me to lie for you.

MARTY: Yes, I do.

FRANK: I'm a terrible liar. She'd see right through me.

MARTY: How do you know until you try?

FRANK: Look, I'm not going to tell her where you were. I mean, I couldn't because I don't know.

MARTY: I was at Dock's. That's on the West Side.

FRANK: I don't want to know. Don't tell me any more.

MARTY: Barbara Schaeffer.

FRANK: I don't want to know who.

MARTY: Barbara Schaeffer.

FRANK: Barbara Schaeffer?

MARTY: See, now you know.

FRANK: I thought she was married.

MARTY: Separated.

FRANK: I didn't know that.

MARTY: More than two months now.

FRANK: I wish you hadn't told me.

MARTY: But you know, and if you don't tell Diane that means you've already lied. Passive shmassive, it's a lie, and if you've gone that far, why not go a little farther for a friend?

FRANK: No, I'm not going to. I'm sorry, you can argue rings around me, but I'm not going to.

MARTY: You don't want to do it.

FRANK: No, I can't.

[*A beat.*]

MARTY: OK, sorry I asked.

FRANK: Don't you understand?

MARTY: Oh, I understand you perfectly. You don't want to do this favor for me. That's your prerogative.

FRANK: I wish you'd understand.

MARTY: It really is a hell of a nice office. You should be very proud.

[*A beat.* DIANE *enters.*]

DIANE: I've found you at last.

FRANK: You have trouble?

DIANE: I was half expecting to stumble on a minotaur.

FRANK: Huh?

DIANE: You know, that monster—the one in the maze.

FRANK: Oh, that's me, I think.

DIANE: Right, some monster. So, you guys ready to go?

FRANK: In a second.

DIANE: Hey, nice view.

FRANK: You like it?

DIANE: That's Jersey, isn't it?

MARTY: You can see thunderstorms, Frank says.

DIANE: Oh really? That must be exciting.

FRANK: What, I don't get a kiss?

DIANE: Absolutely!

[*She kisses* FRANK.]

FRANK: Hey, you look swell.

DIANE: In contrast to—

FRANK: No, of course not.

DIANE: Thank you.

FRANK: That's a nice outfit.

DIANE: I'm glad you like it.

FRANK: It really is.

DIANE [*to* MARTY]: So, how was your day?

MARTY: Fine.

DIANE: You and Jacobs get that thing cleared up?

MARTY: No big problem.

DIANE: I thought you were worried.

MARTY: Not seriously. We sat down; we talked.

DIANE: You compromised.

MARTY: I didn't have to.

DIANE: It must be a relief.

MARTY: And your interview?

DIANE: Nothing definite.

MARTY: But there's interest?

DIANE: They didn't say no.

MARTY: That's half the battle.

DIANE: Yeah.

MARTY: Fingers crossed.

DIANE: You got here early, huh?

MARTY: Just a few minutes ago.

DIANE: You've got a lot of papers on your desk, Frank. You must work awfully hard.

FRANK: It just looks that way. Gives the impression I'm earning my money, when the truth—

DIANE: Oh, no, I know you. Industrious. Kind, loyal, honest, brave. You're the only person I know who lives up to—what is it?—the Boy Scout code?

FRANK: I wouldn't know. I wasn't a Scout.

DIANE: I can see you loaded down with merit badges.

FRANK: Yes, well now, *Touch of Evil* starts at eight, so that means we should figure out what restaurant's near the museum—

MARTY: We should be pushing along, right.

FRANK: There's not a big hurry, but if we want to have a few drinks first—

DIANE [*to* MARTY]: Hey—

MARTY: How are ya?

DIANE: What are you doing?

MARTY: Just saying hi to you.

[*A beat.*]

DIANE: We have to be at the museum at what?

FRANK: Well, by quarter till at least.

DIANE: So, where shall we eat?

FRANK: How does Italian sound, or are you on a diet and don't want that, or what? Chinese?

DIANE: Do you think I should be on a diet?

FRANK: Women always seem to be on diets. Men, too. People in general.

DIANE: Women aren't always on diets. Some women diet. The heavy variety. They tend to diet.

FRANK: I can remember you being on some pretty screwy diets.

DIANE: You think I'm screwy?

FRANK: No, of course not. I didn't say that.

DIANE: I'm sorry. I'm a little weird tonight. The ozone or something.

FRANK: Sure, I mean, air quality does—

DIANE [*to* MARTY]: You didn't get home till really late last night.

MARTY: I know.

DIANE: I wasn't even awake when you got home.

MARTY: I didn't want to disturb you.

DIANE: Listen to the man! My favorite thing in the world is to wrap my arms around him in bed and he says he doesn't want to disturb me. And you got up and left early this morning, too.

MARTY: I know. I had to get out.

DIANE: Away from me?

MARTY: No, no, of course not. I just had to leave.

DIANE: Why?

MARTY: I had someplace to be.

DIANE: Oh.

MARTY: Preparing for the Jacobs thing, you know.

DIANE: Yeah.

FRANK: Do you want me to leave? Would you rather be alone or—

DIANE [*interrupting*]: I promised myself I wasn't going to ask this question. I mean, I was in the bathroom and I combed my hair and I looked in the mirror and I said to myself, "You're looking good, Diane. You're looking very good."

FRANK: You look terrific.

DIANE: Where were you last night? Where were you till so late?

[*A beat.*]

MARTY: I was with Frank all night long. Isn't that right, Frank?

[*A beat.*]

FRANK: Yeah, that's right. He was. With me. We were—

DIANE: With Frank?

MARTY: Yes. Is that what you were so worried about?

DIANE: Yes, I'm sorry. It's stupid.

FRANK: We were playing—

MARTY: Playing—

FRANK: Poker.

MARTY: Cards. I didn't want to tell you because, well, I know you don't like me gambling.

DIANE: No.

MARTY: And I lost a little last night.

FRANK: Yeah, I zapped him for a little.

DIANE: How much?

FRANK: Forty something. He made me promise not to tell.

DIANE: I see. Well—

FRANK: Tell you what, dinner's on me tonight, OK?

[DIANE *knows. She looks at* FRANK *very directly.*]

DIANE: Why not.

[*A beat.*]

MARTY: I guess we'd better get going, huh?

[DIANE *nods. She exits first.* FRANK *and* MARTY *exchange a look before exiting.*]

PORCH

—for T.

Porch began when a woman I knew told me about being summoned by her dying father to discuss his business affairs. I had a hunch that such a meeting would bring up matters beyond business. This linked with the conversations I had had with a number of women living in New York about the gap between the choices they were making and the values of their parents (raised in the forties and fifties). The gap seemed particularly pronounced when they were from small towns.

At the time, I had very few coherent ideas about craft, so this was written mostly on instinct. I was living in Greenwich Village in an apartment on the top floor that tended to bake in the summer. A nearby air-conditioned all-night café beckoned. The owners didn't seem to mind if I nursed a cup of coffee for hours and scribbled on legal pads. My most vivid memory of writing *Porch* is of sitting early in the morning knocking out most of the first draft of the scene between Amy and Sam in one stretch in longhand.

After a very useful, unreviewed workshop at the Arena Stage in Washington in 1977 (rehearsals began a few days after the confetti from Jimmy Carter's inaugural parade was cleaned up), the play received its formal premiere almost as an afterthought at the Encompass Theatre, a company devoted mostly to musical theater. Artistic director Nancy Rhodes had taken my recommendation to produce Marc Blitzstein's *Regina,* the opera version of Lillian Hellman's *The Little Foxes.* Visiting rehearsal one day, I was reminded that one of the scenes in the opera took place on a front porch. I suggested that since we already had a set that would work for my play, it would cost next to nothing to put it up on nights when *Regina* wasn't being given. Nancy agreed, and we rehearsed mostly in the loft apartment of our leading lady, Polly Adams.

The show had a stroke of luck. Richard Eder, who was the first-string critic for the *New York Times* that season, had read and liked *Something Wonderful Right Away,* and that moved him to come to see the show. In those days, before reviews made their first appearances on the Internet, you had to hang around Times Square to get an early crack at the papers. The company and I waited on the second floor of Sardi's for director Nan Harris to return from getting the first printing. The huge smile on her face as she bounded up the stairs was the first inkling that the review was good. I felt as if Eder had opened a door and welcomed me to my professional life as a playwright.

Victory Gardens had been considering the play but had made no commitment at the time the *Times* notice came out. The review prompted artistic director Dennis Zacek to schedule *Porch* for the small second stage. I flew into Chicago in 1979 to see final rehearsals and was dismayed to find that the town had been hit by its most severe blizzard in decades. I was very pleased by the rehearsal I saw, but I doubted that anybody would trudge through streets filled with six-foot-high snowdrifts to see a little play by somebody nobody had heard of. Richard Christiansen and most of his colleagues wrote reviews that made short work of my pessimism. The run sold out instantly, chairs were added to the theater, an extension was scheduled, and the production was brought back to play on the main stage for runs over the next two summers. And then Zacek was good enough to ask me if I was working on anything else.

Looking at *Porch* now, what strikes me is that I was writing about three people who were older than I was when I wrote it (twenty-five) and who had had experiences that I hadn't had yet. It turned out to be uncomfortably accurate in predicting some of what would become my own story.

Porch received its first public presentation at the Arena Stage in Washington, D.C., in 1977 as part of the In the Process series. It was directed by Thomas Gruenewald, with the following cast:

Mr. Herbert .... Mark Hammer
Amy Herbert .... E. Katherine Kerr
Sam Darrow .... Gary Bayer

Porch received its formal premiere off-off-Broadway in November 1978 at the Encompass Theatre, under the direction of Nan Harris, with the following cast:

Mr. Herbert	Conrad McLaren
Amy Herbert	Polly Adams
Sam Darrow	Gary Bayer

Porch received its Chicago premiere in February 1979 at the Victory Gardens Theater under the direction of Tom Mula. The set was designed by Tom Beall. The cast included the following:

Mr. Herbert	Raoul Johnson
Amy Herbert	Sonja Lanzener
Sam Darrow	David Stettler

Porch was produced off-Broadway in New York by the Lamb's Theatre Company in November 1984, under the direction of Nan Harris, with sets by Michael C. Smith, lighting by Marc D. Malamud, costumes by Neal Bishop, and production stage management by Steve Zorthian. The cast was as follows:

Mr. Herbert	Clarke Gordon
Amy Herbert	Jill Eikenberry
Sam Darrow	Gary Bayer

CHARACTERS

Mr. Herbert
Amy Herbert
Sam Darrow

[*The time is 1975. The front porch of a house in Taylor Ridge, an Ohio college town. The house is solidly middle class, of pre–World War II vintage. It is decorated with a few pieces of porch furniture and bordered by a wooden railing. Upstage, a door leads into the house. There are also a few windows looking out onto the porch. Downstage, steps lead to the sidewalk and street. It is a cool August evening. At rise,* HERBERT, *an older man, enters from the house with ill-concealed difficulty. His daughter* AMY *is behind him, watching with concern. At one point she reaches out to help him. He resists.*]

HERBERT: What do you think you're doing?

AMY: Trying to help.

HERBERT [*settling into a chair*]: I can make it on my own steam.

AMY: I don't see the point in having a wheelchair if you don't use it.

HERBERT: I agree with you. I'll call the rental place and have them come and fetch it. I don't need the damn thing.

[AMY *turns to go back into the house.*]

Where you going?

AMY: I forgot your blanket.

HERBERT: I don't need a blanket.

AMY: It's liable to get chilly.

HERBERT: I don't need a blanket, so will you stop fussing and sit down?

[*She sits.*]

Good.

AMY: Dad, why did you get the wheelchair if you weren't going to use it?

HERBERT: Are we still talking about that?

AMY: Yes, we're still talking about that.

HERBERT: It wasn't my idea. It was Wolf's.

AMY: Isn't that what you pay a doctor for—to give you advice to follow?

HERBERT: I don't know what you pay a doctor for. From habit, I suppose.

AMY: Ever think a doctor might know what's best?

HERBERT: You think doctors know everything?

AMY: I think Dr. Wolf knows more than you about—

HERBERT: That's good to know. I'll let him take over the store while I'm gone, see how well he can run it.

AMY: You know that's not what I meant.

HERBERT: You said that he knows more than I do.

AMY: It wouldn't hurt you to follow his orders and use the chair.

HERBERT: I'm not one to give in to a little pain.

AMY: You're not one to give in, period.

HERBERT: That's right . . . Five years? Six?

AMY: What?

HERBERT: Last time we sat out here together.

AMY [*mildly accusatory*]: Eleven.

HERBERT: That long?

AMY: Yes.

HERBERT: Around this time of year, too, wasn't it? Yes, you were going to go back to school in a few weeks, and you were talking about changing your major. Switching to journalism. And we talked about it. What was it you were majoring in before?

AMY: French history.

HERBERT: That's right. Never thought much of that, I must confess. Didn't seem to me there was much you could do with it. Journalism struck me as more practical. Bet it comes in handy on your job, huh?

AMY: It's been useful.

HERBERT: You ever choose anything by someone from around here?

AMY: Choose?

HERBERT: A book by someone in this area. Your book club.

AMY: I don't really do the choosing. I just make recommendations.

HERBERT: But your opinion does carry weight.

AMY: Why? Is there someone you think I should know about?

HERBERT: No, I just thought it would be funny, kind of a funny coincidence, if you were to choose a book written on paper from my store.

AMY: I see what you mean.

HERBERT: Being at both ends.

AMY: That would be funny.

HERBERT: We could be held liable under the Taylor Act.

AMY: The Taylor Act?

HERBERT: You know, the antitrust—

AMY: I think that's the Sherman Act.

HERBERT: I think you're right. The Sherman Act. To break up monopolies. We could be held liable, as I say, catching them coming and going.

AMY: Well, if any of your customers have manuscripts, I'll be glad to—

HERBERT: Hell, I just sell them paper. I don't know what they put on it. Most of my business is to students. Do a brisk trade in paper, typewriter ribbons, and CliffsNotes.

[*A beat.*]

I wonder what the Taylor Act is. Do you know?

AMY: Not offhand.

HERBERT: I'll probably remember when I'm not thinking about it.

[*A beat.*]

You still have a good appetite. The way you wolfed down your food.

AMY: I was pretty hungry.

HERBERT: Didn't finish your ice cream. Here I make a point of getting your favorite flavor, you barely touch it.

AMY: My favorite flavor?

HERBERT: Butter pecan.

AMY: No, I was always partial to fudge ripple.

HERBERT: But you liked butter pecan, too.

AMY: That wasn't me.

HERBERT: Fudge ripple?

AMY: Then, now, and forever.

HERBERT: I'm sorry. I didn't mean to force an unappealing flavor on you.

AMY: I'm not complaining.

HERBERT: Butter pecan was Jeremy. That's right.

AMY: It was nice of Mrs. Ellis to come over and put together dinner.

HERBERT: She's been very neighborly since my discomfort began, helping me keep the house straight, stopping by with food. A real Good Samaritan. I've half a mind to steal her away from her husband. Of course, she's not as good a cook as your mother was, but I'd say she does all right.

AMY: I wish I could do half as well.

HERBERT: Maybe while you're here, you can stop by their place; she can show you some of her secrets.

AMY: Maybe.

[*A beat.*]

HERBERT: What are we talking about cooking for?

AMY: What do you want to talk about?

HERBERT: It's up to me, huh?

AMY: Not if you don't want to. We could go in and watch TV.

HERBERT: No, I like sitting out here. Besides, I'll do enough TV watching in the hospital. If I'm lucky.

[*A beat.*]

Damn it, I wish they'd put me under sedation for the whole thing. Not just the operation but the whole stay. The idea of being cooped up in a hospital . . .

AMY: Let's go in. Aren't you getting chilly?

HERBERT: So tell me.

AMY: Tell you what?

HERBERT: Bring me up-to-date. You don't write very often. Not that I'm blaming you. I'm a little surprised you write to me at all. And that you came out here, if you want to know the truth.

AMY: I wanted to come out before.

HERBERT: I wanted you to come before. I should have said so. And maybe *you* should have said something.

[*A beat.*]

Bet you don't breathe air this fresh in New York. Good to be outside. Clean out your lungs.

[*A beat.*]

Maybe the operation's a blessing in disguise. At least this way, no matter what happens, we've seen each other again. How did I get started on this? Oh yes, I was asking you about what all's been happening. You still seeing that fellow? The one you wrote me about that time. What was his name? You know, the corporation lawyer.

AMY: Stuart?

HERBERT: That's the one. Stuart. Still seeing Stuart?

AMY: No, we parted company a long time ago.

HERBERT: I thought you liked him.

AMY: I did like him.

HERBERT: I thought it was stronger than that.

AMY: It was, for a while.

HERBERT: Only for a while?

AMY: It passed.

HERBERT: You talk about him like he was a kidney stone. "It passed."

AMY: You asked me if I'm still seeing him. I'm not still seeing him.

HERBERT: Why not? What happened?

AMY: Nothing happened. We just woke up one day and realized it was over, that's all.

HERBERT: You catch him running around with other women? That it?

AMY: No, that wasn't it.

HERBERT: Or was it the other way round? Did you meet someone you liked better?

AMY: OK, yes, there was someone else.

HERBERT: Aha, I knew there had to be a reason. So tell me about this someone else.

AMY: Another lawyer.

HERBERT: Another lawyer?

AMY: Not corporation. I met him at a block association meeting.

HERBERT: Does he have a name?

AMY: Scott. Scott Pierson.

HERBERT: Good-looking fellow?

AMY: I'd say so.

HERBERT: Well off?

AMY: Pretty well.

HERBERT: And you're happy with him?

AMY: No.

HERBERT: You aren't happy?

AMY: I'm happy enough. I'm not happy with him. I'm not with him any longer.

HERBERT: Someone else?

AMY: Someone else.

HERBERT: You move around, don't you?

AMY: I guess so.

HERBERT: No guessing about it. You move around.

AMY: All right, I move around. So?

HERBERT: You know the old expression, "A rolling stone—"

AMY: I'm not trying to gather moss.

HERBERT: You know what I'm saying. You're not about to get a family started unless you settle with someone.

AMY: I'm not about to get a family started, period.

HERBERT: You don't want a family?

AMY: Let's not get into a discussion about this, OK?

HERBERT: I don't understand a woman who doesn't want a family.

AMY: Dad, I don't want to talk about it. So why don't we drop the subject right now?

HERBERT: OK, OK . . . So, who are you with now? You said you were seeing someone.

AMY: I'm seeing someone, yes.

HERBERT: What's his name?

AMY: Phillip Sternberg.

HERBERT: Another lawyer, I'll bet.

AMY: No, this one's getting a degree in philosophy.

HERBERT: Do you mean to say he's a student?

AMY: At Columbia.

HERBERT: But that makes him how many years younger than you?

AMY: I don't know.

HERBERT: Yes you do.

AMY: What difference does it make?

HERBERT: I'm just curious.

AMY: Something like eleven or twelve years.

[*He whistles.*]

HERBERT: That doesn't bother you? Being so much older?

AMY: No, it doesn't bother me. Does it bother you?

HERBERT: Why should it bother me?

AMY: Why *does* it bother you?

HERBERT: It doesn't bother me. Doesn't bother me at all. You can choose your beaux from the third grade if you want.

AMY: You mean I have your permission?

HERBERT: Now you know I didn't mean it like that. Don't put words into my mouth. It doesn't matter to me how much younger the man you go out or stay in with is. Just so long as you're happy.

AMY: That's good, because that's the way I feel, too.

HERBERT: I just find it curious. A girl with your looks and your brains, you shouldn't be having any trouble finding a man older than you.

AMY: Tell you what, Dad. The next man will be at least forty-three. How's that?

HERBERT: What do you mean "the next man"? Are you planning on dumping poor Phillip so soon?

AMY: No, I was making a joke. A funny.

HERBERT: I thought so, but I didn't know whether to laugh. The way you go through men. Or should I say, the way men go through you?

AMY [*drily*]: Ha, ha.

HERBERT: I can make jokes, too, can't I? So, this boy of yours, Phillip, he's at Columbia?

AMY: Yes.

HERBERT: Can he find time to study between occupying buildings?

AMY: What?

HERBERT: Columbia—isn't that where they take over the buildings?

AMY: That was a few years back. Like a decade ago?

HERBERT: I'm not up-to-date.

AMY: Not as regards Columbia.

HERBERT: And other things?

AMY: Does it concern you? Do you *want* to be up-to-date?

HERBERT: How would I do that?

AMY: I could send you some pamphlets.

HERBERT: Would they help me understand you better?

AMY: Not a chance.

HERBERT: Not much point to it then. So, does he take you to the school prom? Phillip?

AMY: I don't think Phillip dances.

HERBERT: Of course he dances. That's what kids do; they dance.

AMY [*irritated*]: How about a little canasta?

HERBERT: Don't take me so seriously. I'm just trying to get a rise out of you. It was always so easy to get a rise out of you. When you were a little girl, all someone had to do was look at you cross-eyed and you'd be on the floor, kicking your heels and screaming and crying . . . Philosophy, huh? What do you do with philosophy?

AMY: Teach and write books.

HERBERT: He expects to support you like this?

AMY: No, he doesn't expect to support me.

HERBERT: You're going to support him?

AMY: Nobody's going to support anybody.

HERBERT: Besides, in a week or so, you'll have dumped poor Phillip for another lawyer. No, better yet—a law student. Right?

AMY: Dad—

HERBERT: Oh, now I remember what the Taylor Act is. That's when you take someone across the state line for immoral purposes, right?

AMY: No, that's the Mann Act.

HERBERT: The Mann Act, huh? What is it when you do that with children—the Child Act? Because that's what they'll get you on if you start choosing them any younger.

AMY: That's enough. All right?

HERBERT: Hey, you're taking me seriously again. Don't take me so seriously. I'm just having a little fun with you. I haven't seen you in so long. You're telling me about this man and that man and it's hard for me to keep them straight. If I'm stepping on your toes, I apologize. You should really learn to laugh at yourself more. Be less rigid. You were always so serious. Men like a sense of humor in a woman. I don't know how you got to be so glum. Your mother had a sense of humor. I have a sense of humor. And your brother—

AMY: Yes.

HERBERT: He'd be almost twenty-eight now. A man. On his own. A good job somewhere. Maybe a few people working under him. With a house, married. I'd probably be a grandfather by now. Doesn't look as if there's much chance of my seeing that happen the way things stand.

AMY: I guess not.

[*A beat.*]

HERBERT: What do you figure you'll do with the store if I don't make it?

AMY: I haven't thought about it.

HERBERT: Let's think about it now. It's doing well. You saw the books. It's a good store.

AMY: I know that, Dad.

HERBERT: It could provide you with security. I mean, it's not going to make you rich. You don't get rich selling floppy disks and notebooks and ink. But there's the university nearby, so it's steady. And there's talk they may build a junior college here, too. That won't hurt.

AMY: I'm not certain I have the temperament to run a store.

HERBERT: Don't underestimate yourself, Amy. I think you would do just fine.

AMY: No, it's not that I think I couldn't. I just don't feel that it would be right for me.

HERBERT: I'm not trying to force you.

AMY: I don't want to leave New York.

HERBERT: You wouldn't have to leave. Just fly back here once in a while to make sure the place hasn't burned down. Nothing says you'd have to live here.

AMY: If I were going to run the store, I would want to be here.

HERBERT: Of course that would be best.

AMY: But I don't want to be here. Anyway, it's not going to happen.

HERBERT: What you're saying is that you're going to sell the store.

AMY: The store isn't mine to sell.

HERBERT: But when it is—

AMY: I think it's premature to talk about it.

HERBERT: If we wait till the store is yours to talk about it, the conversation's liable to be very one-sided.

AMY: I don't have anything else to say on the subject.

HERBERT: It's a good feeling to look at it and be able to say, "This is mine. This wouldn't be here without me." But then, you never did have a special feeling for it. Maybe you thought that it was a little ridiculous I did.

AMY: I don't think it's ridiculous. I just don't feel the way you do, that's all.

HERBERT: Jeremy was different. When you and he would help me with inventory, you would do the work conscientiously enough, but it was always work to you. Something to get done. But I remember Jeremy asking me once, "Dad, all of this is ours, isn't it?" He appreciated.

AMY: I'm not Jeremy.

HERBERT: No, you're not.

[*A beat.*]

Is that someone coming up the walk? Hello?

[SAM *enters.* AMY's *age. Casually but neatly dressed. He carries a newspaper.*]

SAM: Mr. Herbert.
HERBERT: Is that Sam Darrow?
SAM: Yes, sir, it's me.
HERBERT: How about that?
SAM: I think this is your paper. I found it in a bush—
HERBERT: I was wondering what happened to that. Thank you.
SAM: It was out there in—
HERBERT: Come on and join us. Come on, I won't bite you.

[SAM *joins them on the porch and hands* HERBERT *the paper. He doesn't sit.*]

SAM [*awkwardly*]: Hello, Amy.
AMY: Sam.
SAM: You're looking well.
AMY: Thank you. So are you.
SAM: It's been a long time.
AMY: Yes.
SAM: Too long.

[*She has no answer for this.*]

I thought it was you. I was just driving by, you know, and I saw the light on the porch. And I thought I saw you, but I wasn't sure. So I parked up the way a little and thought I'd walk back and see if it really was you.
AMY: It is.
SAM: Yes, I see. It's good to see you again.
HERBERT: Sit down, Sam. Rest your feet.
SAM: Well, actually, I thought I might use your bathroom first?
HERBERT: Oh, sure. You remember where it is, don't you?
SAM: Yes, I remember.

[*He exits into the house.*]

HERBERT: Well, how do you like that?

AMY: I don't know.

HERBERT: Aren't you happy to see him?

AMY: I haven't decided.

HERBERT: Decided? I'm not asking you to vote on a referendum. I'm asking you what you feel. You don't decide what you feel.

AMY: What's he doing here?

HERBERT: Don't ask me. I'm not him.

AMY: Dad, I want to know what he's doing here.

HERBERT: You heard him. He was passing by and he saw you.

AMY: That's what he said.

HERBERT: You don't believe him? You think he's lying?

AMY: You didn't have anything to do with it?

HERBERT: Me?

AMY: You didn't call him perhaps?

HERBERT: Why should I call him?

AMY: You didn't call and suggest he drop by?

HERBERT: You think I called him?

AMY: I wouldn't put it past you.

HERBERT: That's a hell of an answer! Wouldn't put it past me. What's that supposed to mean?

AMY: It means I think it's something you could do.

HERBERT: There are lots of things I could do. I could scratch my elbow. You wouldn't say you wouldn't put it past me to scratch my elbow.

AMY: Scratching your elbow wouldn't be sneaky.

HERBERT: I don't understand your attitude, Amy.

AMY: I think you do.

HERBERT: No, I don't.

AMY: Do you want me to spell it out?

HERBERT: Even if I had called him—which I didn't—but if I had, what would have been the harm?

AMY: I don't like being manipulated.

HERBERT: Who's manipulating you?

AMY: What is the point of this?

HERBERT: You have some funny ideas in your head, young lady.

AMY: I don't know what you're thinking will happen.

HERBERT: I don't think anything will happen. I haven't had time to think, what with your being so suspicious, putting me on the defensive.

You think I'd be so devious, you must have a pretty low opinion of me.

AMY [*overlapping above after "devious"*]: That's a very good word for it.

HERBERT: And you must have a pretty low opinion of Sam if you think he's lying.

AMY: How did he know I was here?

HERBERT: He saw you. He was driving by and he saw you.

AMY: Why was he on this street?

HERBERT: It's a public street. Why shouldn't he use it?

AMY: I think it's awfully coincidental.

HERBERT: All right. Believe what you want to believe.

AMY: It strikes me as quite a coincidence that he should just happen to be driving past with us out here.

HERBERT: Look, if you don't like him being here, tell him to go away. It doesn't matter to me. It wasn't me he came to see. I really don't understand your attitude. I can remember a time when you thought you couldn't breathe without him. This is quite a change, suddenly not wanting to see him.

AMY: It's not suddenly. It's been a long time. And anyway, I didn't say that I don't want to see him.

HERBERT: That's the impression you're giving.

AMY: What's more, I never said that I couldn't breathe without him.

HERBERT: Well, you did an awful lot of breathing *with* him.

AMY: It's not the same thing.

HERBERT: So you're right and I don't understand. OK. It doesn't matter to me. You do what you want to do. You always do. Since when did you give a damn what my opinion is?

AMY: I don't like being manipulated, that's all.

HERBERT: Is this what New York has done to you? Made you suspicious?

AMY [*hearing* SAM *coming and signaling* HERBERT *to be quiet*]: Never mind.

[SAM *enters.*]

SAM: Well—

HERBERT: Have a seat.

SAM [*sitting*]: Thank you.

HERBERT: Would you like something? Are you hungry?

SAM: No, I've eaten.

HERBERT: Something to drink, then? Cup of coffee, or would you like a real drink? I have some bourbon.

SAM: No, thanks.

HERBERT: If you're sure.

[AMY *gets up and exits into the house.*]

SAM [*watching* AMY *leave*]: Thanks anyway.

[*Visibly dismayed by* AMY's *departure,* SAM *looks to* HERBERT *as if to ask, "What do we do now?"* HERBERT *signals they should keep talking as if nothing's happened.*]

HERBERT: What are you doing these days?

SAM: Uh, pretty much the same thing.

HERBERT: Photography, wasn't it? You take pictures.

SAM: Sometimes. I get a job here and there.

HERBERT: Weddings and that sort of thing?

[AMY *returns with coffee and a blanket. She tosses the blanket to* HERBERT. *He makes a point of dropping it onto the floor next to him.*]

SAM: In spring I've got the high school graduation pictures. For the yearbook, you know.

HERBERT: You do those?

SAM: Every spring.

HERBERT: Not so long ago, it was the two of you being photographed for that.

SAM: Sometimes it doesn't seem so long ago.

HERBERT: Must take you back, being in the old high school.

SAM: Yes, it does.

HERBERT: Run into your old teachers?

SAM: A lot of them are still there. I'm on a first-name basis with some of them now. But, you know, even though I've been out for years, it still feels a little strange not calling them Mr. or Miss or whatever.

HERBERT: Of course, some of them are Ms.'s now.

SAM: Yes, some of them.

HERBERT: I think that's awfully silly.

SAM: Calling them Ms.?

HERBERT: It's got a period in it, like an abbreviation, only it isn't one. It doesn't stand for anything. And pronouncing it's a problem. Not easy to do. Ms. . . . Doesn't feel natural.

AMY: Excuse me, Sam, what year is this?

SAM: Year?

AMY: Year. Like on the calendar.

SAM: Uh, 1975. Why?

AMY: Just checking.

HERBERT: She's making a point, aren't you?

AMY: Who me?

HERBERT: This is her clever New York way of saying how behind the times I am. This whole discussion, right? Miss, Mrs., Ms. Well, for your information, Amy, I find very few women in this town are using *Ms.* Even among your friends the Democrats.

AMY: Who? Names, I want names.

HERBERT: You don't just overturn years of linguistic tradition because someone comes up with an idea of how to advertise a magazine.

AMY: Yup, that was the reason.

HERBERT: There are some women who find *Miss* and *Mrs.* very useful. Some of them worked very hard to land husbands, and they want people to know they made it. Others like to let it be known that they're available.

SAM: Which are you, Amy?

HERBERT: She certainly isn't a Mrs.

SAM: Never got married?

AMY: Nope, never did.

SAM: I was married. For a while.

AMY: So I've heard.

SAM: It didn't work out. She was a nice person, but it didn't work out. Nobody's fault.

HERBERT: Seeing someone else?

SAM [*evasively*]: Well, I spend most of my time at the store.

HERBERT: Oh.

SAM: You can't make a living doing graduation pictures.

HERBERT: You have a store?

SAM: I'm a partner in a camera shop. In Willow Mill.

HERBERT: That new shopping mall?

SAM: Right.

HERBERT: Doing well?

SAM: Can't keep people from taking snapshots. That and videotape. I do all right. It's a good little store.

HERBERT: Maybe I'll come out and visit, after they let me out.

SAM: That's right. I heard something about you going to the hospital?

HERBERT: Tomorrow. They're going to do some structural renovations. That's what brought Amy out, you know. Just in case.

SAM: I'm sure you'll be fine.

HERBERT: These doctors know what they're doing, I guess.

[*A beat.* HERBERT *starts looking through the paper.*]

You hear about this?

SAM: Sir?

HERBERT: Avery Morse?

SAM: Running again. Oh yes.

HERBERT: You'd think that man would have the sense to give up.

SAM: Running must be in his system.

HERBERT: Losing must be, too. His daughter got married, didn't she? What's her name?

SAM: Julia.

HERBERT: Got married last spring.

SAM: April. It was one of mine.

HERBERT: One of your what?

SAM: I took the pictures.

HERBERT: Nice affair?

SAM: Oh yeah.

HERBERT: Fancy, I'll bet. Avery always liked a good show.

SAM: It was pretty impressive.

HERBERT: I'll bet. I hear she's expecting already. Another few months, they'll be calling you to take pictures on the bearskin.

SAM: I expect so.

HERBERT: Going to make old Avery a grandfather. You'd think that would satisfy him, but no, he's got to try running again. Oh well—

[*He turns a page or two.*]

I didn't know that was going to be on.

SAM: What's that?

HERBERT: *Roman Holiday*. That was a nice picture. You ever see it?

SAM: I don't think so.

HERBERT: Amy's mother and I saw it at the Varsity when it first came out. Very old-fashioned and romantic. Audrey Hepburn's in it. I'd kind of like to see it again. What time you got?

SAM [*checking his watch*]: About eight ten.

HERBERT: It's only just started. You know, I think I will watch it.

[HERBERT *gets up.*]

SAM [*starting to rise*]: Maybe I'd better be going—

HERBERT: No, no, you stay where you are. That's OK. I'm sure you two would like an opportunity to talk anyway. A lot of catching up to do.

SAM: It's been a while.

HERBERT: Sure, you two talk. It's a nice night for it. Nice seeing you again, Sam.

SAM: You, too, sir.

HERBERT: Come around more often.

SAM: I'll do that.

[HERBERT *smiles and exits into the house. A beat.*]

AMY: Subtle, isn't he?

SAM: He'll be all right, won't he? I mean, tomorrow?

AMY: There's no telling.

SAM: What do the doctors say?

AMY: It could go either way. He's got a good chance.

SAM: Oh, he'll make it. All that energy and determination. He'll make it all right.

[*A beat.*]

I gather you two have patched things up? About . . .

AMY: We're avoiding the subject.

SAM: Probably for the best.

[*A beat.*]

So, how are you?

AMY: I'm all right.

SAM: This is the first time you've been back?

AMY: The first time since Jeremy—

SAM: Yeah, I heard about that. I wanted to come by to offer my condolences. But I didn't think it would be tactful; though I wanted to talk to you. You never answered any of my letters.

AMY: I thought that would be for the best.

SAM: Yeah, that's what I figured you figured. It must have been pretty hard for you coming back that time.

AMY: It wasn't pleasant, no.

SAM: It didn't help things between you and your—

AMY: No.

SAM: I'm sorry. You probably don't want to talk about it, do you?

AMY: If you don't mind.

SAM: I shouldn't have just dropped in. I probably should have called first, huh?

AMY: But you didn't know I was here. You just saw me when you drove by.

SAM: I mean, I could have gone to a phone booth and called instead of just barging in—

AMY: But you weren't sure it was me.

SAM [*scrambling to cover*]: I was pretty sure—

AMY: Sam, he asked you to come.

SAM: He tell you that?

AMY: He didn't have to.

SAM: You always were perceptive.

AMY: It was an awfully flimsy story.

SAM: That's the way he wanted it. I figured, "What the hell."

AMY: Sometimes he's so childish.

SAM: Oh, I don't know.

AMY: It's embarrassing.

SAM: Don't you think you're overreacting?

AMY: Probably. But I'd have to be out there where you are in order to see it for myself.

SAM: Is that where I am—out there?

AMY: I can see that I won't be able to say a word safely. You're going to pick up on every nuance, aren't you?

SAM: I'm sorry.

AMY: I'm nervous.

SAM: Me, too.

AMY: My turn to say I'm sorry.

SAM: It's understandable.

AMY: You always were good at understanding.

SAM: Each of us has his talents.

[*Pause.*]

AMY: Are you sure you don't want something? A Coke or something?

SAM: You know, I think I'll take you up on that.

AMY: A Coke?

SAM: Sure, if you've got one. A Coca-Cola.

[*She exits.* SAM *begins to look through the pictures in his wallet, finds the one he was looking for. A beat.* HERBERT *pops his head out through the doorway.*]

HERBERT: Everything all right out here?

SAM [*putting the photo away again*]: She's just gone to get me a Coca-Cola.

HERBERT: Oh, good. Good.

[AMY *returns.*]

AMY: I think the commercial's over, Dad.

[HERBERT *nods and exits.*]

Checking up on us, huh?

[SAM *shrugs.* AMY *laughs and hands* SAM *the Coke.*]

SAM: Thanks. Oh, hey, I've got something here.

AMY: What's that?

SAM: Let me fish it out.

[*He pulls out the snapshot and shows it to her.*]

You remember this?

AMY: That's me, isn't it?

SAM: Don't you remember?

AMY: Where am I in this shot? Where was it taken?

SAM: In the ravines.

AMY: That's right. Oh yes, I remember when you took that. You'd just gotten that new camera, right?

SAM: The Leica. And I asked you if you'd like to model for me so I could try it out.

AMY: I was sure you just wanted to get me alone in the ravines. I was so certain it was a come-on.

SAM: If that's what you thought, why'd you say yes?

AMY: It had been a pretty boring summer till then. I said to myself, "Why not?" Imagine my disappointment when all you did was take pictures.

SAM: Not what you'd anticipated, huh?

AMY: I was half expecting you to ask me to take off my clothes for nude studies.

SAM: The thought crossed my mind.

AMY: It did, huh?

SAM: Not seriously. Just a passing fantasy. Something you think about and it makes you smile to yourself. Nothing I seriously considered acting on, though.

AMY: Why not?

SAM: Partially because I wouldn't have had the nerve to ask. And partially because you wouldn't have said yes.

AMY: I don't know about that.

SAM: You wouldn't have actually done it.

AMY: I might have.

SAM: Oh, come on—

AMY: I might have done it, just to prove something.

SAM: Prove what?

AMY: That I wasn't ashamed of my body or some such nonsense. There's always something you can prove. I just might have done it.

SAM: I was pretty happy with the way things turned out as it was. I mean, I accomplished my purpose.

AMY: Which was what?

SAM: Sort of what you said. To get you alone. But to talk. I was hoping it might lead to us getting together, and it did. So, I was very happy.

AMY: We were always bumping into each other anyway. At parties and at the lake. You could've talked before.

SAM: You were intimidating enough without having all the others there, too.

AMY: I was intimidating?

SAM: A little.

AMY: Tell me, how was I intimidating?

SAM: First, you were a girl—

AMY: Uh-huh?

SAM: And I was always shy of girls. Or I was then. And there was also the fact that during the school year, you were going to college in New York while I was sticking it out here in the boondocks.

AMY: So you thought I was more worldly, was that it?

SAM: Sort of. But anyway, I really liked you. I mean, I'd liked you from way before—from high school.

AMY: You sure took your time.

SAM: Like I say, I was shy.

AMY: Four or five years is awful shy.

SAM: I was afraid if I'd asked you for a date—I don't know, you would have laughed or something.

AMY: So you came up with the modeling idea?

SAM: That way, if you said no, I could've rationalized you were saying no to modeling, not to me. I think I was more afraid of rejection than just about anything else, except maybe the draft.

[AMY *offers the picture back to him.*]

Would you like to keep it?

AMY: But it's yours.

SAM: I've got the negative.

[AMY *smiles and puts the picture away.*]

AMY: Kids really go through a lot of shit, don't they? I know I used to take things so seriously.

SAM: You don't take things seriously now?

AMY: I've stopped thinking in absolutes.

SAM: How do you mean?

AMY: When I was that age, I kept looking at situations like—well, I wouldn't be able to go on living if I didn't get that English paper in on time or wasn't asked to the homecoming dance. It seems to me that I faced so many more crises then. Is it my imagination or are the kids more relaxed these days?

[SAM *doesn't know how to answer this.*]

Well, you see them when you take the yearbook pictures—

SAM: You can't tell from that. They've got their Sunday duds on and their hair combed. The rest of the year, the way they go around—I'm sure most of them have trouble recognizing each other in those books. There they are, all dressed up, smiling away, showing all their teeth, except for the ones wearing braces, who smile like their lips were glued together. Occasionally, though, you get these characters who insist on holding serious expressions.

AMY: I was one of those.

SAM: So aware that they're about to step out on life's great journey.

[AMY *mimics purposefulness.*]

Yeah, like that. Sometimes it's hard to keep from laughing. There's this determined eighteen-year-old kid staring off into the future with pimples all over his face.

AMY: You never see pimples on graduation pictures.

SAM: Of course not. I touch them out. Years from now, somebody looks at his graduation picture, he doesn't want to be reminded of what a lousy complexion he had. So I touch them out.

[*A beat.*]

You remember Bubber Margoshes?

AMY: I remember the name.

SAM: He was in Mr. Lawrence's homeroom.

AMY: Oh, the lummox who was always getting into trouble.

SAM: That's the one. He used to beat the crap out of me after school. Sometimes really stomped me bad. Well, a couple of years ago, I was taking pictures—graduation pictures—and, son of a gun, there was Bubber's younger brother. Another holy terror, I could tell. With a complexion that looked like a relief map of the Rockies. I know it was vindictive of me, but I didn't touch up that picture at all. The way I shot it was the way it ran in the book. So Bubber's baby brother will always be remembered with a lumpy face.

[*They're laughing together now.*]

AMY: So, there are satisfactions in your life?

SAM: Some. What about you?

AMY: I'm getting by.

SAM: What are you working at?

AMY: I'm an associate editor for a book club. I do a lot of reading.

SAM: Sounds like interesting work.

AMY: It's not bad.

SAM: So you're happy.

[AMY *shrugs in response.*]

AMY: What did he say, when he called?

SAM: You mean—

AMY: Yeah, Dad. What was that like?

SAM: He was very polite. I think he must have felt uncomfortable.

AMY: I wonder why.

SAM: It was a surprise, his phoning. Inviting me over.

AMY: Kind of a switch from threatening to have you arrested.

SAM: I don't blame him, you know. About that. The way he took it. Boy, I was teed off at the time, though. Charging over and telling me off like that in front of my parents. After he left, I went up to my room and, jeez, the speeches I came up with! In my head, you know.

AMY: Good stuff?

SAM: Poetry. Too bad I couldn't think of any of it when he was there. I started writing a letter to him. Why waste all that good material, right? I was working on it when he came back later that night. He didn't exactly apologize to me, but he allowed as how he'd gotten carried away a little. We talked a bit, and he asked me what I was planning to do about it.

AMY: And you said you would do the right thing.

SAM: I meant it. And I would have.

AMY: I know.

SAM: So he drove me over here.

AMY: Ah yes, that was a cheerful scene.

SAM: I wish I could have given you more support. Backed you up better.

AMY: You didn't have to give me support.

SAM: But I was responsible.

AMY: Now don't you try to co-opt my responsibility. I made all my decisions consciously.

SAM: Did you consciously intend to get pregnant?

AMY [*concedingly*]: No, that just happened.

SAM: Well, it didn't *just* happen.

AMY: True. But it could have been prevented.

SAM: I should have taken precautions. But I was afraid of offending you.

AMY: I don't follow.

SAM: I'd mailed away to one of those places listed in the back of magazines. The ads for a "super-sensitive assortment" for two fifty. I was too timid to go to the drugstore, right? Every day I would wait for the mailman because I wanted to get my hands on them before my mother saw the box and was tempted to open it and see what was inside. Finally they came, in the proverbial plain brown wrapper.

AMY: So why didn't you use them?

SAM: Well, like I say, the first time I was afraid of offending you. I thought you would think my carrying them would mean that I was expecting it.

AMY: All right, that was the first time. But after that?

SAM: After that, I was afraid you'd think I was taking it for granted. Or that it would make it seem less romantic or something. I guess I had some pretty screwy ideas at the time.

AMY: No pun intended.

SAM: No, no pun intended. These days, they practically hand them out in high schools.

AMY: Times change. How's that for a profound comment?

SAM: I don't care what you say, I should have supported you. I should have told him what I thought. Your dad.

AMY: Which was what?

SAM: That you had a right to make up your own mind. Even if I didn't agree. And that he was off base calling you down for what you'd decided. It was three or four in the morning when he finally drove me home. We were quiet all the way back. I guess he was thinking about what had happened, and I certainly wasn't about to start a conversation. Anyway, we pull up in front of my house, and I'm going to get out, but he reaches over and holds my arm. Not like he's going to hurt me, but just to get my attention, you know? And he says, "Listen, I want you to know that I think you're not a bad kid. I don't hold it against you what she decided tonight. I know you were willing to meet your responsibilities like a man, and I respect you for it." And he stops talking, and I don't know whether he expects me to say anything or not. But I can't say anything. I just sit there, and he holds on to my arm for a while, like he's forgotten about me. Then, finally, he lets go, and I get out of the car, and he drives away. And I hear later that you went back to New York to finish college. And I write letters that aren't answered.

[*A beat.*]

And now here we are as if nothing's happened.

AMY: A lot has happened.

SAM: Yeah, but we're out here again. Back out on the front porch, talking like we used to.

AMY: I miss porches.

SAM: You're still a Midwesterner at heart. Porches, rocking chairs, and cornflakes.

AMY: We do have cornflakes in New York. And I have a rocking chair. And I've got a balcony I sometimes sit on.

SAM: You share the balcony?

AMY: Share?

SAM: I guess what I'm so subtly trying to ask is if you live with someone.

AMY: I can't do that.

SAM: You've tried?

AMY: Once.

SAM: You didn't get along?

AMY: It wasn't his fault. He was very good and more than reasonably patient and put up with a lot of nonsense. But after a couple of weeks, I got edgy. I was always aware of tension in the back of my neck. And a kind of—claustrophobia. Only the barriers weren't physical. It was as if I were cornered in a kind of emotional space. Am I making any sense? I moved out after a little less than three months. I just couldn't hack it. I'm not one of those people with a talent for cohabitation. I cannot share an apartment. I have to have—oh, Jesus, how do I put it? I've got to know that, at any given moment, I have it within my power to be private. To shut the door if I want and sit down in my rocker and be free from other people's rhythms. Removed from them. Or as removed as you can be in the middle of a city. And not to have to consider anybody.

SAM: Sounds lonely.

AMY: I'm not a recluse. Not really. I just have to know that I can be alone when I want. That precludes living with another person.

SAM: You ever wonder what would have happened if we'd gone through with it? Gotten married, had the kid?

AMY: Oh, sure, I wondered. But mostly I was pretty sure I'd done the right thing.

[*A beat.*]

You didn't really want to marry me, did you?

SAM: Part of me wanted to very badly. But I didn't want us to get married because we had to. I figured that would be starting off on the wrong foot. So when you said no, I was kind of relieved. And I really thought that one day we would get married, but because we wanted to. But you went away, and that was it.

AMY: And you married someone else.

SAM: That's the way it happened. They're in Minneapolis now. She moved there after the divorce, with our daughter, remarried.

AMY: You have a daughter?

SAM: Jennifer. She's in the second grade, or will be this fall. I see her during vacations. Minneapolis, too far to go to see her on weekends. But during vacations, we have fun, the two of us. We have a pretty rowdy time.

AMY: You miss her.

SAM: I miss them both. Her and her mother. The divorce wasn't my idea. It's funny. All those things you were talking about—the claustrophobia, the tension—I feel all that, too, only for me it's because there's no one there.

AMY: You thinking of getting married again?

SAM: I'd like to. Frankly I'm scared of asking. Still scared. Isn't that something? What were we talking about? Right, Jennifer. Wait a sec—speaking of photos, I've got one of her, too.

[*He pulls out his wallet and finds it.*]

There.

AMY: She's a charmer all right.

SAM: Very bright kid. It's a real pleasure watching her grow. She's going to be something fine. The guy who marries her is going to be one lucky fellow.

[*A beat.*]

Listen to me. She's barely seven and already I'm giving her away.

[*He puts the photo and wallet away.*]

AMY: I'm glad you didn't break this out while Dad was still here.

SAM: Why?

AMY: Don't you know why you're here?

SAM: Sure, because I wanted to see you.

AMY: I mean why Dad asked you to come.

SAM: I think, in case something went wrong—you know, to have someone you could lean on.

AMY: There's more to it than that.

SAM: There is?

AMY: He wants to be a grandfather.

SAM [*startled*]: Oh, son of a gun!

AMY: Yup.

SAM: That's why he asked me—

AMY: I guess he figured if it happened once, it can happen again.

SAM: Are you sure? Did he say that?

AMY: You heard him.

SAM: When? What are you—

AMY: When he was talking about Julia Morse's wedding and how she's expecting a baby. And that comment about how happy old man Morse must be now that he's going to be a grandfather? That's where that came from.

SAM: Boy! That's—what a thing to put on you. No wonder you were uncomfortable. I mean, if I'd realized this was what he was up to—

AMY: You wouldn't have come?

SAM: I probably would have come, but I'd have gotten that whole thing clear early on.

AMY: Well, it's clear now. Right?

SAM: Yeah. Boy!

[*He shakes his head. A pause.*]

Though, you know, I understand what he's feeling. Not that I approve of what he's trying to do or the way he used you.

AMY: And you.

SAM: And me, yes. But still, I can—I have those feelings inside me, too. I mean, I would like Jennifer to grow up and have kids. And I'd like to have another kid myself. The thing is to leave something behind that people can see you in.

AMY: Isn't that an awful selfish reason to have kids? Self-perpetuation? I mean, maybe there's no unselfish reason to have kids. I don't know.

SAM: That's a pretty negative way of looking at things.

AMY: But I think we're all selfish. To a degree. I don't think there's anything wrong with that. But you can be selfish without using someone else to satisfy your . . .

[*A beat.*]

Oh hell, let's stop this abstract navelizing.

SAM: Huh?

AMY: Staring at our own navels.

SAM: We could stare at each other's navels.

AMY: That your idea of a good time?

SAM: Depends on the circumstances. Are you an innie or an outie?

AMY [*goofing around*]: You don't remember? I'm disappointed!

SAM: I'm sorry.

AMY: A fine romantic you are! Don't even remember. These are the things a true romantic remembers. That and the dress I was wearing on our third date and the candy bar that melted in your pocket at the stadium.

SAM: It was a lapse. A regrettable lapse.

AMY: Get your act together, boy.

SAM: I will. I promise. Am I forgiven?

AMY: "What the hell," she said magnanimously!

[*A beat.*]

SAM: You plan on going out to see your mom and Jeremy?

AMY: Visit the cemetery?

SAM: I'd be happy to drive you out—

AMY: No, I don't think so. I doubt it. I don't know.

SAM: What—would that be too sentimental a gesture?

AMY [*surprised*]: Where did that remark come from?

SAM: Uh, forget it. I'm sorry. It's late, and—

AMY: Things slip out.

SAM: Yuh.

AMY: You've got me pegged as pretty hard bitten, haven't you?

SAM: I didn't say that.

AMY: Tough lady with skin of leather.

SAM: That's not what I meant.

AMY [*seriously considering it*]: Maybe there's something to what you say. Maybe I think it would be too sentimental to go out there.

SAM: You want to know what I think?

AMY: What do you think?

SAM [*tentatively*]: I think you're afraid to be sentimental. I think you're afraid it would be seen as a weakness.

AMY: No, I just don't want to give in to—

[*She stops herself short.*]

Funny. That's what Dad said earlier.

SAM: About being sentimental?

AMY: About giving in. He wouldn't use the wheelchair. He said it would be giving in.

SAM: You're your father's daughter.

AMY: Why do I flinch when you say that?

SAM: Could be you don't want to be anybody's anything.

AMY: My father's daughter. That sounds so possessive. Jeremy, though, he was his father's son. He was pleased when people would say there was a resemblance. I was a little jealous actually. I mean, it's fathers and daughters who are supposed to be extra close, right? But—

[*A beat.*]

You know, the lousy thing is I resent the hell out of Jeremy for dying. I do. If he hadn't had that accident, he would have gotten married, had kids, all of it. Then maybe Dad would have accepted—not approve. There was no way he would have approved. But I thought, eventually, when Jeremy has his first kid, Dad would have what he wanted and I would be off the hook. Only it didn't work out that way. And now I'm stuck being Dad's only chance.

We had a big fight after the funeral. That night—late. We had never really talked about my not having the baby before. And at the airport, through the funeral and dinner, you could hear us avoiding the subject. But that night, all hell broke loose. I hadn't realized how deeply what I'd done had hurt him.

[*A beat.*]

[*Angrily*] God damn Jeremy! If it weren't for his damn motor scooter, I wouldn't have had to go through all this shit. I wouldn't have had to deal with these damn, stupid, irrational guilt feelings for not living up to Dad's expectations. Isn't that pretty? I'm not sad about Jeremy's dying so much for his sake as for my own. Christ, talk about selfish!

SAM: You're being rough on yourself.

AMY [*plowing on*]: Sometimes I wonder, if it weren't for this pressure, would Jeremy matter to me at all? Or would I have forgotten by now? Would I not care, not give a damn?

SAM: Please, stop it! Amy, please?

[*He puts his arms around her to comfort her. They stay like this for several moments. She looks at him. This is the first time they've touched in a noncasual way. For a moment, there is the sense of possibility between them.*]

AMY [*disengaging*]: Well, it's getting late.

SAM: Maybe I should go.

[*A beat. He rises.*]

AMY: Truthfully, it was very good seeing you again.

SAM: Truthfully, it was very good being seen.

AMY: Sorry if I depressed you.

SAM: No, it's—I understand.

AMY: You always were good at understanding.

SAM: So you said.

AMY: Yes, I did, didn't I?

[*A beat.*]

Hey, tell me a joke!

SAM: A joke?

AMY: Sure. Leave me laughing. You must know a good joke.

SAM: It's not enough you want a joke, now you're asking for a good joke.

AMY: I'm not a reasonable person. Come on, you must know one.

SAM: It's not easy to summon one up on the spur of the moment.

AMY: I remove the stipulation that it be good. Go ahead and tell a bad joke.

SAM: How about a good pun?

AMY: There's no such thing as a good pun.

SAM: No, this is a good one. Are you ready?

AMY: Fire away.

SAM: All right—what's the definition of a schizophrenic?

AMY: That's a riddle. You promised me a pun.

SAM: Don't worry, there's a pun.

AMY: All right, I give up. What's the definition of a schizophrenic?

SAM: A person with a bi-psyche built for two.

AMY [*judiciously*]: You're right. That's a pun.

[*She laughs. He's pleased.*]

SAM: Like it?

AMY: Not bad. Where'd you hear it?

SAM: Please, it's an original.

AMY: You made that up?

SAM: Yup.

AMY: Not bad at all.

[*A beat.*]

SAM: So, when do I see you again?

AMY: I don't know.

SAM: You going to be in town for a while?

AMY: I can't say. It really depends on tomorrow. How things turn out for Dad.

SAM: Yeah, I understand. But I was thinking—it would be nice. To see each other again. I really enjoyed tonight, despite—

AMY: Yeah, despite.

SAM: And I'd like to see you some more. So, what shall I do? Shall I call you?

AMY: I guess.

SAM: I won't have to pretend that I just happen to drop by and happen to see you on the porch. That's an improvement.

AMY: Right.

SAM: So, when should I call?

AMY: I don't know.

SAM: I don't guess I should call tomorrow.

AMY: No, that wouldn't be good.

SAM: You'll probably be in and out of the hospital.

AMY: Probably.

SAM: So, the day after?

AMY: If you want.

SAM: I'll call the day after.

AMY: I may still have to be at the hospital.

SAM: Well, you could call me. I'll give you the number.

AMY: No, that's all right.

SAM: I'll write it out.

AMY: Really, it's OK.

SAM: No, I really mean it. I really want us to get together.

AMY: Yes, I know.

SAM: It's been so long. We've barely scratched the surface. So much to catch up on. I mean, it's important.

AMY: Sam—

SAM: The thing is, I still—

[*A beat.*]

I care about you.

[*She turns away.*]

Listen, I understand.

AMY: No, you don't. You don't really.

SAM: It's a scary thing—

AMY: I'm not scared.

SAM: No?

AMY: I don't want it, that's all.

SAM: I can't believe you mean that.

AMY: I do.

SAM: Maybe you think you mean it, but—I know you.

AMY: It's been more than ten years.

SAM: That doesn't matter.

AMY: How can you say that? You don't know what I've done, anything about what I've gone through.

SAM: What do you mean? Did something happen?

AMY: Happen?

SAM: You said about what you've gone through.

AMY: Oh, Jesus—

SAM: You said—

AMY: What I've gone through is ten years, that's all. Ten years changes things.

SAM: It doesn't change who you are.

AMY: I really don't think we should get into this. Why don't we call it a night?

SAM: It's important we talk about this.

AMY: We don't have to talk about anything, Sam. It was very good to see you again, and I like you very much, but that's as far as it can go. Can't you see that?

SAM: I'll tell you what I see—

AMY: I don't want to hear this.

SAM: Someone must have hurt you very badly for you to—

AMY: I said I don't want to talk about it.

SAM: Amy, I understand about being hurt—

AMY: That's enough, OK?

SAM: It scares you.

AMY: Good-bye, Sam.

SAM: But you can't let it keep you from—

AMY: I said good-bye!

SAM: Amy, you have to have someone. You have to share, you have to care about someone.

AMY [*interrupting*]: Jesus, can't you take a hint? Don't you understand what I'm saying?

[*A beat.*]

I *am* involved with someone. I'm living with him. I'm in love with him.

[*A beat.*]

SAM: But, what you said—

AMY: Sam, I haven't seen you in years. I'm not about to tell you all my private . . . I mean, why would I?

SAM: I see. Of course.

AMY: I'm sorry if I gave you the wrong impression. But that's the way it is.

SAM: Well, I uh—I'm bass-ackwards this time, aren't I? Right.

AMY: I'm sorry.

SAM: No, I should have gone while the going was good. You liked the pun. I shouldn't have pressed my luck.

[*A beat.*]

He must be something special, huh? Seeing how you feel about having a private space and everything. Must be quite a guy if he can make you get past that.

AMY: Yes, he is.

SAM: It's just that I felt—that there was a possibility.

AMY [*sympathetically*]: You want someone.

SAM: Yes.

[*A beat.*]

I thought you.

[*A beat.*]

Yes, someone. [*Heading for the steps*] Listen, my best wishes to your dad. I hope it works out.

AMY: Thank you. I'll tell him.

SAM: And, uh—take care, huh?

AMY: You, too.

SAM: Yuh.

[*He nods, smiles. A moment's pause, then he turns and exits down the walk. She watches him go. She sits, picks up the blanket* HERBERT *discarded earlier, wraps herself in it. Sits quietly for several beats.* HERBERT *enters.*]

HERBERT: He's gone.

AMY: Yes.

HERBERT: Going to see him again?

AMY: No.

HERBERT: I guess you grow out of some friends.

[*A beat.*]

If it comes to it, you'll sell the store, won't you?

[*A beat.*]

AMY: Yes.

HERBERT: And the house.

AMY: Yes.

HERBERT: Too bad about Sam. I liked him.

AMY: So did I.

[*A beat.*]

HERBERT: You lied to that boy. What you said about living with someone, being in love—that was a lie.

AMY: It was for his sake.

HERBERT: I'm sure.

[*Pause.*]

I wish you could lie to me.

AMY: Dad . . .

[*A beat.*]

HERBERT: It's getting late. We'd better go inside.

[*He reaches out to touch her shoulder. She holds onto his hand. A beat. The lights fade to black.*]

THE VALUE OF NAMES

—for Sheridan

My friend Kate Draper had news. She had just been cast in her first Broadway show, *A Day in Hollywood, A Night in the Ukraine.* Always looking for things that would (theoretically) complicate the lives of my friends, I asked her what her father, the famous blacklisted dancer Paul Draper, would say if she were in a show directed by Jerome Robbins, who had named names to the House Committee on Un-American Activities in the fifties. Her response—Tommy Tune was directing, not Robbins. And I said, "But *if* . . ." She thought he would disapprove but probably wouldn't say anything. And I thought that if the father would say something, that would make a play.

The script benefited mightily from being developed in the New York Writers Bloc. I originally thought of it as a four-character piece, the fourth character being Norma's boyfriend. For three weeks running I brought in material on this assumption, and for three weeks running my colleagues told me that three of the characters claimed their attention, and the boyfriend was a lox. They were right. He was just there to elicit information from the others. I got rid of him. The Bloc probably saved me months of work. This is one of the reasons I believe in getting feedback on pieces as I'm writing. Incidentally, the member of the Bloc who consistently read Benny for me was Donald Margulies, who is indeed quite a good cold reader in addition to being a fine writer.

The Value of Names premiered at the Actors Theatre of Louisville on November 4, 1982, as part of its Shorts Festival directed by Emily Mann, with the following cast:

Benny Silverman	Larry Block
Norma Silverman	Robin Groves
Leo Greshen	Frederic Major

The Value of Names received its Chicago premiere at the Victory Gardens Theater on March 30, 1983, directed by Sandy Shinner, with the following cast:

Benny Silverman .... Shelley Berman
Norma Silverman...................................... Jill Holden
Leo Greshen.. Byrne Piven

A revised version of the play premiered at the Hartford Stage Company on February 10, 1984, directed by Emily Mann, with the following cast:

Benny Silverman .... Larry Block
Norma Silverman................................. Robin Groves
Leo Greshen...................................... Alvin Epstein

The Value of Names received its New York premiere at the Vineyard Theatre on June 1, 1989, directed by Gloria Muzio, with the following cast:

Benny Silverman .... John Seitz
Norma Silverman.................................. Ava Haddad
Leo Greshen................................. Stephen Pearlman

The Value of Names was produced on radio by Los Angeles Theatre Works in 1995 under the direction of Gordon Hunt, with the following cast:

Benny Silverman .... Garry Marshall
Norma Silverman.................................. Sally Murphy
Leo Greshen................................. Hector Elizondo

The Value of Names was produced by the Nebraska Repertory Theatre on July 10, 2002, directed by Jim Glossman, with the following cast:

Benny Silverman .... Jack Klugman
Norma Silverman..................................... Sarah Yorra
Leo Greshen....................................... Louis Zorich

The Value of Names was produced on tour in 2005 in a production directed by Jim Glossman, with the following cast:

Benny Silverman .... Jack Klugman
Norma Silverman.......................... Megan Muckelmann
Leo Greshen...................................... Louis Zorich

The Value of Names was produced in 2006 at the George Street Playhouse in New Brunswick, New Jersey, directed by Jim Glossman (and subsequently at the Falcon Theatre in Burbank, California), with the following cast:

Benny Silverman .... Jack Klugman
Norma Silverman.................................... Liz Larsen
Leo Greshen...................................... Dan Lauria

CHARACTERS

Benny Silverman
Norma Silverman
Leo Greshen

[*The play is set in 1983 on a patio high up in hills overlooking the Pacific Ocean in reach of Los Angeles. Upstage is* BENNY SILVERMAN's *house. It is the house of someone very comfortably off. The patio may be entered either through a door from the house or through a gate that leads directly from the road. At rise,* BENNY *has an easel set up and is painting the view from his patio. He is in his late sixties or early seventies and appears to be in fine health.* NORMA *is in her twenties. A few seconds of quiet.*]

BENNY: Does it sound too Jewish?

NORMA [*to audience*]: No, hold on. First, a couple of things you should know: It's 1983. A patio up in the hills overlooking Malibu. Over there, the Pacific Ocean. Next to me, my father. On the whole, I have less trouble with the Pacific.

BENNY [*with the tone "Are you finished?"*]: OK?

NORMA: Sure. Go ahead.

BENNY: Does it sound too Jewish?

NORMA: Pop—

BENNY: You're changing your name. Stands to reason there's something about the one you've got you don't like. Or maybe find inconvenient.

NORMA [*to audience*]: I should have known he'd take it like this.

BENNY: Could put you at a disadvantage. A name like Silverman. Some parts—the casting directors won't even look at you. I know. Say, for instance, they do a new version of *The Bells of St. Mary's*. Casting people see the name Norma Silverman, what are they going to say? "Nope, don't call her. A person obviously without nun potential. Get me an O'Hara or a Kelly. Get away with this Silverman." And there goes your chance to play Ingrid Bergman. Of course, Bergman, too, is a name that's a little suspect.

NORMA: Pop—

BENNY: But then, one look at her, that question's laid to rest. Even if she did play Golda Meir once. One look at that nose of hers. That was not a Jewish nose. But then—thanks to the magic of science—who can tell from a nose?

NORMA: Of course.

BENNY: I could show you Horowitzes and Steins and Margulieses with noses on them look like they belong to Smiths. Very funny seeing a Smith nose on a Horowitz. Or a Horowitz nose on a Smith, although this is rarer.

NORMA: They don't transplant noses.

BENNY: You want to know why?

NORMA [*with a sidelong look to audience*]: OK, why?

BENNY: Run the risk of the body rejecting. Sure, it's a big problem. Heart transplant, kidney transplant—the body sometimes says, "No, thank you. Take it away." A case like that all that happens is maybe someone dies. But a nose transplant—could you imagine the humiliation? Walking down the street, maybe you hiccup, a slight tearing sensation, and suddenly there's a draft in the middle of your face. You look down on the pavement, see two dainty nostrils staring up at heaven.

NORMA: Are you finished?

BENNY: Are you?

NORMA: With what?

BENNY: This nonsense. This changing-your-name nonsense.

NORMA: It's not nonsense. I'm going to do it.

BENNY: Fine. So do it. So what do you want from me?

NORMA: I don't want from you. I just thought I should tell you.

BENNY: OK, you've told me. So what do you want me to say? You want me to say congratulations? Like you're having a baby—congratulations? You're having a new name—how wonderful! And who's the father of this new name? I know who the father of the old name is. I see him sometimes on the late movie.

NORMA: OK, Pop.

BENNY: It's not OK. But never mind, we won't talk about it.

NORMA: Fat chance.

BENNY: So what else is new? A sex change?

NORMA: It doesn't have anything to do with Jewish or not Jewish.

BENNY: What *has* it to do with?

NORMA: You.

BENNY: Oh. *I'm* the to-do-with?

NORMA: Here we go.

BENNY: *I'm* the reason you're changing your name?

NORMA: Do you want me to explain now? Or shall I give you a little room for a tirade?

BENNY: What tirade?

NORMA: The tirade you're gearing up for.

BENNY: Who, me?

NORMA: I wish you'd understand.

BENNY: What's to understand? You're changing your name. You're changing your name because it's my name. This makes me feel instantly terrific and wonderful. It makes me feel how glad I am to have my daughter's love and respect. How fulfilling it is to be a parent. How worth it all it's all been. Would you like a little coffee?

NORMA: Look, every time I've ever done anything, every time I've ever been reviewed, they always put in that I'm your daughter. My name is not Norma Silverman. My name is Norma Silverman Benny Silverman's daughter.

BENNY: So what are you trying to do—convince people you're the product of a virgin birth?

NORMA: I'm very proud of being your daughter. But I would like, for once, when I get on a stage, for them to see me. Not just see you in me. There's a comparison implied there. "Is she as good as—"

BENNY: Aren't you?

NORMA: I don't think I should have to fight that. You really don't want to understand, do you?

BENNY: Who put you up to this?

NORMA: What?

BENNY: This is your mother's idea, isn't it?

NORMA: No.

BENNY: I recognize the style.

NORMA: What do you mean?

BENNY: Right after the divorce, she got her driver's license changed back to her maiden name. Sarah Teitel. And her checking account and her magazine subscriptions and all the rest. Sarah Teitel. Didn't want to be known by her married name anymore, thank you very much. Oh no. Said she wouldn't use it ever again. You know what I did? I made the alimony checks out to "Mrs. Benny Silverman." Would have loved to see her face when she had to endorse them.

NORMA: She didn't have anything to do with this.

BENNY: Maybe not, but she didn't tell you no.

NORMA: Actually, she told me you'd probably scream your head off, but she understood.

BENNY: That's generous of her.

NORMA: She respected my decision. Because that's what it was, Pop—my decision. She didn't enter into it. It's something I decided to do by myself, for myself. It's what I wanted.

BENNY: Fine—you wanted, you got.

NORMA: You know something—if you look at it the right way, it's a compliment.

BENNY: It is?

NORMA: If you look at it the right way.

BENNY: Let's hear this right way.

NORMA: Never mind.

BENNY: No compliment?

NORMA: Help.

BENNY: First it's out with the name, then it's good-bye compliment. Beats me why I should give you a cup of coffee.

NORMA: I don't want a cup of coffee.

BENNY: I can understand that. If I were you, I'd have enough trouble sleeping at night.

NORMA [*referring to the painting*]: I like it.

BENNY: Do you know anything about art?

NORMA: Do I have to know something about art to like it?

BENNY: If you knew something about art, you'd be able to appreciate the shadings, the nuances—all the really subtle reasons why this is lousy.

NORMA: One of the things I love about you is this terrifically graceful way you have of accepting compliments.

BENNY: I like my compliments honest.

NORMA: What's not honest? I said I like it. I *do* like it. I didn't say that it's good.

BENNY: Oh, so you *don't* think it's good.

NORMA: Obviously I'm not entitled to think it's good *or* bad. I'm not even entitled to like it. So what *am* I entitled to? Statements of verifiable fact only? OK, a statement of verifiable fact: you are painting a painting, and it's sitting on an easel.

BENNY: Thank you, I'm flattered.

NORMA: And what would be so terrible if I liked it?

BENNY: Anybody can like. To like doesn't take any great skill, any great powers of discernment.

NORMA: I see. Only people with certifiably elevated taste are entitled to like something.

BENNY: Do you know what Monet or Chagall would say if they saw this?

NORMA: What?

BENNY: "Benny, stick to your acting."

NORMA: So why don't you?

BENNY: I like it.

NORMA: *You* like it?

BENNY: Yeah.

NORMA: I thought you said it's lousy.

BENNY: It *is* lousy.

NORMA: It's lousy but you like it.

BENNY: It's *because* I know that it's lousy I *can* like it.

NORMA: Come again?

BENNY: I don't pretend it's good. I don't delude myself. All I can say is that standing here, doing this, I enjoy myself. It doesn't have to be good for me to enjoy myself.

NORMA: Someone should make you a ride in an amusement park.

BENNY: You really like it?

NORMA: Yes.

BENNY: When I finish, it's yours. I hope you treat it better than other things I've given you. Like my name.

NORMA: OK, Pop—

BENNY [*referring to a playscript near her*]: I've read this script of yours.

NORMA: I didn't write it.

BENNY: Well, you're going to be in it.

NORMA: That still doesn't make it mine.

BENNY: It makes you associated with it.

NORMA: As in guilt by association?

BENNY: Who said anything about guilt?

NORMA: Your tone does. You don't like the play.

BENNY: It's OK for what it is. Are you really going to take off your clothes?

NORMA: Not clothes. Just my top.

BENNY: Your top isn't clothes?

NORMA: I'm not taking off my clothes, plural. I'm taking off a piece of clothing, singular.

BENNY: A piece of clothing, singular, that covers up parts of you, plural.

NORMA: It's not a big deal. A lot of plays these days call for it.

BENNY: That excuses everything.

NORMA: I didn't realize there was anything to excuse.

BENNY: It's your business.

NORMA: It is, you know.

BENNY: You knew what was in the script before you signed the contract?

NORMA: Of course.

BENNY: It's your business. It's not my ass people will be looking at.

NORMA: It's not my ass either.

BENNY: Just your boobies.

NORMA: That's right.

BENNY: I never had to do that. Of course, who would pay to see my boobies? Or my ass, for that matter?

NORMA: Who knows, somebody might.

BENNY: Nobody I'd want to meet.

NORMA: I knew you were going to pick up on that. Out of everything in the script that was the one element you were going to bring up.

BENNY: You like this play?

NORMA: I like it very much. I like my part very much. I feel very lucky to have landed it.

BENNY: All right.

NORMA: It's my business?

BENNY: Who else's?

NORMA: Not yours?

BENNY: Never.

NORMA: Well, I'm glad we got that settled.

BENNY: There was never any issue.

NORMA: Could have fooled me.

BENNY: And your mother?

NORMA: What about her?

BENNY: She doesn't have any opinion?

NORMA: All she wanted to know was if it's in—

BENNY AND NORMA [*together*]: Good taste.

BENNY: Of course, I'm used to a different kind of play. The kind with ideas and metaphors.

NORMA: I think this play is metaphoric.

BENNY: There is nothing metaphoric about an attractive young woman with her top off.

NORMA: That moment you keep harping on is about vulnerability.

BENNY: In your mind it may be about vulnerability. Maybe in the playwright's mind. In the audience's mind it will be about tits. The women out there will be thinking, "Gee, I couldn't do that. Well, maybe I could do that. But how many margaritas would it take?" Meanwhile, the guys in the audience will be thinking—well, you *know* what they'll be thinking. And their wives will know what they're thinking. And the women will look at their husbands like they're saying, "Yeah, and what are you gawking at?" And the guys will go, "Hey, I'm not gawking." And the women'll go, "Oh, yeah, right." And the guys will go, "Hey, but it's OK: this isn't tits, this is art. I'm having a catharsis here. Swear to God." You're up there acting your heart out; in the meantime, they've forgotten your character's *name.*

NORMA: Could be the audience is more sophisticated than you think.

BENNY: Don't believe me then.

NORMA: It's not a question of my believing you or not. I believe that you see things the way you see things. I just don't. But things have changed in the theater since you got started. I know it's hard to believe, Dad, but Clifford Odets is dead and gone.

BENNY: Clifford Odets? He was dead and gone even before he was dead.

NORMA: Maybe you'd like to recommend a good hotel.

BENNY: Hotel? For what?

NORMA: To stay in.

BENNY: You don't like the bed in your room?

NORMA: The bed's fine.

BENNY: I should hope so. The mattress was rated a best buy from *Consumer's Union.* What are you talking about, a hotel? What have I got a house with three bedrooms for, so that you can pay money to strangers to sleep someplace?

NORMA: Look, the next few weeks aren't going to be easy for me. It's a new script, and what's undoubtedly going to happen is that, after I've finally memorized the lines, they're all going to be changed on me during rehearsal.

BENNY: That goes with the territory.

NORMA: What I'm concerned about is what goes with *this* territory. Staying here.

BENNY: A nice view of the Pacific where occasionally a whale swims by, spouts off.

NORMA: And you.

BENNY: I don't swim anymore.

NORMA: You do your share of spouting off.

BENNY: That's me—Benny the whale.

[BENNY *laughs and goes back to his painting.*]

NORMA [*to audience*]: I was fifteen years old, pushing a shopping cart at the A&P, when I found out what he'd been through. There were two people standing in line ahead of me, so I checked out the magazine rack to see what I could waste a few minutes with. And there was a caricature of my father grinning out at me from the cover of *TV Guide*. At the bottom it said, "Benny Silverman of *Rich But Happy*." That was the name of the situation comedy he played a crazy neighbor on—*Rich But Happy*. So, of course I'm eager to see what it has to say about him. Maybe he'll mention me or Mom, though at that point they'd been divorced already ten years or so. So I'm standing in line at the A&P, smiling, reading about how he's buddies with all the technicians on the set, about a practical joke he played on the producer once, about how the younger actors on the show revere him as a comic genius, and so forth and so on. And then there was this classic *TV Guide* transitional sentence. Something about—"But Benny Silverman still has vivid memories of the black days when his chief concern was not fine-tuning a laugh but fighting for the right to practice his craft." This was followed by how he was named in front of the House Committee on Un-American Activities. And how he had been subpoenaed to appear, and how he did appear but did not cooperate. And then, years of not being able to find work. I was in the middle of this when it was my turn at the checkout counter. I paid for the groceries, and I took them home and dumped them on the kitchen table. And I asked my mother whether it had been by planning or oversight that nobody had ever told me a word about it.

BENNY [*pulling her back into the scene*]: Planning. I asked her not to.

NORMA: Why?

BENNY: It happened before you were born. It had nothing to do with you. Why should you be bothered by it?

NORMA: You expected me never to find out?

BENNY: What did it matter whether you found out or not?

NORMA: If it didn't matter, why keep it from me?

BENNY: You were a kid. Your mother and I figured, between homework and puberty, you had enough to handle. What did you need to know about something that took place years before you were even conceived?

NORMA: It might have helped me to understand you better.

BENNY: Understand what?

NORMA: Why you are what you are. Why you do what you do.

BENNY: You expect to understand all that? Nothing like modest ambitions.

NORMA: I had to go to the library, for God's sake. I had to look up your name in indexes. I had to *read* about you.

BENNY: Well, at least some good came of it. It was always murder to get you to crack a book.

NORMA: Can I ask you something?

BENNY: No. What is it?

NORMA: There was another book I found, on political theater. And there was a picture. A photo of the Labor Players—

BENNY [*correcting*]: The *New* Labor Players.

NORMA: Maybe seven or eight of you in the picture. And standing next to you is Leo Greshen, and your arm is around his shoulder.

BENNY: That was a fake arm. They touched that arm into the picture.

NORMA: He was a friend of yours.

BENNY: He gave that appearance for a while.

NORMA: So what did he say?

BENNY: Look it up. The transcript's public; it's easy to find.

NORMA: I don't mean his testimony. I mean what did he say to you?

BENNY: Why you want to dig into this is beyond—

NORMA: Did he call you afterwards? Try to explain?

BENNY: Not afterwards, before. Squealer's etiquette. Sort of like an arsonist calling up ahead of time. "Hello, I'm going to burn your house down. Thought you might like to know." Only instead—"Hello, I'm going to burn your career down." "Thanks a lot, Leo. Hope to return the favor someday."

NORMA: But he was a friend. Didn't he give you reasons?

BENNY: Oh, everybody knew the reasons why. He had the prospect of directing his first picture, and he didn't want this to blow it for him.

NORMA: He said this to you? That was why he was going to testify?

BENNY: Did you know "testify" and "testimony" come from the same Latin root as *testes*, as in "balls"? I'm not making this up. In Rome, if you wanted to make a big point that something you said was true, when you said it, you'd grab your balls. Which is why I don't think what he said to the committee really qualifies as testimony. How could it? The man had no balls to grab.

NORMA: I shouldn't have had to find out that way—reading it in a book.

BENNY: "Find out." You talk as if you'd uncovered something shameful.

NORMA: Being ashamed of something is one reason why someone may keep something secret.

BENNY: I was not ashamed. I *am* not ashamed. Perhaps I had a very good reason for not telling you.

NORMA: Such as what?

BENNY: To protect you.

NORMA: To protect me from something you weren't ashamed of. Sure, that makes sense.

BENNY: Do you remember the Epsteins?

NORMA: The Epsteins?

BENNY: The Epsteins, the Epsteins.

NORMA: Why?

BENNY: Do you?

NORMA: I think so.

BENNY: They lived in your aunt Bertha's building.

NORMA: All right, yes, I remember the Epsteins. So?

BENNY: All right. One night, your mother and I were at the Epsteins'. Ten thirty, eleven o'clock, their daughter Becky comes in. She's coming home from a date with someone her parents don't approve of, which is to say someone who isn't Jewish. An argument starts. Didn't they tell Becky not to see him? She doesn't care what they told her. She has a mind of her own, her own life to lead, she'll make her own decisions, et cetera. If she wants to go out with him she'll go out with him, and it's just too damn bad if her parents don't like it. And it keeps going like this, back and forth, more and more heat and passion and arm waving. Finally, her mother cries out, "This is what I survived Buchenwald for? For a daughter with a mouth like this?" I shudder to think how much time that girl probably ended up spending on a psychiatrist's couch.

NORMA: So you think they shouldn't have told her?

BENNY: I think it's not right to bludgeon other people with your suffering.

NORMA: There's a difference between bludgeoning and telling.

BENNY: There's a difference between everything and everything else. You can draw distinctions till you're blue in the face.

NORMA: Don't dance away from me like that. We're talking about something here.

BENNY: All right, so I was a little overprotective. When did this become a felony? But what did you learn that was so valuable? That some son of a bitch, in order to save his own ass, got up in front of some other sons of bitches and said he'd seen me a handful of times in the same room with another group of sons of bitches.

NORMA: And you didn't work for years after that.

BENNY: This was all way before you were born. Do you ever remember going to bed hungry because I couldn't provide? No. So it didn't touch you. So why are you complaining? Are you complaining because you didn't have pain? Or are you complaining because the pain you did have isn't the pain you wanted to have? Maybe you can give Becky Epstein a call, see if she wants to trade. Or maybe she'll give you the name of her shrink. You can go lie on his couch and complain about how awful I was that I didn't lift up my shirt and show you ancient scars.

NORMA: Just because I didn't know about it doesn't mean that it hasn't touched me.

BENNY: Enough already. Are we going to go over all this again?

[*A beat.*]

So, what name now? So when I look in the program I know which one is you.

NORMA: Norma Teitel.

BENNY: Teitel?

[NORMA *nods.*]

You sure this wasn't your mother's idea?

[*A beat.*]

NORMA: Hey, are you glad I'm here?
BENNY: How could you doubt?

[*They both smile. During* NORMA's *subsequent speech,* BENNY *hauls his easel and canvas and paint into the house. He is back on the patio at the conclusion of the speech.*]

NORMA [*to audience*]: And you know something? We get along OK for a little over a week. And the play's coming along well, too. And then our director has a stroke. They take him off to the hospital, where they tell us the prognosis is, thank God, good. But that leaves us without a director. The producers call a hiatus for a couple of days so they can put their heads together and come up with a new director. And then I get a call and they tell me who they've decided on. And that their offer has been made and accepted. I tell them I have some problems with their choice. I explain why. They say they hope I will stay with the show, but that I have to decide quickly. "Think about it seriously," they say. I promise I will. And then I tell Pop.
BENNY: Do you tell me because you want my advice?
NORMA: I tell you because I think you should know. I mean, it's partially for your sake I'd be doing it. If I did it.
BENNY: Quitting?
NORMA: Yes.
BENNY: Well, it *is* your decision.
NORMA: I know.
BENNY: I will only say one thing, and this is not to in any way influence your decision, but—if you were to stay with the play, I wouldn't be able to go to it.
NORMA: You hate him that much?
BENNY: I used to go to see his stuff. And when it was good work, I'd be angry. And when it was bad or flopped, I'd get satisfaction. And then I thought to myself, "What am I doing to myself? I mean, this is stupid. I've got myself to the point where I'm happy about bad work

and miserable about successes." I was letting the guy twist me into knots, plus a percentage of my ticket money was going into his pocket so that I was paying for him to do this to me. So I stopped. I don't go to see his stuff; I don't go to see the stuff of some of the others. And do you know something? The world doesn't end because I miss a play or a movie.

NORMA: So there are people whose work you won't go to see.

BENNY: I think that's what I said.

NORMA: Because of their political beliefs?

BENNY: Because of the way they *expressed* these beliefs.

NORMA: I guess you wouldn't work with them either.

BENNY: No, I wouldn't.

NORMA: When you were on *Rich But Happy,* did the issue ever come up? Was there ever a time when the producer wanted to hire one of these guys that you wouldn't work with?

BENNY: No, they knew not to do that.

NORMA: They knew there were certain people you didn't want hired.

BENNY: They were sensitive to the way I felt.

NORMA: Was there a list?

BENNY: What?

NORMA: Of people you wouldn't work with. Did you write up a list?

[*A beat.*]

BENNY: Cute.

NORMA: Well, I'm your daughter.

BENNY: What you're describing is not the same.

NORMA: You weren't hired, and you turned around and saw to it that other people weren't hired.

BENNY: There's a difference. There's a distinction.

NORMA: I'm sure there is.

BENNY: To anybody with a pair of eyes in her head.

NORMA: Explain the distinction to me.

BENNY: I don't have to defend myself to you.

NORMA: All right.

BENNY: What—do you think I should forget? Would you expect me to work with, for instance, a Nazi?

NORMA: Nazi?

BENNY: You know from Nazis, don't you? They're the guys who had the franchise on swastikas before the Hell's Angels. Let's say I'm in a movie, OK? I'm going to do a scene with this guy. While we're waiting to shoot, we're sitting around, we're kibitzing. I tell an anecdote. He laughs and says, "You know that reminds me of something funny that happened when I was in the SS."

NORMA: Right.

BENNY: So according to you what I should say back is, "Hey, Fritz, want me to cue you on your lines?"

NORMA: Why is it whenever you get mad, you reach for a Nazi?

BENNY: What are you talking about, "reach for a Nazi"?

NORMA: You do, you know.

BENNY: You make it sound like a soft drink. "Worked up a thirst? Reach for a nice, refreshing Nazi!"

NORMA: It's like a conversational preemptive strike. Whenever you don't agree with me, it always comes around to Nazis or anti-Semitism. First is my name too Jewish. Then it's Becky Epstein and the Holocaust. And now, even this, in come the jackboots again.

BENNY: "Even this"? What "this" are you saying "even this" about?

NORMA: McCarthyism, the blacklist—

BENNY: And you don't think that was anti-Semitism? Look at who was on the committee. Martin Dies. Harold Velde. Karl Mundt.

NORMA: Oh come on, everybody with a German name isn't an anti-Semite. Besides which, there were a lot of people on the committee who weren't German.

BENNY: That's right, Nixon isn't German. And we all know what a warm feeling he has for people of—how would he put it?—Hebraic persuasion? And as for the guys he and his buddies went after—

NORMA: All Jews, right?

BENNY: Let's just say you wouldn't have had trouble raising a minyan. Oh, and the fun the committee had with the Jewish names! You can't tell from reading the transcripts—how they punched them, mispronounced them, tried to make them sound sinister and alien. Carnovsky, Papirofsky, Ruskin. Ever hear anything so suspicious in your life? And did they have a field day with the ones who had *changed* their names! "You call yourself 'Holliday' but your real name, the name you were born with, is what? Tuvim?" As if they were talking to a criminal trying to hide something. You're going to tell me that wasn't anti-Semitism?

NORMA: That's not my point.

BENNY: Oh, I know what your point is.

NORMA: I never said you should work with Nazis.

BENNY: So, it's OK with you if I don't? I mean, you won't disapprove if I turn down a contract to costar with Dr. Mengele?

NORMA: There *is* a difference between Mengele and Nixon.

BENNY: You're absolutely right—one murdered Jews; the other only made it hard for them to eat.

NORMA: OK, go ahead, twist everything.

BENNY: And you weren't twisting? That comment about my having a list?

NORMA: I was just raising what I thought was an interesting question.

BENNY: I was kept from working because some of the views I used to have suddenly weren't popular anymore. If I prefer not to work with people who kept me from working or gave support to people who kept me from working, I think I'm within my rights.

[*He exits into the house.*]

NORMA: Pop . . .

[*She follows him off, hoping to calm him down. A second after she exits,* LEO *enters. Like* BENNY, *he is in his late sixties, early seventies. He looks around the patio. He knows he is trespassing, but he is mentally prepared to face whoever might come out and face him. He is casing the place when* NORMA *returns to the patio. Initially, because of where he stands, she doesn't see him.*]

LEO: Miss Teitel?

[*Startled, she turns to look at him.*]

NORMA: You're Leo Greshen.

LEO [*with a smile*]: Guilty. I thought rather than ring the doorbell I'd just come around. I hope you don't mind.

NORMA: They told you.

LEO: Our beloved producers? Yes. At first, I couldn't figure it out. They said your father was somebody I used to know and that that was the reason why. And I kept thinking, "Teitel. When did I ever know a guy named Teitel?"

NORMA: My mother's name.

LEO: You changed it from Silverman?

NORMA: Yes.

LEO: Benny must love that. Why?

NORMA: Personal reasons.

LEO: You and he have a falling out?

NORMA: No.

LEO: OK.

NORMA: This is his house. I'm staying here.

LEO: Point taken.

NORMA: I shouldn't have said anything to them.

LEO: "Them" meaning our producers?

NORMA: I shouldn't have told them.

LEO: What then? Just walked out without warning?

NORMA: Of course not. I haven't decided to leave. All I said to them was that I was thinking about it. It didn't occur to me that they'd tell you.

LEO: Not to mention my popping up unannounced.

NORMA: There's the telephone.

LEO: True, but I've heard that the view here is terrific.

NORMA: Yes, well, there it is.

LEO: Very pretty.

NORMA: The blue part is the Pacific.

LEO: Somehow I never could live in L.A. Oh, I usually have a good time here. But I'm really a lazy bastard at heart, and this climate would probably aggravate that. Too easy to forget that time is passing when there's basically only one season. You're from the East, too, aren't you?

NORMA: New York.

LEO: Sure, you know what I mean. Every three months, you've got another season kicking you in the ass, telling you that the meter's ticking. One moment you're trying to find your sandals, the next you're digging galoshes out from the closet. Keeps you alert.

[*A beat.*]

Is he here?

NORMA: Inside. Probably taking a nap.

LEO: Ah.

[*A beat.*]

Did he ask you to drop out?

NORMA: No.

LEO: But he's not terribly happy about it. About the idea of you working with me.

NORMA: Did you think he would be?

LEO: How is he anyway?

NORMA: Fine.

LEO: He's a talented man, your father. We did a lot of work together.

NORMA: I know.

LEO: He told you?

NORMA: Not really. I did some reading.

LEO: Reading?

NORMA: Yes.

LEO: What did he do—hand you a bibliography and tell you there'd be a quiz?

NORMA: There are certain things he just never talks about.

LEO: And I'm one of those things. Right.

[*A beat.*]

You know, there were once these two guys named Stalin and Trotsky. They were both bigwigs in the Russian Revolution.

NORMA: You don't have to patronize me, Mr. Greshen. I do know who Stalin and Trotsky were.

LEO: In my experience, that puts you firmly in the minority of the people your age. Their idea of history is when the Beatles first appeared on *Ed Sullivan.* Anyway, as you apparently know, after Lenin died, Stalin took over and tossed Trotsky out of Russia. Parenthetically, Trotsky was later murdered with a pickax. One of these days, Brian de Palma will make a movie about this. But, if you were an earnest young student of history while Stalin was in power—at Moscow U., say, or Petrograd Prep—you would have searched in vain to find any mention of Trotsky's part in the revolution in the state-approved texts. In the jargon of the time, he became a nonperson.

NORMA: Your point is?

LEO: Your father has the makings of a fine Stalinist historian. Never talks about me at all, huh?

NORMA: A little—recently, when I asked him. But not very much. The subject's painful for him, I guess.

LEO: Believe it or not, there was a time when he didn't hate my guts. But I don't imagine that was in your reading.

NORMA: You were both members of the New Labor Players.

LEO: Actually, I was one of the founders. A fellow named Mort Kessler was one of the other actors. He also wrote a lot of stuff. That's how he got started as a writer. Anyway, one day he brought in this piece—it was about Saint Peter and about how two or three fat cats con their way past him into heaven. [*Remembering title*] *Capitalist Heaven*— that's what we called it! Well, of course, as capitalists always did in our subtle little plays, they set up an exploitive society—turned the poor cherubim into wage slaves in the harp factory, clipped their wings, et cetera. Anyway, we didn't have a Saint Peter, and somebody knew your father. They had seen him do imitations or something at a party. So I met him. He was working in the garment district. I suggested he might have more fun earning next to nothing with us than earning almost next to nothing hauling around big rolls of fabric. He believed me. And that's how he became an actor. He was a terrific Saint Peter. Who would have guessed he would end up in a swanky place like this? Talk about capitalist heaven.

[*A beat.*]

NORMA: Did you want to see him?

LEO: I came out to see you.

NORMA: Yes, but this is his house. You must have known there was a reasonable chance of running into him.

LEO: I'm not afraid of that.

NORMA: I didn't say you were.

LEO: I'd like you to stay with the show.

NORMA: Have you seen any of my work?

LEO: The producers seem to think you're good.

NORMA: But you've never seen me do anything?

LEO: Nope.

NORMA: If I were to leave, it wouldn't be difficult for you to find someone else.

LEO: That's true.

NORMA: There are lots of good actresses.

LEO: A dozen or so at least.

NORMA: It might be easier for you.

LEO: Thank you for your concern, but I think I could bear up. I long ago accepted the fact that Mother Teresa would beat me in a popularity contest.

NORMA: I don't see why it would be worth it to you.

LEO: Why is your understanding so important?

NORMA: Because, if I were to stay, I'd like to know on what basis.

LEO: That you do your job. What other basis is there? You fulfill a contract that was negotiated in good faith. Or don't you think you can play the part?

NORMA: I can play it.

LEO: It's not unheard of for an actor to come up with a convenient excuse to leave if he thinks he's out of his depth.

NORMA: I can play the part.

LEO: I believe you. Now, as for me, you acknowledge that I probably can do that job I've been hired for. True?

NORMA: Yes.

LEO: Then isn't that all we need be concerned about?

NORMA: I should just do my work and go on about my business.

LEO: It's called a professional attitude.

NORMA: You wouldn't be trying to prove something to my father?

LEO: What would I be trying to prove?

NORMA: You can't tell me the fact that I'm his daughter doesn't enter into this somewhere. Let's face it, I'm being kind of difficult here. And it's not as if I have any real reputation or track record that you should have to put up with it.

LEO: Wait a second. Do you want me to fire you?

NORMA: I didn't say that.

LEO: What do you want?

NORMA: Mr. Greshen, I happen to believe I'm good at what I do. I happen also to have a well-known father who's also an actor.

LEO: That can be an advantage.

NORMA: It's an advantage I don't want. Whatever my career is, wherever it goes, I want it to be on the basis of what I do myself. One of the real kicks of getting this part was that they hired me without knowing who my dad is. I mean, they hired *me*.

LEO: I understand.

NORMA: Well, now I get the feeling that it's because of him you want me to stay.

LEO: Isn't it because of him you're thinking of leaving?

NORMA: Those are two separate issues.

LEO: I don't think so.

NORMA: But it *is* because of him you want me to stay. At least partially.

LEO: If you've got to know, it's because I don't like being walked out on. All right?

[*A beat.*]

Jesus, even if I *didn't* know you're Benny's daughter, I'd probably guess. You're a lot like him, Miss Teitel. By the way, that's a compliment.

[BENNY *enters. At first,* NORMA *sees him and* LEO *doesn't. Then* LEO *senses his presence and turns around.*]

BENNY: Very difficult to nap. All this back-and-forth outside my window.

LEO: Hello, Benny.

BENNY: She's right, you know.

LEO: Oh?

BENNY: If you think you're going to prove something to me—

LEO: No?

BENNY: You proved all that you had to prove to me a long time ago. That fabulous phone call.

LEO: The book is closed, huh?

BENNY: That's the way it is.

LEO: You know, I've got an aunt Sadie, still has my cousin Ernie's baby shoes. A friend of mine, he saves matchbooks from restaurants. But you—you collect old injuries.

BENNY: A shame, isn't it?

LEO: I think so.

BENNY: A shame and a waste. You feel sorry for me.

LEO: I do.

BENNY: I am touched by your concern.

LEO: I can tell.

BENNY: No, really. It comes a little late. But what's thirty years in the grand scheme of things?

LEO: I've always been concerned.

BENNY: "'I weep for you,' the Walrus said, 'I deeply sympathize.'" You know, I believe him. I believe his tears are genuine. I have my doubts about the Carpenter, but the Walrus is a feeling man. Or as feeling as a walrus can be. You, too, Leo.

LEO: Same old Benny.

BENNY: Some people are born walrus, some people achieve walrus, and some have walrus thrust upon them. You can't blame the people who are *born* walrus. After all, that's all they know. But the ones who *choose* it—

LEO: It's all nice and simple for you, isn't it?

BENNY: Why don't I throw you off my patio?

LEO: Maybe you don't want to.

BENNY: Why wouldn't I want to?

LEO: It's been almost thirty years.

BENNY: You say that as if there's a statute of limitations.

LEO: *Are* you going to throw me off your patio?

BENNY: I'm thinking about it.

[*A beat.*]

You want a beer?

LEO: Couldn't hurt.

BENNY [*to* NORMA]: You want to bring this bastard a beer?

NORMA: What about you?

BENNY: Why not?

[NORMA *exits.* LEO *sits.* BENNY *picks up a bowl of chips, offers him some.* LEO *takes a few.* BENNY *grabs some chips for himself and sits. For a while, they sit and munch chips in silence.*]

LEO: She looks like her mother.

BENNY: We're divorced.

LEO: I heard. I'm sorry.

BENNY: She isn't. She's a very happy divorcée. She's told me so herself.

[*A beat.*]

So you're coming back to the theater. What happened? The movies go sour on you?

LEO: The movies are going fine. As a matter of fact, in a couple months I start a new one.

BENNY: But you're directing this play.

LEO: I wasn't aware of any rule that if you do one you can't do the other.

[NORMA *returns with two beers. She hands one to* LEO *during the following. He nods thanks.*]

No, the producers were in a bind. They needed a director. They talked to my agent. The timing worked out OK. I read the script.

[NORMA *now hands* BENNY *his beer.*]

BENNY: You like it?

LEO: It's a little lighter than I usually do, but I thought it might be fun to direct.

BENNY: Fun to look at my daughter's chest?

[NORMA *wishes the ground would open up.*]

LEO: Huh?

BENNY: The scene she takes her top off.

LEO: Oh that.

BENNY: Yes, that.

LEO: I told the playwright I want to cut that. I don't like naked actors on the stage. Distracts from the play.

BENNY: Oh.

LEO: You don't agree?

[BENNY *shrugs, but he sends a pointed look in* NORMA's *direction.*]

NORMA: I think I'm going to take a drive.

BENNY: Where to?

NORMA: Nowhere in particular. Just a drive. Things to think about.

BENNY: I see.

NORMA: Besides, you probably want to be alone, right?

BENNY [*not replying to her line*]: Will you be gone long?

NORMA: I don't know.

LEO: I'm glad I had a chance to meet you, Miss Teitel.

NORMA: Mr. Greshen.

[*She exits.*]

LEO: You should let her do the play, Benny. It's a good part. People will notice. She'll be on her way.

[BENNY *laughs.*]

What?

BENNY: Good thing you didn't say that in front of her.

LEO: What?

BENNY: About my "letting" her. She would have laughed in your face.

LEO: Is that so?

BENNY: The idea that I have anything to do with what she decides.

LEO: Not a thing, huh?

BENNY: Do you think I *let* her go into acting?

LEO: No?

BENNY: If you knew how hard I tried to keep her out of this business. And you can see how successful I was.

LEO: She never consults you.

BENNY: Who's around to consult? This is the first time we've actually laid eyes on each other in almost two years. She's in New York; I'm here.

LEO: And the telephone hasn't been invented.

BENNY: Why should she care about my opinion?

LEO [*anticipating* BENNY *saying this*]: You're just her father.

BENNY: What do you think? She does your show, I'm going to cut her out of my will?

LEO: Apart from everything else, whether or not the show does well, I think she'd find it a valuable experience.

BENNY: You want me to tell her that? You want me to put in a good word for you, Leo?

LEO: When's the last time *you* did a play?

BENNY: Half dozen years ago.

LEO: Which?

BENNY: *Front Page.*

LEO: Who'd you play?

BENNY: Pincus.

LEO: Remind me.

BENNY: The little schmuck with the message from the governor.

LEO: Bet you were good.

BENNY: Me? I was terrific.

LEO: Not a big part, though.

BENNY: It was one of those all-star casts. Limited run.

LEO: Ah.

BENNY: I did it for the fun of it.

LEO: Was it fun?

BENNY: Sure.

LEO: So why not anything since?

BENNY: Wasn't *that* much fun.

LEO: Oh.

BENNY: Besides, nobody's sent me a script I really wanted to do in a long time. God, the things they call musicals these days! Most of them seem to be about some kid screaming how he wants to be a star. I've also been sent a lot of plays about people dying. You think they're trying to tell me something? Sometimes you get an adventurous blend of the two—about celebrities who die. From what I can tell, nobody's writing about anything anymore but show business and cancer. As if there were a difference.

LEO: You don't think you're overstating the case?

BENNY: Not by much, no.

LEO: You could always revive *Capitalist Heaven*.

BENNY: At least that was about something.

LEO: Yeah, about twenty-five minutes.

BENNY: You didn't think so at the time.

LEO: At the time was at the time.

BENNY: What a way with words you have!

LEO: We were talking about you doing a play.

BENNY: Why should I haul my ass down to some drafty theater eight times a week? It's not like I need the money.

LEO: That I noticed. [*Referring to the house*] Is the inside as nice as the outside?

BENNY: You'll have to take my word.

[*A beat.*]

LEO: When did you start painting?

BENNY: How do you know I'm painting?

LEO: I could pretend to be Sherlock Holmes and say it's the smudge of blue on the side of your thumb.

BENNY: Did Norma tell you?

LEO: Nobody told me. I saw.

BENNY: Saw what?

LEO: One of your paintings.

BENNY: Where?

LEO: I was at someone's house. There was a picture on the wall. A view from this patio.

BENNY: I paint it a lot. Monet had water lilies and haystacks. Silverman's got smog.

LEO: Anyway, I told him I liked it, and he said you painted it.

BENNY: He?

LEO: Mort Kessler.

BENNY: I didn't know you and Morty were in touch.

LEO: More than in touch.

BENNY: Oh?

LEO: We get together whenever I'm out here. Or he gives me a call when he's east. Sure.

BENNY: From what happened I wouldn't say it was all that sure.

LEO: Oh, we patched all that up a long time ago.

BENNY: Patched it up?

LEO: There was a fund-raiser. Somebody did a dinner in their home, for the farmworkers, I think. One of those, I don't know. As it happened, Morty and I found ourselves seated near each other. He pretended I wasn't there for a while. Then I remember some woman walked by with impossibly blonde hair. Well, the lady I was with made some comment like, "Do you believe that hair?" And Morty said, "Hey, I happen to know her mother was a natural fluorescent." I laughed. He looked at me. You can't ignore a man who laughs at your joke, right? And we started talking, and before the evening was over we were friends again.

BENNY: He never said.

LEO: Probably thought it would upset you.

BENNY: Why should it upset me who he chooses for friends? Just surprises me a little, that's all.

LEO: Like I said, we patched it up.

BENNY: He always did have a forgiving streak. You know, a couple weeks ago, I even heard him say something nice about his third wife.

LEO: He didn't forgive me. I didn't ask him to forgive me. I don't ask anybody to forgive me.

BENNY: He may have done it without your asking. Without your permission. He's got a sneaky side.

LEO: I don't think so. I don't think forgiving had anything to do with anything. I think he just put it aside. Somewhere along the line, he must have weighed things in the balance—

BENNY: And put it aside.

LEO: Yeah.

BENNY: First he weighed it, then he patched it, then he put it aside. Where? In storage?

LEO: In the past, where it belongs.

BENNY: Well, he never told me.

LEO: He knows you had strong feelings.

BENNY: I still do.

LEO: I guessed as much. But I suppose you're entitled.

BENNY: Thank you.

[*A beat.*]

LEO: So, how are you feeling?

BENNY: How am I feeling about what?

LEO: The question is health, Benny, not opinions.

BENNY: I'm feeling fine.

LEO: You've recovered.

BENNY: What am I supposed to have recovered from?

LEO: Morty said something about you in the hospital.

BENNY: Oh, that. Nothing dramatic. Just a little prostate trouble.

LEO: How much is a little?

BENNY: It got to the point where it was taking more time for me to pee than to prepare my taxes. The doctor kind of thought maybe we should do something about that. So did my accountant.

LEO: So you went to the hospital. How was that?

BENNY: Not too terrible actually.

LEO: Did they knock you out?

BENNY: No. They gave me a spinal. That just anesthetizes you from about the navel down. The upper part stays wide awake. As a matter of fact, they asked me did I want to watch.

LEO: And?

BENNY: I took a pass.

LEO: If you could take a pass, you wouldn't have needed the operation.

BENNY: Anyway, I said no, thanks, my idea of entertainment was not to watch them drill for oil in my privates. So they put up a sheet to block the view, and they called in a Roto-Rooter man. A few hours, and that was it.

LEO: So it was all right.

BENNY: All right? What are you talking about? Better than all right! Fantastic! Really, Leo, you should give it a try.

LEO: I mean it healed nicely. No complications.

BENNY: Such an interest you take! What—you want to make an on-site inspection?

LEO: Maybe some other time.

BENNY: Nope, you had your chance. For a while there I had to avoid orange juice, grapefruit juice, pineapples—

LEO: Why?

BENNY: Citric acid, you know. Stings like crazy.

LEO: Right.

BENNY: But it's fine now.

LEO: Well, that's good news.

BENNY: Jesus.

LEO: What?

BENNY: I remember when we used to talk about girls and the revolution. Now—

LEO: You want to talk about girls, I'll be glad to talk about girls.

BENNY: Morty keeps you posted on my health.

LEO: He doesn't hand me bulletins or anything, but I like to keep track of the old gang.

BENNY: You heard about George.

LEO: I saw it in the *Times*. Christ, every morning, opening the god-damned *Times* to find out who I've survived.

BENNY: I know.

LEO: You went to the funeral?

BENNY: They didn't have a formal funeral. There was a kind of memorial thing.

LEO: What was that like?

BENNY: Sort of fun actually. Everybody got up, told stories.

LEO [*laughing*]: Oh?

BENNY: No, the clean ones.

LEO: Must have been a short memorial.

BENNY: They read some from his file. You know, he got the stuff the FBI kept on him under the Freedom of Information thing.

LEO: Sounds like a lot of laughs.

BENNY: Did you ever hear about when he was in the army?

LEO: I know that he was in the army—

BENNY: About when he was in the hospital in the army?

LEO: Wait a second? About the FBI agent?

BENNY: Came to question the other guys in the ward about him—

LEO: I've heard it, yeah.

BENNY: Didn't recognize him. Gave a testimonial to his own—

LEO: Yeah, I heard it.

BENNY: They asked him his name—

BENNY AND LEO: Jake Barnes.

BENNY: You heard it.

LEO: I heard it.

BENNY: You ever send for your file?

LEO: What for?

BENNY: To see what they said about you.

LEO: What for?

BENNY: I sent for mine.

LEO: To see what "they" said about you?

BENNY: What are you smiling about?

LEO: You remember the end of the second part of *Faust*?

BENNY: It doesn't spring to my lips, no.

LEO: Goethe.

BENNY: All of a sudden this is *GE College Bowl*.

LEO: He talks about the eternal feminine. The last line is something about constantly pursuing the eternal feminine.

BENNY: So?

LEO: So, instead of the eternal feminine, for you it's the eternal they. They do this; they keep you from doing that. Always *they*.

BENNY: Not always, Leo. Sometimes it's *you*.

LEO: So you sent for your file.

BENNY: I sent for my file.

LEO: Anything interesting?

BENNY: Great nostalgia value. Lists of the petitions I signed, the magazines I subscribed to. Some bastard even showed up at one of the benefits I performed at. "Subject performed allegedly humorous routine—"

LEO: "Allegedly humorous." He said that?

BENNY: Fucking critics, they're everywhere. You remember—just after Sarah and I got married, I had to go out of town on that tour?

LEO: *Native Son,* wasn't it?

BENNY: Probably. Anyway, Sarah was doing real well in radio then, so she didn't want to go out with me. So we wrote each other a lot. Some of it was personal stuff.

LEO: You mean love letters?

BENNY: Well, yeah, I guess you could call them that. Anyway, I'd lost the originals a long time ago in one of our moves. But, like I say, I had the FBI send me my file, and they must have kept a mail cover on us, because there they were—all the letters I'd lost. A lot of them anyway.

LEO: They Xeroxed your letters?

BENNY: Xeroxed? In nineteen forty—

LEO: Right.

BENNY: No, someone actually typed them up. Probably anchored them with a book or something so they'd lie flat, be easier to type from. You know Sarah's handwriting—probably had to hire a cryptographer to decipher. Sarah and I were waiting for the final divorce paper when I got that file from the feds.

[*A beat.*]

I almost sent her copies.

LEO [*gently*]: Almost?

BENNY: What purpose would it have served? It was all over between us by then.

LEO: Benny, what happened?

BENNY: Well—

LEO: The two of you—I've never seen a couple like—

[BENNY *suddenly realizes how close he's got to the old friendship. He forces himself to pull back.*]

BENNY: No, I'm not going to talk about that.

LEO: If there's something you want to—

BENNY: Not with you.

[*A beat.*]

LEO: OK.

BENNY: Anyway, I get some satisfaction out of knowing that the SOB who wrote that is probably dead now.

LEO: Or maybe having a prostate operation of his own.

BENNY: He should only have it done without a spinal.

[*A beat.*]

How's your beer?

LEO: Fine.

[*A beat.*]

I was given an honorary degree, you know. Last spring.

BENNY: In what—communications?

LEO: A doctor of letters, actually. Avery College, New Hampshire. For my body of work. That's how they phrased it. Sounds cadaverous, doesn't it? "Here lies Leo Greshen's body of work." I had to laugh when I was told. But I said sure. Sure, I'd be honored to be honored. And, generous fellow that I am, I say I'll throw in a seminar on directing or some damn thing. They couldn't be happier. I'm met at the airport. I have dinner with a bunch of deans and professors and nice faculty wives, faculty husbands, whatever. Some nice stroking. Springtime in New Hampshire. Who could object to that? So I'm scheduled to speak to this media studies class. The guy who runs the class introduces me. My pictures, the plays I've directed, blah, blah, blah, and would you please welcome. Applause. All very nice. He asks me questions. I answer. I make jokes. He tosses in a quip or two like a regular Dick Cavett. Everything's bopping along well. About forty-five minutes of this, he says he's going to open the floor to questions. Four or five hands shoot up. I see this one intent kid off to the side, near the window. Skinny kid with eyes like lasers. I look at him and I know he's going to ask it. I just know it. But my friend, the would-be Dick Cavett, calls on some girl who asks me how it was to work with so-and-so, and I tell an amusing story and everybody laughs in the right place except for the kid with the laser eyes. I've barely finished my amusing story when his hand shoots up again. The professor again chooses another hand. Bearded kid wants to know if I storyboard when I'm in preproduction. I tell another amusing story. Soon as I'm finished with that one, again that kid's hand shoots up. Again my host chooses another hand, but I interrupt him. I say, "Wait a second. There's a young man over there by the window seems to have something urgent to ask. Yes, son, what is it?" Yes, son, I'm thinking, go ahead and prove how brave and liberal you are. Nail me in front of all your nice classmates and your nice teacher on this nice, nice campus in New Hampshire. "Yes, son," I say, "what's your question?" He doesn't disappoint. No sooner has he said the magic words "House Committee on Un-American Activities" than my friend the professor interrupts, says that we are not here to discuss that. "We are here to discuss Mr. Greshen's art, Mr. Greshen's craft. We are here to learn what we can from Mr. Greshen's years of experience in the theater and film. Politics has nothing to do with it." And he asks if there are any other questions. I answer two more, and my friend the professor wraps it up by thanking me on behalf of the class for my generosity and candor. Applause. My host and I go to the faculty lounge. He buys me a drink and tells me that he's sorry about the boy's rudeness. Apparently that boy has a habit of stirring things up. And that was why my friend hadn't wanted to call on him. He was trying to protect me. Seems like this kid had circulated a petition calling on the college to rescind the honorary degree. That it would not redound to the school's credit to honor a stoolie. This was not quite how my friend put it, but that was the gist of it. So there was a ceremony, I got my degree, shook a lot of nice hands, and went home. And all through this I was thinking of how I should have answered the little bastard.

BENNY: And what would you have said?

LEO: That he hadn't earned the right to ask me that question. He hadn't earned the right to brandish his moral indignation in my face.

BENNY: That's a nice snappy reply. Maybe you'll have another opportunity to use it.

LEO: Oh, I don't lack for opportunity. Even after all these years, it knocks with regularity. I'm constantly being offered forums for public confession. Really, it's very touching to know how many people are concerned about my moral rehabilitation. So eager to help me get this awful weight off my shoulders. This one woman—from some French film journal—for some reason I agreed to be interviewed for an article she was writing on my films. Turned out to be structuralist bullshit. Anyway, in the middle of it—here we go again. To be fair, we'd had a bottle of wine and we were getting along. Anyway, I informed her as affably as possible that I really didn't want to get into that subject. And she leaned forward and took my arm with that easy familiarity that a shared bottle of wine can encourage, she took my arm and looked into my eyes and said, "But Leo . . ." Not "Monsieur Greshen" but "Leo," right? "But Leo," she said, "you will feel—how do you say it?—the relief, no?"

BENNY: And you don't think you'd feel relief?

LEO: Benny, please. To step into a mess of dog shit once—that's something that can happen to anybody. To intentionally step into the same dog shit again—

BENNY: What dog shit is that?

LEO: Look, I've been through this before. "Leo, get up, get it off your chest. You'll feel better, swear to God." All I had to do was submit to a nice dirty ritual of public cleansing. Did you read the Navasky book?

BENNY: I glanced at it.

LEO: Well, I think a lot of it is double-talk. But he got that part right. The ritual part. Get up in front of the committee, admit your errors. Prove how repentant you are—*demonstrate* your sincerity by naming a few names, you'll emerge redeemed, rehabilitated. Decent American folks will be happy to shake you by the hand, slap your back, let you do your work. Now, though, different political truths are operative, as the saying goes. Now I'm told that I bought the moral equivalent of a pig in a poke. I got myself the wrong brand of cleansing and rehabilitation. There's a new improved formula. Yes, there is! This season, if I want to be cleaner than clean, I'm supposed to get up and say I done wrong when I said I done wrong before. I'm supposed to do a mea culpa over my other mea culpa. Only instead of doing it in front of a mob of congressional Neanderthals, I'm supposed to confess to someone like Navasky or that French structuralist or that kid at Avery College. And after I choke out my apology, Navasky, on behalf of his enlightened readers, will dispense absolution. "Go and sin no more." In my book, it's the same damn ritual of public cleansing, only some labels have been changed to conform to the spirit of blacklist chic. Well, like I say, I stepped into that shit once. I'm not doing it again. Not even for you, Benny. And believe me, you're about the only reason I'd think of doing it.

BENNY: Sounds like you've got this all thought out.

LEO: It's not like I haven't had the time.

BENNY: Just one problem, Leo. When you called me up that night, you didn't call me because you thought you were right. You called me because you felt lousy about what you were going to do.

LEO: Benny, I never claimed to feel good about it.

BENNY: But you did it.

LEO: Only a fool fights the drop.

BENNY: You want to translate?

LEO: You've seen enough cowboy movies. If the bad guys have got the drop on you, it's crazy to draw on them. You're only going to get gunned down. Can't fight if you're dead.

BENNY: So now we're cowboys?

LEO: Thank you for taking what I have to say seriously.

BENNY: Seriously, OK. Leo, not only did you not fight the drop, you helped the bad guys gun down some good guys. What would the kids in the balcony say if Roy Rogers shot Gabby Hayes?

LEO: Bad guys, good guys

BENNY: It's your analogy.

LEO: I said nothing about good guys.

BENNY: Oh, I see: there were no good guys?

LEO: Present company excepted, of course.

BENNY: No good guys. Well, that makes it nice and convenient, doesn't it? If everybody's equally scummy, then the highest virtue is survival. That must make you pretty goddamn virtuous. You should write a book about your philosophy, Leo. Really. I've got the title for you: *Charles Darwin Goes to the Theater.*

LEO: Being a victim doesn't automatically entitle you to a white hat, Benny. It's that old liberal impulse—romanticize the persecuted.

BENNY: What the hell would you know about liberal impulses?

LEO: Hey, I've got my share of them.

BENNY: You—a liberal? Don't make me laugh.

LEO: I sure wouldn't want to do that, Benny—make you laugh.

BENNY: Maybe you're a checkbook liberal. You send in contributions to those ads with pictures of kids starving in South America, a couple bucks to the ACLU—

LEO: More than a couple of bucks, but never mind—

BENNY: More than a couple? Well, hey, that changes my opinion completely.

LEO: I'll tell you where I part company with a lot of them, though. I won't romanticize. Just because someone's a martyr doesn't make him wise and good and pure. Sure, I sent in money to Joan Little's defense fund, but that doesn't mean I'd trust her to babysit my grandchildren.

BENNY: The guys the committee went after weren't accused of murder, just of having believed in something unpopular. And the ones who wouldn't buckle under—out with the garbage.

LEO: Which is exactly what they did to each other when they were members of the party. Those bastards were always browbeating each other, excommunicating each other for not embracing "the correct revolutionary line." Do you remember when the party endorsed Henry Wallace for president? Lenny Steinkempf got up in a meeting, said he thought it was a crappy idea. So what did the party do? They threw him the fuck out. And after *they* threw him out, his *wife* Elaine, being a loyal party member, *she* threw him out. As far as I was concerned, facing the committee was an exercise in déjà vu. Believe me, Nixon and Mundt could have taken lessons from some of those old Commies. I wasn't about to put my dick on the block for any of those guys. Why should I keep faith with them when they couldn't keep faith with themselves?

BENNY: The point wasn't to keep faith with *them.* Leo, don't you remember anything about how or why we put together the New Labor Players?

LEO: Oh, for Christ's sake!

BENNY: For Christ's sake what?

LEO [*laughing*]: Benny, you aren't seriously going to hit me with the New Labor Players?

BENNY: And why not?

LEO: All that agitprop bullshit, the slogans, screaming our lungs raw—

BENNY: Worthless?

LEO: Not worthless, exactly—

BENNY: Then *what*, exactly?

LEO: All we ever did was play to people who felt exactly like we did. Invigorating—sure. Fun—absolutely. And a great way to meet girls. But don't try to tell me we ever accomplished any great social good. I doubt that we ever changed anybody's mind about anything.

BENNY: That's how you measure it?

LEO: You measure it differently?

BENNY: Seems to me there's some value in letting people know—because they laughed or maybe cheered at the same time as a bunch of other people—letting them know they aren't alone. That there are other people who feel like they do.

LEO: Maybe we should have broken out some red pom-poms while we were at it.

BENNY: Pom-poms?

LEO: Hey, if you're going to cheerlead, you should have pom-poms. "Give me a *P*, give me an *R*, give me an *O*, give me an *L*!"

BENNY: Leo—

LEO [*continuing*]: "Whaddaya got? Proletariat! Whaddaya got? Class struggle! Whaddaya got? Dialectical materialism! Rah, rah, rah!"

BENNY: Some terrific joke, Leo. Very funny.

LEO: What's funny is you telling me this stuff.

BENNY: What's funny about that?

LEO: You think I don't know my own spiel when I hear it?

BENNY: Your spiel?

LEO: Of course my spiel. "Class consciousness is the first step. Through theater we give dramatic form to our lives and hopes and so create our identity and the identity of our community." You like it? I've got another three or four hours of this. Rousing stuff, huh?

[*A beat.*]

BENNY: Yeah, I thought so.

LEO: Oh, I convinced myself pretty good, too. But I'm not a twenty-two-year-old kid anymore, and neither are you. And I'm not going to let you get away with pretending that *Capitalist Heaven* and the rest of it was any great golden age of drama. Face it, Benny, it was amateur night.

BENNY: I'm not talking about how sophisticated or how professional. Leo, what I'm saying is that when we started, all right, we may not have had much polish or technical expertise, be we did have a sense of purpose. There was a *reason* I started acting. There was a *reason* Mort Kessler started writing. There was a *reason* you started directing. And then came a point you gave up your reason so you could keep on directing.

LEO: Maybe directing *was* my reason.

BENNY: What—directing anything?

LEO: Of course not.

BENNY: You say of course not, but I don't take it for granted that there are things you wouldn't direct. Before the committee—yes. But after?

LEO: So all of a sudden I'm a whore. Of course, it isn't whoring to do some dumb-ass sitcom. What was it called—*Rich and Happy?*

BENNY: *Rich But Happy.*

LEO: I stand corrected. Truly edifying, uplifting stuff. My God, in the old days, if somebody had told you that's what you'd end up doing! *Rich But Happy.* I mean, back then just the *title* would have made you gag!

BENNY: I had to live.

LEO: So did I, Benny. So did I.

BENNY: But if I did crap—and God knows I'm not holding up *Rich But Happy* as an example of high culture—but if I did crap, I didn't destroy other people to do it.

LEO: I don't happen to think that the work I did after that *was* crap. As a matter of fact, a lot of it was damn good.

BENNY: If you do say so yourself.

LEO: You're going to tell me that it wasn't? Oh, I know this riff. If a guy's politics aren't approved, aren't correct, then he can't be any good as an artist. I bet you're one of those people who think God took away Frank Sinatra's voice as a punishment for voting Republican.

BENNY: I'm not talking party affiliation—

LEO: I know what you're talking about: in order to be an artist, you've got to be a certified good guy.

BENNY: Being a mensch enters into it, yes.

LEO: And if he isn't, you feel cheated. Shortchanged. Well, if art by bastards upsets you so much, you should drop everything right now, go into your library and toss out anything you have by Robert Frost. Now there was a world-class shit! And how about Ezra Pound! And let's not bring up Wagner!

BENNY: I don't have any Wagner in my house.

LEO: No? Well now *there's* a brave stand! My hat's off to you, Benny! Keep those doors guarded. Be vigilant! Hey, you can't be *too* careful. I mean, you never know when somebody might try to sneak the fucking *Ring Cycle* into your house without your knowing it, right?

BENNY: This I'm enjoying—you linking arms with Wagner!

LEO: Tell me something, if you found out that Charles Dickens shtupped ten-year-old boys, would that make him any less of a writer?

BENNY: Well, it sure as hell would make a difference in how I read *Oliver Twist.*

LEO: Whatever you or anybody else thinks about me as a person, I did good work, Benny. Not just before. After, too.

BENNY: I wouldn't know about after. I didn't see most of it.

LEO: Well, you missed some good stuff. If you don't want to take my word for it, you can take it from the critics. You can look on my fucking mantle in New York at the prizes and the plaques—

BENNY: I'm sure they would blind me.

LEO: They mean something, Benny, even if it's fashionable to sneer at them. They mean that a lot of people thought that the work was good.

BENNY: And that's important to you.

LEO: Yes, it is.

BENNY: You like having the good opinion of others.

LEO: Is that a crime?

BENNY: No, I don't think it's a crime. I like it, too. I'm just sorry to have to tell you that you haven't got my good opinion, Leo.

LEO: And I'm sorry to have to tell you I don't give a damn.

BENNY: Then why are you here?

LEO: Because I don't want your goddamn daughter walking out of my goddamn play.

BENNY: Fine, you told her that. So why are you still here?

LEO: Because I'm a masochistic idiot!

BENNY: What, you expected me to throw my arms open?

LEO: No.

BENNY: Then what?

LEO: Damn it, Benny—thirty years! It's been more than thirty years! We're going to start *dying* soon!

[*A beat.*]

While there's still a chance.

[*A beat.*]

BENNY: Leo, you got a car?

LEO: Yeah. Why?

BENNY: Let's say for the sake of argument there's someplace you want to go. So you go to your car, put the key in the ignition—nothing. It isn't working. But there's this place you want to go. You want to go there real bad. You take a look in my garage, what do you know?—I've got a car. A car in good working condition. It's got a few years on it, but it runs fine. We're talking about a respected make. So you ask me, can you take my car? I say no, I'm sorry, I've made plans, I need it. You tell me about this place you want to go, how important it is to you to get there. I say I'm sorry, but no, I can't let you have my car. What do you do? You take it anyway. Now what do you figure I do in a situation like this? Call the cops, of course. Give them your description and the license number, they take off after you. What happens if they catch you? You end up being charged with grand theft auto. All right, you didn't steal my car. But there *was* someplace you wanted to go, and the only vehicle you could get your hands on was something else that belonged to me.

[NORMA *has entered during the above. Neither* BENNY *nor* LEO *betrays any notice of her presence, which is not to say that they don't know she's there.*]

Something that belonged to me, something that belonged to Morty, something that belonged to a few other guys. I don't know how you did it with them, but I get the famous phone call. You call and tell me what you're going to do. You cry about the pressure. You tell me how much getting to this place you want to go means to you. You want me to tell you, "Sure, Leo, go ahead. Take it for a drive. Barter it for the good opinion of a bunch of cynical shits. Buy yourself a license to work." But it doesn't play that way. I say no. And the next day, you go into that committee room, and you use it anyway. The difference between that and you taking my car—my car you can return.

[*A beat.*]

Leo, I'm not Morty Kessler. I won't put it aside.

[*A beat.*]

Norma, Mr. Greshen dropped by to ask you about his show. Why don't you tell him what you've decided?

[*A beat.* NORMA *doesn't respond.*]

Norma?

[*A beat.*]

LEO: Miss Teitel, I would appreciate it if you would call me later.

[NORMA *nods.* LEO *exits. A beat.*]

NORMA: OK, I think I've got it now.
BENNY: What is that?
NORMA: Why you didn't throw him out before. All these years, you've been thinking, working up what you would say if you ever met him again—
BENNY: Who wanted to meet him again?
NORMA: I'm saying *if.*
BENNY: I did my best to make sure that wouldn't happen.
NORMA: I'm sure you did.
BENNY: I gave up my favorite Chinese restaurant. A place I knew he sometimes ate. Never went back. Last thing I wanted was to see him.
NORMA: Last thing, huh?
BENNY: If you'll have the stenographer read back the transcript, I think you'll see that's what I said.
NORMA: I know you said it—
BENNY: But you—with your years of wisdom and experience—you see the deeper truth, is that it?

NORMA: Maybe *at first* you didn't want to meet him again—

BENNY: Oh boy, here we go—

NORMA: Maybe in the beginning—

BENNY: I can see where all this is heading. I didn't, but really underneath it all, I did.

NORMA: After all, you had the speech ready. What good is a speech if you don't give it?

BENNY: And there it is, folks—my soul naked and quivering.

NORMA: Then why did you come out in the first place? If you knew who I was talking to—

BENNY: This isn't a Chinese restaurant. This is my patio. I won't stop coming here.

NORMA: That's not what I'm saying.

BENNY: Oh, you grant me the right to step out on it if and when I please?

NORMA: Sure, and it pleased you to do it then because he was out here.

BENNY: I should hide inside?

NORMA: Nobody said anything about hiding.

BENNY: What about Leo? It sure pleased *him* to barge in here uninvited.

NORMA: We're not talking about him.

BENNY: No? Oh, I see, *you're* setting the agenda here. The topics of discussion. Sorry, Mr. Chairman.

NORMA: Mr. Chairman?

BENNY: "Mr. Silverman, you aren't being cooperative. If you would please answer the question. Did you or did you not know that the American Committee for Spanish Freedom was a Communist front organization?"

NORMA: Pop—

BENNY: "And just exactly who was present that night in Mr. Kessler's house?"

NORMA: If you can't tell the difference between me and the committee—

BENNY: The tone is similar, believe me.

NORMA: You're misunderstanding—

BENNY: I don't know what you think you're accusing me of—

NORMA: I'm not accusing you—

BENNY: No?

NORMA: I'm not disagreeing with anything you said to him.

BENNY: Then what? That I said it at all?

NORMA: Never mind.

BENNY: What—are you afraid I lost you your job?

NORMA: No.

BENNY: That's it, isn't it?

NORMA: The job isn't yours to lose.

BENNY: Right. Your decision.

NORMA: That's what he said.

BENNY: And you can take it from me, he's a man to be trusted. Yes, sir.

NORMA: I just hope you got what you wanted.

BENNY: And what might that be?

NORMA: I don't know. Satisfaction?

BENNY: No way to get satisfaction.

NORMA: Then why do it?

BENNY: Sometimes you do a thing because you've got the right to do it. Or don't you think I have the right?

NORMA: Of course you've got the right. And I've got the right to do some things, too.

BENNY: Like to judge me, my behavior? Well, I beg to differ, kiddo. You haven't earned it.

NORMA: Oh, so it's like with the painting. I don't have the proper background, so I can't appreciate it. Because I didn't suffer through the blacklist, I can't have an opinion.

BENNY: Have any opinion you want, but don't expect me to get all worked up about it.

NORMA: No, of course not. Who the hell am I, anyway? If I happen to think that walking around spitting battery acid at the world is no kind of a life—

BENNY: I don't have to listen to this.

NORMA: Pop, he did a shitty thing to you. No argument. But after all of these years, to let it keep eating at you, to let it take over your life—

BENNY: "A shitty thing." Your command of the language—"a shitty thing." Like maybe he stole a girl from me or got drunk and peed in my swimming pool. It goes beyond. You think something happens and that's it, it's over with? That it's gone and remote because you can stick a date to it and a lot of calendars have been tossed out in the meantime? All those books you've read, all that time in the library, you still don't understand a thing.

[*A beat.*]

I was an actor. Basic to being an actor is the fact that you can't do it by yourself. It's not like plumbing or fixing shoes or painting a picture. You've got to do it *with* other people in the *presence* of other people. If someone does something to cut you off from them, you're not an actor anymore. I don't care what you call yourself or what you put on your résumé, you're not. You can't grow; you can't develop. You're not allowed to be what you could. You aren't even allowed to be who you are. You're an exile. Not just from your profession, your business. You're an exile from yourself. That's what Leo did to me when he said my name. This charming fellow with all of his stories and his reasons. Sorry, yes. I'm sure he is. But that's what he did.

NORMA: And that's what you want me to do to myself. Because you couldn't work, you want me to refuse to work. Doesn't what you were saying apply to me as well? About needing other people to be an actor? You were entitled to work. Aren't I entitled, too? Or am I supposed to give up my entitlement because I'm your daughter?

BENNY: But with *him.*

NORMA: Since when do you have to like everybody you work with?

BENNY: Fine, you want the part, you keep the part. It's your decision.

NORMA: Pop—

BENNY: No, I think it's a terrific career move. And as far as your not liking him goes, I'll bet you get past that. I'll bet you two get along great. After all, so much in common: he steals my name, you throw it away.

NORMA: What do you want? You want me to blacklist myself?

BENNY: I want you to go ahead and do what you're going to do and spare me the hypocrisy of pretending that you give a good goddamn about what I want.

[BENNY *exits. A beat.* NORMA *turns to the audience.*]

NORMA: That afternoon, I move to a motel. We go back into rehearsal a couple days later, a couple of weeks later we open. True to his word, Pop doesn't come to the opening. The next day, I drive over to see him.

[BENNY *enters with brushes and paint, goes to the easel. He begins to work. A beat.*]

BENNY: The reviews?

NORMA: Mostly good.

BENNY: What about for you?

NORMA: Also good.

BENNY: Congratulations.

NORMA: Something I want to show you.

[*She takes out a program.*]

BENNY: Oh?

NORMA: The program.

BENNY: What about it?

[NORMA *opens it to a specific page, hands it to him.*]

NORMA: Here.

BENNY: Your bio? I'm familiar with your credits.

NORMA: I added a line to the end.

[*A beat.* BENNY *looks at it, reads.*]

BENNY: "Norma Teitel is the daughter of actor Benny Silverman."

[*He hands the program back to her.*]

It's not enough.

[*A beat. She stands there as he goes back to painting. The lights fade on them.*]

NOTES

In 2006, I attended a trim little production of this play by the Square One Theatre Company in Stratford, Connecticut, and stood up afterward to discuss the show with the audience. A woman toward the back of the house got up and said, "You'd have no way of knowing it, but that's my life you put onstage." She had come to the show unaware of the subject matter and was surprised by the story of a young woman who learns that her father had been blacklisted in the fifties and realizes the degree to which his experience has shaped her own life. In the case of the woman in the audience, her father had been Bob Roberts, the man who produced the classic John Garfield films *Force of Evil* and *Body and Soul.* (Garfield himself had run afoul of the House Un-American Activities Committee. Julie Garfield, his daughter, has told me that she holds the committee responsible for the stress that led to her father's early death from a heart attack.) Despite having produced two hit films, when the red scare hit postwar Hollywood, Roberts found himself unemployable in the States. He fled the country for the United Kingdom. "That's why I speak this way," the woman in the audience said in a crisp British accent.

I asked her if her father had worked on the *Robin Hood* TV show in England. A number of the American refugees from the blacklist worked on the Richard Greene series, seeing in the life that Robin Hood's merry men lived as outlaws in Sherwood Forest something akin to their lives as exiles from their home country. "No," she said, "he never worked as a producer again."

While I was beginning work on this script, the Dramatists Guild sponsored a series of programs reuniting key figures of the original productions of classic plays. The guild announced that playwright Arthur Miller and director Elia Kazan would appear together to talk about the premiere of *Death of a Salesman.*

Garson Kanin (who had a piece of immortality of his own as the author of the classic comedy *Born Yesterday*) was moderating with his usual understated wit, easily drawing from the two men the familiar details of how a script provisionally titled *The Inside of His Head* found its final name, despite the misgivings of a backer who thought a play with the word "death" in its title would scare away audiences. After maybe a half hour of informative back-and-forth, Kanin asked if anyone in the audience had any questions.

A young man got up. I can't claim to remember the exact words, but the gist was this: "We've just elected Ronald Reagan to the presidency. It's recently come to light that in the fifties, when he was head of the Screen Actors Guild, Reagan passed names of members of his union on to be blacklisted. Given your own experiences, do you have any comment?" It was clear the "experiences" to which the young man was referring were Miller's and Kazan's different reactions to being summoned to testify in front of Congress in the fifties.

Kanin interrupted. "We're not here to talk about politics," he snapped. "We're here to talk about *Death of a Salesman*. Does anybody have a question about *Death of a Salesman*?"

I don't recall Kazan betraying any reaction to this development. He sat quietly, seemingly unfazed. Miller, too, sat quietly. Someone else in the audience asked a question more appropriate for the occasion, and the event went on without further bumps.

As much as I disagreed with what Kazan had done, I couldn't help but feel a twinge. It occurred to me that he was like Jacob Marley in *A Christmas Carol*, except he didn't get to wait till death to drag his chains around. No matter where he went, somebody was ready to clobber him. That's where the passage about Leo's visit to Avery College came from.

Incidentally, *The Value of Names* was produced and published before Kazan's autobiography, *Elia Kazan: A Life*, was published. I was startled to find that in his book Kazan made a similar comment to that of Benny about Odets being dead before he was dead, and he quoted the same passage that Leo references from the second part of *Faust*. Obviously I couldn't know what would be in his book, and I rather doubt he read my play.

I should acknowledge a debt. An actor friend named John Randolph, himself a blacklist victim, heard I was writing the play and thought I would be interested in the files the government had kept on him (which he acquired through the Freedom of Information Act). Indeed, in those pages were copies of love letters he and his wife, Sarah Cunningham, had exchanged when separated by work during the early days of their marriage. Yes, someone on the government payroll had actually typed copies. I asked for John's permission to include this in the play, and he gave it.

AMERICAN ENTERPRISE

—for Joyce Sloane

I had had a very good run of luck in Chicago theater. Within five years, six of my plays were produced there; three (*Porch*, *Ties*, and *The Value of Names*) had gone on to extended runs, and one (*Ties*) had been adapted for public TV.

But all of them had been on contemporary subjects. All of them had called for relatively small casts. And none of them had anything to say about Chicago.

I decided I wanted to write a play that told a story about the town where I had been raised and whose community made me feel so welcome.

Inside an exhibit at a visitors' center on Chicago's Michigan Avenue there used to be two dioramas of the city's history. One depicted Mrs. O'Leary's cow starting the Chicago Fire and the other the Saint Valentine's Day massacre. Add to that the Chicago Black Sox baseball scandal and the Democratic convention in 1968 and you probably have a list of those events most Chicagoans are aware of in their town's past.

Obviously there was more there. I started to dig. I had the good fortune to stumble onto a book called *Altgeld's America* in which Ray Ginger wrote with great vitality about the saints and sinners of the city in the years surrounding 1900. (It's out of print but well worth an online search.) One of the chapters was devoted to Pullman and the town he built and named after himself. Something about his mission intrigued me.

I began to research the story and the times, and it soon became apparent that the key task of writing the play would be to figure out what to leave out. There was so much fascinating material. How could I omit Clarence Darrow and Jane Addams? How could I omit the Haymarket Riot and Governor John Peter Altgeld's pardons? How could I omit the irony that Pullman, who had made his fortune partially because of Lincoln's assassination, ultimately would be succeeded in his company's presidency by Lincoln's son Robert?

Well, I had to omit these things or the play would be long and shapeless. Organizing the material into a coherent whole demanded I figure out what my through line was. An article by Jane Addams comparing Pullman to King Lear got me started thinking about Pullman as a would-be father who failed. That would tie together the story of his relationship with his children and his relationship with the people in his town, to whom he often referred as his children.

Then I had another piece of luck. While looking through a muckraking book dating from the 1890s called *If Christ Came to Chicago,* by William T. Stead, I discovered J. Patrick Hopkins—a young man who began by schlepping around planks in the Pullman lumberyard, rose in the Pullman community with Pullman's help, was instrumental in challenging Pullman's authority in the town, and through a twist of circumstance that no fiction writer would have had the gall to contrive, became mayor of Chicago and one of Pullman's most bitter political enemies. I couldn't have invented a better counterweight for my central character.

My father, James, was living in the Chicago area while I was working on the play in New York. He was kind enough to dig up and send to me a lot of the historical material I needed. My brother Stuart at the time was working in Washington, D.C., and through his contacts was able to secure a copy of the transcript of the Federal Strike Commission.

That transcript was a gold mine. Obviously, I drew upon it for the scene in which Pullman testifies before the commission, but it was also valuable in that it gave me access to the language and logic of many other key players at the time.

I finished a draft of the play and sent it out. I was disappointed to discover that, although there was general appreciation for the script (it was the basis of my grant from the New York State Council for the Arts), there was little eagerness to produce it professionally. Didn't I have a new script with fewer characters? It seemed I'd written something too big.

Then the late Michael Maggio, who was then artistic director of the Northlight Theatre in Evanston, Illinois (at the time just blocks from the house in which I'd been raised), came up with an offer to hire a group of actors to workshop the script for two weeks. And what an exciting two weeks they were! I found many useful cuts, and through group experiments and improvisations led by Michael I reorganized much of the material. It was during this period, for instance, that Michael suggested that Hopkins's speech in favor of the town being annexed to Chicago be run in counterpoint to Oggel's sermon against it. This looks like an inevitable and logical passage now, but it took workshopping to find this and other solutions to the dramatic problems of the script.

Michael was scheduled to direct the premiere at Northlight, but health problems led him to resign from his position there, and the artistic director who succeeded him chose not to honor the theater's commitment to produce the play.

I was happy that this is where Deborah Dixon, then of the Kennedy Center, came in. She had become interested in my writing when she saw the premiere of *The Value of Names* at the Actors Theatre of Louisville. Over lunch at the Kennedy Center, she asked me what I was working on. I told her I had written a play nobody could afford to put on. She asked to see it. After reading it, she said, "We might be able to help you with this."

The help came in the form of a $35,000 grant from the Kennedy Center–American Express Fund for New American Plays to support a production. With this money, Chicago's Organic Theater was able to undertake the project. The Organic's then artistic director Richard Fire assigned the project to a director named Wes Savick and budgeted another two workshops, which further refined the script. At the end of this process, we were ready to go into production.

Now, about the style of the piece. Because this was a Chicago story, my instinct was to employ a theatrical form born in Chicago— story theater, as developed by Second City founder Paul Sills. In this form, actors alternate between playing characters and stepping outside those roles to narrate their characters' actions in the third person. They may switch modes at a moment's notice. By this definition, David Edgar and Trevor Nunn's adaptation of *Nicholas Nickleby* and Jean-Claude Carrière and Peter Brook's collaboration on *The Mahabharata* are story theater pieces.

Incidentally, whenever lines are assigned to the ensemble, they are intended to be distributed among individual members of the ensemble except when otherwise indicated. This is not to be an occasion for choral speaking. Whenever an em dash (—) appears at the beginning of a line for the ensemble, it is an indication that a new cast member should speak. I use this convention in *The Action Against Sol Schumann,* too.

The play opens with a song, and there are other songs in the piece, but this is not a musical any more than is *Nicholas Nickleby* (which also employs songs). I wrote music and lyrics for four of the numbers; the others originated in the late 1800s. They are "Porters on a Pullman Train" (lyrics by Charles D. Crandall, with new music by Michael Vitali), "Maggie Murphy" (music and lyrics by Ned Harrington and Drave Braham), "Step by Step" (traditional Irish song, lyricist anonymous), and "The Pullman Strike" (music by Lewis Hall and lyrics by William M. Delaney).

Much of the text is adapted from primary sources, which means people talked the way they do in the play. The challenge for contemporary American actors accustomed to scripts filled with false starts, fragments, and hesitation is to embrace the language. In those days, long before technology piped drama, information, and music directly into people's living rooms, speeches and debates were considered entertainment. The audience may not have been exposed to as many books and periodicals as we are today, but they relished the prospect of hours of stirring oratory, and from the evidence of the speeches of the time, they were expected to be sophisticated listeners. Transcripts of Debs's speeches, for instance, are filled with extended quotes from Shakespeare and a suppleness and expressiveness of language that we would be surprised to hear from a contemporary labor leader—or indeed, in this age of sound bites, from most other sorts of leaders.

As the action bounces from location to location, the play calls for an environment rather than a conventional representational set. The sets in both the Chicago and the New York productions used the Corliss Engine as a metaphor—a big, hulking, gleaming thing with pistons that suggested nineteenth-century industry. Both designs also made use of multiple levels, a balcony being useful for the orators. An occasional piece of furniture—a desk, a chair, a table—may be brought in by members of the ensemble. Flags and banners were used liberally in both productions. I urge designers and directors to make the transitions between scenes as speedy as possible.

American Enterprise premiered at the Organic Theater in Chicago on March 6, 1991. It was directed by Wesley Savick. The set design was by Richard and Jacqueline Pernod, lighting design by Kevin Snow, and costume design by Yslan Hicks. Michael Vitali was music director and sound designer. The play opened with the following cast:

George M. Pullman . . . . Gary Houston
Beman; Jackson . . . . Edmund Wyson
Rev. E. C. Oggel; George Pullman Jr. . . . . Michael A. Krawic
Superintendent; John Peter Altgeld;
   Mayor Carter Harrison . . . . Phillip East
J. Patrick Hopkins . . . . Larry Russo
Clayton . . . . McKinley Johnson
Heathcote . . . . Chris Farrell
Stephens; Harahan; Commissioner Wright . . . . L. D. Barrett
Priest; Eugene V. Debs . . . . Juan Ramirez
Thomas Wickes; Commissioner Worthington . . . . . . Peter Garino
Jennie Curtis . . . . Tonray Ho
Florence Pullman . . . . Paula Harrington
Soloist . . . . Jamie O'Reilly

The production was made possible by a major grant from the Fund for New American Plays, a project made possible by the John F. Kennedy Center for the Performing Arts, with support from the American Express Company in cooperation with the President's Committee on the Arts and Humanities. Additional support came from the Theatre Communications Group.

American Enterprise was subsequently produced by the New York State Theatre Institute in Troy, New York, with Patricia Di Benedetto Snyder as producing director. The production was subsequently moved to Saint Clement's Church in 1994. It was directed by Patricia Birch, with set by Richard Finkelstein, costumes by Brent Griffin, lighting by John McLain, sound by Matt Elie, additional vocal arrangements and musical direction by Betsy Riley, and production stage management by Heather J. Hamelin. The cast was as follows:

George M. Pullman . . . . John Romeo
Railroad Owner; Heathcote;
   Commissioner Worthington . . . . Joel Aroeste

Railroad Assistant; Porter; Servant . . . . Jack Seabury
Club Attendant . . . . Jason W. Bowman
Beman; Eugene V. Debs; McCormick; Priest . . . . . Gerard Curran
Rev. E. C. Oggel; Field . . . . John T. MacGuire III
Florence Pullman; Jennie Curtis . . . . Erika Newell
J. Patrick Hopkins . . . . Erol K. C. Landis
Clayton; John Peter Altgeld; Jackson; Porter . . . . Bernard J. Tarver
Stephens; Harahan; Agent . . . . Paul Villani
Secretary . . . . Tracey E. Madison
George Jr.; Paymaster . . . . David Bunce
Thomas Wickes; Commissioner Wright;
    Porter . . . . Marshall Favtora
Soloists . . . . Betsy Riley, Kelly Sweeney
Mayor Carter Harrison; Swift; Cosgrove . . . . Michael Steese
Ensemble . . . . Laura Roth, Allison Sharpley

CHARACTERS

George M. Pullman
J. Patrick Hopkins

The following roles are divided up among the ensemble members: Businessmen (First, Second, and Third), Woman Customer, Railroad Owner, Assistants, Travelers (First, Second, Third, Fourth, Fifth), Club Attendant, Stockholders (First, Second), Beman, Junior, Florence Pullman, Rev. E. C. Oggel, Passengers (First, Second, Third, Fourth, Fifth), Pullman Resident, Thomas Wickes, Men (2), Woman, Superintendent, Clayton, Stephens, Heathcote, Messenger, Secretary, Jackson, Agent, Priest, Ely, Foreman, Eugene V. Debs, Soloists (male and female), Orator, Mayor Carter Harrison, Jennie Curtis, Paymaster, Reporters (First, Second, Third, Fourth, Fifth), Delegate, Second Delegate, Chairman, Harahan, Railroad Officials (First, Second, Third), Servant, Judge, Federal Marshal, John Peter Altgeld, Observers (First, Second, Third, Fourth, Fifth), Commissioner Wright, Commissioner Worthington, Billings, Citizens (First, Second)

ACT 1

PROLOGUE

[*The play is set in Chicago in the last third of the nineteenth century. The* ENSEMBLE *gathers in a chorus arrangement. A conductor steps forward with a pitch pipe, then leads the* ENSEMBLE *in a song.*]

ENSEMBLE: Neighbors, shall we promise now
    Someday under spreading bough
    We'll know joy only peace can endow?
    Shall we plant a tree?

    Shall we see the cutting take root?
    Shall we watch it flower and fruit?
    Shall our will remain resolute?
    Shall we plant a tree?

    A tree for shelter.
    A tree for shade.
    A tree for all to share.
    A tree whose arms reach up to the sky!
    Shall we see this—you and I?

    Though we hail from separate parts,
    Common purpose gathers our hearts.
    This is where the future starts.
    Shall we plant our tree?
    Yes, we'll plant our tree!

[*The following speeches are distributed among the* ENSEMBLE.]

    —This is the story of a man who had good intentions.
    —And how those intentions led him to try a noble experiment.
    —And how that experiment didn't exactly lead where he hoped.
    —This is the story of an American enterprise.
    [*Singing*] Though we hail from separate parts,
    Common purpose gathers our hearts.
    This is where the future starts.
    Shall we plant our tree?
    Yes, we'll plant our tree!

SCENE 1

ALL: Chicago!

ENSEMBLE: —And there's a fortune to be made.

—If you have the right idea.

FIRST BUSINESSMAN: Harvesttime. The wheat stands tall and you have your choice: hire six men or put this beauty to work in your fields.

ENSEMBLE: The reaper.

FIRST BUSINESSMAN: The McCormick reaper.

ENSEMBLE: One hundred twenty dollars on the installment plan.

FIRST BUSINESSMAN: Don't be left behind.

ENSEMBLE: And Cyrus McCormick makes his fortune in—

ALL: Chicago!

ENSEMBLE: —And there's a fortune to be made.

—If you have the right idea.

SECOND BUSINESSMAN [*advancing on a* WOMAN CUSTOMER]: You have a fine house, and why not? You've earned it. But to make that house a home you need—

[*The* ENSEMBLE *splits into two groups that, on their lines, advance on the* WOMAN CUSTOMER.]

FIRST ENSEMBLE GROUP: Persian rugs—

SECOND ENSEMBLE GROUP: And hand-painted china—

FIRST ENSEMBLE GROUP: And lace—

SECOND ENSEMBLE GROUP: And tableware—

SECOND BUSINESSMAN: Courtesy and convenience at our State Street address.

[WOMAN CUSTOMER *gives* SECOND BUSINESSMAN *money.*]

WOMAN CUSTOMER: And Marshall Field makes his fortune in—

ALL: Chicago!

ENSEMBLE: And there's a fortune to be made—

[PULLMAN *steps forward.*]

PULLMAN: This is what it means to travel overnight by railroad today:

[*Members of the* ENSEMBLE *mime a very disagreeable rail journey. One of them plays a passenger; the others jostle and push and otherwise manhandle him, finally tossing him to the floor.*]

Narrow, uncomfortable berths. Linen that is either filthy or nonexistent. Noise, dust, smoke. Sleep is out of the question. The traveler arrives at his destination rumpled, exhausted, debilitated. He must rest a day, perhaps two, before pursuing his business. Result: loss of time and consequent income. I now have the pleasure of introducing the Pullman alternative.

[*During the following, the* ENSEMBLE *again mimes a rail journey. This time, however, the passenger is pampered and caressed, at one point being hoisted on their shoulders as if sleeping comfortably in a berth. By the end, he has been set gently down on his feet and politely awakened. In short: a wonderful time.*]

Twice the standard number of wheels, springs, shock absorbers. Cushioned seats that convert into real beds with clean sheets and pillowcases. Result: a smooth ride, a luxurious sleeping experience. The traveler arrives refreshed, ready to face the challenges of the day. I present to you the Pullman car—the railway car that makes travel a pleasure.

[*The* RAILROAD OWNER, *a prosperous man with a stovepipe hat, steps into the car with his* ASSISTANT *in tow.* PULLMAN *watches as the* RAILROAD OWNER *looks around. In the meantime, the* ASSISTANT *begins measuring dimensions unobtrusively. Note: during the following,* PULLMAN'*s attitude is consistently genial, if a little distant. If any of the things that the* RAILROAD OWNER *says to him in the following scene upset him, he takes care not to let it show. A beat.*]

RAILROAD OWNER: Cherrywood?
PULLMAN: Yes.

[*The* RAILROAD OWNER *nods appreciatively. Looks at another detail.*]

RAILROAD OWNER: Velvet?
PULLMAN: Yes.
RAILROAD OWNER: Aren't you a little worried?
PULLMAN: About—
RAILROAD OWNER: Some of our ridership are not—shall we say, very refined? Traveling salesmen and so forth. What's to keep them from climbing into your clean beds with their boots on, spattering mud on your sheets?
PULLMAN: The car will tell them not to.
RAILROAD OWNER: In addition to everything else, the car *talks*?

PULLMAN: It is my belief that people behave better when they are in a refined and aesthetic environment.

RAILROAD OWNER: An interesting theory. What if you're wrong?

PULLMAN: I lose.

RAILROAD OWNER: What is it you want, exactly?

PULLMAN: A trial run on the line between Chicago and Springfield.

RAILROAD OWNER: A trial—on what terms?

PULLMAN: Three months. You collect the basic fare, I collect an additional fare when a passenger chooses to ride in my car.

RAILROAD OWNER: And the advantage to me is—

PULLMAN: More people will ride your train. The more people ride your train—

RAILROAD OWNER: The more basic fares I collect.

PULLMAN: That's the idea.

RAILROAD OWNER: And if it doesn't work out that way? If I'm not happy at the end of three months—

PULLMAN: I unhook my car, we shake hands, and that's the end of it.

[*The* RAILROAD OWNER *considers this for a second and then nods.*]

RAILROAD OWNER: You may have yourself a deal.

ASSISTANT: Uh, sir—

RAILROAD OWNER: Bennett?

ASSISTANT: Perhaps you should take a look at this—

[*The* ASSISTANT *shows the* RAILROAD OWNER *some figures he's marked down.*]

RAILROAD OWNER [*to* ASSISTANT]: You're sure?

ASSISTANT: I double-checked.

RAILROAD OWNER: We seem to have run into a little problem here, Mr. Pullman.

PULLMAN: Oh?

[*During the following,* PULLMAN *continues to smile politely, dealing with the* RAILROAD OWNER's *objections with slightly condescending patience. The* RAILROAD OWNER, *too, gives a great show of geniality tinged with condescension. The politeness masks the impatience they both feel having to deal with what each considers the other's denseness.*]

RAILROAD OWNER: Station platforms are built on the assumption that all railroad cars conform to a standard width.

PULLMAN: Yes.

RAILROAD OWNER: Mr. Bennett here tells me your car is wider than that standard.

ASSISTANT: By a good two feet.

PULLMAN: Yes.

RAILROAD OWNER: You're aware of this?

PULLMAN: I am aware.

RAILROAD OWNER: You knew that the car you were building was two feet wider than the standard and you built it anyway.

PULLMAN: I needed these dimensions to accommodate all the features I'd designed. The pulleys, the plumbing—

RAILROAD OWNER: Yes, yes, but how do you expect the train to come into the station? If the car is too big—

PULLMAN: You have saws.

RAILROAD OWNER: Saws?

PULLMAN: I assume your platforms are made of wood.

RAILROAD OWNER: Oh, cut back the platforms?

PULLMAN: As you point out, my car won't fit otherwise.

[*A beat.*]

RAILROAD OWNER: How much did it cost you to build this?

PULLMAN: Twenty thousand dollars, more or less.

RAILROAD OWNER: Investors?

PULLMAN: No.

RAILROAD OWNER: Your own money.

PULLMAN: Yes.

RAILROAD OWNER: Why would somebody spend twenty thousand dollars of his own money to build a railroad car that can't run?

PULLMAN: It *can* run.

RAILROAD OWNER: All I have to do is—

PULLMAN: Cut back the—

RAILROAD OWNER [*overlapping*]: The platforms, yes, I know. But why would I want to do that?

PULLMAN: It's a good car.

RAILROAD OWNER: It's a beautiful car. What I'm trying to understand is why you didn't build this beautiful car so as to conform to the standards.

PULLMAN: I wouldn't have been able to accommodate all of the special features I had envisioned. The pulleys, the plumbing—

RAILROAD OWNER: But even if you had to give up one or two of the things you *envisioned,* it still would have been a better car.

PULLMAN: *Better* is not necessarily good.

RAILROAD OWNER: It might just be good *enough.*

PULLMAN: My name is on what I build. When people see my name, I don't want them to think, "Oh, that's George Pullman. What he builds is good *enough.*"

RAILROAD OWNER: Have you ever heard of the word "compromise"?

[*A beat.*]

PULLMAN [*a little steel glinting through the smile*]: Our conversation appears to be over.

RAILROAD OWNER: If you ever build a practical version of this, do let me know.

PULLMAN: I have built what I intended.

[*The* RAILROAD OWNER *shakes his head, and he and his* ASSISTANT *exit the car. The* RAILROAD OWNER *moves onto a platform—an area we will later identify as the Chicago Club—where he joins three other* BUSINESSMEN.]

THIRD BUSINESSMAN: So what is Pullman doing with it?

SECOND BUSINESSMAN: His precious car?

RAILROAD OWNER: He's got it sitting on a siding gathering dust.

SECOND BUSINESSMAN: The man won't bend.

PULLMAN [*to audience*]: Why should I compromise? One compromises when one is wrong or when one is compelled to. I am not so compelled. And I am not wrong.

RAILROAD OWNER: Pigheaded. Just plain pigheaded.

PULLMAN: I prefer to call it determined. When I first arrived here—this was in 1855—Chicago was one big muddy swamp.

SECOND BUSINESSMAN: Oh, Christ, here comes that story again.

FIRST BUSINESSMAN [*anticipating*]: "People were in such a rush—"

[*During the following speech, the* BUSINESSMEN *and* RAILROAD OWNER, *shaking their heads, exit, leaving* PULLMAN *alone onstage addressing the audience.*]

PULLMAN [*blithely continuing*]: People were in such a rush to throw up buildings, they didn't bother to notice that they hadn't built them on proper foundations. They built too low. At times, Lake Michigan was practically lapping at the doorsteps. The cellars were constantly flooded. A proper drainage system was impossible. The answer was obvious—raise the buildings. Raise the buildings? No, no, I was told, that was impossible. I said, let me see what I can do. We agreed on a test case: the Tremont Hotel. I calculated it needed to be raised eight feet. I engaged twelve hundred men, positioned them by forty-eight hundred jackscrews. I won't go into the mechanics of it. But, at my signal, each man turned four jackscrews. And the building rose. Within an hour, it was raised by eight feet, and without spilling a single drop of tea from a cup in the tearoom. After that, I had all the work I wanted. I had arrived in Chicago with next to nothing in my pocket. Within a year, I was worth—well, let's just say neither I nor my family has wanted for anything since. This is the power of determination.

[*A beat.*]

I am right about my car. They may not see it now, but that's all right. If something has value, it will find its time. I have confidence.

ENSEMBLE: —April 15, 1865:
—This morning, despite the best efforts of attending surgeons, President Abraham Lincoln died of an assassin's bullet.
—Mrs. Lincoln accompanies her husband's body on its long journey home.

WOMAN: When she arrives in Chicago, she is on the verge of physical collapse.

ENSEMBLE: There are doubts as to whether she will be able to bear up under the strain of the final ride to Springfield.

[PULLMAN *steps forward, locates Mrs. Lincoln beyond the proscenium.*]

PULLMAN: Mrs. Lincoln, may I offer you the use of my car?

[RAILROAD OWNER *turns to the* ASSISTANT.]

RAILROAD OWNER: Where do we keep the saws?

ASSISTANT: The saws?

RAILROAD OWNER: The saws. The goddamn saws, goddamn it.

ASSISTANT: All of the platforms?

RAILROAD OWNER: Between here and Springfield.

ASSISTANT: But we can't do that.

RAILROAD OWNER: Would you like to tell that to Mrs. Lincoln?

[RAILROAD OWNER *gives* PULLMAN *a disgruntled look.* PULLMAN *nods.*]

WOMAN: Mrs. Lincoln expresses her gratitude to Mr. Pullman for the comfort of his car.

ENSEMBLE: And suddenly everyone wants to ride in it.

PULLMAN: And so the Pullman Palace Car Company is born.

FIRST TRAVELER: Dear Mr. Pullman: I had the very great pleasure of riding in one of your sleepers on the twelfth of this month and may I say I have never enjoyed a trip by rail more.

SECOND TRAVELER: Dear Mr. Pullman: there was a time when I would have scheduled two days to recover from a railway journey, but I arrived refreshed and ready to do business. You have my thanks and my congratulations.

[*The following speeches are contrapuntal. After each "Dear Mr. Pullman" and the first few words, the next speaker joins in until all are speaking at once.*]

THIRD TRAVELER: Dear Mr. Pullman: I cannot begin to tell you how very much I enjoyed riding in your lovely car. The service was exemplary and the hygiene impeccable. I shall certainly commend it to those friends of mine planning to travel.

FOURTH TRAVELER: Dear Mr. Pullman: I had heard from friends of your extraordinary car and the comfort it affords, but was not prepared for the joy of the actual experience. I use the word "joy" and that is exactly what I mean, for that is the only word to describe the sensation.

FIFTH TRAVELER: Dear Mr. Pullman: I had always thought the phrases "railway travel" and "comfort" to be mutually exclusive till I rode in your commodious car. It was worth every penny of the two-dollar surcharge.

[*As the previous ends, the* FIRST TRAVELER *chimes in.*]

FIRST TRAVELER: It's a godsend!
ENSEMBLE: And so George Pullman, too, makes his fortune in—
ALL: Chicago.

SCENE 2

[*The* CLUB ATTENDANT *steps forward.*]

CLUB ATTENDANT: And now he lunches regularly in the Chicago Club
with other men of means.

[PULLMAN *moves to the area where the Chicago Club is located. He nods hello
to the* THREE BUSINESSMEN *sitting there and sits off to the side. The* CLUB
ATTENDANT *approaches the* BUSINESSMEN.]

Another brandy, sir?
SECOND BUSINESSMAN: What? No, no, thank you.
FIRST BUSINESSMAN: Newspaper.

[*The* CLUB ATTENDANT *hands a paper to the* FIRST BUSINESSMAN, *who
begins reading it. Something catches his attention. He grunts and hands the
paper to the* SECOND BUSINESSMAN, *who looks at it and hands it to the* THIRD
BUSINESSMAN, *who looks at it and puts the paper down.*]

FIRST BUSINESSMAN: A militia.
SECOND BUSINESSMAN: I don't know.
FIRST BUSINESSMAN: No, I'm telling you—a militia. That's what we need.
CLUB ATTENDANT [*to audience*]: A strike in Baltimore has touched off
demonstrations and violence.

[*The* FIRST BUSINESSMAN *looks at the* CLUB ATTENDANT *who takes this as
his cue to exit.*]

SECOND BUSINESSMAN: So you're suggesting, what? That the government should put together some kind of military force to—
FIRST BUSINESSMAN [*interrupting*]: An army, yes. Trained to deal with
this sort of thing.
SECOND BUSINESSMAN: But is that a proper function for government?
The country doesn't own these businesses, we do. So why should the
country—

FIRST BUSINESSMAN [*interrupting*]: We are *building* this country. What we do is in the national interest. No, I go farther: what we do *is* the national interest. It's only right that the nation defend us.

SECOND BUSINESSMAN: But with an army? Armies are for war.

FIRST BUSINESSMAN [*referring to the newspaper*]: People getting killed; property going up in flames. You don't call that war? No, sir, if my factory is going to be attacked, I want some kind of militia to stand in front of it.

PULLMAN: You wouldn't need a militia if they didn't think of you as the enemy.

THIRD BUSINESSMAN: I like the way you say "you."

FIRST BUSINESSMAN: I didn't know that you had resigned from the club, George.

PULLMAN: Have you ever seen the sort of neighborhood where the workers we employ live? Have you been to the First Ward?

THIRD BUSINESSMAN: Oh, George—

PULLMAN: The ugliness, the relentless filth. A bar every third building to take their money and ravage their minds. Brothels to corrupt their morals and spread disease. The air stinks with death and despair. If this were your life, how much affection would you have for a system that places you there?

FIRST BUSINESSMAN: That's right—I personally drove every one of them there and put a bottle in his hands.

PULLMAN: When I built my first sleeping car, I was told I was crazy. Putting in carpeting, fresh linen—they said the passengers would destroy it. In point of fact, people behave better in my cars than they do in their own homes.

FIRST BUSINESSMAN: I assume there's a point to this.

PULLMAN: The more artistic and refined a man's external surroundings—

FIRST BUSINESSMAN [*finishing* PULLMAN'S *sentence*]: The nicer person he is.

PULLMAN [*finishing the sentence his way*]: The better and more refined the man. If we put our men into a decent environment, we won't need an army.

FIRST BUSINESSMAN: I have to hand it to you, George. You've sure solved that.

THIRD BUSINESSMAN: Now, now.

FIRST BUSINESSMAN: No, really, why didn't we think of it before? All we need for peace and harmony is to give everyone his own personal Pullman car.

PULLMAN [*coolly*]: Good afternoon, gentlemen.

[*He rises.*]

THIRD BUSINESSMAN: Oh now, George—you must cultivate a sense of humor.

PULLMAN: I am not aware of being deficient in that regard.

ENSEMBLE: Pullman makes up his mind to act on his theory.

[*A pair of* ASSISTANTS *enter. One pulls down a banner reading "Welcome, Pullman Stockholders—1880!"*]

PULLMAN: Gentlemen, in the thirteen years since it was incorporated, the Pullman Company has built thousands of sleeping cars and seen them adopted by railroad lines coast to coast. In addition, we are now constructing restaurant and chair cars as well as operating facilities for the repair of railway carriages. All this accompanied by a steady eight percent dividend and stock whose par value has more then doubled.

[*Cheers from* STOCKHOLDERS *planted in the audience.*]

Thank you. Today I have the honor and pleasure of introducing to you the newest and perhaps the boldest undertaking of our company. The fulfillment of the Pullman philosophy.

[*A signal to his* ASSISTANTS. *A black-and-white rendering of the town of Pullman is unfurled, accompanied by a dramatic change of lighting and a drumroll. An* ASSISTANT *hands him a pointer.*]

These will be the factory works, where we will continue to make and service the Pullman Palace cars. We will also begin to accept orders from the railroads for the construction and maintenance of other cars. On the other side of this avenue—the residential section. Different zones for different classifications—homes for executives here, for workingmen with families there. You get the idea. This is the hotel, which will be named for my daughter Florence. And this, something rather special—we call it the Arcade. It will include various shops and businesses, the library and a theater to rival any in Chicago.

FIRST STOCKHOLDER [*rising in the audience*]: Excuse me, Mr. Pullman, did I hear you say something about a theater?

PULLMAN: Yes.

FIRST STOCKHOLDER: This company is going to build a theater?

PULLMAN: Without a theater we wouldn't have a proper town.

SECOND STOCKHOLDER [*rising*]: You are going to build an entire town?

PULLMAN: That is the plan, yes.

FIRST STOCKHOLDER: Excuse me, but when I bought shares in the Pullman Company, it was on the understanding that its business was railroad cars, not real estate.

PULLMAN: The people who work in our new factory will need to live somewhere.

FIRST STOCKHOLDER: But since when is it our responsibility to build homes for them?

PULLMAN: It may not be our responsibility, but it is in our interest.

FIRST STOCKHOLDER: I don't see—

PULLMAN [*interrupting*]: If you will allow me to explain?

[*A beat.*]

Thank you. This will be a very handsome town. Quite in contrast with the slums most workers are used to living in. And as there will be indoor plumbing and a strictly enforced policy to keep out—shall we say, undesirable elements?—I expect we will have the benefit of a clean, sober, healthy, and consequently happy citizenry. Happy workers, gentlemen, do not strike. Moreover, I have determined that their output is of increased quality and quantity.

SECOND STOCKHOLDER: I gather you have likewise determined that your stockholders will pay for this philanthropy?

PULLMAN: It's not philanthropy. To receive charity robs a man of his dignity, his self-respect. No, we will give away nothing. People will work in our factories. We will pay them fair market rates. They will live in the town. They will pay us fair market rent. The company will make a profit on both enterprises. Both the company and the workers will prosper. Far from being philanthropy, it is a system designed to make philanthropy unnecessary. By doing good, we will do well. Call it an experiment in enlightened capitalism.

FIRST STOCKHOLDER: What if I don't want my money financing your experiment?

PULLMAN: It was one of my experiments that founded this company. This has helped make you rich. If you no longer trust my judgment, then by all means, sell your stock. You will find no shortage of people who will be happy to relieve you of it.

[*A beat.* PULLMAN *turns away. Lights shift for the construction scene.*]

ENSEMBLE: Pullman has purchased four thousand acres on which to build his town—

PULLMAN: Several miles south of the malign influences of Chicago.

ENSEMBLE: The project has been designed by a young architect by the name of—

BEMAN [*to audience*]: Beman.

ENSEMBLE: Construction begins.

BEMAN: As the buildings rise, the architect comes to George Pullman with a suggestion.

PULLMAN: And what is that, Mr. Beman?

BEMAN: I'd like to propose a name.

PULLMAN: A name?

BEMAN: For the town.

PULLMAN: What might that be?

BEMAN: Well, uh, Beman.

PULLMAN: Beman?

BEMAN: I'm very proud of the way this is turning out.

PULLMAN: Beman.

BEMAN: If you would do me the honor of considering it.

PULLMAN: What do you say we name it after both of us?

BEMAN: How?

PULLMAN: We'll take the first syllable of my last name and combine it with the second syllable of your last name.

[*A second while* BEMAN *figures this out, smiles wanly.* PULLMAN *turns to audience.*]

And they say I have no sense of humor.

BEMAN [*to audience*]: As the crowning touch to his grand design, Pullman buys an engine—

PULLMAN: And not just any engine—the Corliss engine.

[*The map of the town is pulled down, revealing a representation of the Corliss engine upstage.*]

BEMAN: It weighs over three hundred and fifty tons and generates twenty-four hundred horsepower.

PULLMAN: Placed on permanent display behind plateglass windows, it is the beating heart that drives the town of Pullman.

ENSEMBLE: A ceremony marks the opening of the town. [*Introducing*] The Reverend E. C. Oggel, the Presbyterian minister of the town—

[PULLMAN, JUNIOR, *and* FLORENCE *take seats on a platform as* OGGEL *rises. Members of the Chicago Club watch from the side.*]

OGGEL: Walk through this town. Nowhere will you find a gaming table, a barroom, or a brothel. And nowhere the attendant miseries of degradation, drunkenness, and disease. Observe instead clean, self-respecting homes. Homes of honest, God-fearing workmen. Pullman will continue to build railroad cars. But better than factory, and richer than material production, shall be the manhood that will be developed here.

[*The following is another contrapuntal* ENSEMBLE *piece similar to the previous sequence featuring letters from happy passengers.*]

FIRST PASSENGER: Dear Mr. Pullman: I write to express my heartfelt admiration for the town which has the honor to bear your name. The streets, the gardens, the thousand and one details delight the eye and ennoble the spirit. You have cause to be proud of this astonishing achievement and I salute you for it.

SECOND PASSENGER: Some men talk, some men do. What George Pullman has done on the banks of Lake Calumet gives physical expression to the American ideal at its highest. By harnessing philosophy to action, he has wrought a revolution.

THIRD PASSENGER: I have visited the Taj Mahal and the gardens of Versailles. But glorious as these wonders are, to my mind they cannot compare to the community you and your inspired architects have constructed. My congratulations.

FOURTH PASSENGER: Pullman is the only city in existence built from the foundation on scientific and sanitary principles. The health of the town is exceptional, and the moral tone of the workmen remarkable.

FIFTH PASSENGER: To go from the filthy tenements of Chicago to the clean and hygienic homes of Pullman is akin to an ascent from Hades to paradise. The enlightened citizen must join his fellows in crying, "Bravo!"

ALL PASSENGERS: Bravo!

PULLMAN RESIDENT: Pullman takes particular pleasure in walking through the town on Saturdays—

FLORENCE: With his daughter Florence.

PULLMAN: The sight of children playing tag in the park—

FLORENCE: The men engaged in athletic contests—

[PULLMAN *sees a* WOMAN *with a watering can standing with her back to him. He signals to a man we'll later come to know as* WICKES, *who in turn signals offstage. A second later, an* ASSISTANT *hurries onstage with a basket of flowers that he gives to* PULLMAN. PULLMAN *approaches the* WOMAN. *She senses his presence and turns.*]

WOMAN: Mr. Pullman, I—

PULLMAN: I'm sorry, I didn't meant to startle you. I was just admiring the care you've taken with your garden. I hope you'll accept this as a token of appreciation. It is a pleasure to have you living in this town.

[*He hands her the flowers. She is pleased and a little dumbfounded. Impulsively, she kisses his cheek.* PULLMAN *blushes but is not displeased.* PULLMAN *returns to* FLORENCE *and takes her arm. As he turns, several townspeople gather.*]

ENSEMBLE: And, on Sundays, there are free concerts in the park featuring performers drawn from the ranks of the Pullman workers.

[TWO MEN *step forward and sing "Porters on a Pullman Train."*]

TWO MEN [*singing*]: We need no introduction.
    You can see who we are—
    Porters on a Pullman train,
    Standing at the platform of the sleeping car—
    Ready, quick, and willing to explain,
    Explain where you're located.
    But we must be remunerated.
    Don't forget a friendly tip.

We think you oughta
Give us a quatah
For then you'll have a very pleasant trip.

Porter, porter—give us more air!
Porter—I'm just about froze!
Porter—this pillow is hard as a rock!
Porter—the window, please close!
Porter—come here!
Porter—stay there!
All night the people complain.

We are porters,
Dandy porters.
We are handy Pullman porters
And we run on the vestibule—
Run on the vestibule—
Run on the vestibule train!

[*Now a* WOMAN *of the town steps forward to sing "Oh, Leave a Light." After the first time through, she sings it again, joined in harmony by a* MAN.]

WOMAN [*singing*]: Oh, leave a light
To guide me back.
Oh, leave a light so bright
That when I'm lost
And so alone
I can raise my eyes
And find my way back home,
And find my way back home.
Oh, leave a light
So I can see.
Oh, leave a light for me.

[*Lights up on the* FIRST *and* SECOND BUSINESSMEN *in the Chicago Club. The following is played over underscoring.*]

SECOND BUSINESSMAN: Beautiful.
FIRST BUSINESSMAN: I suppose.
SECOND BUSINESSMAN: What's bothering you?

FIRST BUSINESSMAN: Nothing.

SECOND BUSINESSMAN: Are you that upset he's made a success of it?

FIRST BUSINESSMAN: Every honeymoon comes to an end.

SECOND BUSINESSMAN: A worm in every apple, huh? I feel sorry for you.

FIRST BUSINESSMAN [*referring to* PULLMAN]: I feel sorry for *him*.

[*The music comes to an end.* PULLMAN *and* FLORENCE *applaud and exit as the next scene begins.*]

SCENE 3

[*A sign: hiring today.* HOPKINS *enters for an interview with* SUPERINTENDENT.]

SUPERINTENDENT: Name?

HOPKINS: Hopkins. J. Patrick Hopkins.

SUPERINTENDENT: Age?

HOPKINS: Twenty-two.

SUPERINTENDENT: Ever been married?

HOPKINS: No, sir.

SUPERINTENDENT: Any outstanding debts?

HOPKINS: None.

SUPERINTENDENT: Do you drink?

HOPKINS: No, sir.

SUPERINTENDENT [*handing him a slip*]: Report to the lumberyard.

[HOPKINS *nods and goes to the lumberyard.* SUPERINTENDENT *exits as* CLAYTON, STEPHENS, *and* HEATHCOTE *enter. During this next dialogue, they begin to work with one another.*]

CLAYTON: You play the cornet?

HOPKINS: Excuse me?

CLAYTON: The cornet.

HOPKINS: Oh no, I'm afraid I'm not musical. Back home in Buffalo, the priest called my singing a venial sin.

CLAYTON: Too bad. We could use a cornet player.

[*They begin to work together.*]

HOPKINS: We?

CLAYTON: The band. Stephens here and I are in the band.

HOPKINS: Are you any good?

STEPHENS: We'd be better if we still had our old cornet player.

HOPKINS: Something happened to him.

HEATHCOTE: He was invited to leave town.

HOPKINS: A pleasing personality?

STEPHENS: Couldn't stop using offensive language.

HEATHCOTE: Words like "union" and "organize"—

CLAYTON: He also showed up to work drunk a lot.

STEPHENS: You'll find out they keep a pretty close eye on you here, Mr. Hopkins.

CLAYTON: Would you rather move back to the First Ward?

STEPHENS: I'm not saying that.

CLAYTON: Do you miss the rats?

STEPHENS: That's not what I'm saying.

CLAYTON: If you're so unhappy—

STEPHENS: There's more to happiness than good sewers.

HEATHCOTE: Welcome to Pullman, Mr. Hopkins.

SUPERINTENDENT: The superintendent is impressed by Hopkins's work in the lumberyard.

ENSEMBLE: —Mr. Pullman is told of the young man's industry and good nature.

—Soon after, Hopkins advances to the storekeeping department.

—A little later, he is appointed timekeeper of the store.

—Then general timekeeper.

MESSENGER: Then, one day: [*to* HOPKINS] Mr. Pullman wants to see you.

HOPKINS: Me?

MESSENGER: At your earliest convenience.

[HOPKINS *approaches* PULLMAN.]

HOPKINS: Mr. Pullman?

PULLMAN [*shaking hands with him*]: Hopkins. I'll call you Pat, if you don't mind. Have a seat.

HOPKINS: Thank you.

PULLMAN: I understand you're from New York.

HOPKINS: Upstate New York, yes, sir.

PULLMAN: I am, too. In fact, I wasn't much older than you are now when I came to Chicago. A fine time. A lot of opportunity if you had a clear idea of what you wanted to do and took the bit between your teeth. Tell me about your schooling.

HOPKINS: Not much to speak of. Only a few years really.

PULLMAN: Why no more?

HOPKINS: I was pretty young when my father died—

PULLMAN: And you had a mother and the other children to support.

HOPKINS: Yes, sir, that's the way it was.

PULLMAN: Education is a fine thing. But even without formal education, a man with determination can make his way. I had very little formal schooling myself, you know.

HOPKINS: No, I didn't realize.

PULLMAN: Oh yes, I wasn't born to all this. Seven brothers and sisters. My parents couldn't afford to send us to school. I had to begin work when I was fourteen. Started off as a clerk. Forty dollars a year.

HOPKINS: I've tried to continue studies on my own.

PULLMAN: Yes, I see that from your record.

HOPKINS: My record?

PULLMAN: At the library. What you've been borrowing. [*Pulling out sheet*] Hopkins, J. Patrick. You're eleven days overdue on *Stettler's Approach to Modern Accounting*.

HOPKINS: I'm not quite finished with it.

PULLMAN: Books on accounting, engineering—isn't that rather dry stuff for a young man to spend his own time on?

HOPKINS: I like to know how things run.

PULLMAN: The company paymaster is retiring. The job is yours.

[*A beat.*]

Nothing to say?

HOPKINS: This is—

PULLMAN: A surprise?

HOPKINS: Yes, sir.

PULLMAN: That was the idea.

[SECRETARY *enters.*]

SECRETARY: Excuse me, sir.

PULLMAN: Yes?

SECRETARY: Your son is here.

PULLMAN: Did we have an appointment?

SECRETARY: No.

PULLMAN: I'm busy.

SECRETARY: Do you want me to tell him that?

PULLMAN: Tell him he's being paid for a full day's work, and I expect him to do it. If he wants to see me, he should make an appointment like everybody else.

[JUNIOR *has entered during the last of this.*]

JUNIOR: Thanks, Pop. Nice to know you're willing to treat me as well as everybody else.

PULLMAN: I didn't invite you in.

JUNIOR: You canceled the contract with Fleischer.

PULLMAN: Yes.

JUNIOR: The contract I negotiated.

PULLMAN: We can get the linen from Nickerson and Company for half what Fleischer's asking.

JUNIOR: Not according to Nickerson's price list.

PULLMAN: You don't rely on the price list. We're dealing in bulk. If you had bothered to contact Nickerson directly—

JUNIOR: The point is I set up a purchase, and you canceled it.

PULLMAN: Because I arranged for better terms.

JUNIOR: Don't you care what this makes me look like?

PULLMAN: What does it matter what Fleischer thinks?

JUNIOR: Not just Fleischer. The others in my department. They all know about it.

PULLMAN: I wish you were as concerned about my good opinion as you are about theirs.

JUNIOR: How am I supposed to command any respect if you undercut me?

PULLMAN: George, as you can see I am in a meeting. You will oblige me by returning to your desk.

[*A beat.*]

JUNIOR [*to* HOPKINS]: Excuse me.

[JUNIOR *exits with* SECRETARY.]

PULLMAN: I'm afraid my son has a few problems to . . . sort out. It takes some people a little longer to find their feet.

HOPKINS: Yes, sir.

PULLMAN: One must be patient.

[*A beat.*]

So what do you say, Pat?

[HOPKINS *looks confused.*]

The job. Do I have a new paymaster?

HOPKINS: Oh, uh, yes, sir. Thank you, sir.

PULLMAN: You're entirely welcome.

[PULLMAN *shakes* HOPKINS's *hand.* HOPKINS *leaves the office. The* SUPERIN-TENDENT *hands him a jacket and tie, befitting his new position. He smiles.*]

SCENE 4

[*A street in the town.* JACKSON *and* AGENT *in midconversation.*]

AGENT: The Arcade Theater?

JACKSON: On March 31.

AGENT: And just what do you want to rent it for, Mr. Jackson?

JACKSON: A lecture.

AGENT: Called?

JACKSON: "Britain's Title to the Northwest."

AGENT: Concerning?

JACKSON: Britain's title to the Northwest.

AGENT: You can have the market hall.

JACKSON: Excuse me, but you mustn't have heard me correctly. I said I wanted the Arcade Theater.

AGENT: Yes, Mr. Jackson, and I said you can have the market hall.

JACKSON [*acquiescing*]: The market hall.

AGENT: I'll need a deposit.

JACKSON: Jackson goes about publicizing his lecture.

[JACKSON *gives* AGENT *one of his handbills, then goes out into the audience to distribute more, ad-libbing about the virtues of his lecture. The* AGENT *looks at the handbill and passes it to the* SUPERINTENDENT. *The* SUPERINTENDENT *gives it a look, then goes to* PULLMAN. *They have a muffled conference. The* SUPERINTENDENT *turns to* AGENT, *tears the handbill.* AGENT *nods.* AGENT *calls out to* JACKSON.]

AGENT: No point handing out any more of those. Your lecture's been canceled.

JACKSON: Canceled?

[JACKSON *runs back to the stage to the* AGENT.]

There's a conflict. A booking for the hall.

JACKSON: But you said it was free then.

AGENT: I was wrong.

JACKSON: I saw your calendar. There was nothing else written in.

AGENT: You want to take a look at my calendar? You want to see if there's something written in there or not?

JACKSON: People will show up—

AGENT: We'll put up a sign to explain. Here's your deposit.

JACKSON: No.

AGENT: You don't want your money?

JACKSON: We have a contract—

AGENT: Which is null and void owing to a prior engagement.

JACKSON: We'll see about that.

[PULLMAN *and* HOPKINS *are in conference, speaking in muffled tones.* JACKSON *approaches.*]

Mr. Pullman?

PULLMAN: Yes?

JACKSON: Just a moment of your time. My name is Jackson.

PULLMAN [*shaking his hand*]: Yes, Mr. Jackson, how may I be of help?

JACKSON: I contracted for the use of the market hall tonight. Today your agent told me there was a mistake in the scheduling. Something about a prior commitment.

PULLMAN: Then he owes you your deposit.

JACKSON: Mr. Pullman, I've advertised; I've sold tickets. Canceling would mean a substantial loss to me.

PULLMAN: I'm sorry to hear it, but there's nothing to be done.

JACKSON: Well, actually I *do* have an idea: I understand there's no performance tonight in the Arcade Theater. It was, in fact, my first choice.

PULLMAN: For your lecture?

JACKSON: Oh, you've heard about it?

PULLMAN: I've heard about its subject. I must say that, given the uncertainty of the times, I see no need to agitate the public on labor questions.

JACKSON: My lecture is not on labor questions. It concerns constitutional issues.

PULLMAN: The word "monopoly" appeared on your handbill.

JACKSON: Yes, but not in the context of the labor question.

PULLMAN: I'm sorry, Mr. Jackson, but I am determined that nothing of questionable character be presented in my halls.

JACKSON: Questionable character?

PULLMAN: Good day, sir.

[PULLMAN *turns away.* JACKSON *leaves the area;* HOPKINS *is looking after him.*]

ENSEMBLE: That night, Jackson arrives at the market hall. A crowd has gathered.

AGENT: You might as well go home. The building's closed.

JACKSON: What about that so-called prior engagement?

AGENT: Postponed. Policy dictates that the hall is not to be used when repairs are necessary.

JACKSON: What needs to be repaired?

AGENT: The gas meter.

JACKSON: What's wrong with it?

AGENT: Do I look like an expert? It's broken. That's all either of us needs to know.

[HOPKINS *steps forward.*]

HOPKINS: Unlock the door.

AGENT: Mr. Hopkins, I have orders.

HOPKINS: I'll take the responsibility.

AGENT: But Mr. Pullman said—

HOPKINS: That's all right. Now, the doors—

[AGENT *opens the doors.*]

JACKSON [*to* HOPKINS]: Thank you.

[*Others follow* JACKSON *off. Lights shift.* PULLMAN *enters.*]

PULLMAN: I was under the impression I gave an order.

HOPKINS: It wasn't a very good lecture, and there wasn't anything in it about labor—

PULLMAN: That's not the issue, Pat. Did I or did I not give an order?

HOPKINS: Yes, sir.

PULLMAN: And are you or are you not in my employ?

HOPKINS: Yes, sir.

PULLMAN: If you are willing to enjoy the benefits of this company, you must show some responsibility to it, and to me.

HOPKINS: I understand, sir. But there was a large crowd. Canceling the lecture wouldn't have made them very happy.

PULLMAN: There are sufficient resources in this town to make them happy without wasting their time and money on crackpot speeches.

HOPKINS: If I'd known it would upset you—

PULLMAN [*irritated*]: I'm not upset. I am disappointed.

[*A beat. More controlled.*]

This town works because there is a system. Perhaps the reason for everything in this system is not evident to you, but I ask you to trust that there is indeed a reason for all of it. Upset the equilibrium and you invite chaos.

HOPKINS: Yes, sir.

PULLMAN: I don't mean to be severe. I suppose I should take your age into account. Your lack of experience. Perhaps you'd be more likely to understand the business perspective if you had one of your own.

[*A beat.*]

Would that interest you?

HOPKINS: I'm sorry—

PULLMAN: A business of your own.

HOPKINS: Well, of course I've thought about it, but I'm not in a position—

PULLMAN: Never mind about your position. Yes, I think it could be very useful in developing your character further. If you were to open a store in town, for instance. Learn something about caution, prudence, sound business practice—

ENSEMBLE: And with the financial assistance of his employer, Pat Hopkins establishes a business—

[*A slightly drunk* JUNIOR *enters, carrying a bottle and looking bitterly at* HOPKINS.]

JUNIOR: The Arcade Trading Company—
ENSEMBLE: Located in the Arcade, selling a variety of clothing and utensils.

[*During this, the* SUPERINTENDENT *hands* HOPKINS *more impressive clothing to change into.*]

HOPKINS: At the same time, he maintains his position of paymaster of the Pullman Company.
JUNIOR: Business flourishes, and he moves into one of the finest houses in the town.
PULLMAN: Nothing like a little success to reinforce the correct values.

[PULLMAN *turns his attention to* JUNIOR, *who now sits in a disheveled state in another area of the stage representing* JUNIOR'*s bedroom.* FLORENCE *enters and tries to run interference as* PULLMAN *approaches* JUNIOR.]

FLORENCE: He isn't feeling well.
PULLMAN: I'll just look in on him.
FLORENCE: Perhaps later might be better.
PULLMAN [*gently but determined*]: Florence—

[*She stands aside.* PULLMAN *approaches* JUNIOR. FLORENCE *stands nearby.*]

You didn't report to work today, George.
JUNIOR: I'm not feeling well.
PULLMAN: So your sister tells me. A cold?
JUNIOR: I'll be all right tomorrow.
PULLMAN: Perhaps I should send for the doctor.
JUNIOR: It's not necessary.
PULLMAN: No, I can see you're taking care of yourself.

[*He pulls out a liquor bottle* JUNIOR *has hidden.*]

What's the recommended dosage?
JUNIOR: To be used as required.
PULLMAN: *Do* you require this?
JUNIOR: No.

PULLMAN: If I thought you did, I'd have to make arrangements for you to take the cure. That's not something I should like to see get about.

JUNIOR: It would be an embarrassment for you, wouldn't it, Pop?

PULLMAN: You're my son.

JUNIOR: Really? Then who is that other fellow?

PULLMAN: What are you talking about?

JUNIOR: Did it ever occur to you maybe *I* would have liked a business in the Arcade myself?

PULLMAN: Mr. Hopkins has demonstrated a sound character and a sense of responsibility.

JUNIOR: Perhaps you should adopt him.

PULLMAN: That will be enough of that.

JUNIOR: Better yet, send him to me and I'll sell him my name. God knows it's been of little use to me.

PULLMAN: If it weren't for your name, you'd probably be—

FLORENCE [*interrupting*]: Father!

[PULLMAN *stops, looks at her, then turns back to* JUNIOR, *composure largely regained. He now speaks with a gentler tone.*]

PULLMAN: We can do better than this, can't we, son? It's only a matter of determination.

JUNIOR: Yes, sir.

[*A beat.* JUNIOR *exits abruptly.* FLORENCE *follows him off. Lights shift. Looking across the stage,* PULLMAN *sees* HOPKINS *enter, dressed rather formally, and approaches him.*]

PULLMAN: Are you ready, Pat?

HOPKINS: I'm a little nervous.

PULLMAN: Nothing to be nervous about. I propose you, Arthur seconds you, a vote, and that's all there is to it. I suggest you give your tie some attention.

HOPKINS: What? Oh yes, thank you.

[HOPKINS *fixes his tie.* PULLMAN *leads Hopkins to the Chicago Club.* HOPKINS *sits as* PULLMAN *speaks.*]

PULLMAN: Gentlemen, not many years ago a young man without a penny to his name applied for a job in my town. Today that young man is paymaster of the town and the owner of one of its leading businesses. He has achieved much and I expect will achieve more in the years to come. I take pride in nominating Patrick Hopkins for membership in the Chicago Club.

THIRD BUSINESSMAN: I second the nomination.

FIRST BUSINESSMAN: Any opposed? Congratulations, Mr. Hopkins.

[HOPKINS *shakes hands with a number of the others.*]

MALE ENSEMBLE [*singing*]: In this world
　　Prosperity comes to few
　　But it came to you
　　And me
　　And me
　　And me.
　　But there's
　　Something else that goes hand in hand.
　　You must understand.
　　You must see

　　It's a trust,
　　God's bounty is a trust.
　　It's not yours, it is His that He's lent you.
　　Give daily thought
　　Daily thought to Him who gave you what you've got.

　　It's a trust.
　　God's bounty is a trust,
　　This great and good fortune He's sent you.
　　Make a solemn vow
　　A solemn vow
　　To be the best kind of rich you know how,
　　To be the best kind of rich you know how.

SCENE 5

[*As* BUSINESSMEN *exit, a* PRIEST *enters. Several members of the* ENSEMBLE *form a congregation.*]

HOPKINS: Patrick Hopkins is a Catholic.

[*He moves to the congregation.*]

In time, the congregation of which he is a member grows to such a size that it desires to build a church.

PRIEST [*to* HOPKINS]: The proposed site is land owned by George Pullman just outside of the town.

[HOPKINS *nods and looks to* PULLMAN.]

HOPKINS: After some negotiation—
PULLMAN: Pullman gives tentative permission to build.
HOPKINS: Thank you, sir.

[*The congregation disburses.*]

PRIEST: But the deed has not been formally transferred when—

[ELY *approaches* WICKES, *handing him a card.*]

WICKES [*reading*]: Richard T. Ely, *Harper's Magazine.*
ELY: My editors have asked me to write an article about the town—how it works, what it means.
WICKES: What it means, Mr. Ely, is the future.
ENSEMBLE: And Thomas Wickes, vice president, gives him a tour of Pullman.
WICKES [*to* ELY]: The sewage from the town is collected in that great tank over there, then it's pumped to the Pullman farm for use as fertilizer. [*Removing a carrot from his pocket and offering it to* ELY] From our farm.
ELY [*taking the carrot*]: Very efficient. Which house does the Pullman family live in?
WICKES: Pardon me?
ELY: Where in the town?
WICKES: Mr. Pullman doesn't keep a house here. When it's necessary for him to be here overnight, he stays in a suite reserved for his use in the Hotel Florence. The Pullman family residence itself is on Prairie Avenue.
ELY: In Chicago proper.
WICKES: Yes.

ELY: My confusion. I assumed that if a man built a town to his specifications, he would naturally live there.

WICKES: The town was built to help elevate the characters of his employees. Mr. Pullman does not need to live here.

ELY: Point taken.

WICKES: We shall be looking forward to your article. May I escort you to the train station?

ELY: Thank you, but I'm not leaving yet.

WICKES: Oh?

ELY: I'd like to get some sense of the town from the workers' point of view.

WICKES: Oh, well, that's easy enough to arrange. [*To* CLAYTON, *who is passing by*] You there.

CLAYTON: Me, sir?

WICKES: Mr. Ely is a journalist. He wants to know what you think of living here in Pullman.

CLAYTON: It's very clean.

ELY: Yes.

CLAYTON: We're very happy.

WICKES: There, you see? [*Sending* CLAYTON *on his way*] Now, you still have time to catch the five fourteen back to Chicago.

ELY: Thank you, but I think I will stay on for a few more days.

WICKES: Ah, well, if there's any way in which I can be helpful to you.

ELY: I won't hesitate; I promise.

[ELY *shakes* WICKES's *hand and goes off on his own.* WICKES *calls the* FOREMAN *over.*]

WICKES [*to* FOREMAN]: Have someone keep an eye on him.

FOREMAN: Yes, sir.

WICKES: Discreetly.

[*Shift focus to* PRIEST *and* ELY. *During the rest of* ELY's *visit, the* FOREMAN *does indeed keep his eye on* ELY *and notes with whom he talks. In the background of the scene between* ELY *and the* PRIEST, *a* WOMAN *with a clipboard is approaching various townspeople, collecting signatures.*]

ELY: It's a very impressive church, Father.

PRIEST: The stone was hauled all the way from New England.

ELY: Very handsome.

PRIEST: It's too bad nobody uses it.

ELY: The residents of Pullman—they're not concerned with spiritual matters?

PRIEST: Oh yes, only none of the denominations here can afford to rent it. The Pullman Company is determined to make a profit on it.

ELY: A profit on the church?

PRIEST: My congregation is planning to build a church on Pullman property outside of the town. We should take possession of the deed shortly. Uh, you won't mind a little advice, Mr. Ely?

ELY: Anything you think might be helpful, Father.

PRIEST: Put away the notebook. If the men see you writing in it, they may think you're reporting to management. You're not likely to learn much that way.

[ELY *nods and puts away the notebook. The* WOMAN *with the petition approaches* ELY.]

WOMAN: Would you be interested in—oh, you're not from around here.

ELY: No.

WOMAN: I'm sorry.

[*She starts to move away.*]

ELY: Uh, excuse me. What is that?

WOMAN [*cautiously*]: A petition.

ELY: May I see it?

WOMAN: It's a matter of local interest.

ELY: I'd like to see it if I may.

[*The* WOMAN *looks to the* PRIEST, *who indicates that it's OK. She hands* ELY *the petition.* ELY *reads it.*]

Do many of the people here feel like this?

WOMAN: Some do; some don't.

ELY: I see.

WOMAN: We're not saying anything against the town, or Mr. Pullman—

ELY: No, of course not.

WOMAN: It's a fine place to live. The schools, the parks . . . But some of us think it might be better if—

[*She nods toward the petition.*]

ELY: Yes, I understand.

[*The* WOMAN *holds out her hand for the petition.* ELY *returns it to her. He nods and moves away. She looks after him, then moves on.*]

ENSEMBLE: The town eagerly awaits Mr. Ely's article in *Harper's Magazine.*

[ELY *sits and begins to write. He looks up and sees that all eyes are indeed upon him, then turns away and continues writing. He finishes with a flourish and turns around holding his manuscript. As he does so, copies of the magazine are distributed among the company, including* PULLMAN *and* WICKES. ELY *turns and begins to recite from his article.*]

ELY: A social experiment on a vast scale! What is seen in a walk or a drive through the streets is so pleasing to the eye that a woman's first exclamation is certain to be—

WOMAN: "Perfectly lovely!"

ELY: And indeed what might have been taken for a wealthy suburban town is given up to busy workers. In a hundred ways one sees in Pullman today evidences of its founder's foresight.

WICKES [*to* PULLMAN]: Very well expressed.

ELY: But certain unpleasant features of social life are soon noticed by the careful observer.

PULLMAN: What?

ELY: Though built near Chicago, the town has been designed by its namesake to be independent of that city. Consequently, it is governed not by the democratically determined will of the residents but by George M. Pullman himself. The books in the library are books Pullman chooses, the lessons taught in the schools are those he endorses, the businesses are those he approves. In designing his model town, Mr. Pullman has diminished the residents from citizens to serfs. Mr. Pullman hopes his community will serve as an example for other companies to follow. A patriotic American must reply, God forbid. We must not embrace the gilded cage as a substitute for personal liberty.

PULLMAN [*putting aside the magazine quietly*]: He doesn't understand.

[PULLMAN *turns to the* FOREMAN. FOREMAN *points to the* PRIEST. PULLMAN *nods.* PULLMAN *and the* FOREMAN *exit. The* PRIEST *looks down. He crosses the stage, encountering* HOPKINS, *who nods a greeting. The* PRIEST *stops him with a look.*]

PRIEST: I am sorry to say that I am no longer to have the privilege of serving you as your priest. I shall miss your friendship.

HOPKINS: Why?

PRIEST: Mr. Pullman informed the archdiocese it had a choice to make—me or the deed for the church. I gather he took exception to my conversation with Mr. Ely.

[HOPKINS *and the* PRIEST *shake hands. The* PRIEST *exits.* HOPKINS *looks sharply in the direction of* PULLMAN, *who doesn't notice* HOPKINS's *look. The* WOMAN *with the petition appears some distance away.* HOPKINS *goes across the stage, stops her. Initially she is nervous.* HOPKINS *signs the petition. He goes to another area of the stage. The* FOREMAN *has seen this. The* WOMAN *exits, followed by the* FOREMAN. HOPKINS *is notified by the* SECRETARY *that* PULLMAN *wants to see him. With an air of determination,* HOPKINS *goes to* PULLMAN *in his office.*]

PULLMAN: Somebody has been forging your name.

HOPKINS: Forging?

PULLMAN [*showing him the petition*]: It's a very good forgery. If I didn't know you better, I'd say that this was your signature.

HOPKINS: How did you get this?

PULLMAN: It's in my interests to know who is doing what here.

HOPKINS: It's not a conspiracy; it's a petition.

PULLMAN: It's a call for the destruction of this town.

HOPKINS: It's a call to annex the town into the city of Chicago. To incorporate it.

PULLMAN: Which would lead to its destruction. The point of founding this place was to be removed from Chicago and its corruption. Why should we embrace what I have taken pains to shield us from? Now, we'll run an article in the town paper to the effect that your name has been forged on this thing. I have the editor waiting in the next room.

[*He rises to get the editor.*]

HOPKINS: Don't.

PULLMAN: The sooner we can disassociate you from these, these Democrats, the better.

HOPKINS: I don't choose to be disassociated. I am a Democrat.

PULLMAN: You never told me.

HOPKINS: With all due respect, sir, it was none of your business.

PULLMAN: This company is my business, and I won't have you working against its interests.

HOPKINS: I don't think that I am.

PULLMAN: I don't care what you think.

HOPKINS [*quietly*]: I know. That's one of the reasons I signed the petition.

[*A beat.*]

PULLMAN [*awkwardly*]: Perhaps I did not make myself clear.

HOPKINS: In what way?

PULLMAN: Pat, everybody has a public side and a private side.

HOPKINS: All right.

PULLMAN: Now, your private side has nothing to do with me. Think what you want to think, believe what you want to . . . Vote Democrat if you feel you must. But you're a member of management; you represent the company. You're a public figure. You're a public figure because I chose to *make* you one. By hiring you, promoting you.

HOPKINS [*quietly*]: Have you been unhappy with my work?

PULLMAN: Of course not.

HOPKINS: I've been a competent paymaster?

PULLMAN: There's more to holding down a position than just doing the work.

HOPKINS: I see, it's not enough for me to hold my position; I must also hold yours.

PULLMAN: To not publicly express opinions which conflict with company policy.

HOPKINS: Sir, I am very mindful of all that you have done for me. I'm very grateful.

PULLMAN [*interrupting*]: Which is why you signed that petition.

HOPKINS: The two are not connected.

PULLMAN: Don't you have any idea of the plans I have for you?

[HOPKINS *looks at* PULLMAN, *not understanding what he's getting at.* PULLMAN *proceeds rather stiffly.*]

I'm in my sixties. In good health, thank God, but someday somebody else will have to run this company. My son has demonstrated no particular aptitude, so it's logical I should look for somebody who does. This is what you put at risk.

HOPKINS [*simply*]: And what do you require of me? A promise I'd never do anything you wouldn't?

PULLMAN: Assurances that the company would hold to the principles on which it was founded.

HOPKINS: And if I don't subscribe to those principles?

PULLMAN [*flaring*]: You damn well should. They're what put you where you are. Who were you? What were you? A young man with little education, no money, and no prospects. You started here in the lumberyard, and now look at you. This system has worked for you. It is a gesture of the purest perversity to try to dismantle it.

HOPKINS: I don't see it that way.

PULLMAN [*making a plea*]: Haven't you got the sense to bend?

HOPKINS: Mr. Pullman, you are a man of principle. It is one of the reasons why people respect you. Why *I* respect you. What you have built you have built without compromising your principles.

PULLMAN: Yes, well?

HOPKINS: How much respect would you have for me if I were to compromise mine?

[*A beat.*]

PULLMAN: Please clean out your desk before the end of the day.

[HOPKINS *exits* PULLMAN's *office.* OGGEL *enters. He and* HOPKINS *both appeal to audience during the following.*]

OGGEL: My text today is from Isaiah: "Woe unto them that join house to house, that lay field to field until there be no place; that they may be placed alone in the midst of the earth."

HOPKINS: Proposition!

OGGEL: I also refer you to the old children's verse: "Come into my parlor, said the spider to the fly."

HOPKINS: That the town of Pullman be conjoined with and part of the city of Chicago.

OGGEL: The law of self-preservation has always led mankind to avoid everything that has a propensity to devour. We rightly fear that which would absorb us, rob us of our character, our life, our soul.

HOPKINS: The annexation question is put onto the ballot.

OGGEL: And so I say to you beware. The only annexation one ought to think of is to the church and Sunday school. Let us pray.

HOPKINS: Despite Reverend Oggel's stirring oration—

OGGEL [*disappointed; to* PULLMAN]: The referendum passes.

HOPKINS: Pullman is no longer a separate town but part of the city of Chicago. One of many neighborhoods.

[HOPKINS, OGGEL, *and* PULLMAN *exit. Lights shift, and* DEBS *is revealed speaking to a group of* ENSEMBLE *members.*]

DEBS: What can we do for labor?

ENSEMBLE: —Introducing Eugene Debs.

—A man with a new idea.

DEBS: "What can we do for labor?" Where have we heard that question before? Where haven't we heard that question? I will lay you odds that wherever a master wielded his whip above the bowed backs of slaves, some tenderhearted, sympathetic, paternalistic soul asked, "What can we do for the slaves?" Well, the time is coming when "What can we do for labor?" will be replaced by another and more manly question: "What can labor do for itself?"

ENSEMBLE: —Previously, there had been some labor groups organized along craft lines.

—Engineers had belonged to an engineer's union.

—Conductors to a conductor's union.

—And so on.

DEBS: Such specialization has undercut our ability to fight for common interests.

ENSEMBLE: Debs and his colleagues hammer out the constitution for a—

ENSEMBLE [*in unison*]: New organization!

DEBS: Any man or woman who works in any capacity whatsoever in the rail industry is welcome to join—

ENSEMBLE [*in unison*]: The American Railway Union!

[*Lights fade on* DEBS *and his followers.*]

SCENE 6

ENSEMBLE: —For several years, Chicago has been in competition with
several eastern cities—
—who shall remain nameless—
—for the right to host an international trade and cultural exposition.
—Finally, the decision is announced.

[*The* ENSEMBLE *cheers.*]

PULLMAN: Now we will show the world what we can do.

ENSEMBLE: —And so a huge white city rises on the banks of Lake
Michigan.
—It is called the Columbian Exposition.

[*A sheet is pulled as if to unveil a statue. Underneath is a male* SOLOIST *dressed as Columbus. He sings.*]

SOLOIST: Four hundred years ago
More or less,
Christopher Columbus
Stood on the brink of a new world.
Four hundred years have passed
And just like him,
Here we stand
On the brink of a new world.

[*A* FEMALE SOLOIST, *also extravagantly attired, enters and joins him.*]

SOLOISTS: But you don't have to set to sea to see it,
Nor sail away to foreign shore
Just hurry to the city of Chicago
To see what lies in store!

ENSEMBLE: Come and see tomorrow at the fair!
Come and see the
Bright and gleaming future that is shimmering there!
A Mr. Otis says

Why climb up stairs
When you can use his new
Invention?
Cordially he
Welcomes you to come and ride
The elevator.
Won't you come and step inside?
It will sweep you off the ground
And lift you to the sky.

Come and see tomorrow at the fair.
Come and see the
Splendid new inventions to eliminate care!
In exhibition they
Have on display
A giant whirligig
They call a
Dynamo. It
Generates electric power,
Rumbling as its
Sparks go flying in a shower.
We will all be
Plugged into its magic by and by.

[PULLMAN *appears on a platform and, over underscoring, speaks to the* ENSEMBLE *below.*]

PULLMAN: I am pleased so many of you have toured our exhibit here at the exposition. If you are interested in further aspects of the Pullman system, I urge you to visit the Pullman community. Complimentary trains are standing by for your convenience.

[PULLMAN *exits as an* ORATOR *appears on another platform.*]

ORATOR [*singing*]: The ceaseless march of civilization
Westward, ever westward,
Has founded here in America's heartland,
The greatest city of modern times.
Chicago, the peerless, has been selected
For this great celebration

Which gives new fire to human progress
And sheds its light upon ages to come!
ENSEMBLE: So much to see.
So many things to sample.
There isn't time enough to do it all!

Come and see tomorrow at the fair!
Come and see the
Promise and the plenty that we all soon will share!
Come see
Tomorrow being born!

[*The number concluded, members of the* ENSEMBLE *crowd around* HARRISON.]

ENSEMBLE: Carter Harrison, the mayor of Chicago, makes a speech at the Columbian Exposition.
HARRISON: And so, I say to you that genius is but another word for audacity. This exposition has been a celebration of Chicago's audacity. Chicago has chosen a star, has looked upward to it, and knows nothing she cannot accomplish.

[*The* ENSEMBLE *applauds.*]

ENSEMBLE: —With the sound of applause still in his ears, the mayor goes home for lunch.
—A madman shoots him dead.

[HARRISON *tumbles forward and disappears into the* ENSEMBLE.]

—A special election is held to finish the mayor's term. And the winner is—

[HOPKINS *emerges from the* ENSEMBLE.]

HOPKINS: At the age of thirty-five, J. Patrick Hopkins is the mayor of the city of Chicago.
PULLMAN: Including the town of . . . the neighborhood of Pullman.

[*A moment as* HOPKINS *and* PULLMAN *look at each other. Then* HOPKINS's *supporters raise him onto their shoulders and carry him off, leaving* PULLMAN *alone on a quiet stage. A beat.* PULLMAN *looks after him for a second, then turns away. He holds his position as the lights fade.*]

ACT 2

SCENE 1

ENSEMBLE: —The exposition closes.

   —The visitors leave and take their money with them.

   —The streamers and tents are pulled down.

   —Tens of thousands roam the city, looking for work that isn't there.

   —The depression of 1893 has arrived in Chicago.

HOPKINS: Mayor Hopkins authorizes the use of City Hall and other public buildings as shelters for the indigent at night.

ENSEMBLE: Each morning, he arrives to find the hallways crowded with those who have spent the previous evening sleeping on the cold floors.

HOPKINS: And he thinks of his arrival in Chicago some years before, when he had no more in his pocket than do these men.

[*A street in the town of Pullman. The* SUPERINTENDENT *addresses workers.*]

SUPERINTENDENT: If I may have your attention. Due to the loss in revenue, the Pullman Company regretfully deems it necessary to cut wages by twenty-five percent, effective immediately.

JENNIE: Sir?

SUPERINTENDENT: You are?

JENNIE: Jennie Curtis. I have a question.

SUPERINTENDENT: Yes, Miss Curtis?

JENNIE: What about the rents?

SUPERINTENDENT: I don't catch your meaning.

JENNIE: The wages are being cut. Will the rents also be cut?

SUPERINTENDENT: My announcement is exclusively regarding wages.

[SUPERINTENDENT *exits.*]

ENSEMBLE: Payday.

[*A line to a desk behind which sits a* PAYMASTER. STEPHENS *and* CLAYTON *and others are in line.* PAYMASTER *opens for business.* STEPHENS *approaches.*]

PAYMASTER: Name?

STEPHENS: Stephens.

PAYMASTER: Department?

STEPHENS: Repair.

[PAYMASTER *thumbs through a box of envelopes, pulls out one, hands it to* STEPHENS. STEPHENS *steps aside as* CLAYTON *approaches the desk.*]

PAYMASTER: Name?
CLAYTON: Clayton.
PAYMASTER: Department?
CLAYTON: Carpentry.

[*During the previous lines,* STEPHENS *has opened his envelope, looked at his paycheck. He returns to the window.*]

STEPHENS: You've made a mistake.
PAYMASTER: I beg your pardon?
STEPHENS: This check is made out for seven cents.
PAYMASTER: Yes.
STEPHENS: I work for two weeks and you tell me all I've earned is seven cents?

[PAYMASTER *flips through a book.*]

PAYMASTER: You earned $9.07. You owe nine dollars in rent for your home. Nine-oh-seven minus nine.
STEPHENS: Seven cents.
PAYMASTER: Seven cents.

[STEPHENS *grabs the* PAYMASTER *by the front of his shirt.*]

STEPHENS: Give me the rest of it.
CLAYTON: Stephens—
STEPHENS: The rest of it.

[SUPERINTENDENT *enters.*]

SUPERINTENDENT: Give it to him.

[STEPHENS *relaxes his hold.* PAYMASTER *counts out some money, gives it to* STEPHENS. SUPERINTENDENT *turns to* STEPHENS.]

I wish you luck finding another job, Mr. Stephens.

[STEPHENS *looks at him darkly, then exits.*]

If anyone else would like to terminate his employment with the Pullman Company, now is the time to say so.

[*Silence.* SUPERINTENDENT *turns to* PAYMASTER.]

Continue, please.

PAYMASTER: Name?

[SUPERINTENDENT *approaches* PULLMAN *and* WICKES *in* PULLMAN's *office.*]

PULLMAN: A grievance committee?

WICKES: Shall I send them away?

PULLMAN: No, I'll see them.

WICKES: I don't think this is a good idea.

PULLMAN: Are we to be afraid of our own men? [*To* SUPERINTENDENT] Show them in, please.

[*The committee—including* HEATHCOTE, CLAYTON, *and* JENNIE—*approaches* PULLMAN. *The* SUPERINTENDENT *stands to the side.*]

HEATHCOTE: Mr. Pullman, I'd like to thank you for this opportunity to—

PULLMAN: Mr. Heathcote, is it?

HEATHCOTE: Yes, sir.

PULLMAN [*to* SUPERINTENDENT]: What department?

SUPERINTENDENT: Frame construction.

HEATHCOTE: Mr. Pullman, I've worked and lived in this town for five years. Most of them happy ones.

PULLMAN: I'm very glad to hear that.

HEATHCOTE: But the wage cuts of the past several months . . . There is no way for me and my family to keep head above water. I am here in the hope that, as reasonable men, we might be able to work something out.

PULLMAN: You're asking me for yourself.

HEATHCOTE: For myself and for the others.

PULLMAN: What others?

HEATHCOTE: Who work for you, sir. We're their representatives.

PULLMAN: Mr. Heathcote, if you want to come to me, man to man, and say, "Mr. Pullman, my wages are too low," fine, we can talk about that. I accept you as representing your own interests. But I cannot accept you as a representative of any other person or persons in the employ of this company.

HEATHCOTE: I have been elected—

PULLMAN: You have not been elected by me.

HEATHCOTE: I am not here to represent your interests.

PULLMAN: If what you have to tell me isn't in my interest, why should I talk to you?

HEATHCOTE: Because it is in your interest to keep this plant open.

PULLMAN: Mr. Heathcote, let me show you something. [*To* WICKES] Hand me that ledger, will you?

[WICKES *does.* PULLMAN *opens it.*]

This is what it costs this company to build a railway car. This is at the current level of wages. [*Pointing to another page*] And this figure represents the per-car price under the most recent car order this company secured from the owners of the Lake Shore Limited. This is how much the Lake Shore Limited is paying this company for one car. You will observe which figure is the greater. [*Closing the ledger*] Every car this company builds represents a loss. A loss to me, a loss to the stockholders. Nevertheless, I continue to secure contracts. Why? To keep the factory gates open. To keep you gainfully employed, to keep this town alive. Management is making sacrifices. I do not think it is unreasonable to ask you and your friends to make some sacrifices, too. If we keep faith with each other, if we ride out this depression, we will see prosperity again and I assure you wages will return to their previous level.

JENNIE: But what do we live on in the meantime?

PULLMAN [*to* SUPERINTENDENT]: Who?

SUPERINTENDENT: Jennie Curtis. A stitcher in the furnishings department.

JENNIE: I am president of Girls' Union Number 269.

PULLMAN [*showing a small smile*]: Well, President Curtis, if you feel the terms this company offers are unacceptable, you have the perfect freedom to secure work elsewhere.

JENNIE: Where?

PULLMAN: I'm afraid I cannot advise you on that. I am sorry for your troubles, but their solution lies not in my hands but in the economy.

[*A beat. The committee exits.*]

WICKES: You handled them well, sir.

PULLMAN: Handled? All I did was tell them the truth. You should have greater faith in the power of reason.

[PULLMAN *exits.* WICKES *turns to* SUPERINTENDENT *and gives him a look.* SUPERINTENDENT *nods.*]

ENSEMBLE: The next morning, members of the grievance committee are informed—

FOREMAN: There is no longer sufficient work to warrant your continued employment.

[*The workers behind the committee shout in protest.*]

PULLMAN [*to* WICKES]: You what?

WICKES: I had them dismissed, of course.

PULLMAN: That was not my intention.

WICKES: Would you like me to rehire them?

[*A beat.*]

PULLMAN: No, we can't do that. It would appear that we did so under compulsion.

HEATHCOTE: Three thousand workers put down their tools and walk off the job.

ENSEMBLE: —The machinery lumbers to a halt.

—Inside the plant, all is still.

SCENE 2

[REPORTERS *enter, looking to* WICKES *and* HEATHCOTE *for the story.*]

WICKES [*to* REPORTERS]: It will not inconvenience the company to have the shops idle at this time.

HEATHCOTE [*to* REPORTERS]: We have been working for less wages than will maintain our families. On that one proposition we refuse to work any longer.

WICKES: To tell the truth, for some months we have been operating primarily to give the men employment.

OGGEL [*climbing into his pulpit*]: George M. Pullman, his services to his age, his country, and humanity.

FIRST REPORTER: Reverend Oggel's Sunday sermon.

OGGEL: The Savior has said that no man buildeth a house before he has considered the cost. Aesop says that half a loaf is better than none. One should not throw away dirty water until he has secured some clean.

FIRST REPORTER: Who said that?

SECOND REPORTER: John the Baptist.

STEPHENS: Pullman paid him to give that sermon!

SECOND REPORTER: Paid?

STEPHENS: Reverend Oggel. Paid him three hundred dollars!

HEATHCOTE [*mocking shock*]: We are loathe to believe such ugly charges, but the strike committee will investigate the matter.

[*The* REPORTERS *and* HEATHCOTE *begin to advance on* OGGEL.]

OGGEL [*getting down from his pulpit*]: I regret that my usefulness among the workmen of Pullman is a thing of the past.

[*He exits.*]

THIRD REPORTER: A dance is held for the benefit of the strikers.

[*The* FEMALE SOLOIST *who sang "Leave a Light" in the first act now, accompanied by two members of the* ENSEMBLE, *sings a popular song of the period as the dance begins.*]

FEMALE SOLOIST: On Sunday night, 'tis my delight
    And pleasure don't you see,
    Meeting all the girls and all the boys
    That work downtown with me.
    There's an organ in the parlor
    To give the house a tone,
    And you're welcome ev'ry evening
    At Maggie Murphy's home.

[JENNIE CURTIS *approaches* HOPKINS *with a white ribbon in her hands.*]

JENNIE: Mr. Mayor—

HOPKINS: Good evening, Miss Curtis.

JENNIE: If you would allow me the honor—

HOPKINS: The ribbon?

JENNIE: A symbol of sympathy.

HOPKINS: On condition you allow me the honor of this dance.

[JENNIE *attaches the white ribbon to his sleeve. They dance as the* FEMALE SOLOIST *reprises a bit of her song. At the conclusion of the dance,* HEATHCOTE *rises to speak.*]

HEATHCOTE: If I may have your attention . . . I am happy to announce that our friend, Mayor Hopkins, has offered a room on the second floor of his store for the use of the strike committee. In addition, he is contributing twenty-five thousand pounds of flour and another twenty-five thousand pounds of meat to the cause.

[*Strikers applaud.*]

We have another special guest tonight. You've all heard of the recent strike against the Great Northern Railroad out west and of its happy outcome. I'm delighted to introduce to you the architect of its success, Eugene Debs.

DEBS [*rising to applause*]: Today one of the officers of the Pullman Company said that you could not hold out against the company more than ten days longer. If it is a fact that after working for George M. Pullman for years it takes but ten days to reduce you to rags and starvation, then Pullman must stand revealed to the world as a self-confessed robber. But Mr. Pullman and his officers are making the mistake of their lives if they think they are going to reduce you to subjugation in so short a time. This strike is going to be won. If it takes months it will be won. And it will be won because you are in the right.

[*Applause.* HEATHCOTE *takes* DEBS *aside.* HOPKINS *stands next to* DEBS, *listening during the following scene.*]

HEATHCOTE: Mr. Debs, I'd like to thank you for coming here tonight.

DEBS: My pleasure.

HEATHCOTE: May I assume then you will call for the membership of the union at large to support our strike?

DEBS: We will issue a statement of support, of course.

HEATHCOTE: I mean something stronger than that. The union convention is being held in Chicago next week. Seems to me that would be the perfect time to announce a general action against Pullman.

DEBS: To take what form?

HEATHCOTE: The refusal of all union members to work any train that carries a Pullman car.

DEBS: A sympathy strike.

HEATHCOTE: A boycott.

DEBS: Which would become a strike. That would put us in a contest against every railroad line in this country.

HEATHCOTE: You won out west.

DEBS: That was against but one railroad line. You're asking us to take on all of them. We have to choose our fights very carefully. I don't think this is one we can afford to get into.

HEATHCOTE: Perhaps the rest of the membership will feel differently.

DEBS: You're thinking of addressing the convention on this matter.

HEATHCOTE: I am the chairman of a local; I have that right.

DEBS: Mr. Heathcote, our cause has a number of friends in high places. Perhaps they can prevail upon Mr. Pullman to agree to arbitration.

HEATHCOTE: I doubt it.

DEBS: We must at least give him the opportunity to turn us down or else we risk losing public support. Please give me your word you will do nothing until this avenue has been exhausted.

HEATHCOTE: I think it's a waste of time.

HOPKINS: If there's a chance of solving this thing without open confrontation, we must take it.

DEBS: Do I have your word?

[HEATHCOTE *hesitates, then nods.* DEBS *shakes* HEATHCOTE's *hand.* DEBS *turns to* HOPKINS. HOPKINS *nods and heads toward the Chicago Club as* JENNIE CURTIS *ties a white ribbon to* DEBS's *sleeve.*]

HOPKINS: A few days later, Mayor Hopkins enters the Chicago Club. [*To* PULLMAN] Mr. Pullman.

PULLMAN: Mr. Mayor.

HOPKINS: This is an extremely painful situation. You must know the affection most of the workers hold for you. They are well aware of all you have done for them in the past.

PULLMAN: Indeed.

HOPKINS: No good can come of a prolonged strike—either for them or for you. There is still a chance of ending this business. If you would agree to arbitration before a panel of neutral observers—

PULLMAN: Do you know I was just thinking—

HOPKINS: Sir?

PULLMAN: I was the one who nominated you for membership in this club.

[PULLMAN *gets up.*]

Good day.

[*He turns away from* HOPKINS.]

SCENE 3

[*A banner proclaiming* American Railway Union Convention—1894 *is rigged over the stage.* DEBS *is attending business on the platform as* HEATHCOTE *and* JENNIE *approach him.*]

HEATHCOTE: Mr. Debs—

DEBS: You still want a boycott.

HEATHCOTE: We've done what you asked.

DEBS: I know.

HEATHCOTE: We've tried to approach Pullman a dozen different ways. He refuses to discuss even the idea of arbitration. He is a closed door. We have done all we can do by ourselves. We have no alternative but to turn to the union for support.

DEBS: Mr. Heathcote, if we take on this fight, in six months there will *be* no American Railway Union.

HEATHCOTE: You know our situation in Pullman. You know this is our only hope.

[*A beat.*]

DEBS: I can't prevent you from bringing the issue to the floor.

HEATHCOTE: Would you if you could?

[*A beat.*]

DEBS: The whole point of a union is that members determine their *own* course of action. It is the central principle on which it was founded.

HEATHCOTE: So if the membership adopts our cause, you will support it?

[*A beat.* DEBS *nods. The delegates to the convention stand in dim light downstage, facing the audience and looking up.* HEATHCOTE *turns to* JENNIE CURTIS, *gently indicates the podium. The idea of speaking to such a crowd obviously gives her pause. She hesitates, but* HEATHCOTE *encourages her. She takes the podium. Initially, she is shy, tentative. But, as she gets into the body of the speech, the passion of her cause bolsters her.*]

JENNIE: I feel a little lost here. Making a speech. I'm not a speaker. I'm a stitcher. My name is Jennie Curtis. I worked in the repair-shop sewing room. And the other girls, they made me, uh, they elected me president of the girls' union. It's a queer feeling. Someone—you know, another girl who you work with—looks at you and calls you president. But—

[*A beat.*]

I was on the committee that went to talk to Mr. Pullman. We went to him for—not for justice. But for just a chance to live. They'd cut our paychecks to the point where—

[*A beat.*]

For instance, carpets. All right: a year ago, we got a dollar a yard for carpets. This year, that went down to twenty cents. A three-window drapery used to be a dollar fifty. This year, eighty cents. I could give you more numbers but the point is—the point is the wages have all been cut way down.

[*A beat.*]

In fairness, I have to say that we used to be allowed to make two dollars and twenty-five cents a day, which was very good wages for a girl. But which we did earn. But that was a year ago. At the time we went out on strike, I was earning on average eighty cents a day.

[*A beat.*]

As you may know, the town of Pullman is built alongside Lake Calumet. Since the strike began, some of us . . . We don't have the money to buy groceries, so we've been fishing in the lake. Just to be able to put something on the table. Well, we've just been told that we will no longer be *permitted* to fish from Pullman property. However, they did tell us that we're free to pick through the hotel's garbage for whatever food a customer might not have been able to finish.

[*A beat.*]

So we come to you. We ask you to help. We ask you to join us. By ourselves, we have so little hope of success. That's really all I have to say. Thank you.

DELEGATE: Mr. Chairman!

DEBS: The chair recognizes Mr. Cosgrove.

DELEGATE: I move that it be the voice of this convention that the American Railway Union declare a boycott on the Pullman Palace Cars.

DEBS: Is there a second?

SECOND DELEGATE [*in the audience*]: So seconded!

DEBS: All in favor?

ENSEMBLE: Aye!

DEBS: Opposed?

[*No answer.* DEBS *looks at* HEATHCOTE.]

The motion is carried.

[*The stage fills as railway union members sing "Step by Step."* DEBS *joins* HEATHCOTE, JENNIE, *and the others in the singing.* DEBS *doesn't look particularly happy, but his course of action is determined.*]

ENSEMBLE: Step by step the longest march
Can be won, can be won.
Many stones can form an arch,
Singly none, singly none.
And by union, what we will
Can be accomplished still.
Drops of water turn a mill,
Singly none, singly none.

[*At the number's end, the union members, in high spirits, exit together, leaving* DEBS *alone—upset at the way things have gone, but determined to meet his responsibilities. Across the stage,* PULLMAN *appears.* DEBS, *still on the platform, looks down at* PULLMAN *for a second, then exits.* PULLMAN *turns into the beginning of the next scene.*]

SCENE 4

[PULLMAN *is at a table with a number of other well-dressed businessmen, including the* CHAIRMAN *and* HARAHAN.]

PULLMAN: The issue is a simple one: who is to run our businesses—we who have founded and developed them or the people we employ? I submit that this is the essence of the contest in which we find ourselves.

CHAIRMAN: Thank you, Mr. Pullman. [*To audience*] A meeting of the officers of the country's major railroads.

HARAHAN: Mr. Chairman?

CHAIRMAN: Mr. Harahan.

HARAHAN: I'd like to follow up on some of the issues Mr. Pullman has raised.

CHAIRMAN: Certainly.

HARAHAN: Gentlemen, listening to Mr. Pullman, I think it's obvious we are in the presence of a visionary. He had a vision. Of course, lots of us have visions. But what makes our friend here different . . . He acted on his. Gave it substance and form. He decides to build a town for his purposes and to his specifications. And he does it. If he decides to name it for himself, well, who has better right? But there's more. Mr. Pullman decides that it's not enough to design a town. He's going to roll up his sleeves, take a crack at designing some people, too. What's a model town without model citizens? So he does his homework. He goes to an authoritative text, makes a few notes. Takes a handful of clay, shapes it just so, makes some figures in his own image.

PULLMAN: What?

HARAHAN [*continuing*]: Which just may be where he went wrong. Now he's got himself a town full of people who are just as pigheaded as he is.

PULLMAN: Sir!

HARAHAN: I think they deserve each other.

CHAIRMAN: Mr. Harahan, the point of this meeting is to come up with a course of action. Have you one to suggest?

HARAHAN: I do indeed: let's do nothing. I think it's always the best policy to keep out of family quarrels.

CHAIRMAN: May I suggest that we don't have that luxury. Mr. Debs and his friends have decided not to handle any train with a Pullman car on it.

FIRST RAILROAD OFFICIAL: Which leaves us with two choices. We either keep the cars on the trains, in which case almost nothing moves. Or we cut them out, in which case we've just given Mr. Debs the best news of his life.

SECOND RAILROAD OFFICIAL: That's a hell of a choice.

THIRD RAILROAD OFFICIAL: There's one other choice.

SECOND RAILROAD OFFICIAL: Yes?

THIRD RAILROAD OFFICIAL: The attorney general of the United States has been good enough to remind me that it is a federal offense to interfere with the delivery of the United States mail.

CHAIRMAN: I don't see how that's relevant to the topic at hand. Debs's boycott isn't against the post office; it's against Pullman cars.

THIRD RAILROAD OFFICIAL: Yes, but what do you suppose would happen if every train carrying a mail car also happened to carry a Pullman? How much mail do you think would get through? Who would be liable under the law?

[*A beat. The idea sinks in. They smile.*]

CHAIRMAN: A very profitable meeting, I think.

[*The officials prepare to exit.*]

PULLMAN: Mr. Chairman—

CHAIRMAN: Yes?

PULLMAN: There are other avenues I thought might be worth—

CHAIRMAN: I'm sure if you put them down on paper—

PULLMAN: If I may have just a moment—

THIRD RAILROAD OFFICIAL [*with a smile*]: You just aren't getting the drift, are you, George? We aren't interested.

CHAIRMAN: Perhaps we might—

THIRD RAILROAD OFFICIAL [*to* CHAIRMAN]: No, I think he should understand this. [*To* PULLMAN] You were invited to this meeting only as a courtesy. We don't want to hear your ideas. We don't want your opinions. They are irrelevant. You are irrelevant.

PULLMAN: This strike is against my company.

THIRD RAILROAD OFFICIAL: That is merely a technicality. You have blundered into this situation. Now, it so happens that we may be able to use your blunder to our advantage. The fact that we do so, though, has nothing to do with any personal regard or respect for you. We do not work for you, nor are any of us so unlucky as to live in your town. We do not have to listen to your philosophy. So, in the future, why don't you spare yourself and us the bother of your presence?

[*A beat.* PULLMAN *turns away.*]

SCENE 5

[FLORENCE *meets* PULLMAN *as he leaves the meeting. She escorts him across the stage as a* SOLOIST *from the* ENSEMBLE *sings, "The Pullman Strike."*]

SOLOIST: Near the city of Chicago
 Where the bosses hold full sway
 The workingmen of Pullman
 Are battling for fair play.
 But Pullman would not listen
 To the workingmen's appeal
 And scorned their mute advances,
 No sympathy did feel.

[*Arriving at* PULLMAN'*s house,* PULLMAN *is helped into a dressing gown by the* SERVANT.]

SERVANT: Would you like me to prepare your bed?

PULLMAN: Not yet, thank you. Does anybody know where George Junior is?

FLORENCE: I don't think he's home yet.

PULLMAN [*snapping*]: I did not ask where he isn't; I asked where he is.

[FLORENCE *is stung by this.* PULLMAN *bites back on his immediate flash of regret and turns to the* SERVANT.]

 Do *you* know?

SERVANT: No, sir.
PULLMAN: Thank you.

[*The* SERVANT *exits.*]

FLORENCE [*an offer*]: Father?
PULLMAN [*firmly*]: Good night, Florence.

[*A beat.*]

FLORENCE: Good night.

[FLORENCE *exits. A beat.* JUNIOR *enters the house, a little drunk, sees his father.*]

PULLMAN: Good evening.
JUNIOR: Good evening, sir.

[*He begins to turn away.*]

PULLMAN: Join me?
JUNIOR: Sir?
PULLMAN: I was wondering if you'd care to join me.
JUNIOR: You want my company?
PULLMAN: Please.

[JUNIOR *hesitates, then he approaches.*]

JUNIOR: A hard day?
PULLMAN: I've seen easier.
JUNIOR: You gave them your best advice.
PULLMAN: I tried.
JUNIOR: They didn't agree?
PULLMAN: I'm afraid they don't see things—
JUNIOR: As clearly as you do?
PULLMAN [*nodding*]: The larger principles.
JUNIOR: You tried to explain—
PULLMAN: Yes.
JUNIOR: But prejudices, preconceptions—
PULLMAN: Well—
JUNIOR: People can be so damn stubborn.

[JUNIOR *goes to a sideboard and pours himself a large drink. He looks straight at his father.*]

You've got my sympathy, Pop.

[PULLMAN *doesn't respond, just watches him as* JUNIOR *raises the glass to his lips. He stops.*]

I'm sorry. Where are my manners?

[JUNIOR *pours a drink and hands it to his father.* JUNIOR *picks up his drink again, mimes a toast, then raises the glass to his lips.* PULLMAN, *too, raises the glass to his lips. The crash of glass from offstage. The* SERVANT *and* FLORENCE *enter.* PULLMAN *looks at them expectantly.*]

SERVANT: The parlor window. Somebody threw a rock.

FLORENCE: He seems to have run away.

PULLMAN: Pullman orders a heavy guard to surround his house for the duration of the strike.

[*He turns his back on the next scene.*]

SCENE 6

DEBS: A man who will destroy property or violate the law is not a friend but an enemy to the cause of labor!

[DEBS *is handed an envelope. He opens it and begins to read. As he reads to himself, the* JUDGE *stands up.*]

JUDGE: From the United States Circuit Court to Eugene Victor Debs and the American Railway Union: You are hereby restrained, commanded, and enjoined absolutely to refrain from in any way interfering with, hindering, obstructing, or stopping any mail trains or any other trains engaged in interstate commerce.

DEBS: President Grover Cleveland orders federal troops to Chicago to enforce the injunction.

HEATHCOTE: The arrival of federal troops triggers violence.

DEBS: Riots erupt in railroad yards around the city.

JENNIE: Boxcars are overturned and looted.

DEBS: People die.

HOPKINS: One evening, Mayor Hopkins sees a red glow on the horizon. A fire. The Columbian Exposition. Buildings that housed exhibits of an America to come burn to the ground. The wind scatters the ashes over the city.

DEBS: We've lost.

[HOPKINS *turns to look at* DEBS. *A* FEDERAL MARSHAL *approaches* DEBS.]

FEDERAL MARSHAL: Are you Eugene Victor Debs?

DEBS: I am.

FEDERAL MARSHAL: I have a warrant for your arrest.

HOPKINS: The strike is over.

PULLMAN [*turning around*]: The Pullman Company reopens its doors.

SCENE 7

[HEATHCOTE *and* JENNIE *are discovered standing together holding a letter.*]

HEATHCOTE: To his excellency, John Peter Altgeld, governor of Illinois: Starvation stares us in the face. You are the last hope for relief.

JENNIE: Signed—the citizens of Pullman.

[*During the following exchange between* ALTGELD *and* PULLMAN, HOPKINS *stands near* ALTGELD.]

ALTGELD: Mr. Pullman: today, I received an appeal from the people of Pullman for aid. These people live in your town and were your employees. Many of them have practically given their lives to you. I would very much like to learn from you what proposals you might have for alleviating their situation.

PULLMAN [*looking at* HOPKINS]: There is no reply.

ALTGELD: What the hell is going on up there?

[ALTGELD *and* HOPKINS *are met by a delegation including* HEATHCOTE, WICKES, *and three* REPORTERS. HOPKINS *runs interference for* ALTGELD *with the* REPORTERS, *escorting* ALTGELD *to* HEATHCOTE *and* JENNIE.]

HOPKINS: Governor, this is Mr. Heathcote. He's the chairman of the relief committee.

HEATHCOTE: Thank you for coming, sir.

ALTGELD: I wish I could say it's my pleasure.

WICKES: Governor? I'm the second vice president of the Pullman Company.

ALTGELD: Mr. Pullman is not here.

WICKES: No, sir. If I might have the honor of being your guide?

ALTGELD: To what purpose?

WICKES: To assist in making essential discriminations.

[ALTGELD *turns away from* WICKES *to* HEATHCOTE. WICKES *removes himself. As* ALTGELD, HOPKINS, HEATHCOTE, *and* JENNIE *tour the town, they periodically stop and face upstage to look at what the* REPORTERS *describe. The* REPORTERS *stay in fixed positions, working hard to keep their growing anger in check.*]

FIRST REPORTER [*to audience*]: Governor John P. Altgeld toured the town of Pullman today to investigate reports of widespread suffering among the defeated strikers.

[OGGEL *appears on a platform to reprise excerpts from his opening-day speech.*]

OGGEL: Walk through this town. Nowhere will you find a gaming table, a barroom, or a brothel. And nowhere the attendant miseries of degradation, drunkenness, and disease.

FIRST REPORTER: Dennis Halloran and his three children occupy a furnished flat on Fulton Avenue.

SECOND REPORTER: They had received help from the relief committee—

THIRD REPORTER: But that organization has run out of supplies.

SECOND REPORTER: All he has left is a small quantity of flour.

OGGEL: Observe instead clean, self-respecting homes. Homes of honest, God-fearing workmen.

THIRD REPORTER: Across the street—Mr. and Mrs. John O'Connor.

FIRST REPORTER: They, too, are without food.

THIRD REPORTER: Says Mrs. O'Connor—

SECOND REPORTER: "If it were not for the baby, I would not care."

OGGEL: Pullman will build cars. But better than factory, and richer than material production, shall be the manhood that will be developed here.

THIRD REPORTER: Mrs. Charles Longstone is found dying of consumption.

SECOND REPORTER: The physician believes—

FIRST REPORTER: If she had nourishment at the time her sickness first showed itself, she might have recovered.

[ALTGELD, HOPKINS *standing beside him, turns to address* PULLMAN.]

ALTGELD: Mr. Pullman: no matter what caused this distress, it must be met. I will be glad to see you if you care to make any reply. Yours respectfully, John P. Altgeld.

PULLMAN [*looking at* HOPKINS]: Sir: I do not doubt that there are many cases of need caused by the refusal of the employees for more than two and one-half months to earn offered wages in excess of three hundred thousand dollars. I am likewise certain that such cases have been made more severe by the refusal of many to apply for their old places after the strike was practically over. We now have a full force engaged sufficient to facilitate the execution of all work in hand. I regret to say we are not in a position to engage any more at this time. Very respectfully yours, George M. Pullman, president.

ALTGELD [*heatedly*]: I cannot enter into a discussion with you as to the merits of the controversy between you and your former workmen. Six thousand people are suffering for want of food, four-fifths of them women and children. I am now compelled to take those steps I feel necessary. Respectfully yours—

[ALTGELD *turns away from* PULLMAN.]

The good people of this state cannot allow women and children by the hundreds to perish of hunger. I call upon all humane citizens to contribute what they can toward the relief of these people.

[*Another contrapuntal section.*]

FIRST OBSERVER: Representing the Ladies Aid Society of Evanston, I write to inform you that three wagons containing food and clothing will arrive tomorrow to be distributed to the beleaguered citizens of Pullman. We only wish to God we could send more.

SECOND OBSERVER: The *Chicago Tribune* wishes to announce that it has contributed two hundred dollars to the good cause of relieving destitution in the town of Pullman. In addition, the *Tribune* will accept contributions on behalf of the Pullman Relief Fund.

THIRD OBSERVER: On behalf of the board of directors, am donating a railroad car containing meat and provisions. Loading same today. Will arrive at Pullman Saturday for distribution. Signed, Swift and Company.

FOURTH OBSERVER: Dear Mr. Pullman: I read of the report of conditions in your town in today's *Chicago Times*. I cannot fathom how you can be so indifferent to the suffering borne in a town that bears your name. If you do not wish the name Pullman to be synonymous with "callous," I urge you to act, and act now.

FIFTH OBSERVER: The events of the past few weeks only confirms the doubts raised by Mr. Ely in his prescient article in the *Harper's Magazine*. Pullman represents a tide in industrial feudalism which must be beaten back. It is a disgrace!

[*The word "disgrace!" is echoed, then—quiet.* REPORTERS *turn to* PULLMAN.]

PULLMAN: No. No comment.

SCENE 8

[PULLMAN *takes a place before three commissioners*—WRIGHT, WORTHINGTON, *and* BILLINGS. *Note that during most of the following scene,* PULLMAN *stays calm and courteous, as if he sees his task to be to patiently explain a civics lesson to slightly rude boys. It is only toward the end of the scene that he begins to understand that things are slipping from his control.*]

WRIGHT: State your full name.

PULLMAN: George Mortimer Pullman.

BILLINGS [*to audience*]: President Cleveland has ordered a commission to investigate the causes of the strike.

WRIGHT [*to* PULLMAN]: You are the president of the Pullman Palace Car Company?

PULLMAN: Yes, sir.

WRIGHT: Please describe the nature of your company.

PULLMAN: Its main objects are the manufacture and operation of sleeping and parlor cars as well as the manufacture of cars for the general market.

WRIGHT: When was the town of Pullman established?

PULLMAN: The first stone was laid in May 1880, I think.

WRIGHT: Generally, what was the idea behind its development?

PULLMAN: Our hope was to create a harmonious setting for our business as well as to encourage our employees to improve themselves intellectually and morally.

WRIGHT: So you built homes.

PULLMAN: The company did, yes. Houses and apartments.

WRIGHT: And offered them for rent.

PULLMAN: Yes.

[WRIGHT *nods and yields the floor to* WORTHINGTON, *who now takes over the questioning.*]

WORTHINGTON: Now, I understand that when the threat of a strike first appeared, you refused to consider the possibility of arbitration.

PULLMAN: That is correct.

WORTHINGTON: Why?

PULLMAN: It would have meant compromising a principle.

WORTHINGTON: Which principle?

PULLMAN: That one should have the right to manage his own property.

WORTHINGTON: Well, for the sake of argument, let's suppose that a board of arbitration had examined the matter and had said, "Yes, we accept your statement that you're losing money; but with a body of workmen that have been with you some time, you ought to divide with them a little, give them at least enough to live on."

PULLMAN: The wage question is settled by the law of supply and demand.

WORTHINGTON: Supply and demand. Fair market.

PULLMAN: That is the system under which we live. In this particular case, a mutual sacrifice had to be made. The Pullman Company had to use its profits as a cushion so as to underbid and thus win contracts it would not have ordinarily won, and the men had to work a little harder and at the new wages as they had been adjusted. I would have been very glad to pay the men higher wages if business conditions had so warranted.

WORTHINGTON: But given the conditions, you felt you had to reduce them.

PULLMAN: I believe I have said so, yes.

WORTHINGTON: Your company has had a phenomenal success financially, has it not?

PULLMAN: I'm not sure I know what you mean by "phenomenal."

WORTHINGTON: It was initially capitalized by the sale of a million dollars worth of stock. Is that figure accurate?

PULLMAN: To the best of my recollection.

WORTHINGTON: And now, according to the figures I have at hand, the stock is valued at thirty-six million dollars. From one million to thirty-six million. And with dividends of never less than eight percent and sometimes as high as twelve percent. That sounds like a successful enterprise to me.

PULLMAN: There have been some good years.

WORTHINGTON: Even last year. With the country in the middle of a depression, you were still able to declare a dividend of two million eight hundred thousand dollars.

PULLMAN: Through prudent investments and sound business practices—

WORTHINGTON: Mr. Pullman, don't you think it would have been right for a corporation that has been so successful to have borne some losses for its employees? To have shared some of its profits with them?

PULLMAN: I can see no way to justify taking stockholders' money and distributing it in wages above the fair market level.

WORTHINGTON: Not good business?

PULLMAN: Certainly not during the middle of a depression, and not at a time when we have been taking contracts at a loss.

WORTHINGTON: All right, what about during those many years when you were not taking contracts at a loss? Did you ever voluntarily increase the wages of your employees?

PULLMAN: No, sir. Neither did I increase the rent.

WORTHINGTON: You have never divided any profits with them in any shape or form?

PULLMAN: The Pullman Company divides its profits with the people who hold shares in it.

WORTHINGTON: And it divides the losses among the workers whose industry made those profits possible.

PULLMAN [*with heat*]: That is your construction. [*More coolly*] It has always been the company's policy to pay fair market level.

WORTHINGTON: And in a depression that fair market level is naturally depressed?

PULLMAN: That is the way of things.

WORTHINGTON: What about the wages of the officers of the company? Were they reduced?

PULLMAN: No, sir.

WORTHINGTON: Were the salaries of the superintendents and foremen reduced?

PULLMAN: If I were to arbitrarily reduce the salaries of my officers, I would probably lose them.

WORTHINGTON: You might reduce your own perhaps, but not theirs.

PULLMAN: I might.

WORTHINGTON: Did you reduce your own?

PULLMAN: Did I—

WORTHINGTON: *Did* you reduce your own salary?

[*A beat.*]

PULLMAN: No.

WORTHINGTON: You did not.

PULLMAN: I did not.

WORTHINGTON: You don't consider that it might have been a gesture that would have been appreciated by your employees?

PULLMAN: I don't consider that it would have made any significant difference to the financial situation of the company.

WORTHINGTON: I see. That will be all.

PULLMAN: I don't feel that I need to justify to you—

WRIGHT: Thank you, Mr. Pullman.

BILLINGS: The strike commission releases its report.

[WORTHINGTON, WRIGHT, *and* BILLINGS *stand in unison.* PULLMAN *remains seated.*]

While impressed by the design behind the town of Pullman, the commission expresses its opinion that—

WRIGHT: When the depression of 1893 came, morally calling for concessions as to wages and rents, this very wealthy corporation resisted all attempts at conciliation.

WORTHINGTON: The commission believes that had the Pullman Company pursued a different policy, the strike and the consequent loss of property, wages, and life would have been prevented.

PULLMAN [*quietly*]: So, that's it then. They say that it's our fault. My fault.

[*Lights shift and* HOPKINS *steps forward forcefully. In the original production, he emerged from the audience.*]

HOPKINS: No! I'm sorry, sir, I don't mean to interrupt but I have to protest.

[*Paying him no attention,* WRIGHT, WORTHINGTON, *and* BILLINGS *exit.* HOPKINS, *in one pool of light, continues his speech while* PULLMAN, *in a separate and different-colored spot, remains seated. Even when he seems to address* PULLMAN *directly,* HOPKINS *does not face* PULLMAN *but addresses the audience.* PULLMAN, *however, does look directly at* HOPKINS.]

The world knows that I have had my differences with Mr. Pullman, but I cannot stand by and see this injustice done. To lay all responsibility at his door . . . Did he direct the strategy of the response to the strike? No. For this, one must look to the General Managers' Association, which ignored his every attempt to advise. Did he call in the federal troops? No. This action was urged by the attorney general of the United States in complete disregard of Mr. Pullman. Was he responsible for the fiscal policies that resulted in the depression of 1893 and that precipitated this crisis? I would remind you all that these conditions occurred during the administration of a president who is a Democrat and in a state whose governor is a Democrat. Mr. Pullman, a staunch Republican, obviously cannot be held responsible for the effects of policies he has never supported. To saddle him with the responsibility for the unfortunate events of this past summer is scapegoating, pure and simple. A few years ago, you called him genius. He is the same man. A few years ago, you hailed him for his vision, his compassion. He is the same man. A few years ago, you pointed to his achievements and told your sons and daughters that he represented the zenith of American aspirations and ideals. George Pullman is still the same man. In 1865, an assassin tore from us our greatest president. Are we any less assassins to so wantonly destroy the character of one of our greatest citizens? For myself, I most heartily regret any part I may have inadvertently played in this travesty. Effective immediately, I resign the office of the mayor of the city of Chicago.

[*The lights shift around* PULLMAN *to general lighting.* PULLMAN *is back in his home. We should gradually realize that he has been dreaming this reconciliation. The* SERVANT *enters, carrying a wooden lap desk.*]

SERVANT: Sir?

HOPKINS: I shall devote all of my efforts to assisting him who has proved himself to be my best friend in whatever way he may direct.

SERVANT: Mr. Pullman?

HOPKINS: And now, in the witness of you all, I ask his pardon for any injuries that I have done him. Please, sir—

SERVANT: Sir?

HOPKINS: I ask your forgiveness.

[HOPKINS *reaches out downstage and kneels. With great magnanimity,* PULLMAN *reaches out to him.*]

SERVANT: Mr. Pullman, sir? What are you looking at?

[PULLMAN *looks around.*]

Excuse me, sir . . . Are you all—

PULLMAN: I'm fine, thank you. I was just—

[*A beat.*]

Daydreaming.

[HOPKINS's *spot goes out and* HOPKINS *exits. A beat.* PULLMAN *turns to the* SERVANT.]

What is it?

SERVANT: You asked me to fetch your lap desk.

PULLMAN: Oh. Yes, thank you.

[*The* SERVANT *directs a member of the* ENSEMBLE *to bring in the stand, on which lie paper and a pen.* PULLMAN, *still recovering from his reverie, approaches it and picks up the pen.*]

SERVANT: October 1897: George Pullman writes a letter to the new grandson born to him by his daughter Florence.

PULLMAN: My dear grandson: in honor of your birth, I have placed in trust an amount sufficient to perpetually endow in your name a bed in Saint Luke's Hospital. I do this so that any sick child whom you may choose can always have the benefit of kind care and skillful treatment. I hope your life may be successful, and that you will always remember that good actions speak louder than do spoken words. Very affectionately, your grandfather, George M. Pullman.

[PULLMAN *signals* SERVANT.]

SERVANT: Sir?

PULLMAN [*handing* SERVANT *the lap desk*]: See to this, will you?

SERVANT: Yes, sir.

[PULLMAN *suddenly winces.*]

Sir?

PULLMAN: It's the heat. I'll be all right in a second.

[*A beat.*]

There. That's better.

[*Suddenly,* PULLMAN *is stricken again by a pain in the chest. He reaches out but cannot speak. The* SERVANT *puts down the lap desk and rushes to him. He helps him off the stage.*]

ENSEMBLE: The doctor arrives too late to be of any assistance.

FIRST CITIZEN: Had he been better known, he would have been better liked.

SECOND CITIZEN: He did a great deal of good, even if he was not thoroughly understood by a part of the public.

FLORENCE [*dressed in mourning*]: He loved his town as he loved his children.

JUNIOR: One of his children discovers a measure of his father's love when the will is read.

ENSEMBLE: —"Inasmuch as my son has never developed a sense of responsibility, I am compelled to limit provisions for his benefit."

—Nevertheless, George Pullman Jr. is heard to remark that he intends to visit his father's grave regularly.

JUNIOR: Yeah, with my dog.

[FLORENCE *gives* JUNIOR *a sharp look.* JUNIOR *turns away.*]

REPORTER: Eugene Debs, no longer imprisoned for his part in the strike, is asked for his comment.

DEBS: Mr. Pullman would not arbitrate. Now he is on an equal footing with those who worked for him.

[*The* FEMALE SOLOIST *begins a reprise of* "Leave a Light," *over which the following is played.*]

ENSEMBLE: —Special precautions are taken to prevent any possible interference with his remains by those who disagreed with him in life.

—The body is placed in a mahogany casket.

—The casket is secured within a sheath of tar paper.

—The tar paper is surrounded by a layer of asphalt.

—And the asphalt is sealed within a block of steel-reinforced concrete
the size of a drawing room.

—It takes two days to fill in the grave.

HOPKINS: And so George Pullman lies undisturbed for the ages.

[*"Leave a Light"* is finished and the play ends.]

NOTES

How much of the story in the script is true? The vast majority, actually.
In fact, much of what might seem most likely to be invention is true. In
no particular order, here are the details.

Pullman's story about raising the Tremont Hotel is true, as are the
Mary Lincoln incident, the joke he made about naming the town after
Beman and himself, and most of the other public actions he is represented as taking in the play. His love for his daughter Florence is well
documented. He had two sons, both of whom disappointed him greatly
and both of whom he more or less disinherited. I needed only one.

Jackson did indeed contract the market hall to give his speech and confronted Pullman directly when the hall was taken away from him. Contrary
to the play, however, Hopkins did not intervene. Jackson, in fact, never got
to give his talk on "Britain's Title to the Northwest." Dramatic license.

Pullman did indeed run the priest out of town because he was unhappy
with the priest's sentiments. The deed for the church was made condi-
tional upon the priest's being transferred.

During the strike, Pullman's advice was indeed ignored by the railroad owners, and a man named Harahan did rise during a meeting and
give him a tongue-lashing.

The scene in front of the strike commission is a condensation of
Pullman's actual testimony with just a little fiddling for dramatic purposes.

Pullman was buried in the manner described. His grave is in Chicago's
Graceland Cemetery. Junior's line about visiting his father's grave with
his dog is from the record.

Altgeld was governor of Illinois at the time, and nearly everything he says in the play—including his correspondence with Pullman—is adapted from the record. His tour of the town is true. The people described as suffering were real people.

Debs's speeches, too, are quoted from the record, and his desire to keep the American Railway Union out of the Pullman strike is documented. When the membership voted for the strike in spite of Debs's sentiments, he assumed his responsibilities and led what he believed to be a doomed effort.

Oggel was indeed a minister in the town, and most of what he says here he was quoted as saying in accounts of the time; the account of his last sermon and the rumors that hastened his departure are also true.

Jennie Curtis, too, was a real person and did everything she does in the play—along with Heathcote, she was a member of the committee that called on Pullman, she did dance with Hopkins at the benefit, and she did give the speech at the railway union convention that stirred the membership to vote for a sympathy strike.

Richard T. Ely toured Pullman and wrote the famous article on it for *Harper's*. Most of his speech is excerpted from that article.

As for Hopkins—he did indeed come to Pullman as a young man and begin by working in the lumberyard. The idea that Pullman saw in him something of a surrogate son is dramatic license but not inconsistent with known facts. As I mentioned previously, Pullman was very disappointed by his sons, and this young man, a charming go-getter, must have stood in dramatic contrast to them in Pullman's eyes. In any case, Hopkins rose swiftly in the company and opened a store in the Arcade (though I confess to having fudged the details regarding the degree of Pullman's support in opening the store), and Pullman fired him from his job as paymaster upon learning of his advocating the annexation of the town into Chicago. (In reality, Pullman fired Hopkins twice. After the first time, he discovered that nobody understood Hopkins's system of bookkeeping. He rehired him, gave him an assistant, and when the assistant had mastered the system, fired Hopkins again.)

Mayor Carter Harrison was indeed assassinated after giving a speech at the exposition, and Hopkins was elected to fill out his term, making him mayor of Chicago when the strike started. (Elected at age thirty-five, there is a good chance he was the youngest mayor in Chicago's history.)

Hopkins was rebuffed by Pullman in the Chicago Club when he tried to get his former employer to agree to arbitration, and he did indeed show open support for the strikers by attending their dance and contributing large quantities of flour and meat to the cause. After the strike, he was instrumental in relief for the strikers.

Much of the town of Pullman still exists. In fact, the villain in the film version of *The Fugitive* lived in Pullman, and those with quick eyes can spot Hopkins's house and the church. The Hotel Florence is undergoing restoration by the Historic Pullman Foundation; visitors can view Pullman's private rooms and have a meal in nineteenth-century surroundings. I strongly recommend visiting the town with a copy of William Adelman's guide *Touring Pullman*. Published by the Illinois Labor History Society, it is available through the Chicago Historical Society.

I've tried to present the facts in a way that tells a complete and coherent tale. It is, however, necessarily only a complete tale, not the complete tale. Anyone interested in Pullman and his time will find that further exploration yields more compelling material.

I am particularly fond of a passage the original director, Wes Savick, got me to write. In the original draft, after the sequence in which Pullman testifies in front of the commission, I had written a scene in which Pullman attends a performance in his theater of *King Lear*. Sitting in a box, he looks across the hall to see Hopkins sitting in another box. As Lear rages onstage about the ingratitude of children, Pullman begins to hyperventilate.

Wes suggested gently that maybe this was just a bit obvious. A little sarcastically, I replied, "What would you prefer? A scene where Pullman dreams Hopkins is apologizing to him?" Wes smiled and said, "Try it." I did. He was right. It's better.

At this point, I'd like to pay tribute to my two directors. I was happy with both productions, but they were very different. The lights never faded in Wes Savick's production; the action ricocheted from one area of the stage to another in the theatrical equivalent of jump cuts. Patricia Birch was more interested in creating a sense of the ongoing life of the town and brought her choreographer's eye to running the major scenes in counterpoint with a constant flow of activity in other corners of the stage.

They came up with very different solutions to staging the ending of the play. Pat set up a tableau of all the actors; they barely moved a muscle during the story of Pullman's funeral. Then, right at the end, one of the businessmen in the Chicago Club raised a drink to his lips as the lights faded. Lovely and understated.

Wes surprised me by introducing—in the last thirty seconds—a contemporary tour guide leading a bunch of tourists (dressed in T-shirts and jeans and so forth) through Graceland Cemetery (where Pullman is buried), telling this story of a hundred years ago while the ghosts of the past look on. Neat.

WITH AND WITHOUT

—for Kristine Niven

There is no rule that says how plays must be built.

Yes, I do believe there are craft principles of dramatic writing that one ignores at one's peril. I wrote a book called *The Dramatist's Toolkit* (published by Heinemann) to articulate these principles as I understand them and apply them in my own work.

But the fact that the vast majority of contemporary plays are written by single writers at keyboards doesn't mean that every script has to be generated in this way. *With and Without* is a case in point.

I used to be associated with Alice's Fourth Floor, a small theater on Forty-second Street's Theatre Row. When I floated the proposition of working improvisationally with member artists, Susann Brinkley, the space's artistic director, offered me a weekly slot in the space to give it a try.

The first thing I had to do was to establish some common language with the actors and writers who joined me. Theatrical improvisation is not simply a matter of actors leaping onto a stage and blurting out whatever occurs to them. Just as jazz musicians must be familiar with key signatures and meters, and have some working knowledge of the principles of harmony and counterpoint, so improvisational actors work from a set of shared understandings.

In an interview I did with longtime improvisational actor-director Del Close (which appears in my book on The Second City, *Something Wonderful Right Away*), Del summarized what he saw as the theoretical underpinnings of the work:

1. Don't deny verbal reality. If it's said, it's real. "What about our children?" "We don't have any." That's wrong. Same is true with

physical reality. If another actor physically establishes something, it is there and you mustn't do anything that says it's not there.

2. Take the active as opposed to the passive choice. Of course, this means a great deal. It means you are free to choose on a stage. Which, if you choose to ponder that for a second, means you are in an existentialist state of living your life in public.

3. The actor's business is to justify. What this came out of was a time when one of the actresses in [the] St. Louis [company of the Compass Players] said, "The character I'm playing in the scene wouldn't *do* that. How can I justify doing that?" Elaine [May]'s response: "The actor's job *is* to justify."

Various improvisational companies, directors, and teachers over the years have invented hundreds of theater games—structures that enable actors to spontaneously and cooperatively generate theatrical activity. I drew on some of these games to develop the common language I needed the members of my workshop to speak. We began to be able to listen to one another and build scenes jointly.

"Jointly" is an important word. One of the key distinctions between working improvisationally and writing at your desk is that the former is a social activity and the latter is not. Working alone, of course, you have complete control over what you produce. This also means that you have only your own resources on which to draw.

Working improvisationally, you must give up your authorial control to have the benefit of the creative resources of the group. Though an improvisational scene may have its genesis in an individual's idea, when you're genuinely improvising, everyone present has a determining influence on the action.

For example, you might begin by setting up and playing a simple courtship scene set in a restaurant. Then another actor may come in and introduce an additional element that changes its direction—say, because of a flash flood, the restaurant is surrounded by water, and nobody will be able to leave until tomorrow morning. You may continue to play the courtship scene, but it necessarily will be influenced by the changed circumstance.

As I mentioned earlier in this book, the short piece "Cover" was created when two friends and I improvised our way through an outline I had devised. I long wanted to try to build a full-length piece this way. One day in the workshop an idea presented itself. Three men and two women were present, and trying to figure out a situation that would support this configuration, I proposed we play a scene about three couples who are in the habit of vacationing together. We had arrived at the house we had jointly rented only to discover that one of the wives hadn't shown up and probably wouldn't. This meant that the other two couples are left to cope with the abandoned husband.

No, the scene we played then was by no means a finished product, or even something that might have entertained an outside audience. But there was enough promise in what resulted that I thought there was a play to be developed out of it.

At this point, I stepped in as playwright and reorganized the material. In the interest of writing a small-cast play, I decided it would concern two couples, not three. Looking to write a play emphasizing good roles for actresses (it's no secret that there are fewer good roles for women than men), I decided that instead of a missing wife I would deal with a missing husband.

At that point, I began private improvisational sessions with two of the actresses, Beth Lincks and Kristine Niven. I would set up circumstances for scenes, and then the three of us would let fly with a tape recorder running. Through these sessions, I learned a lot about the characters and the quality of their relationships and their histories. I learned how they interact and what their differing philosophies are. And learning these things made it possible for me to create a plot to accommodate them. In the end, maybe 5 percent of the dialogue came directly from our improvisations, but with the characters' voices now in my head, it was easier to write dialogue for them.

Incidentally, Beth, writing under the pen name of Arlene Hutton, has since become a popular playwright herself, her best-known play being *Last Train to Nibroc*.

With and Without received a workshop production under the sponsorship of Artistic New Directions at the Frog Pond Theatre in Upper Jay, New York, on July 15, 1994, directed by Michael Gellman, with the following cast:

Jill	Kristine Niven
Mark	Dan Daily

Shelly .... Beth Lincks
Glen .... Erol K. C. Landis

With and Without was recorded for WFMT's Chicago Theatres on the Air on April 13, 1995, in a coproduction with the Victory Gardens Theater of Chicago under the direction of Sandy Shinner, with the following cast:

Jill .... Lindsay Crouse
Mark .... Michael Tucker
Shelly .... Jill Eikenberry
Glen .... Tim Halligan

With and Without formally premiered at the Victory Gardens Theater of Chicago on November 10, 1995, under the direction of Sandy Shinner, set design by Bill Bartelt, lighting by Chris Phillips, costumes by Margaret Morettini, sound and props by Galen G. Ramsey, and the production stage manager was Christi-Anne Sokolewicz, with the following cast:

Jill .... Annabel Armour
Mark .... James Sherman
Shelly .... Linnea Todd
Glen .... Marc Vann

With and Without received its New York premiere at the 78th Street Theatre Lab on February 14, 1998, under the direction of Michael Montel, with the following cast:

Jill .... Kit Flanagan
Mark .... Reed Birney
Shelly .... Mia Dillon
Glen .... Erol K. C. Landis

With and Without in a revised version opened at the Blueberry Pond Theatre Company on June 16, 2006, under the direction of Jeffrey Sweet, with the following cast:

Jill .... Michelle Best
Mark .... Michael J. Muldoon
Shelly .... Cynthia Granville
Glen .... Francis Callahan

CHARACTERS

Jill
Mark
Shelly
Glen

SCENE 1

[*The time is today. On a deck of a country house, overlooking a lake. A door leads into the house. The deck also has steps down that provide access to a path around the side of the house. Summer, late afternoon. At rise,* MARK *and* JILL *are on the deck. They are in their midthirties to late forties.* MARK *is dressed casually.* JILL, *dressed in city clothes, is fiddling with a Nerf gun.*]

JILL: No, if he shows he'll just show.

MARK: Did he say he might? When you talked to him?

JILL: Mark, this isn't on the basis of talking to him. This is on the basis of living with him. Years of experience and acquired—

[*A beat. She fires the Nerf gun at* MARK. *One of the sponges hits him or lands near him.*]

I've figured out how it works. Aren't I clever?

MARK: I never said otherwise.

JILL: You gonna give that back?

MARK: So you can shoot at me again?

JILL: Doesn't hurt.

MARK: Maybe I just don't want to be a target.

JILL: Where did this come from?

MARK: People we're renting from have a kid. Probably left it out by accident.

JILL [*overlapping*]: No, Russ will either show up or he won't show up. And probably even he doesn't know. And probably he won't know until he finds himself here, or doesn't. He'll just open the door to his car and say, "Oh, look where I am!"

MARK: And act accordingly.

JILL: Or not. He's Russ. Never can tell.

MARK: I'm sorry, Jill.

JILL: Of course you are. I'm gonna change.

[*As* JILL *begins her exit,* SHELLY, *about the* same *age as* MARK *and* JILL, *enters from the house carrying a wicker hamper.*]

SHELLY: I've finished putting the stuff away.

JILL: Back in a sec.

[JILL *exits.* SHELLY *perches on the deck.*]

SHELLY: God damn, Russ. Now I'm going to have to make the pasta instead of the roast.

MARK: What does that have to do with Russ?

SHELLY: Well, *dinner*—

MARK: Yeah?

SHELLY: It doesn't spontaneously generate out of the collective will. "Oh, we're hungry." Bang—there's dinner. It has to be made.

MARK: Yes.

SHELLY: If we were going to eat at seven, I'd have to put the roast in right now for it to be done.

MARK: At seven.

SHELLY: That's how long it takes. But we don't know if we're *going to* eat at seven because we don't know if Russ will show up by then. Pasta, on the other hand—

MARK: It's faster.

SHELLY: He shows up, I can have pasta ready like ten, fifteen minutes later. I can't have the roast ready—

MARK: No, I grasp the concept.

[SHELLY *has pulled a bottle of wine and two wineglasses out of the hamper and poured* MARK *a glass.*]

Thanks. The thing is, we don't know if he's going to show up at all.

SHELLY: Oh, I thought it was a *when* question. But it's *if*?

MARK: Yeah.

SHELLY [*getting the implications*]: Oh.

MARK: Yeah.

[*A beat.*]

SHELLY: So, you and Jill have a good talk?

MARK: Mmmm.

SHELLY: No?

MARK: Well, I want to be there for her, of course.

SHELLY: Of course.

MARK [*nodding*]: On the other hand, I don't want to say anything that will suddenly throw her into—I didn't want her to—to start crying, 'cause then you're supposed to step forward and do that thing—

SHELLY: Which?

MARK: You know, a pat on the back, or hold her.

SHELLY: You don't want that to happen?

MARK: To hold her? No, I really don't. But if she starts crying, what are you going to do? Just stand there and make sympathetic noises?

SHELLY: What's a sympathetic noise?

MARK: You know.

SHELLY: Make me a sympathetic noise. So if I hear it in the future I can identify it.

MARK: "Ohhhhh." Or, "there, there."

SHELLY: "There, there"?

MARK: "There, there."

SHELLY: Oh yes, that would help a lot. "There, there." I'll have to remember that.

MARK: What really *does* help?

SHELLY: It's hard being a sensitive man, isn't it?

MARK: You think I'm not a sensitive man?

SHELLY: I think you're a *very* sensitive man. That's what you want to be, right?

MARK: Yeah, but, you know, in a manly way. Stoic, but in my eyes you can read deep reservoirs of—

SHELLY: Feeling.

MARK: Yes. That's what I'm shooting for. That's my goal.

SHELLY: So what are you afraid of?

MARK: Afraid?

SHELLY: With Jill? That if she, in a fit of whatever, propelled herself into your arms—that what?

MARK: That it might throw a switch on to a track we used to travel down that isn't appropriate to travel down now.

SHELLY: Meaning what? That you'll suddenly have this overwhelming urge to start pawing at her clothes?

MARK: Shelly—

SHELLY: Or the other way round?

MARK: Well, don't you sometimes, when you run into old boyfriends—

SHELLY: There are so many of them—

MARK: I'm saying when you *do*, on those rare occasions when you *do*, don't you sometimes find old impulses being triggered?

SHELLY: Not triggered. Remembered. Acknowledged.

MARK: Uh-huh.

SHELLY: Well, of course remembered. I don't forget people. I don't forget that something happened, if something happened.

MARK: But there's a difference between like remembering, oh, once upon a time this person and I, so forth and so on, between *that,* which is an intellectual thing—"I know this," your word: *acknowledge*—between that and the feelings themselves coming back. Echoes of them.

SHELLY: And if she weren't around you wouldn't have to cope with these echoes?

MARK: May I point out something here? Let me point something out. And I'm casting no particular, uh, castings, which is that you're the reason she—

SHELLY: She what?

MARK: You were the one who made the big gesture of "I don't care what happened between you and Mark in the past—"

SHELLY: I didn't. Why should I?

MARK: Not saying you should. But to say, pretty much, "I want you to be a friend of the family." Which I thought was a lovely gesture and much appreciated. And a lot of women wouldn't have done that.

SHELLY: Hey, you're sensitive; I'm noble.

MARK: But you, in a way, have made her more welcome into our lives than I think *I* would have?

SHELLY: Do you *not* want her in our lives?

MARK: I'm just saying that having her in our lives is not always easy.

SHELLY: And you only want friends who are easy.

MARK: It's kind of nice when you're on vacation, yeah. Last time I looked, that's what this was supposed to be. We've got all the fixings—the lake here, a bunch of silly board games—I brought along three paperback novels with guns on the cover. After all the bullshit in the office, I came up here in anticipation of a certain kind of week by way of contrast. And instead—

SHELLY: What is it? Are you afraid if she hugs you you're going to get hard?

MARK: I'm so glad we can have these conversations.

SHELLY: Well, you said triggers. What other triggers could you be talking about? You ever think about her naked anymore? What she looks like?

MARK: I don't know what she *looks* like. It's been years.

SHELLY: What she *looked* like then. Come on, fess up.

MARK: What is the point of asking this question?

SHELLY: You do, don't you? Remember?

MARK: I really don't see the point of asking—

SHELLY: You do, don't you?

MARK: You're just trying to make me blush.

SHELLY: The perils of being a sensitive man. It's OK if you do, you know—remember.

MARK: Let me get this straight: I have your *permission*?

SHELLY: You do it anyway, don't you? *I* do.

MARK: Oh, you think about Jill naked?

SHELLY: You know what I'm saying.

MARK: I know what you're saying. *Why* you're saying it—that's another matter.

SHELLY: Would you look at your shoulders?

MARK: What about them?

SHELLY: They're up around your ears.

MARK: And this signifies what?

SHELLY: OK, OK, I'll stop.

MARK: Who do *you* think about naked?

SHELLY: Never mind.

MARK: Oh, it's OK for you to razz me but—

SHELLY: I did have a life before I met you.

MARK: Is there someone in particular? Or do you mentally skip around between erotic highlights?

SHELLY: I *had* no erotic highlights until you came along.

MARK: I believe you.

SHELLY: Give me your lips.

MARK: You want them so bad, come get them.

[SHELLY *goes over to him and kisses him with serious intention. The kiss ends.*]

More, more, I'm still not satisfied.

[SHELLY *gives him a playful swat, puts her finger to her lips, and nods in the direction of the inside to indicate that she hears* JILL *returning.* JILL *enters in casual clothes.*]

You changed—nice.

SHELLY: Jill, something to drink? We brought some wine up.

MARK: One of Shelly's clients, every Christmas, sends over a case, practically.

JILL: Fine.

SHELLY: It's pretty good stuff.

JILL: Fine. Sure.

MARK [*pouring*]: This is supposed to have a wonderful bouquet. I don't know what that means really. Tell me. *Does* this have a wonderful bouquet?

JILL: Yes. It also has good legs.

[SHELLY *laughs.*]

MARK: Is that actually a real thing?

JILL: Look, you see, you hold it up to the light; you tilt the glass a little. Now, you see where it's falling down on the sides? If it clings to the glass, it has good legs.

MARK: I'm astonished. Shelly, your wine could be a Rockette.

JILL: This is actually very nice.

SHELLY: Could I have some more, too?

MARK: Oh yes, sorry. Of course.

JILL: Somebody should call Russ.

MARK: Why?

JILL: Well, for the obvious reason it would be nice to know if he's coming. Somebody should call him.

MARK: Why do you look at me when you say "somebody"?

JILL: Come on, Mark.

MARK: And what is this hypothetical somebody supposed to say?

SHELLY: That we're preparing dinner and we want to know if he's going to join us for it. Or, if he's coming late, should we tell him where we're going to be—

MARK: Are we going out?

SHELLY: If we want to go out.

MARK: Perfect. You know what to say; you've got the job.

JILL: I think it's better if you do it.

MARK: Why is it better if I do it?

JILL: Because you're a guy.

MARK: What?

JILL: Well, you *are.*

MARK: I'm not disputing that. I'm disputing that my being a guy has anything to do with why it's more appropriate for me to make this call.

JILL: Well, you're a guy, he's a guy, you've got a guy friendship, you and Russ—

MARK: Why is it that two guys—any two guys, any two heterosexual guys—are supposed to be able to talk in a way that . . . I think this idea is a complete fallacy. No pun intended.

[JILL *laughs in spite of herself.*]

JILL: You are so—

MARK [*overlapping*]: I don't play racquetball with him. I don't go drinking with him. If you added up all the time I have spent alone with him since you two got married—

JILL: Don't you like him?

MARK: I like him OK, but he wouldn't be my friend if he weren't married to you.

SHELLY: Why not? He's *my* friend.

MARK: All right, yes, he would have been my friend because he's *your* friend. [*To* JILL] But the fact of the matter is, now he's married to you, and because he's married to you—that's the reason he comes into our life. That's why he'd be here this week, why we've been together other weeks, because of you being a couple. Because these weeks are about two couples sharing this kind of time.

JILL: I still think you should call.

SHELLY: I do, too.

MARK: Excuse me, this is not up to a vote.

JILL: Why won't you?

MARK: He's gonna know that I'm calling not just to find out, "Are you coming up?" And what if he says he's *not* going to come? What then?

JILL: You could ask why.

MARK: See, the thing is, if I do that, he might tell me.

JILL: No, I know what: you should tell him—this is perfect—you should tell him *I* haven't shown up.

SHELLY: You?

JILL: I haven't shown up and you're worried about me.

MARK: But how would we know that you were going to be coming up in a different car from him?

JILL: I called while I was on the road and told you so. Told you that I was on the way.

MARK: Why would you call us on the road?

JILL: I was passing the store in town and wondered if there was something I could pick up for dinner. And so you were expecting me in a few minutes, but that was more than an hour ago and where could I be? Has he heard anything?

SHELLY: So he thinks maybe you've been in an accident?

JILL: Whatever he wants to think. Whatever conclusion he wants to—

SHELLY: But that's a lie.

JILL: I'm not saying you should tell him that I've *been* in an accident.

SHELLY: But to say that you haven't shown up.

JILL: Right.

SHELLY: But you *have* shown up.

MARK: You're right here. I see you.

JILL: A technicality.

MARK: The truth is a technicality.

SHELLY: How would you feel if we did something like that to you?

JILL: How would I know?

SHELLY: You could find out. Whenever someone does stuff like this—

MARK: People find out.

SHELLY: Thank you, I really wanted that sentence finished.

JILL: No, you're right. It was a stupid idea. Besides, Mark couldn't pull it off.

MARK: Gee, I think I'm offended.

SHELLY: You're offended that she says you're not a liar.

MARK: That's not what she's saying. She's saying I don't have the talent to *be* one. That choice of whether or not to lie—that's a moral question. The *ability* to lie—that speaks to competence. She's saying that I'm not competent.

JILL: All right, forget it.

MARK: Thank you, I will.

JILL: But I still think someone should call.

SHELLY: All right, I'll call.

MARK: And what are you going to say?

SHELLY: "Shall we expect you for dinner or not? Are you going to be late?"

MARK: Sounds excellent.

JILL: And if he says he's not coming, ask him why. And maybe what her name is.

MARK: Her name?

JILL: Whoever the bimbo is he's—

MARK [*to* SHELLY]: Uh-huh, see?

SHELLY [*to* JILL]: Are you sure you don't want to call yourself?

JILL: The whole point is what he'd say to you. I know what he'd say to me. He's said it.

MARK: But you want Shelly to ask what *you* want her to ask. Maybe you should hold up cue cards for the conversation?

JILL: Don't talk to me like that.

MARK: Sorry. [*To* SHELLY] But I think if you *do* get him on the phone, the conversation's going to turn to something beyond is he or isn't he going to come up here. And do you want to be part of that conversation?

SHELLY: Well, it's preferable to this one.

MARK: Do you want him to say something to you under pressure that might be irrevocable? Do you want to be the one to have to bring the news of that back?

SHELLY: I'm going to call. I will say what I think needs to be said.

[*She goes inside.*]

JILL: You chicken. You're such a chicken.

MARK: Thank you.

JILL: You've always been a chicken.

MARK: Thank you.

JILL: Well, you *have.*

MARK: That's right. Aren't you glad you didn't end up with a chicken?

JILL: If you'd ended up with me, you wouldn't have been a chicken.

MARK: By definition.

JILL: Well, it's true, isn't it?

MARK: Absolutely, yes; it's true.

JILL: Well, it is.

MARK: I'm not going to disagree with you.

JILL: You're too chicken to disagree with me.

MARK: Probably.

JILL: You're so tentative, so fucking cautious.

MARK: If you mean I don't dive into a swimming pool unless I'm sure there's water in it—

JILL: You don't dive into a swimming pool unless it's heated to precisely 89.2 degrees.

MARK: Excuse me, are you insulting me?

JILL: Of course I'm insulting you.

MARK: Just checking.

JILL: What the fuck do you *think* I'm doing?

MARK: No, if I have a choice between being called an asshole and someone who likes to swim in a warm pool—

JILL: Oh, shut up.

MARK: On the other hand, if you'd called me a Rush Limbaugh fan—

JILL: Stop being rational! God damn, I'm so tired of that tone—

MARK: What tone?

JILL: You explaining the ramifications of everything. Don't you ever have an impulse? Or did you have it removed surgically—

MARK: What?

JILL: Whatever organ or gland it is that secretes impulses, spur-of-the-moments?

MARK: I think you mean spurs-of-the-moment.

JILL: Stop it! Just stop it!

[SHELLY *returns.*]

SHELLY: What's he doing?

MARK: Being too rational.

SHELLY [*offhandedly*]: Yeah, that's annoying, stop it.

JILL: So?

SHELLY: I called.

MARK: Were you able to get a signal?

SHELLY: I had to use the landline.

MARK: You keep track of how many minutes? If we have to reimburse—

SHELLY: I've got minutes left on one of my discount calling cards.

JILL: Excuse me, this is fascinating, but—

SHELLY: Sorry.

JILL: You called. And?

SHELLY: No answer on his cell. And no message thing.

JILL: Huh.

SHELLY: So then I tried his number at your place. I left a message on his machine.

JILL: How many rings? Two or four?

MARK: What difference does that make?

SHELLY: Toll saver.

MARK: What's that?

SHELLY: It's a feature on some answering machines. You put it on toll saver, if there are messages waiting, it rings twice before it answers. If there are no messages, it rings four times.

MARK: So, if it rang four times, what would that mean?

JILL: It would mean that he's picked up my messages. That what I said wasn't enough to get him to call me here. It was four rings, right?

SHELLY: I'm sorry.

JILL: Well, no, it just gives me more information to work with. He heard my messages, he erased them, he didn't call here. It gives me a better idea where I stand.

MARK: I don't see how that's necessarily true.

JILL: You know, your opinion on this is real valuable.

SHELLY: Hey now—

JILL: Can I have another glass? [*To* MARK] Don't look at me like that. It's wine.

[SHELLY *pours* JILL *another glass.*]

SHELLY: So, are you up for linguine?

[*Lights out.*]

SCENE 2

[*An hour or so later. Sunset.* MARK *is alone on the deck.* SHELLY *enters.*]

MARK: You know what we could do.

SHELLY: What?

MARK: Leave.

SHELLY: Just do that, huh?

MARK: Yeah.

SHELLY: Leave?

MARK: Toss our stuff into the back of the car, hit the road—

SHELLY: Say good-bye or not?

MARK: Maybe wave to her. Jill's still on the phone, right?

SHELLY: Still, yes.

MARK: Good. She's on the phone, we wave, "See you." When she finally gets off the phone, in a couple hours, she realizes that we didn't mean "see you later," we meant "see you—"

SHELLY: "Much later."

MARK: We could be back to the city in time for *The Daily Show*. Have a glass of wine. Congratulate each other over a narrow escape.

SHELLY: And what would she do?

MARK: That would be up to her. She's an adult.

SHELLY: Drink?

MARK: Probably.

SHELLY: Cry?

MARK: She's gonna do that whether we're here or not. I mean, she's mapped out this week for misery. The question is whether it's solo or communal.

SHELLY: And the money we blew to rent this place? We kiss that off?

MARK: The point of this was to spend a nice relaxing week with our friends. Since only fifty percent of our friends showed up, and she is not making for a relaxing time—

SHELLY: Her feelings would be badly hurt.

MARK: On the other hand, we might reach the end of the week alive.

[*A beat.*]

SHELLY: You're not serious.

MARK: Of course not.

SHELLY: You're just saying this in the spirit of—what?

MARK: Yeah. Exactly.

SHELLY: Irony.

MARK: That, too.

SHELLY: A little sardonic humor to cover the compassion you really feel.

MARK: You've got me nailed. That's me.

SHELLY: How soon do you want to leave?

MARK: You're kidding, right?

SHELLY: Yeah.

MARK: Damn.

SHELLY: We can't.

MARK: I know.

SHELLY: We *can't*.

MARK: I know we can't.

SHELLY: Damn.

MARK: You want me to rub your neck?

SHELLY: You think it needs it?

MARK: It's so knotted up it looks like a piece of challah. Come on—sit.

[SHELLY *sits in front of* MARK, *who begins to rub her neck.*]

SHELLY: I envy bastards.

MARK: How so?

SHELLY: It must be so liberating. Like—who is it? "Now is the winter of our discontent."

MARK: Richard the Third.

SHELLY: You remember Olivier in the movie? How much fun he had? All that twinkling evil. "This is what I'm gonna do." Murder, seduction, betrayal. Those two kids. No apologies, no scruples, no hesitations. Just blast away.

MARK: Of course he died at the end.

SHELLY: Of course he died. In the classics, there has to be balance, justice. Classical literature—he *has* to be punished.

MARK: As opposed to real life?

SHELLY: Hey, Franco died of old age. So did J. Edgar Hoover. So did my grandma Ruth. You never met her.

MARK: And I am thankful for it.

SHELLY: Mean. And never pretended to be anything but.

MARK: What was her excuse? The Depression?

SHELLY: She didn't make any excuse. If you had something and she wanted it, she'd say, "Give me that." And if you asked why, she'd say, "Because I want it more than you." And she did. She wanted Grandpa. He was married to someone else. So what. She wanted him, she got him, and once she got him, she made his life miserable.

MARK: You've inherited genes from this person?

SHELLY: It was like she figured out that if she got rid of her conscience there wouldn't be any friction.

MARK: Friction?

SHELLY: Yeah. I mean, let's say you have the impulse to do something, something crummy. Like, "Oh, I'd like to ram that jerk in the red car." You'd do it—right?—if it weren't for friction.

MARK: You're talking moral friction?

SHELLY: Some voice—some Elmer Fudd voice that pops up with things to consider. Like fairness, or other people's safety or feelings, or the rule of law.

MARK: Yours sounds like Elmer Fudd?

SHELLY: What does yours sound like?

MARK: James Earl Jones.

SHELLY: Ooooh.

MARK: What's that smell?

SHELLY: Over there—that guy is barbecuing.

[MARK *picks up binoculars.*]

MARK: Yup. Oh, he's wearing one of those joke barbecue things.

SHELLY: What, aprons?

MARK: Yeah.

SHELLY: What's it say? What's the joke?

MARK: I can't see. Something about meat. Something about eating meat.

SHELLY: Thank you, I get the idea.

MARK: You want to look?

SHELLY: What I want is your hands.

MARK: You got it.

[*He puts down the binoculars and returns to rubbing her neck.* SHELLY *begins to moan from the neck rub.*]

Does that mean that feels good?

SHELLY: Mmmmm.

MARK: How come I never hear that sound in bed?

SHELLY: You should rub my neck in bed.

MARK: Thank you very much.

[*He stops rubbing her neck.*]

SHELLY: Oh come on, a joke.

MARK: Yeah, well there've been a lot of jokes like that flying around here tonight. Jokes of that ilk.

SHELLY: What ilk?

MARK: It's kind of a therapeutic thing, right?

SHELLY: What is?

MARK: She makes a crack, you make a crack, I'm supposed to be a good sport. Laugh along.

SHELLY: You think we're picking on you?

MARK: On what I represent.

SHELLY: Oh? What do you represent?

MARK: People with dicks.

SHELLY: You represent them, do you? All of them?

MARK: Not of my choosing. But, since I am the one person in the vicinity at the moment who matches that description, I seem to have been elected by default.

SHELLY: It must be a burden.

MARK: Just because Russ and I have this one anatomical characteristic in common doesn't mean that we share other characteristics as well.

SHELLY [*intending it as a joke*]: Well, you're all no damn good.

MARK: That's supposed to be funny, right?

SHELLY: Oh, come on.

MARK: No, this is just what I mean. It's the one easy put-down that's still socially acceptable. Can't put down blacks, can't put down gays, can't put down Jews—that marks you as a racist or a redneck. But men—the one category that's always fair game.

SHELLY: No, there's one other group.

MARK: Yeah, what?

SHELLY: Lawyers.

MARK: Well, *they* deserve it. Hey, you can't tell me that there's any comparison between men and lawyers. I mean, the idea is insulting.

SHELLY: Except, of course, a lot of lawyers are men. Most of them, in fact.

MARK: Coincidence, pure coincidence. You know you've got half of us believing it.

SHELLY: Half of who?

MARK: Us.

SHELLY: People with dicks?

MARK: Half of us do believe it.

SHELLY: You've taken a poll?

MARK: We walk around in a state of constant apology and guilt. "We're sorry, we're sorry." Like being born a man automatically puts us under a presumption of schmuckiness. "What do you expect from him? He's just a man after all. Doesn't know any better."

SHELLY: Mark, stop now. Please.

[*A beat.*]

MARK: All right. But—

SHELLY: "All right, but?"

MARK: I'm just suggesting it would be a little bit easier—if we're going to stay—

SHELLY: You said you wanted to stay.

MARK: I do want to stay. We're going to stay. But I would appreciate it if you didn't help her get out her anger at men in general by beating up on me in particular. I'm not the one who dumped her, if that indeed is what has happened.

SHELLY: All right, yes. I'll try.

MARK: Thank you.

SHELLY: It's just I'm at kind of a loss. What to say to her, what to do.

MARK: If you hadn't introduced them to begin with—

SHELLY: Excuse me?

MARK: Jill and Russ. If you hadn't tried to be the matchmaker—

SHELLY: I should have known better?

MARK: Well—

SHELLY: I should have foreseen—

MARK: Why not?

SHELLY: I don't see how—

MARK: The probability anyway.

SHELLY: That this would happen? How on earth could I have foreseen that this would happen?

MARK: Well, it does a lot, doesn't it? More often than not? People don't work out. People fall apart.

SHELLY: So because people mostly don't work, I shouldn't have introduced them?

MARK: Then she wouldn't look at us like it's our fault.

SHELLY: I didn't tell them to get married. I just thought they might show each other a good time.

MARK: Yeah, but even that phrase—"a good time."

SHELLY: What?

MARK: It implies, you know, something that will come to an end. A finite period. Why were you so eager?

SHELLY: Are you asking me to defend myself for trying to make people happy?

MARK: You can't make people happy.

SHELLY: Why not? You make me happy. Usually, generally.

MARK: I don't. I do things. I have good intentions. I try to be considerate and so forth and make choices. The fact is you could be happy or not. You *choose* to be happy. If you wanted to be *not* happy, the same things I do could just as easily piss you off royally. You could go to some support group or something and tell awful stories of how I did the exact same things and they would mostly go, "How do you stand it? Leave the creep."

SHELLY: Well, I'm not going to do that.

MARK: No?

SHELLY: Because I choose to be happy with you.

MARK: Is that true?

SHELLY: Yes.

MARK: You're not just being clever?

SHELLY: I don't *be* that kind of clever.

MARK: Wait a second: you're telling me we're happily married?

SHELLY: Yes.

MARK: Wow.

SHELLY: Yes.

[*A beat.*]

MARK: You want to go upstairs?

SHELLY: We can't do that either.

MARK: Really?

SHELLY: No. Not yet.

MARK: She's on the phone.

SHELLY: Yeah, but she could get off the phone at any time. She *would* get off the phone. If we went upstairs, she *would* get off the phone. And then she'd look for us. Maybe tap at our door. "You guys busy?"

MARK: That's true.

[JILL *enters during the following.*]

SHELLY: Later.

JILL: What later?

SHELLY: I'm going to rub his back.

JILL: Mmmm. Some fun, huh?

SHELLY: What?

JILL: Just what you were looking forward to, yes? Part of me thinks maybe I should leave—

SHELLY: No. And do what?

JILL: Just because my life has turned to puke, why should I junk up your week?

MARK: Hey, are we complaining?

JILL: Not to my face.

SHELLY: We don't want you to go.

JILL: That's the problem. I don't think I *can* go.

MARK: Of course you can't.

JILL: No, I'm talking about reasons of practicality. If Russ magically suddenly does decide to appear. If I've misread him. By the way, I'm going to have to leave money for the phone bill. My cell doesn't get reception here, so I've had to use the landline.

SHELLY: Your phone calls?

JILL: Nothing. Nobody knows where he is, or if they do, they're not telling me. And I understand that. I do. They're his friends mostly. Higher loyalties. Shared histories. If *I* were hiding out with *you,* and I asked you not to tell him I was here if he called, I'm sure you'd respect that. Gee, what do you think? Do you think I sound rational? Do you think I sound fair and reasonable and understanding?

MARK: Completely.

[JILL *picks up* MARK's *paperback.*]

JILL: Are you actually reading this?

MARK: Yes, I believe I am.

[*She puts it down.*]

JILL: What we should do, probably, is rent a video. Something awful. Something we can mock. You ever see *Return to Peyton Place*?

MARK: No.

JILL: It was on one of the cable channels. Russ and I watched it. All these incredible archaic 1950s values topped off with fifties hair and paperback versions of Freud. So-and-so's shocking secret. The scandal that rocked a town.

MARK: Which was?

JILL: Probably somebody slept with somebody they weren't supposed to. Isn't that what it always is? Actually, it's almost quaint. Looking at what was supposed to shocking, daring. Kind of a nostalgia rush. Like Jane Russell's boobs in that western.

MARK: *The Outlaw.*

JILL [*to* SHELLY]: Trust a man to remember that, huh?

[MARK *looks at* SHELLY *pointedly.* JILL *doesn't notice.*]

Sometimes I think—you know, to go back to a world where Jane Russell's cleavage was shocking. Who could be shocked by that today, right? Hell, you see more boobs today in *Disney* movies. Jessica Rabbit.

MARK: I read someplace that he was an ass man.

JILL: Who?

MARK: Disney. That if you look at a lot of the cartoons, you'll see that there's a lot of fanny patting.

JILL: Are you saying Disney had a secret lust for Minnie Mouse?

MARK: Of course, that's exactly what I'm saying.

JILL: Then what *are* you saying?

MARK: Just thought I'd toss in a little ancillary trivia.

JILL: That Disney was an ass man.

MARK: That's what I read. Or heard.

JILL: What does this have to do with what we were discussing?

MARK: Were we discussing something? Something in particular?

JILL: I thought we were. I was making a point, and I don't usually make points if I'm not discussing something. But then you jump in with that Jane Russell thing—

MARK: I didn't bring up Jane Russell. You brought up Jane Russell.

JILL: You brought up Minnie Mouse's ass.

MARK: I brought up Walt Disney.

JILL: Yeah, why did you do that?

MARK: I'm sorry.

JILL: Well, you should be. What does it matter, really, what Walt Disney was? I mean, he's gone, and he's left behind all these wonderful films, so why do you have to attack him?

MARK: Is that what I was doing?

JILL: You called him an ass man.

MARK: You think that was an attack?

JILL: You think that was a compliment?

MARK: I think it's just a comment. With no particular value attached.

JILL: Sometimes I think it would be nice to put up a fence around people and they would be, like, protected people. No matter what you dug up about them, we don't want to know. Like Disney. I don't want to know. Or that stuff about Errol Flynn maybe being a Nazi spy. Or Joan Crawford and the coat hangers. Or whatever Chaplin was supposed to have done. Leave it alone, you know? Leave it alone. What's going to be helped by learning shitty things about people like that? All it does is make you feel like a fool for having enjoyed their stuff. Like you watch this great comedy and somebody tells you this guy who, even though he's been dead fifty years, is making you laugh—but somebody tells you, "Yeah, but did you know he was a drunk and a child molester and he sent Christmas cards to Hitler?" Spoilsports.

MARK: So you're proposing legislation?

JILL: Sure, why not? There's the Endangered Species Act, so why not—

MARK: The Endangered Celebrities Act?

JILL: Not just celebrities. Martin Luther King. Isn't there a point where the good stuff they've done outweighs the smaller shit?

MARK: What do you think, Shelly?

SHELLY [who hasn't been paying attention]: Huh?

MARK: What do you think?

SHELLY: I guess I agree.

JILL: What do you agree with?

SHELLY: That it's a shame that people who've done good things—I mean basically what you said.

MARK: But here's the problem.

JILL: OK, let's hear it.

MARK: Are you saying that people who've done really good things, we should excuse the bad things they do?

JILL: Where's your problem?

MARK: Well, someone might get the idea that you can get a free ride on the shit you do if you do a lot of good stuff. I mean, it could be interpreted as a license. "Oh, I cured cancer, so it's OK for me to rob a convenience store." "Oh, she's a great actress so she can bust up anybody else's marriage she wants to."

JILL: So you're saying you would have given Gandhi a parking ticket.

MARK: I don't think Gandhi owned a car.

JILL: I'm talking about the principle—

MARK: If you're asking me if I think there should be special rules for a certain class of people, no I don't think there should be special rules. I don't think being a celebrity should protect someone from the consequences of behaving badly.

JILL: No, see, this is what you don't get. I'm not talking about *them.* I'm not talking about protecting *them.* I'm talking about protecting *us.*

MARK: What from?

SHELLY: Disillusion.

JILL: See? She gets it. Your wife gets it. Sometimes the heart only can take so much. You don't want more bad news. Especially unnecessary bad news. Stuff that you can't change. I can't change that Errol Flynn was a Nazi spy, if he was. But knowing that changes me. It makes me not be able to enjoy *Robin Hood.* And I'd rather enjoy *Robin Hood* than know something I can't change.

MARK: You'd rather not know.

JILL: I'd rather not know.

MARK: So why have you been on the phone the past hour and a half?

SHELLY: Mark.

[*A beat.*]

JILL: Thank you. That was cute.

MARK: I shouldn't have said that.

JILL: It's not the same thing.

MARK: No, it isn't.

JILL: Russ isn't a celebrity.

MARK: No. What I said was dumb. I apologize.

[*A beat.*]

SHELLY: You said something about renting a video. Is that what you'd like to do?

JILL: I don't know. That sound like fun to you?

SHELLY: Could be OK.

JILL: Where would I go around here?

SHELLY: I think there's a video joint on the main drag. What do you say I go with you?

JILL: No, I'd like to do this by myself. I don't want another opinion in there, because I really intend to rent something terrible.

SHELLY: You'd feel inhibited?

JILL: Yeah. Maybe a monster movie.

SHELLY: OK, but not one of the new ones with the really convincing gore. One of the old ones from the fifties.

JILL: Vincent Price.

SHELLY: I haven't seen one of those in years.

JILL [*to* MARK]: And if you know something nasty about Vincent Price, I don't want to hear it.

MARK: I hear he was a gentleman and a humanitarian.

JILL: Good. And I could get some microwave popcorn. Does that idea appeal?

SHELLY: Sounds good to me.

JILL: I feel pathetic.

SHELLY: You aren't.

JILL: Good, I'm reassured. Oh, Christ.

[JILL *begins to cry.* SHELLY *holds her as* MARK *stays put. A beat.*]

MARK: There, there.

[SHELLY *shoots him a look.* MARK *shrugs. Fade out.*]

SCENE 3

[*Night. Moonlight.* JILL *enters from around the house.*]

JILL [*talking to someone behind her*]: Around this way. Watch your step.

[GLEN, *a casually dressed man in his midforties, now appears behind her. She leads him to the deck. She signals that he should have a seat, puts down her purse, then goes inside the house.* GLEN, *a little ill at ease, looks around a little. Lights suddenly illuminate the deck, and* JILL *emerges with glasses and a bottle of wine.*]

A little light on the subject.

GLEN: Hi.

JILL: This is better, don't you think? At least we'll be able to hear each other.

GLEN: Ernie's usually isn't that noisy.

JILL: "Usually" being when weekend visitors aren't infesting the place?

GLEN: You aren't going to hear me complain about weekenders. Half the businesses in the area would probably go under if it weren't for them.

JILL: But it would be nice if they hadn't discovered Ernie's?

GLEN: Ernie isn't complaining. [*Smiling at her shyly*] And I'm not complaining tonight.

JILL: Wine?

GLEN: Sure.

[*She pours some for both of them. They drink. The sound of a couple's laughter from some distance.* GLEN *looks in the direction of where it came from.*]

Looks like a couple of your neighbors over there are having a midnight frolic.

JILL: Where?

GLEN [*pointing*]: Over there, see?

JILL [*laughing*]: Oh yes.

GLEN: Wonder where the expression came from? The "dipping" part I understand. But the "skinny"? That there is what I call middle-age-spread dipping.

[*Laughs. Slaps his stomach.*]

Like I should talk, right?

JILL: Well, they're having fun. Midnight splash. What the hell.

GLEN: I was in Los Angeles once, stayed with the older brother of a friend of mine. He was a techie at a record company.

JILL: Cool, man.

GLEN: Anyway, his place is up in Laurel Canyon, and one night he has some friends over. Including some ladies. He has a pool—

JILL: I think I see where this is going.

GLEN: Well, I was still young, shy.

JILL: So you didn't?

GLEN: No, actually, I did.

JILL: Your basic birthday suit?

GLEN: God, talk about self-conscious. But the thing is, when I take my glasses off—I'm real nearsighted—

JILL [*signaling that he's not wearing glasses*]: Contacts?

GLEN: Uh, yeah. So, I'm in this pool, but I can't see much of anything. Everything's a blur. And because everything's a blur for me, on some level I kind of believe—

JILL: Everything's a blur for them, too?

GLEN: If I can't see them, how can they see me?

JILL: Logical.

GLEN: I thought so.

JILL: Had a good time, huh?

GLEN: It was fun.

JILL: You were how old? A kid you said.

GLEN: Early twenties.

JILL: You even remember her name?

GLEN: Whose name?

JILL: Whoever she was you ended up with.

GLEN: No, that didn't happen.

JILL: No? All that potential for nooky and nothing? That's all there is to the story? Just that you paddled around bare-assed in the same pool with some women you couldn't see very well?

GLEN: It wasn't only women. But yeah, that was it.

JILL: But this was Laurel Canyon, right? Hippies with dough. Drugs, presumably.

GLEN: Some pot.

JILL: All that stuff working for you and all you did was the backstroke? That's what you call a good time?

GLEN: Actually, there was something nice about being able to all be naked together without feeling the necessity of taking it further. It's like a truce had been declared.

JILL: A truce? From what?

GLEN: The usual will-we, won't-we stuff. Not that anybody said anything like that. Made an announcement or anything. Just there was a sort of understanding.

JILL: A sex-free zone?

GLEN: Huh?

JILL: Like a nuclear-free zone, a sex-free zone.

GLEN: Like that, yeah. No pressure. No expectations. We all felt safe. Like we were all observing, well, like I said—a flag of truce.

JILL: I'd like to know where to get one of those.

GLEN: A flag of truce?

JILL: Sometimes to be able to call a time-out. To be able to say, "Hey, could we, for a little while, put all this crap aside?"

GLEN: You know *The Left Hand of Darkness*?

JILL: No, what's that?

GLEN: Science-fiction novel? Ursula Le Guin?

JILL: I'm not into science fiction. I don't mean that in a snobby way. It's just I haven't read anything later than H. G. Wells.

GLEN: Anyway, she wrote this book that's set on this alien world where there's only one sex.

JILL: One sex like it's the planet of the Amazons?

GLEN: No, it's more—well, they're not exactly hermaphrodites.

JILL: How do these aliens do it, reproduce? Or don't they?

GLEN: They have cycles.

JILL: Cycles?

GLEN: I'm not explaining this right.

JILL: No, cycles how, cycles how?

GLEN: OK, say you're an alien: one part of the cycle you've got male characteristics; the other part you're kind of female.

JILL: So how does the couple thing work?

GLEN: Say you're in an alien relationship—when you're sort of the man, your significant alien other is sort of the woman. A month or two later, it's the other way around.

JILL: Oh, so you take turns having periods. I like that idea.

GLEN: I don't remember the details of the story all that clearly, but I think the point of the book is, if everyone's male sometimes and female sometimes, what changes does this make in the society?

JILL: Probably, you know what, there'd be couples who would be perpetually out of sync—when one's a guy the other's a guy, when one's a woman—right?

GLEN: Sure, star-crossed lovers.

JILL: Though, see, with *my* luck, I'd be the one person in this alien world who had some kind of glandular condition and I'd get trapped somewhere in the cycle, *jammed*—end up combining the worst aspects of both sexes.

GLEN: Oh?

JILL: I'd probably still be stuck with childbirth, *and* I'd be an asshole.

GLEN: The divorce was pretty recent, huh?

JILL: You can tell?

GLEN: It takes one to know one.

JILL: You, too?

GLEN: Yup.

JILL: That was your ex, wasn't it?

GLEN: What was?

JILL: You were yelling at on the phone? At Ernie's?

GLEN: Was I yelling?

JILL: Maybe you were just trying to be heard over the crowd.

GLEN: That was probably it. It can get awfully noisy at Ernie's.

JILL: Particularly with us weekenders.

GLEN: I'm not complaining.

JILL: But I'm right? About who you were on the phone with?

GLEN: How'd you guess?

JILL: I heard the word "visitation."

GLEN: That's what I was supposed to be doing tonight.

JILL: Seeing your kid? Or is it kids?

GLEN: Kid. Son. Darryl.

JILL: So what went wrong?

GLEN: Well, I was running late, so I stopped by Ernie's to use the phone, to call and say that. But that I was on my way. And she says—

JILL: Your ex?

GLEN: She says, "On your way to what? He's not here." I say, "What do you mean, it's my weekend." She says it isn't and she'll check the calendar. And when she does, it turns out it *is* my weekend, but he's away on a sleepover so it'll have to be next weekend I see him. I say I'm busy next weekend. She says something about what it means if I'm too busy to see my son, and so on and so on.

JILL: And that's when you tried to be heard over the crowd.

GLEN: You weekenders are a noisy bunch.

JILL: Sorry about that.

GLEN: But that's how I ended up at Ernie's. [*Referring to the skinny-dippers*] Oh look, they're going in.

JILL: He could afford to cut back on those doughnuts. You like it around here?

GLEN: Oh yeah, this is nice.

JILL: No, I don't mean here, I mean *around* here.

GLEN: You mean to live?

JILL: The city's beginning to get to me. Maybe it's time for me to—

GLEN: I could clear out a corner in my trailer.

JILL: You actually live in a trailer?

GLEN: That's me, trailer trash.

JILL: City's for youngsters. For women it is anyway. Girls. When I was in my twenties, I'd go to a party, I'd know it was my option.

GLEN: What was?

JILL: If something was going to happen. I used to be pretty hot.

GLEN: What do you mean "used to be"?

JILL: A man would come up to me and I had this smile I would turn on. No, not turn on. Turn up.

GLEN: Turn up?

JILL: Like it was on a dimmer switch. Tease it up so it kinda flickered around the edges of my lips.

GLEN: And that smile said what?

JILL: "Tell me why I should care. Why you're worth it."

GLEN: You were a heartbreaker.

JILL: I was cruel. I really was. But you can't get away with being cruel when you're pushing forty. Unless you have money. Then you can hire people to be cruel to. I don't have money. Not *that* kind of money. In case you were wondering.

GLEN: Hey, I'm out of here.

JILL: Men fifteen years ago I wouldn't have looked twice at, probably would have cut short—

GLEN: Back in your cruel days?

JILL: All of a sudden these men—with the thinning hair and the tummies creeping over the belts—they're the ones with the goods. And dames like me—we're a glut on the market.

GLEN: Don't talk like that.

JILL: No, I have a healthy opinion of myself. A healthy appreciation of my gifts. But the city is lousy with gifted ladies of a certain age. Straight, single guys, on the other hand—

GLEN: A rare commodity?

JILL: Sometimes I look around, try to find someone to fix up some of my divorced girlfriends with. Something even vaguely suitable. And I'd think, thank God I'm not one of them. How lucky I am. Was.

[*A beat.*]

You'd make out like crazy in the city.

GLEN: Is that so?

JILL: No, you really would. Straight, presentable, charming—

GLEN: Thank you.

JILL: I'm not kidding. Clean you up, put you in a decent jacket, you could write your own ticket. You've got talent, kid.

GLEN: Tell you what, you can be my personal manager.

JILL: Maybe I'll take you up on that.

GLEN: I thought you were going to move up here.

JILL: Into your trailer. That's right.

GLEN: Well, give me a few years. Maybe I'll give the city a shot.

JILL: Why the wait?

GLEN: Darryl.

JILL: Your son.

GLEN: Got to be around for my kid. If he needs to call me. His mother's crazy, you know.

JILL: I think so.

GLEN: Not a bad person exactly, but her wheel's definitely slipping off the axle. He needs to know he's got one parent he can depend on. Till he takes off for college anyway.

JILL: What's that—four years? Five?

GLEN: About.

JILL: You let me know when. Course, I reserve the right of first refusal. Kidding. What do you do anyway? You a teacher? You talk like a teacher.

GLEN: I've done some different things. These days, I'm mostly a carpenter. Cabinet work. Building decks like this one.

JILL: And how *is* this deck? Your professional opinion.

GLEN: Good job.

JILL: I work with carpenters sometimes.

GLEN: Really, how?

JILL: If I need something built for a function.

GLEN: A function? What do you—

JILL: I'm a partner at Iris Broder Promotions.

GLEN: And that is—

JILL: Events planning.

GLEN: And that is—

JILL: Say you've got a daughter's getting married and five, six hundred grand to do it up right.

GLEN: Five, six hundred grand?

JILL: Hey, I know one topped a million two.

GLEN: So you do what?

JILL: Conceptualize, organize, schedule. If we're doing something on a gypsy theme, maybe I'll fly violinists in from Budapest. Or if I need a gazebo to be built in the ballroom at the Saint Regis, I'll work with designers. Keep an eye on construction.

GLEN: Carpenters.

JILL: And electricians, yeah. Though I don't really deal directly at that level. That's for the person I've brought in to supervise to handle. And then, you know, photographers. Sometimes it's on a level where there's press to deal with.

GLEN: Are there enough weddings to make a living at this?

JILL: Not just weddings. Benefits. *Some*body has to plan Carnegie Hall's hundredth birthday. These things don't take care of themselves. *Some*body has to plan when Queen so-and-so of Pottsylvania comes to visit.

GLEN: And you're that somebody?

JILL: Well, not those particular gigs, but stuff like that. It's like being a producer.

GLEN: A lot of people work on these things, huh?

JILL: For the big projects, it can go north of a hundred.

GLEN: And you're the boss.

JILL: Oh, I don't know.

GLEN: You said you hire people—

JILL: Some.

GLEN: And you can fire them.

JILL: Yeah.

GLEN [*making his case*]: You're the boss.

JILL: I'm *a* boss.

GLEN: *Do* you fire people?

JILL: I try to hire the right people to begin with so I don't have to.

GLEN: But you *have* fired people?

JILL: Part of the job.

GLEN: You set standards, and if people don't meet them—

JILL: First, maybe a warning shot over their head.

GLEN: A touch of the whip?

JILL: Just to get them focused. Mostly it works.

GLEN: But sometimes—

[*He signals, "out of there."*]

JILL: Part of the job.

GLEN: And if you fire them from one job, you're not likely to hire them for another.

JILL: No.

GLEN: So when you're in the neighborhood, people are on their best behavior.

JILL: Yes, I inspire fear. No, I'm pretty easy to get along with. Long as you do your job.

GLEN: I'll remember that.

JILL: Doing this kind of work can spoil you. You make a decision, you tell people the way you want it—

GLEN: They do it.

JILL: But outside of work . . . People have this annoying tendency to do what *they* want to do.

GLEN: And you can't fire them.

JILL: There are days I'd like to. Like my mother. She'd open an envelope from me, there's this pink slip, maybe a little handwritten note. "Thanks for all your hard work, but we're downsizing the family. Best of luck in your future parenting career."

GLEN: Well, I don't know what you'd do up here.

JILL: No?

GLEN: I don't guess there's much money to be made planning events in these parts. Unless you wanted to organize the wet T-shirt competition at Ernie's.

JILL: I don't think I'm qualified.

GLEN: Well, you could pick up some bucks if you *won* the wet T-shirt competition.

JILL [*wryly*]: I don't think I'm qualified.

GLEN: So what brought you to Ernie's anyway?

JILL: Well, I went out to rent a video. But Friday night, the pickings are pretty thin. There I was, holding *The Mighty Ducks* in one hand and *Porky's III* in the other, seriously debating which was the better choice . . . Then I saw Ernie's through the window.

GLEN: So if the video selection had been better, you and I wouldn't have met.

JILL: Talk about fate.

GLEN: And I was right? The divorce is pretty recent?

JILL: So recent it hasn't happened yet. Part of the reason I'm here actually. Visiting with friends.

GLEN: That's who *you* called from the bar.

JILL: Didn't want them to worry about me. They're nice people.

GLEN: They have names?

JILL: Mark and Shelly. I knew Mark back in college. Actually, we lived together for a couple years after. Mark and me.

GLEN: What broke you up?

JILL: We were awfully young. Too young to be thinking about permanent. So, yeah, we broke up, thinking that maybe someday, after we had enough mileage, we'd check each other out again. And a year or two later—surprise, surprise—he met Shelly and they got married. And, you know, I wanted to dislike her. I really did. But somehow I couldn't manage it.

GLEN: You all ended up being friends?

JILL: Isn't that nauseating? Actually, she's the one who introduced me to Russell. My husband. My soon-to-be ex-husband.

GLEN: Breaking up's a bitch.

[*A beat.*]

Sometimes when I'm on the phone with her, just the sound of her voice—

JILL: Oh, yeah, right—

GLEN: For years, that was programmed into me. "That's the voice of the person I love."

JILL: Conditioned response?

GLEN: The sound triggers this wave of feeling—

JILL: Must be what ex-Catholics go through when they hear organ music.

GLEN: And then, right after that first wave of, "Oh, she's the person I love," there's a second wave—

JILL: —that says, "Hey, wait a minute."

GLEN: I would really like to know when that goes away. So that when I hear her voice, it's just another voice.

JILL: Do you think that ever happens?

GLEN: I sure hope it will. I've noticed it's changed the way I answer the phone.

JILL: How did you used to answer the phone?

GLEN [*lightly*]: Hello?

JILL: And now?

GLEN [*neutrally*]: Hello?

JILL: And that's why?

GLEN: Well, it could be her. Don't want to answer [*lightly*] "Hello?" if it's her.

JILL: You afraid that she'll think that you're happy?

GLEN: I say it that way and it's her, I have to do a whole readjustment thing.

JILL [*darkly*]: What—"Oh, it's you?"

GLEN: Like in music, a modulation to a different key.

JILL: Major to minor?

GLEN: I do the modulation too abruptly, she gets offended and pissed off. So I do this more neutral "Hello."

JILL: This leaves you positioned to modulate to whatever key you want.

GLEN: Maximum flexibility.

JILL: So it's like the doorbell rings, and you're looking through the peephole first.

GLEN: Well, we're grown-ups now. You can't be a grown-up and automatically assume that whatever comes over the phone is going to be good news.

JILL: Is that what being a grown-up means? Living in the expectation that you could be whacked at any time?

GLEN: Yeah. But there's some good stuff, too. Being able to stay up as late as you want. Not having to take phys ed. Not having to eat beets.

JILL: Not to mention you can run for president.

GLEN: Don't think that's an option for me.

JILL: Something scandalous in your past?

GLEN: Well, I did hold up a bank.

[*She laughs.*]

No, really.

JILL: You held up an actual bank?

GLEN: Over in Spring Hill, one town over that way.

JILL: You're serious.

GLEN: Uh-huh.

JILL: Wow.

GLEN: I used to do a little coaching for the high school track team.

JILL: What does that have to do with—

GLEN: Well, I was on the way to a practice session. I stopped in at the Spring Hill branch of my bank to pick up some cash. I'm standing in line, and I put my hand in my pocket and realize I have a starter's pistol with me.

JILL: So the idea just popped into your head.

GLEN: I get the money, no problem. I jump in my car and I'm driving away and I go about two blocks and I stop. And I think, "Did I just do what I think I did?" And I look down at the seat next to me and there's this money there. "Yeah, I guess I did."

JILL: "Oh shit?"

GLEN: So I get out of the car and I flag down a cop. What do I want, he asks me. I tell him that I've just done something I think he'd find of interest.

JILL: He must have gotten a kick out of that.

GLEN: Made his day. Made my year. Actually more like six months with good behavior. My behavior was very good. I was a model prisoner. The warden said so himself.

JILL: They put you away?

GLEN: Yes, they did.

JILL: But didn't they understand you'd flipped out?

GLEN: That's why it was only six months. Armed robbery charge, I could have still been in there. I think I got a pretty good deal actually.

JILL: Why'd you do it? Do you know?

GLEN: Well, some of it was money, obviously. The divorce was getting under way and that wasn't cheap. But I thought about it a lot afterwards—I had six months *to* think about it—and I think it was that so much of my life was stuff that was happening *to* me. Just me reacting to whatever garbage was being fired my way. A sustained defensive posture. And for a second there, with that pistol in my hand, I had the illusion that *I* was setting the agenda for once. What I did might have been stupid—*was* stupid—but it was an action I was taking.

JILL: Your *choice* to be stupid.

GLEN: Funny thing, my son—

JILL: Darryl?

GLEN: It's about the only thing he's shown me any respect for.

JILL: Holding up a bank?

GLEN: He's thirteen. Here.

[*He reaches for his wallet.*]

JILL: Picture time?

GLEN: Sorry if it's corny.

JILL: No, no, it's nice corny. Let's see—

[*She looks.*]

Yeah, that's a thirteen-year-old boy, all right. He'll grow out of that.

GLEN: You think?

JILL: *You* did.

GLEN: The divorce wasn't my idea.

JILL: Another guy?

GLEN: Mmmmm.

JILL: That must have done wonders for your ego.

GLEN: Made me stand real tall in my son's eyes. Thirteen years old—you have all these semiadult impulses and appetites, but you don't have the power to do anything about them. So you look around for someone to identify with who's got muscle.

JILL: Vin Diesel, the Rock, Spiderman.

GLEN: You sure don't look at a dad who couldn't hold the family together. That's the first job of a dad, and he thinks I blew it.

JILL: But robbing the bank—

GLEN: The most dumb-ass thing I've done in my life, and that's what he gives me points for.

JILL: Well, you know it's just a matter of time before he grows up and sees you clearly and maturely and learns to hate you for who you really are.

GLEN: You read about how kids take after their parents? For his sake I hope not.

JILL: Hey, you want to take a break from beating yourself up?

GLEN: And do what?

JILL: Well, I have an idea.

[*Over the following, she disappears through the door.*]

GLEN: Where you going?

JILL: Hold on. You'll see.

[*Slow, romantic music begins from offstage. She returns carrying the boom box it's coming from.*]

This should do it.

GLEN: Do what?

JILL: It's called atmosphere.

GLEN: Oh?

JILL: Or did you think I invited you out here to talk about social themes in genre fiction?

GLEN: I'd like to know why.

JILL: Why what?

GLEN: Me. Why me?

JILL: Are you complaining?

GLEN: No, not at all. But it would be nice if I could believe there was something about me in particular—

JILL: Well, that goes without saying.

GLEN: My eyes.

JILL: Yeah, that's it.

GLEN: It's one of my better features, my eyes.

JILL: That's what did it for me. I got the feeling there's all kinds of stuff going on behind there.

GLEN: You're very perceptive, you know that?

JILL: So I was right?

GLEN: Oh yeah, there's lots of stuff going on behind there.

JILL: Well sure. I'm not into, you know—

GLEN: Meaningless, anonymous sex?

JILL: Sure. It's too dangerous.

GLEN: If you had known I was a bank robber?

JILL: Well, it's not like you do it all the time. It's not like that's your vocation.

GLEN: No. Strictly amateur standing. I should tell you something.

JILL: What?

GLEN: I really haven't been with anybody else since my wife and I broke up. The divorce.

JILL: Me neither.

GLEN: Oh, well, then you understand.

JILL: We can take it real easy, if that's what you want.

GLEN: It's not that I'm made out of china.

JILL: No, I do understand. But while we're talking, if there's something you used to do with her—with your wife—in bed, you know?

GLEN: Like what?

JILL: Oh, scratch her head or something—like a habit thing—if you could do me the favor of not doing that with me.

GLEN: OK.

JILL: Tonight's going to be whatever it's going to be, but I would like it if it's me you're with, not that I'm a stand-in. Or a lie-in.

GLEN: You got it.

JILL: All right then.

GLEN: Shall my lawyer call your lawyer, draw up the contract?

JILL: Huh?

GLEN: A joke.

JILL: I don't understand it.

GLEN: We've just gone through this negotiation.

JILL [*laughing*]: Oh. Yes.

GLEN: I mean, we've basically decided what we're going to do and we haven't even touched each other.

JILL: We should get around to that.

GLEN: Break the ice a little.

JILL: Every journey begins with one step.

[*A beat.* GLEN *goes to her and kisses her.*]

GLEN: Hello.

JILL: Hello.

GLEN: This could work.

JILL: For tonight anyway.

[*She kisses him, then leads him into a dance. The door opens and* MARK *enters.*]

MARK: Jill—

JILL: Mark. I thought you guys were asleep.

MARK: Well, no.

JILL: We didn't wake you?

MARK: No.

[JILL *turns off the boom box.*]

JILL: Glen, this is Mark. One of the friends I was telling you about.

GLEN: Hello.

JILL: Where's Shelly?

MARK: Up in our room.

JILL [*to* GLEN]: Shelly is Mark's wife.

GLEN: That's right.

MARK: Jill, could I have a word with you for a second?

JILL: What kind of word?

MARK: Something to discuss.

GLEN: Why don't I hit the john?

MARK: Good idea. Inside and to the right.

GLEN: Got you.

[GLEN *exits into the house.* JILL *and* MARK *look at each other for a second.*]

JILL: What?

MARK: Do I need to say it?

JILL: You don't approve.

MARK: This is a mistake, Jill.

JILL: I'm very grateful for your assessment.

MARK: Not just my assessment.

JILL: Shelly's, too?

MARK: You know it's the wrong thing to do.

JILL: You can see deep in my heart, huh? You can tell this?

MARK: I don't need to see deep in your heart to know.

JILL: Mark, you're about to embarrass yourself.

MARK: I don't think so.

JILL: Mark, this is not a subject on which you are entitled to offer an opinion. Not one I have to take seriously anyway.

MARK: Look, I understand what's going on here. You're angry, you're hurt. Russ has behaved badly, but that doesn't mean it's a good idea for you to—

JILL: I thought you didn't like Russ—

MARK: I like Russ OK.

JILL [*continuing*]: So what are you doing, acting like a human chastity belt for him?

MARK: I'm not doing anything *for* him—

JILL: Is this you keeping faith with the code?

MARK: Code? What code?

JILL: One guy to another.

MARK: Oh, for Christ's sake—

JILL: Like you're bound to act as his stand-in?

MARK: This has nothing to do with him—

JILL: Then why are you getting involved?

MARK: It has to do with you.

JILL: What you think's best for me.

MARK: Yes.

JILL: Thank you. I'm touched. Butt out.

MARK: Jill—

JILL: You've proved how concerned you are about me.

MARK: What does that mean?

JILL: Think about it.

MARK: Let's not dig up ancient bullshit.

JILL: That's how you characterize it.

MARK: What's going on is not about what happened between you and me a hundred million years ago—

JILL: Oh, it's up to *you* what this is about?

MARK: What's going on is right here and now. This guy you've picked up.

JILL: How do you know he isn't an old friend I happened to meet?

MARK: He isn't.

JILL: How do you know?

MARK: He's not an old friend. You met him in a bar.

JILL: How do you know? Were you listening in?

MARK: It's obvious.

JILL: How?

MARK: I'm not blind.

JILL: Right now I wish you were. Blind *and* deaf.

MARK: Jill—

JILL: Not to mention mute.

MARK: You pick this guy up, you tell him a lot of lies—

JILL: What lies?

MARK: How you're almost divorced. That we suggested you come up to console you.

JILL: How would you like it if I put a glass to the wall and listened in on you and Shelly?

MARK: It wasn't a matter of putting a glass to the wall. That's our window up there.

JILL: And you couldn't close it out of respect for my privacy?

MARK: Jill, we're friends. This guy can't be important enough for you to risk screwing up our friendship.

JILL: Then why did you come out here, if he isn't that important?

MARK: I don't want to see you get—

JILL: Hurt? Is that what you were going to say?

MARK: All right, if you don't give a damn about yourself, then how about us?

JILL: What's it your concern? It isn't you he's going to sleep with.

MARK: Maybe Shelly and I don't want a stranger under our roof.

JILL: What do you mean your roof? You put up half for the week. Does putting up half make it yours?

MARK: We put up half under the assumption of what this week would be.

JILL: Yeah, well it isn't. So does that give you veto power?

MARK: It's Russ's money, too. He wouldn't approve of you doing this.

JILL: Russ no longer has power of approval. He gave that up when he defaulted this week. Anyway, he's probably out there boffing some bimbo even as we speak.

MARK: Well, if he is, that doesn't make it right.

JILL: Of course it doesn't make it right, but how is that relevant? The question is whether you and Shelly have the authority to tell me what I can do. You are not my parents or my legal guardians, so I submit you have no such authority.

MARK: You don't think we have any rights in this?

JILL: Not as regards my behavior.

MARK: You don't think Shelly and I have the right not to share an intimate environment with some guy we don't know, much less trust?

JILL: Then lock your door.

MARK: That's no answer.

JILL: I don't owe you an answer. You've turned into such a smug, arrogant, self-righteous jerk—

MARK: Call me names if you want to—

JILL: And I don't need your permission to call you names, thank you.

MARK: He's not staying here.

JILL: And how are you going to enforce that? You going to throw him out? Physically?

MARK: I will do what I have to.

JILL: Just a little clue to you, as a friend—you don't have the equipment to carry off the macho pose.

MARK: Is this what it all comes down to? You taking cheap shots at me?

JILL: Disillusioning, ain't it?

MARK: Jill, please.

JILL: Fuck off, Mark.

[*The sound of a car engine turning over.*]

What's that?

[*She runs around the side of the house, calling out.*]

Glen! Glen! Come back here! You dickless bastard!

[*The sound of the car driving away.* MARK *picks up her purse, takes out her keys. Hearing her returning, he puts the purse down in a place different than where he found it. She reenters, notices the purse is in a different place. She looks at him suspiciously.*]

Were you in my purse?

[*She looks in her purse. She looks up at* MARK.]

OK, hand them over.

MARK: Jill—

JILL: Give them to me now.

MARK: Don't you think you ought to—

[JILL *suddenly socks him one, knocking him on his ass. His hand flies open and the keys fall onto the deck.* JILL *scoops them up and runs off the deck and disappears offstage. The sound of her car starting and driving away.* MARK, *a little stunned, gets up as* SHELLY *emerges.*]

SHELLY: What?

MARK: Jesus, what a punch.

SHELLY: He hit you?

MARK: No, *she* did. She wanted her keys. Her car keys.

SHELLY: What about him? The guy?

MARK: He took off, drove away. Said he was going in to use the john and slipped out the front door. I think maybe he heard what was going on between Jill and me.

SHELLY: Wouldn't be surprised. I heard it and I was upstairs.

MARK: That's what she wanted her car keys for.

SHELLY: To chase after him?

MARK: I guess. I don't know. I can't believe it—she hit me. I haven't been hit since Gus Teddis nearly broke my nose in high school.

SHELLY: You aren't going to hold that against her.

MARK: Why not?

SHELLY: She's upset.

MARK: What if I got upset and walloped her?

SHELLY: That would be different.

MARK: Because I'm a guy? It's OK to punch out guys?

SHELLY: OK, come on, enough.

MARK: You think this is funny, don't you?

SHELLY: No, I don't. Do you want some help?

MARK: I don't need help.

SHELLY: Hey, I'm sorry.

MARK: Let's just go to bed, OK? Let's just get some sleep.

SHELLY: OK. Let me just pick up—

MARK: Don't pick up after her. It's her mess, she should pick up after herself.

SHELLY: Yes, but it's our stuff. Our glasses.

[*A beat.*]

MARK: Do what you want. I don't care.

[*He exits, leaving* SHELLY *alone on the deck. She hesitates for a second, then picks up the glasses and the hamper and exits into the house.*]

SCENE 4

[*The next morning.* SHELLY *is sitting on the deck, reading.* JILL *enters from around the side of the house. She doesn't step onto the deck but leans against the railing.*]

SHELLY: Hello, slugger.

JILL: Where's Mark?

SHELLY: In the shower.

JILL: How pissed is he?

SHELLY: On what scale of measurement?

JILL: Well, what would I have to do to get back into his good graces? A simple apology? Abject groveling? A blow job?

SHELLY: I don't think a blow job would do it.

JILL: Funny, it always used to.

SHELLY: Well, then you'd be stuck with the problem of getting back into *my* good graces. Or does that matter to you?

JILL: Of course it matters.

SHELLY: Is that so?

JILL: What makes you say—

SHELLY [*interrupting*]: Did you think that I would applaud your belting my husband? Did you think that this would endear you to me?

JILL: Sorry. I didn't mean to intrude on *your* prerogatives.

SHELLY: That's another joke, right?

JILL: Oh, lighten up. I didn't maim the guy. In a moment of anger—and I think with some justification—I took a little swing at him.

SHELLY: That little swing has produced a very colorful eye.

JILL: Well, I was frustrated.

SHELLY: If being frustrated justified taking swings at someone, you'd be in a wheelchair now.

JILL: Really?

SHELLY: You're not the easiest houseguest.

JILL: Excuse me, I paid my share for this week. I am your house*mate*. Not a guest.

SHELLY: All right, then don't make us treat you like one.

JILL: I'm not.

SHELLY: We came here to relax, not to look after—

JILL [*overlapping*]: Have I asked you to look after me?

SHELLY: Not in so many words.

JILL: Not in any words at all. Your company, your support, that's appreciated, but—

SHELLY [*overlapping*]: We see what you're going through—you're someone we care about.

JILL: So of course this deep wellspring of compassion licenses you to act like cops?

SHELLY: We're not doing that.

JILL [*overlapping*]: Mark took my keys. Out of my purse. My car keys. Went into my purse when my back was turned and confiscated them. Like he was the fucking highway patrol and I was a drunk. Or do you think that was right?

SHELLY: I'm not saying it was.

JILL: Or do you let him prowl through *your* purse?

SHELLY: Point taken.

JILL: Not to mention sticking his nose into my personal choices. Holding my keys hostage to deny me the *possibility* of choice. I asked him to give them back. He refused. What was I supposed to do?

SHELLY: No, I'm surprised you were so restrained. Especially when chairs were handy and you could have bashed him over the head.

JILL: That would have been excessive. That orange juice looks good.

SHELLY: Help yourself.

[JILL *steps onto the deck for the first time in the scene and pours some juice during the following.*]

JILL: I needed the keys quick if I was going to have any chance of catching up. I needed them.

SHELLY: And *did* you catch up with—what's his name?

JILL [*drinking*]: Yes. He's a nice guy.

SHELLY: Funny, last night I remember you yelling something—something about him being a dickless bastard.

JILL: Well, I was wrong. On both counts.

SHELLY: Uh-huh.

JILL: It's been a while since somebody made me feel like—since somebody looked at me differently than the way they'd look at, I don't know, a bar of used soap.

SHELLY: Last night you felt like new soap?

JILL: Do you want the graphic details?

SHELLY: Would any of them surprise me?

JILL: It was your basic standard-issue sex, and I make no apologies for enjoying it.

SHELLY: He's a nice guy.

JILL: He *is.*

SHELLY: Even if he is a bank robber.

JILL: He's not really a bank robber. Just—

SHELLY: Someone who robbed a bank.

JILL: Yeah.

SHELLY: There's a difference.

JILL: If you heard the whole story, you know that he just flipped out for a moment.

SHELLY: *He* was frustrated, too, right? He robs a bank, you deck my husband.

JILL: It's not the same—

SHELLY [*overlapping*]: No, sounds like you're made for each other.

JILL: It was about consolation. I cried a little on his shoulder, he cried a little on mine.

SHELLY: Another sensitive man.

JILL: It's not like this is the beginning of a great romance. There was no pretending that. We were what each other needed last night. Simple as that.

SHELLY: Then it's lucky you found each other.

JILL: I mean, come on, are you going to tell me you never in your life had a nice therapeutic fuck? I understand what's going on here, you know.

SHELLY: Enlighten me.

JILL: All of a sudden, I'm a threat.

SHELLY: You, a threat? To what?

JILL: You and Mark.

SHELLY: What?

JILL: Sure. Russ and I break up, suddenly you've got failure close up. Like lightning zapped us and you've got the smell of it in your nostrils. And if it could happen to us, if *we* could get zapped, who knows who could be zapped next?

SHELLY: Maybe we're more secure than you think.

JILL: Could you possibly be a little more smug?

SHELLY: I get the weirdest feeling that you want me to apologize to you for something. I can't for the life of me think what. Is it that I'm not miserable? Does misery really love company so much that if I'm not in pain you feel like I'm betraying you somehow? What would make you happier? If I confessed to you that I was having an affair? Or that he beat me or that we take turns having sex with the dog?

JILL: Enough. Sorry. It's just, yeah, it is a little oppressive being around people who get along as well as you guys.

SHELLY: It's not all *Brady Bunch*.

JILL: No, but still you've got something that seems to work. And here I am on the verge of—oh Christ, I don't want to be one of that sad-eyed crowd of disconnected ladies. I don't want to have to learn how to say, "No, I really *enjoy* having my own space." Talking about how much reading I get done. And how *much* I've learned about myself by living alone. I know enough about myself to know that I don't want to know all that much more.

SHELLY: Oh, come on, Jill—

JILL: Loneliness is not an opportunity. It is not a growing experience. It's just fucking lonely.

SHELLY: Well, don't give up so quickly.

JILL: It's not a matter of *my* giving up. You're forgetting, Russ has taken off—

SHELLY: Actually, he called.

[*A beat.*]

JILL: What?

SHELLY: Russ. He called this morning. He said he'd been trying to reach you on your cell but he wasn't getting through. I told him about the hassle with the reception.

JILL: He called here?

SHELLY: Yes. And I answered.

[*A beat.*]

JILL: What did he say?

SHELLY: Well, he asked for you.

JILL: What did you say?

SHELLY: That you were off with a bank robber enjoying some standard-issue sex.

JILL: Please—

SHELLY: I said you went for a drive, you said to think things through.

JILL: And?

SHELLY: He asked how you were.

JILL: Do I have to pull this out of you word by word?

SHELLY: OK, he said he thought maybe he'd screwed up big-time.

JILL: So, I was right. There *is* somebody else?

SHELLY: That was the pretty clear implication—

JILL: Who?

SHELLY: I didn't press him on it.

JILL: I'll bet it's Nancy Latham. I'll just bet it's Nancy Latham. She's got tits and whenever we're at a party together she tells me how lucky I am.

SHELLY: He didn't say. And if I were you, when he gets here I wouldn't bring it up.

JILL: Wait, wait, hold on. When he gets here? He's coming here?

SHELLY: That's part of why he called. To say that he was on his way up. To make sure you'd be here to come up to.

JILL: When?

SHELLY: He's driving from the city. That's—what?—a little less than a two-hour drive? And he called, I guess forty-five minutes ago.

JILL: You told him that it was OK?

SHELLY: It's not my place to say whether it's OK or not. He has a share in this house this week, he has the right—

JILL: And besides, since he's an old friend of yours—

SHELLY: Excuse me, but what do you think you're saying?

JILL: Sorry, sorry, sorry.

SHELLY: I was under the impression you'd like him back. Am I wrong? That you don't want to be—"disconnected" I think is what you—

JILL: Yeah, but on what terms?

SHELLY: Well, I guess that's what you two have to talk about. I am not offering myself as a mediator or a counselor. But my completely unsolicited opinion: it's worth a try. In my experience, sometimes the difference between something working and not working can be whether one person is smart enough not to say something they have every right to say but that could only do damage.

JILL: That one person in this case being me?

SHELLY: Just because you have ammunition doesn't mean you have to use it. Do you want to score every point you can score, or do you want to—

JILL: OK, OK, I get the drift. I do.

SHELLY: I'd *prefer* it if you two stay together. I get tired of penciling in corrections in my phone book.

JILL: So we should stay together as a favor to you. Aside from any cornball considerations like love.

SHELLY: Hey, have you heard me use the word?

JILL: Did he sound miserable?

SHELLY: Russ?

JILL: Tell me he sounded miserable.

SHELLY: Do you want me to lie?

JILL: Do you have to?

SHELLY: No. Not really.

JILL: You've known him. You've known him for years.

SHELLY: And it's on the basis of that I think it's worth it.

JILL: God, I'm so confused.

[MARK *enters through the door wearing a bathrobe. He indeed has a shiner.*]

You're out of the shower.

MARK: There's still plenty of hot water. In case *you're* thinking of taking a shower. Which personally I would recommend.

SHELLY [*cautioning*]: Mark—

MARK [*to* SHELLY]: Don't you think that would be a good idea? You did tell her that Russ is on his way over.

JILL: I heard, yes.

MARK: Not that your hygiene is my business—

SHELLY: Mark, please—

JILL: Look, you're pissed and you have a right to be.

MARK: Yes, I do.

JILL: I shouldn't have slugged you.

MARK: Don't you think it would be better now if I *hadn't* given you the keys?

JILL: Why can't we say the whole thing was real unfortunate and move forward?

MARK: Here's the thing about that word "unfortunate": It implies that fortune—luck, happenstance—had something to do with what went on. That events were somehow outside your control. You didn't *do* anything. Things *happened* to you. You didn't make any choices. This huge boulder of circumstance bore down on you and poor you, you just couldn't get out of the way.

JILL: What is this—the relay scolding team? Shelly already worked me over pretty good, you know.

SHELLY: I did, Mark. I spanked her good.

JILL: And I am sorry I hit you.

MARK: Fuck being hit. Who cares? Fine. It doesn't matter. That really doesn't matter. The bigger thing that I'm concerned about is Russ is going to show up pretty soon and you're going to ask us not to say anything.

SHELLY: Why should we say anything?

JILL: Why should you say anything?

SHELLY: When he called and asked for her, I said she was upset and took her car out. I did not lie to him.

MARK: Oh no, it's not lying to not say something. I see. It's not lying.

JILL: Mark, what is your problem?

MARK: My problem is that you went out and spent the night with this guy.

JILL: You don't know that. You don't know what I did. You're assuming.

MARK: Oh, give me credit, I'm assuming right.

JILL: But you don't know. So if you don't know—

MARK: Then what's your story? After you punched me and took the keys? Where did you go? What did you do?

JILL: I don't have to tell you that. Look, if I don't say anything, then you don't know anything, and then you don't have to lie.

MARK: Deniability, huh?

JILL: You self-righteous son of a bitch, why are you doing this? Why are you attacking me?

MARK [*raising his voice for the first time*]: Because you did the wrong thing! You did the wrong thing! What you did was wrong! It was not the correct thing to do!

JILL: And you never did anything like this? You never picked up somebody? You never . . . With somebody you met in a bar or at a party?

MARK: Not while I was married.

JILL: Well, last night I didn't know whether or not I was still married. I did not know that.

MARK: So you don't know where you stand for a few hours and that gives you license to—

JILL [*overlapping*]: Why can Russ go off with somebody and I can't?

MARK: I'm not suggesting that he can—

JILL: I don't see you hollering about Russ.

MARK: Russ isn't here for me to holler at.

JILL: Like you would.

SHELLY: Time out! Time out! Can I ask a simple—what are we going to do when Russ gets here?

MARK [*at the top of his lungs*]: *Good question! Just* what I'm asking!

[*A beat.*]

SHELLY: I want to apologize for my husband.

MARK: You haven't got the right to apologize for me. If I do something wrong, it's up to me to apologize. And I'm not, and I won't.

[*A beat.*]

SHELLY [*gently*]: Jill, why don't you go inside? Do what you have to do.

JILL [*nearing tears*]: Shelly, please don't let him—

SHELLY: Don't worry.

JILL: Please.

SHELLY: Go inside now. Take care of yourself. Go on.

[JILL *hesitates, then goes inside. A beat.* SHELLY *turns on* MARK.]

I'm not recognizing you.

[*A beat.*]

MARK: What do you propose?

SHELLY: That we give them a chance. Jesus Christ, it's hard enough for people to manage. Why do you have to make it harder?

MARK: And so they make up—

SHELLY: I hope they do—

MARK: And what? We just go on? The four of us? Dinners, drinks, arguing about the op-ed page like nothing's happened? How are we supposed to do that?

SHELLY: We just will. Get over it. Live with it. There's a friend of yours that called me one night when his wife was out of town, told me he wasn't wearing anything, and could I picture that? You think I don't think of that every time I see him?

MARK: Who?

SHELLY: I'm not going to tell you. Forget it. Get over it. It's meaningless.

MARK: I don't think it *is* meaningless. I'm sorry, I think this is exactly the stuff that does have meaning.

SHELLY: It must be awfully lonely for you—by yourself on top of that mountain.

MARK: I didn't think I was by myself. I thought that you and I basically believed the same things.

SHELLY: I thought so, too. I guess we've learned something.

MARK: I guess so.

[*A beat.*]

I've spent years feeling vaguely guilty about breaking up with her. And it always comes up. Not directly usually. Sometimes it's a joke. But—spoken or unspoken—the accusation that I'm responsible for what's become of her. If I hadn't called it quits all those years ago—

SHELLY: You're tired of it.

MARK: I'm real tired of it.

SHELLY: So this is what? You getting even?

MARK: No.

SHELLY: Are you sure?

[*A beat.*]

What if I tell you that she told me nothing happened?

MARK: Last night?

SHELLY: What if I tell you that she caught up with that guy, and he was so upset by you bursting in on them that he told her that it wasn't worth the trouble?

MARK: And she didn't come home until this morning?

SHELLY: She was angry, she was embarrassed. She slept in her car.

MARK: She'd rather that I think she spent the night with that character than tell me that?

SHELLY: Think about it.

MARK: But why would that be—

SHELLY: Think about it. You're a smart guy. You're a sensitive man. Think about it.

MARK: Well, I guess I can see how that—

SHELLY: You can't let her know that I told you. It's important to her.

MARK: She said this to you? That this is what happened?

SHELLY: Yes.

[*A beat.*]

MARK: OK.

[*A beat.*]

SHELLY: I figure tonight I can make the roast.
MARK: Yeah, that sounds good. That could work.

[*Fade out.*]

BLUFF

—for Lanford Wilson

A word about dedications.

I have dedicated a couple of plays to the women who were gracing me with their company at the time of their composition (including my ex-wife). I have dedicated other plays to actors for whom I was intending to provide parts. In other cases, I have dedicated plays to people to thank them for kindnesses shown or to express appreciation for happy collaborations from the past. This dedication is motivated by something different.

Lanford isn't a particularly close friend of mine. I have known him since that day I approached him during the first run of *Hot L Baltimore*, and over the years we have had a few conversations over cups of coffee or sitting on panels or in meetings. Still, I felt moved to dedicate this one to him. He thanked me but wondered why. And I told him that I was doing so to acknowledge the debt this play owes to his work.

Truth be told, there is nothing in here in terms of plot or character that has been lifted from his work. But two of his plays, *Lemon Sky* and the one-act *The Great Nebulae of the Orion*, introduced me to new theatrical possibilities, and I can't imagine having written this script without seeing those shows. Today it's popular to talk about metatheater, pieces that allow for a repertoire of techniques in which characters slip in and out of various levels of reality, sometimes playing scenes naturalistically and sometimes acknowledging and addressing the audience.

One passage in *Lemon Sky* is particularly striking: the lead character (named Alan and based on Lanford himself) sits chatting with a young woman he used to know and she shares with him—and the audience— the story of how she died in a stupid car accident. The young woman isn't played as a ghost—no spooky music, no eerie lighting effects. (In the effective film version, the two sit next to each other on stools in some unspecified bar.) Given that she is dead, the scene is not realistic, but the interaction is credible because we feel that this is just how this unstable young woman *would have* talked about her death if she were able to have a conversation with Alan.

I knew that I wanted *Bluff* to build to the point at which a person who is not physically present during a confrontation nevertheless is in the scene because the confrontation could only have happened given her presence in the adversaries' lives and thoughts. In order to have license to pull this off, I had to plant the license to play with theatrical time and space and to break the fourth wall earlier in the script. That such a thing could be accomplished without confusing the daylights out of the audience is something that was suggested by Lanford's remarkable plays.

I've seen a number of successful productions of this play, but the design that worked best for me was something that director Sandy Shinner, 78th Street Theatre Lab producer Eric Nightengale, and I improvised out of what was handy at 78th Street. The theater there has brick walls that we kept exposed. On either side and upstage, the actors sat on chairs in full view of the audience whenever they weren't involved in action. A large rectangular platform, maybe eighteen inches tall, sat on the stage at a modest angle, and the majority of the scenes were played on it. However, Georgia, never physically being present in New York, played all of her scenes off the platform. Also, the revolt of the Doubling Actress began with her on the platform playing the bar scene but brought her off the platform when she made a direct appeal to the audience and dealt with the Doubling Actor's attempt to mollify her.

Bluff premiered September 27, 1999, at the Victory Gardens Theater of Chicago (Dennis Zacek, artistic director) under the direction of Sandy Shinner. Scenery by Jack Magaw, costumes by Judith Lundberg, lighting by Rita Pietraszek, sound by Andre Pluess and Ben Sussman, and production stage management by Shane Spaulding, with the following cast:

Neal	Jon Cryer
Doubling Actress	Beth Lacke
Emily	Sarah Trigger
Doubling Actor	Jeff Parker
Georgia	Kristine Thatcher
Gene	Tim Grimm

Bluff was produced at the Shadowland Theatre in Ellenville, New York, in August 2000 under the direction of James Glossman, with the following cast:

Neal	Brendan Patrick Burke
Doubling Actress	Deb Hiett
Emily	Christina Zorich
Doubling Actor	John Henbest
Georgia	Linda Setzer
Gene	John Astin

Bluff received its New York premiere on March 10, 2006, as a coproduction of Artistic New Directions and the 78th Street Theatre Lab under the direction of Sandy Shinner, with the following cast:

Neal	Ean Sheehy
Doubling Actress	Michelle Best
Emily	Sarah Yorra
Doubling Actor	Luke McCloskey
Georgia	Kristine Niven
Gene	Bill Tatum

CHARACTERS

Neal
Emily
Georgia
Gene

The Doubling Actress plays Bonnie and Marta.
The Doubling Actor plays Loring and Fred.

[*The play is set in New York and in the meeting place between actors and audience. It begins with a ghost light onstage.* NEAL *enters and turns off the ghost light, takes it offstage. He,* BONNIE (*played by* DOUBLING ACTRESS) *and* EMILY *arrange themselves onstage.* NEAL *and* EMILY *are wearing winter coats. At* NEAL's *cue, the lights come up onstage.*]

NEAL [*to audience*]: Stan Getz is playing on the CD. Candles are throwing our shadows onto the walls and the ceiling.

BONNIE [*to audience*]: I like the candles. I take a last sip from my wine glass. "OK," I say.

NEAL: "OK?" I ask. I mean, I haven't asked a question.

BONNIE: I raise a single finger to my lips.

NEAL: She's wearing a blouse, which she now unbuttons and discards.

BONNIE: "Your turn," I say. He's wearing a shirt, which he now unbuttons and discards.

NEAL: She smiles and, in one smooth motion, she removes—

BONNIE: My bra. I step forward and press myself against him.

NEAL: I see no reason to object.

EMILY [*to audience*]: Four blocks away, I'm saying good night to some friends in Weaver's. A place in the Twenties. A birthday drink with a friend. Her birthday, not mine. She's decided to stay, but I'd like to get to bed early tonight. So, yes, good night, good night, and I step out of Weaver's and climb the stairs up to the street.

NEAL: We're making our way to my bedroom.

BONNIE: We're kissing—

NEAL: And at the same time she's undoing my belt.

EMILY: It's November. The air is crisp. I can hear the thump of the bass notes from the loudspeakers pound through the closed door behind me. I begin to walk in the direction of the subway.

NEAL: She's just pulled my belt out of the loops when—

LORING [*played by* DOUBLING ACTOR, *entering, to audience*]: A scream.

NEAL: Outside my window.

EMILY: From around the corner.

BONNIE: He steps back from me and goes to the window.

NEAL: Out on the street, three guys are beating the crap out of someone. I open my front closet, pull out a jacket and a baseball bat, and slam out of my apartment—

BONNIE [*to* NEAL]: Where you going?

NEAL: I barrel down the stairs and out the front door and onto the street, yelling—

EMILY: I race around the corner.

NEAL: The three guys take off.

EMILY: They run right past me, actually.

LORING: I'm lying in the street.

NEAL: I'm standing over him.

EMILY [*to* NEAL]: What the hell are you doing to him?

NEAL [*to audience*]: Understandable. She sees me standing over someone, holding a bat.

EMILY: He corrects my wrong impression and suggests we take this guy on the street—

LORING: I can't remember my name.

EMILY: Up to his—

NEAL: Up to my—

EMILY: Apartment.

LORING: What the hell is my name?

NEAL: The idea being to clean him up, check out the damage.

BONNIE: I've been watching this out the window. I've got my clothes back on when they come in.

[NEAL *and* EMILY *ease* LORING *into a seat as* BONNIE *stands by.* EMILY *takes off her coat, puts it over a chair. Except for asides to audience as noted, the scene plays naturalistically.*]

EMILY [*to* NEAL]: Bathroom?

NEAL: That way.

[EMILY *passes* BONNIE, *who is standing and watching, on the way to the bathroom.*]

EMILY: Hi.

BONNIE: Hi. [*Approaching* NEAL *and* LORING; *reacting to* LORING's *injuries*] You know, you should just give them the money. It's not worth it.

NEAL: Bonnie, I don't think this has much to do with money.

BONNIE: So why—

NEAL: This is Chelsea. Who lives in Chelsea?

BONNIE: You—

NEAL [*overlapping*]: Besides me.

BONNIE [*getting it*]: Oh. Right. Jesus Christ. That's why they—Jesus. Animals.

[EMILY *returns with a cloth, some astringent retrieved from the medicine cabinet.*]

EMILY: OK, now, hold still.

[*As* NEAL *holds* LORING's *arm, gently keeping him on the chair,* EMILY *begins to clean* LORING's *face.*]

What's your name?

LORING: My name? That's a hard one right now.

NEAL: Does he have a wallet?

[EMILY *reaches for the inside pocket of* LORING's *jacket.*]

LORING: Hey—

EMILY: It's OK.

LORING: It is?

EMILY: Yes.

LORING: Oh, all right then.

[EMILY *pulls out* LORING's *wallet and looks at an identification card.*]

EMILY: Loring. Loring Foley. That you?

LORING: Yes. Yes, that's who I am. Right. Thank you.

NEAL: Where does he live?

EMILY: Weehawken.

LORING: That's my home. That's not where I live.

[*He laughs.*]

BONNIE: Sounds like he's getting it together.

NEAL: You getting it together?

LORING: Dizzy.

EMILY: He could have a concussion.

BONNIE [*to* LORING]: Do you think you have a concussion?

NEAL: How would he know?

BONNIE: Bite my head off, why don't you—

NEAL [*overlapping*]: Sorry, sorry.

BONNIE: But, Neal, if he's going to be OK—

NEAL: We don't know that yet.

BONNIE: Right.

NEAL: We can't just put a Band-Aid on and shove him back into the street.

BONNIE: Of course not. I didn't say that.

EMILY: Loring, is there someone we should call?

LORING: For what?

EMILY: Family?

LORING: No.

EMILY: You don't have any family?

LORING: They don't have me, you know?

EMILY: What about a friend?

LORING: It's late.

NEAL: They won't mind.

LORING: I don't want them to see me like this. Just give me a little—to sit for a few minutes.

EMILY: Loring—

LORING: I'll be all right. I just need to sit.

EMILY [*to* NEAL]: What do you think?

NEAL: Saint Vincent's is about five minutes away.

LORING [*crying*]: Saint Vincent's!

EMILY: A doctor has to look at you.

LORING: A minute. Dizzy.

[*A beat.*]

BONNIE: Neal, I think—

NEAL: Yes?

BONNIE: Tomorrow's a workday for me.

NEAL: Oh.

BONNIE: Yeah, I think I'll—

NEAL: Yeah, that might be a good idea. Sorry.

BONNIE: It's what happens.

NEAL: I'll call you.

BONNIE: Did I give you my number? I forget—

NEAL [*overlapping*]: Yes, I've got it. You gave it to me at the—

BONNIE: Right. That's right.

NEAL: I'm sorry.

BONNIE: Hey, what you're doing here? What kind of person would complain?

NEAL: I'll get you a cab.

BONNIE: That's OK, Neal. You've got two people you don't know here in your apartment, you should stay. I'll be all right. I'll be all right. See you around. [*To audience*] And that's it for this character. I'll be back later, playing someone else. Hold your breath.

[*She exits.*]

EMILY [*to* NEAL]: Why don't you take off your coat and stay a while?

NEAL: Take off my coat? OK.

[*He takes off his coat and drapes it over a chair. He has no shirt on and there is no belt in his pants.* EMILY *looks at him deadpan.*]

EMILY: One might draw conclusions.

NEAL: Really.

EMILY: Sorry.

NEAL: Give me a second?

[*He goes offstage.* EMILY *returns to cleaning* LORING'S *face.*]

LORING: How does my face look?

EMILY: Your lip's going to be puffy, and you've got some cuts—

LORING: Stitches?

EMILY: I'm not a doctor, but I think they took off before—

LORING [*overlapping*]: Oh!

EMILY: What?

LORING: My ring! My ring is gone!

EMILY: Your ring?

LORING: On my finger. It was—

EMILY: You're sure you had it on?

LORING: I never take it off. It was Joey's. He gave it to me in the hospital. I wouldn't take it off.

[NEAL *returns.*]

NEAL: What's wrong?

EMILY: His ring. He's lost his ring—

NEAL: You think they took it? Those guys?

LORING: I don't remember.

EMILY: Maybe it fell off.

LORING: It could be just lying there in the street.

[*He gets up, sways a little.* NEAL *reaches out to steady him.*]

NEAL: Don't you think you'd better—

LORING: No, I've got to go down. I've got to find it.

[NEAL *and* EMILY *trade looks and put on their coats. Lights shift and they are outside with* LORING, *who is looking on the ground.*]

EMILY: What does it look like?

LORING: A silver band with a blue stone. It was a friend's. The last time I saw him, he gave it to me. It was the last thing—

NEAL: Right here's where I found you.

EMILY: There isn't any gutter here, so it couldn't have gone down—

LORING: It's not fair. It was the last thing—

EMILY: Wait a second.

[*She crosses the street, leans over, picks it up.*]

Silver band with blue stone.

LORING: Oh my God!

[*He runs to her and takes the ring, puts it onto his finger.*]

NEAL: OK, now, you've got to do something for us.

LORING: Do something?

NEAL: You've got to let us take you to the hospital so you can get checked out.

LORING: Well—

EMILY: He's right.

NEAL: Come on now.

LORING: But she said I look OK.

NEAL: Let's just make sure, all right?

EMILY [*to audience*]: And we take him to Saint Vincent's—

NEAL: We're in the waiting room while they look him over.

EMILY: Good thing you don't play tennis.

NEAL: I'm sorry?

EMILY: A tennis racket—not as scary as a bat.

NEAL: I don't know what I would've done if they hadn't run. Made Tarzan sounds, I guess.

EMILY: That would have done it.

NEAL: That's pretty much my inventory of—

EMILY [*overlapping*]: I'm Emily, by the way.

NEAL: Yes, I've been meaning to ask.

EMILY: I've been meaning to tell you.

NEAL: Neal.

EMILY: Yes, so she said.

NEAL: She?

EMILY: Bonnie, your, uh—

NEAL: My "uh"?

EMILY: You mind my asking a question?

NEAL: Something personal and private?

EMILY: What else is worth asking?

NEAL: No, she isn't.

EMILY: I didn't think so.

NEAL: We met tonight at a party.

EMILY: So, tonight was what?

NEAL: It never got to the "what" stage. Not quite.

EMILY: Hence your lack of shirt under the coat. And your lack of belt.

NEAL: They probably have a coffee machine around here.

EMILY: A couple of more questions. If you don't mind.

NEAL: Do I get to ask you some?

EMILY: Oh, is there something you want to know?

NEAL: Why you're asking me these questions.

EMILY: Maybe I'm curious as to what's what.

NEAL: And what use would you make of this information?

EMILY: A person can only act on the basis of what they believe circumstances to be.

NEAL: You're investigating circumstances.

EMILY: Yes.

NEAL: Should I then infer you are contemplating action of some sort?

EMILY: You're teasing me.

NEAL: You make it pretty hard for me not to.

EMILY: Did you say something about a coffee machine?

NEAL: I met Bonnie tonight at a party. I invited her back to my place for purposes I'm sure it won't strain your imagination to, uh—

EMILY: Imagine?

NEAL: Confirmation that this idea was agreeable to her was in the process of being—

EMILY: Expressed?

NEAL: Expressed, yes, when Loring started getting the shit beat out of him.

EMILY: Leading you to pick up your baseball bat.

NEAL: Well, even when you have a hard-on, sometimes priorities are clear.

EMILY [*not turning a hair*]: Good to know.

NEAL: And no, when I invited Bonnie to my place, it was not in the expectation that this would begin a substantial and meaningful chapter in my life. And she was pretty clear about her interests being strictly—

EMILY: Recreational?

NEAL [*nodding*]: Recreational.

EMILY: How do you discriminate, uh, distinguish between people with purely recreational potential and—

NEAL: And?

EMILY: Those with whom you—

NEAL: Well, how does it work for you? Say, you see somebody—you're interested or not on the basis of what?

[*A beat.*]

EMILY: I'm not going to say looks don't count. Not just looks, as in handsome or not. But bearing, demeanor.

NEAL: Poise?

EMILY: Poise, yes.

NEAL: And standing there without my shirt and belt, you thought I was poiseful?

EMILY: Oh yes.

NEAL: Are you seeing somebody or are you also in a recreational phase?

EMILY [*overlapping*]: Nothing's going on that would be a serious impediment.

NEAL: Dinner tomorrow night?

EMILY: I would like to make something clear: I am not a Bonnie.

[LORING *enters.*]

LORING [*to audience*]: I have to wear dark glasses for maybe a week, and I will end up with a little scar. But I got my ring back.

[*He smiles at* EMILY *and* NEAL. *They nod acknowledgment and* LORING *exits.*]

NEAL [*to audience*]: If you travel from one country to another, you know when you're crossing the border. There's a sign, of course. "You are entering the Sovereign State of Such and So." And sometimes some guards and a barrier. This side of the barrier, you're in *this* place and the flag has these colors and the currency has these historic faces on them. And then you drive across a bridge and you're in *that* place. And you pull out a passport and they ask you if you have anything to declare. And they stamp your papers and wish you a nice visit, and on you go. And now the flag has different colors and there are other faces looking serious on your money. This is how you know—these are the things that confirm that where you are is not where you were. OK? But the signs that you've crossed over into new territory with another person, they aren't as well marked. Maybe you don't notice the change itself when it actually happens. It's not like suddenly you feel aglow or anything. I think maybe you just notice that something *has* changed. It's something you catch up to a little after the fact. Maybe you're starting to make plans, and in your mind the plans have the word *we* in them rather than *I*? Or maybe you find yourself reacting in a way differently than you would have before about—I don't know—a song. A song that once you thought was kind of stupid but now, because she likes it, you see all these levels of profundity and meaning in it. Like, what?—"Louie, Louie"?

EMILY: I don't see any levels of profundity in "Louie, Louie."

NEAL: I'm making an example.

EMILY: Well, you could make an example that's true. There is nothing in "Louie, Louie" that is in any way profound. That is the true glory of "Louie, Louie."

NEAL: OK.

EMILY: "Shim-bam-ba-doo-ah, I'm all shook up"—*that's* profound.

NEAL: Isn't it "Shim-*ba*-ba-doo-ah?"

EMILY: No, that's from the Twenty-second psalm.

NEAL: But, and the point I was trying to make before you—

EMILY: I'm a disruptive broad, aren't I?

NEAL: The point is that you realize something *has* changed *after* it's changed because of this.

EMILY: The change you're talking about is the way you feel about this other person.

NEAL: Yes.

EMILY: And you think if you feel it you have to declare it?

NEAL: I'm not saying I expect the other person to.

EMILY: Well, she won't.

NEAL: Is that because she doesn't want to declare or she doesn't have anything to declare?

[*A beat.*]

EMILY: Look, I'm not going to deny that something's happening here.

NEAL: Oh lady, you sweep me off my feet!

[*A beat.*]

EMILY: I'm not going to move into your place. I've seen your place. I've got more room.

NEAL: We could get our own place. One that we choose together.

EMILY: We wouldn't get as good a deal as I've got.

NEAL: But, you know, if I move into your place you'll always think of it as your place, not our place.

EMILY: And how is that bad?

NEAL [*to audience*]: I sublet my apartment to the niece of a friend going to NYU. The niece is, that is—going to NYU.

EMILY [*referring to audience*]: Do you think they care? You can have that closet.

NEAL: I can?

EMILY: I just said that you—what are you laughing—

NEAL: Nothing.

EMILY: Do you want another closet?

NEAL: I like the closet you have chosen for me fine. I think it is a handsome closet.

EMILY: It's just space, you know.

NEAL: I'm sure my clothes won't care where they live.

EMILY: Do I owe you an apology?

NEAL: No.

EMILY: I didn't think so.

NEAL: What side of the bed can I have?

EMILY: Have you ever lived with anybody?

NEAL: No. Have you?

EMILY: No.

NEAL: You think this is something we should be worried about?

EMILY: If one of us had a little more experience at this—

NEAL: If you think it would help, I could go live with someone else for a while first.

EMILY: There's an idea.

NEAL: Sure. Take notes.

EMILY: You wouldn't have to sleep with this other person, would you? The person you would be living with?

NEAL: Nah, I'm sure there are a lot of women in this city want a live-in guy who doesn't put out.

EMILY: If they knew it was in a good cause . . .

NEAL: Maybe where we are isn't so bad. We don't have to unlearn bad habits.

EMILY: Do you have bad habits? Things I should know about? What things about you should I know about?

NEAL: Isn't it enough for you to know I'm nuts about you?

EMILY [wincing]: Can we just—

NEAL: What?

EMILY: Can we just be together and not say a lot of this stuff?

NEAL: You prefer doing to saying?

EMILY: Pretty much.

NEAL: What if, in the process of doing, I can't help but say?

EMILY: OK, but in moderation.

NEAL: All right, but this is—and I'm being candid so you cannot mock me—

EMILY: Enough said, OK? If you don't mind.

NEAL: No, I don't mind.

EMILY: Good.

[She kisses him.]

NEAL [*to audience*]: My clothes and I move in, in April. In June, Emily is on the phone with another hospital. This one in California.

[GEORGIA, *a woman in her fifties or sixties wearing a hospital gown, enters and begins a phone conversation with* EMILY.]

GEORGIA [*to* EMILY]: Don't be silly.

EMILY: I could get some time off from work. [*To audience*] I help raise money for the Urban Appeal. Contributions are tax deductible, by the way. [*To* GEORGIA] I could take a week off, fly out.

GEORGIA: Thank you, honey, but no—I'm fine.

EMILY: I'm still not clear about what happened.

GEORGIA: I don't know, it's a vitamin thing.

EMILY: Vitamin?

GEORGIA: Too much of this, too little of that.

EMILY: And that put you into the hospital?

GEORGIA: Well, I got dizzy and fell down and got banged up a little. How did you find out I was here anyway?

EMILY: Noli called me.

GEORGIA: Noli should keep her nose on her own side of the fence.

EMILY: She did what you or Gene should have done. I was under the impression that I'm a member of this family. That somebody might think to call me about it when stuff that's important happens.

GEORGIA: But that's the point—it really isn't all that important.

EMILY: You're in the hospital.

GEORGIA: Lots of people are in the hospital. Why don't you call *them*?

EMILY: Lots of people aren't my mom.

GEORGIA: Well, right now, if you don't mind, your mom would like to go to the little girl's room, so—

EMILY: Is Gene there?

GEORGIA: Why?

EMILY: Put him on.

GEORGIA: Don't you give him a hard time.

EMILY: I want to talk to him.

GEORGIA: Gene?

[GENE, *in his fifties or sixties, appears.*]

She's going to give you a hard time.

[GEORGIA *exits.*]

GENE: What, did Noli call you?

EMILY: What is this about vitamins? She said something about this being about vitamins?

GENE: She's going to be all right.

EMILY: The way she talked, it sounded like scurvy.

GENE: She could pay better attention to what she eats.

EMILY: And what she drinks?

GENE: She tell you that?

EMILY: What do you think?

GENE: It's under control.

EMILY: Then why is she in the hospital?

GENE: She had an accident. Anybody can have an accident.

EMILY: But accidents are more likely to happen under certain circumstances.

[*A beat.*]

GENE: I'll be coming to New York for a convention about the first week of October. You be in town then?

EMILY: Yes.

GENE: See you then.

EMILY: Call me if there's anything I should—

GENE: I will.

[*He exits.* NEAL *has overheard some of* EMILY's *side of the conversation.*]

NEAL: What was that about vitamins?

EMILY: It's very difficult to meet your nutritional needs if your primary food group is vodka.

NEAL: Who was that you were on the phone with? After your mother?

EMILY: Gene.

NEAL: Who is he?

EMILY: He's married to my mother.

NEAL: Your stepfather?

EMILY: Technically.

NEAL: Technically?

EMILY: He's married to my mother.

NEAL: What, he married her after you were out of the house?

EMILY: No. I've told you about him.

NEAL: No. No, you haven't.

EMILY: He's married to my mom.

NEAL: Yes.

EMILY: His name is Gene.

NEAL: OK.

EMILY: He's a salesman. You'll meet him. You'll see.

[NEAL *moves upstage as* GENE *enters. He and* EMILY *pick up in the middle of a conversation.*]

GENE: Sadists and goofs.

EMILY: I don't know.

NEAL [*to audience*]: It's October now.

GENE: Oh sure. Just take a look.

EMILY: Where?

GENE: Movies, for instance.

EMILY: Oh, well, movies—

GENE: What?

EMILY: You don't expect in *movies*—that's not where you look for facts
　　or reality or anything—

GENE: No, that's my point.

EMILY: What is?

GENE: It's the impressions I'm talking about, not reality. The image.
　　When there's a pattern, you take a look at that. What it means.

EMILY: And the pattern here?

[NEAL *enters with drinks which he hands to them.*]

NEAL: What's the topic?

GENE: Sadists and goofs.

EMILY: Dentists.

NEAL: Of course.

GENE: Did you see that movie, that spy movie?

EMILY: Which one?

GENE: That British actor played a Nazi—

EMILY: Which actor?

NEAL: Which Nazi?

GENE: "Is it safe?"

NEAL: Dustin Hoffman.

GENE: He's not British.

NEAL: He was *in* it. Laurence Olivier was the Nazi.

GENE: That's right. And he's got Dustin Hoffman in the chair and he's holding a drill to his naked tooth, and he says, "Is it safe?"

EMILY: OK, so?

GENE: So what's your impression of Olivier in this picture? I'm not talking about acting, I'm talking about character.

EMILY: Impression?

GENE: Not exactly a nice guy, right?

EMILY: Well, he's a Nazi war criminal.

GENE: Yes, a Nazi war criminal and what else?

EMILY: I don't know.

GENE: What are we talking about here?

NEAL [*raising his hand like he's answering in class*]: Dentists.

GENE: A war criminal *and* a dentist. And what's the effect of that? To link the two in your mind.

EMILY: Oh, come on.

GENE: Come on what?

EMILY: A little far-fetched.

GENE: You wouldn't think so if you were a dentist. That movie is not big with dentists.

EMILY: Well, it's just one movie.

GENE: You want more? OK, how about *Little Shop of Horrors*—Steve Martin? And, what's the name of that book—*Couples*?

EMILY: *Couples*? Are you talking about the novel, Updike?

GENE: Yes.

EMILY: I didn't know you read Updike.

GENE: I read *Couples*. So?

EMILY: I'm just surprised.

GENE [*to* NEAL]: She doesn't think I read.

EMILY: I didn't say that.

GENE: I read all the time.

EMILY: I just didn't think John Updike would be your—

GENE: Speed?

EMILY: Did you like it?

GENE: I liked it OK. I mean, from the blurb on the cover, I thought it was going to be dirtier.

EMILY: You were saying—

GENE [*to* NEAL]: I love to tease her.

NEAL: No kidding.

EMILY: You were saying—

GENE: You remember the dentist in that? In *Couples*?

EMILY: It's been kind of a while.

GENE: Take my word for it, there's a dentist.

EMILY: And he's the villain?

GENE: Worse than that, he's an asshole. He is the asshole of the book. The way he's described—pink. Like a baby. Balding. And a liberal.

NEAL: That's a low blow.

GENE: Huh?

NEAL: Bad enough a dentist who's a war criminal, but a dentist who's pink and balding *and* a liberal!

GENE: Have you ever seen a movie or read a book where a dentist is a hero? Or a TV show? They do stuff about detectives and cops and newspaper reporters. But how about a single series where the hero is a dentist or an oral surgeon?

NEAL: Actually, I *do* know where there's a dentist who's a hero.

GENE: Yeah?

NEAL: *The Complaisant Lover.*

GENE: Never heard of it.

NEAL: It's by Graham Greene. This dentist ends up being the guy you sympathize with.

GENE: That doesn't count. Nobody's ever heard of it.

NEAL: I've heard of it. Does that make me nobody?

GENE [*to* EMILY]: Have *you* ever heard of it?

EMILY: Actually, no.

GENE: If *she* hasn't heard of it, how you going to expect a dentist to?

NEAL: I was just pointing to a case—

GENE: OK, we'll call it the exception that proves the rule. [*Looking out the window positioned downstage*] That building.

NEAL: Which?

GENE: The one that's going up. How high is it planned for?

EMILY: Too high.

GENE: Your view, the river?

EMILY: Will be a fond memory.

GENE: You going to get a discount?

EMILY: Discount?

GENE: Presumably when you rented, it was partially for the pleasure of a river view. That's part of what you're paying for.

EMILY: It's not the landlord's fault they're putting up a building there.

GENE: So you're not doing anything about it?

EMILY: What do you suggest?

NEAL: I was thinking of casting a spell and moving it to the Meadowlands.

GENE: Well, that's a practical plan.

EMILY [*bringing back the subject*]: Dentists. No movies they're heroes?

GENE: Right. It's true.

EMILY: But, come on, how would you make a movie about a heroic dentist? Where would the drama be? The extraction of a wisdom tooth? A life-threatening root canal?

GENE: You think dentists don't lead dramatic lives? You think they don't have dreams and frustrations? You think they don't have accomplishments to be proud of? If you had a tooth that was giving you misery, who would you turn to—Clint Eastwood or a good dentist?

NEAL: Well, Clint—he could punch it out.

GENE: What I'm saying, the point I'm trying to make—it's no accident I'm doing well. I've got the respect of the people I'm dealing with because I give them the respect they are due. Due from you, too, kiddo. Dental supplies paid for your ballet lessons and your braces and college.

EMILY [*to audience*]: I'm biting my tongue.

GENE: I remember seeing your endorsement on a lot of canceled checks.

EMILY: Here we go.

GENE: Hey, you want to ride the pony on Saturday?

NEAL: What?

EMILY: Private joke.

GENE [*to audience*]: First time we laid eyes on each other.

EMILY: Oh, for God's sake—

GENE: I think it's relevant. Come on. [*To audience*] She's nine years old.

NEAL [*moving to the side*]: I'll just give you a little room.

GENE [*to* EMILY]: Don't play it cute.

EMILY: OK, nine.

[GEORGIA *enters, carrying a glass of wine. She moves between* GENE *and* EMILY.]

GEORGIA: She's not usually like this.

GENE: That's OK.

GEORGIA: Emily—

GENE: She's shy.

GEORGIA: Young lady, where are your manners?

GENE: I understand.

GEORGIA: Young lady, be polite. Don't make me ashamed of you. This is a friend of mine. Say hello. This is my friend. This is Gene.

GENE: Maybe now isn't a good time. Maybe another day—

GEORGIA: No. She has to learn. Emily, if you want to ride the pony on Saturday—

GENE: Don't threaten her—

GEORGIA: Excuse me. This is my daughter. I will deal with her the way I—

GENE [*overlapping*]: She's scared.

GEORGIA: She's been brought up to know what good behavior is.

EMILY: Go away.

GEORGIA: What? What did you say?

GENE: She doesn't mean anything.

EMILY: Go away. I don't like you.

GEORGIA: No pony.

EMILY: I don't care.

GENE [*to audience*]: That'll do it.

GEORGIA [*to* GENE]: Is that it? Am I done?

GENE: That was fine, darling.

GEORGIA [*to audience*]: And by the way, just so you don't think I'm some kind of ogre, I let her ride the pony anyway.

EMILY: Mom, a point of accuracy—

GEORGIA: What?

EMILY: You weren't carrying a glass.

GEORGIA: Excuse me?

EMILY: You weren't. Not that day. That was one of your—

GEORGIA: One of my?

EMILY: Good days.

GEORGIA: It's easier when I hold something. Now, if you'll excuse me, I was watching a movie. Fred Astaire. He was dancing on the ceiling. I had to put it on pause.

EMILY: OK.

[GEORGIA *exits.* EMILY *looks at* GENE.]

GENE: "Go away. I don't like you."

EMILY: Oh, for God's sake—I was nine. [*To audience*] Nine.

GENE: I know that. I *said* that.

EMILY: If we went back to when *you* were nine—

GENE: The only thing I'm suggesting is, if we don't always have Kodak moments, it's not entirely to be laid at my door. "Go away. I don't—"

EMILY: Yeah, yeah. Neal? Shall we pick it up?

NEAL: Ready. [*To audience*] He's just asked me what I do for a living. I consider lying.

GENE: Lawyer?

NEAL: Lawyer.

GENE: And you seemed like such a nice fella.

[NEAL *and* EMILY *exchange a look.*]

NEAL: So which one is your favorite?

GENE: Which one what?

NEAL: Lawyer joke. Is it the shark one? "Professional courtesy"?

GENE: That's a good one.

NEAL: Or, "How can you tell when a lawyer is lying"?

GENE: His lips are moving. I like that one, too.

NEAL: How about the one about the lawyer and the dentist?

GENE: That one I haven't heard. How does it—

NEAL [*overlapping*]: This lawyer walks into a bar, and he says, "Is there a dentist here?" And this man at the end of the bar says, "I'm a dentist." And the lawyer says, "Good, at least there's *one* person here everyone hates more than me." He's a pink, balding liberal by the way—the guy at the end of the bar.

[*A beat.*]

GENE: What kind of law?

NEAL: I was tempted to go into robbing the dead, but I settled on winning acquittals for the guilty.

[*A beat.*]

GENE [*to* EMILY]: So, we took this cruise. South Pacific.

EMILY: Oh yes, right, how was that?

GENE: Oh my God—food?

EMILY: I'll bet.

GENE: We'd stop at these islands, you know, for picnics or luaus or whatever they're called. So this one island, it's the pig on the spit and some kind of paste you eat with your fingers and these drinks made of fruits you've never heard of. You think you're drinking juice and the next thing you know you're—well, you're behaving in ways you hope nobody has a camera to get the evidence.

EMILY: You didn't let Mom get too—

GENE: I keep my eye out for your mom, don't worry. But who would've seen her? A bunch of housewives from Topeka who were as schnockered as she was? But this one island—big daylong bash. Lots of food, lots of those fruit drinks, it's pretty warm—

NEAL: The South Seas, sure—

GENE: Right. Well, it's time to go back onto the ship. Course, if it's warm and you've had a lot to drink, you're liable to take an unscheduled nap—the ship stewards are shaking people awake. "Time to go to your cabin, Mr. Packard." Grumble, grumble, they get up, stagger up, *lurch* up the plank. But this one woman, she won't wake up.

EMILY: She wasn't—

GENE: No, not dead, just dead to the world. So they're shaking her and she will not come to. So the social director—there's a schedule, they're supposed to be on their way soon—

EMILY: So?

GENE: This social director, he orders them to carry her aboard—the stewards. The only problem is, we're talking about a woman for whom the word "ample" is insufficient. They bring out this stretcher and it takes four guys, they're heaving her up the gangway or whatever you call it. Huffing and puffing, sweating gallons, muttering words you can imagine. This broad, she's just out of it, snoring. They finally make it up to the top, they toss her onto a deck chair to sleep it off, the ship weighs anchor, and they set sail. Four or five hours later, all of a sudden there's this hollering. This woman. "You shitheads! You sons of bitches!" Turns out she doesn't belong to the ship. She lives on the island where we stopped. She's on the hill, looks down at the beach, sees all of us stuffing our faces, thinks, "Happy days, free eats." Came down to join the party. Next thing she knows, her perspective, she's been kidnapped. She doesn't care if the dance band plays the hustle every night, she wants off the boat.

EMILY: I can imagine.

NEAL: So, what did they do? With her? They turn around and take her back?

GENE: Turn around? This is a huge cruise ship. Turn around to take one person back? You have any idea how much that would cost? No, they took her to the next port and I guess they arranged for her to be sailed or helicoptered back. But that's not the point of the story.

EMILY: What is the point?

GENE: Well, there *is* none. Does there always have to be a point? I just think it's a hoot. The picture of those guys hauling her up the gang-way— [*To* NEAL] So what's your opinion?

NEAL: My opinion?

GENE: Legally. You're a lawyer. Who has a case here?

NEAL: Well, they can't charge her as a stowaway 'cause she didn't board the boat voluntarily. On the other hand, she did eat and drink stuff she wasn't supposed to, so I guess that's technically theft. Of course, who knows what laws would be relevant? If this happened on Pago Pago or something . . . Maybe it's the law on Pago Pago that it's OK to scarf up whatever food you can off the tourists.

GENE: So you wouldn't take the case.

NEAL: I haven't passed the Pago Pago bar exam.

GENE [*to audience*]: What's going on here, my opinion—this boy, Neal, he thought the story was funny.

NEAL [*to audience*]: Actually, yeah, pretty—

GENE [*to* NEAL]: But you can tell *she's* not amused, so you're not going to let on you did, 'cause then she'd think you were a jerk because you laughed at her jerky stepfather's story. But it's OK. No, it really is.

NEAL: Well, I'm glad to hear that.

GENE: We could get along if you want to. You and I.

NEAL: We're getting along.

GENE: Well, I *thought* we were.

NEAL: We are. We don't have to have the same taste in ties to get along.

[GENE *gives him a look, then goes back into the scene.*]

GENE: So what's the story with you two? I mean, you're living together.

EMILY: We're living together. Does it bother you?

GENE: It bothers your mom.

EMILY: She still lives in the fifties.

GENE: Ah, so her opinion doesn't matter. OK.

EMILY: I didn't say that.

GENE: It matters *less*?

EMILY: I didn't say that either.

GENE: I wish you'd tell me what you said so I'd know what you're saying. Or are you saying what you're saying in the *way* that you're saying so that I *won't* know? Is it a way of saying something without saying it so I can't say you said it? Or so that you can say you *didn't* say it?

EMILY: Huh?

GENE: "I didn't say that." You just said that. Twice.

EMILY: OK. What I meant to say—

GENE: I'm listening—

EMILY: What I meant to say is that Mom's values date from the fifties.

GENE: That's when she was a girl, yes.

EMILY: Of course I care about her opinion, of course I care about her feelings—

GENE: I hear a "but" coming, she's gonna say "but"—

EMILY: *However*—

GENE: Sneak.

EMILY: However, but, *notwithstanding*—

GENE: OK.

EMILY: Seeing as how her values were formed at a time when sexuality—when people's attitudes *toward* sexuality—

GENE: You mean shacking up?

EMILY: Screwing without a license, OK?

GENE: OK by me.

EMILY: All I'm saying is that attitudes have changed.

GENE: You betcha.

EMILY: They've changed and she—

GENE: She hasn't.

EMILY: No.

GENE: I'm not arguing with you. Screwing without a license, what the hell. Some of the best screwing is done without a license.

EMILY: You make it sound like driving a gypsy cab.

GENE: I'm talking strictly about your mother's perspective, and since we've established that this isn't worth wasting much concern over—

EMILY: Her values are not my values. I live my life by my own values.

GENE: Of course—who else's would you live by? Certainly not mine.

EMILY: Would you live by mine?

GENE: This screwing-without-a-license stuff is interesting.

EMILY: You get a kick out of saying that, don't you?

GENE: It's your phrase. You said it first.

EMILY: All right.

GENE: It's OK for you to say to me, but not for me to say to you?

EMILY: I said it once.

GENE: Once is tasteful. I get it.

EMILY: So, how long you in town for?

GENE: The conference is this weekend. Today, Friday, Saturday. The executive committee will do something Sunday morning, some planning meeting, but I'm not part of that, thank God.

EMILY: So this is it? Or we'll be seeing you more?

GENE: You want to see me more?

EMILY: I just want to be prepared so that I can practice looking happy if I *have* to see you again.

GENE: It's hard to fake affection, isn't it?

EMILY: Who said anything about affection?

GENE: Tolerance?

EMILY: I wish she'd come out with you.

GENE: You know how your mom is about flying.

EMILY: I'd like to see her.

GENE: So come out and see her.

EMILY: Well, I do.

GENE: It's been two years.

EMILY: I call all the time.

GENE: That's no substitute—

EMILY: Look, I offered to come and she told me not to.

GENE: You offered to come when she was in the hospital from her accident. She didn't want you to see her like that. She's not in the hospital now.

EMILY: Are you going to hit me with a guilt thing?

GENE: I'll take my shots where I can find them.

EMILY: I will, soon as I can.

GENE: Visit?

EMILY: Maybe in the new year.

GENE: The sooner, the better. After all, who knows how much longer—

EMILY: I thought you said she's fine.

GENE: Yes, but you can't take anything for granted.

EMILY: You aren't keeping anything from me?

GENE: I'm keeping lots of things from you, but not about this.

EMILY: She sounds good on the phone. Is that an act?

GENE: No. But don't expect her to take up tennis. Or swimming for that matter.

EMILY [*referring back to his previous line*]: I don't take things for granted.

GENE: I'm not saying you do. All I'm saying is just because something is the way it's been for a long time doesn't mean that it's always going to stay that way. People get old. People have accidents. She'd appreciate a visit.

EMILY: I'll see if I can get away sooner.

GENE: Christmas would be nice. She puts a lot of stock into the holiday stuff. [*To* NEAL] Listen, about my cracks about lawyers—

NEAL: I know: joking.

GENE: Everybody has a job. Everybody makes a contribution.

NEAL: I like to think so.

GENE: See you kids later.

[*He exits.*]

EMILY: You have an opinion?

NEAL: I wouldn't have pictured you being raised by someone like him.

[NEAL *begins to clean up after* GENE's *visit*.]

EMILY: I wasn't. Being in the same house doesn't make him someone who—he's not my father.

NEAL: Of course.

EMILY: He's *not* my father.

NEAL: Did he want to be?

EMILY: Oh, he took a stab at it.

NEAL: Which took the form of what?

EMILY: Every now and then saying no. Laying down the law. That was his phrase for it. "I'm going to lay down the law." Like, by announcing his intention, by saying that it *was* the law, somehow it would *become* the law.

NEAL: So he'd lay down the law and you'd, what—salute?

EMILY: Please. As if I had a choice. If only for my self-respect. Anyway, I could handle him.

[NEAL *finishes cleaning up.*]

NEAL: So if you don't like him, when he comes to town why do you see him?

[*A beat.*]

EMILY: Did I say I don't like him?

NEAL: I don't know where I got that impression.

EMILY: I mean, if he weren't married to my mom—

NEAL: Right.

EMILY: But we've put together something that works. He and I.

NEAL: Yes, I can tell.

EMILY: Whether I like him isn't the important thing anyway. He wasn't my idea. He didn't arrive for my benefit.

NEAL: Your mom's.

EMILY: She had the right. If he was what she—and it's not like she had her pick of a long line of suitors. A woman with a kid, a woman with problems of her own. I mean, I love her, but it's not like she had a lot of options. And why should she be alone if she could find an alternative?

NEAL: And he presented himself as the alternative.

EMILY: OK, so when I first met him, I wasn't nuts about him. But it registered on me, you know, that she was drinking less.

NEAL: When she started to see him?

EMILY: I thought, OK, well, if seeing him means that she drinks less, then maybe there's a point to this.

[GEORGIA *appears.*]

GEORGIA: God, listen to you! So understanding, so—

[*She looks to* NEAL *for help.*]

NEAL: Compassionate?

GEORGIA: Mmmm.

EMILY: Mom, do you remember who you were? Do you remember you when you were young your eyes were clear?

GEORGIA: And your father was alive.

EMILY [*to audience*]: A car accident. When I was seven.

GEORGIA: Well, you live long enough, nobody stays young . . .

EMILY: But you could have come back. You could still have managed it.

GEORGIA: Oh, darling—

EMILY: You could still do it now, if you really wanted.

GEORGIA: You haven't seen me in two years—

EMILY: I bet you could, if you made an effort—

GEORGIA: How can you know what I could do? Please, please don't.

[*A beat.*]

NEAL: I had an aunt. She did things that made people nervous.

GEORGIA: Nervous, how?

NEAL: Talked to people who weren't there. And not real people.

GEORGIA: Not real people who weren't there? If they weren't there, how could they be real or not real?

NEAL: I mean characters in books. When she was a girl, Nancy Drew. When she was older, Heathcliff. Not the cat.

GEORGIA: I never did that. Did I, honey? People who weren't there?

EMILY: No, Mom.

GEORGIA: Even at my worst.

EMILY: No.

NEAL: But she—my aunt—was, well, we didn't use the word "crazy," that would have been—

GEORGIA: Unkind.

NEAL: "Troubled" was what the family settled on. Aunt Agnes was troubled. Well, I was a kid, and I thought, if I sit down and make this plain to her, if I tell her, gently but firmly, that Heathcliff is a character in a book, that she's having conversations with someone that doesn't exist, she would have to recognize the truth and—

EMILY: That would cure her?

GEORGIA: You thought that, you really *must* have been a kid.

NEAL: Well, yes, I was.

GEORGIA: You have this conversation?

NEAL: I tried.

GEORGIA: And?

NEAL: I'm sitting there with her on the swing on the porch. I take her hands in mine. I make my case. I use simple, earnest language. She doesn't say anything. Just looks at me. I wait for a response. I don't know—maybe a promise that she would try, try to *not* be troubled.

GEORGIA: And?

NEAL: She just sits quiet. A couple of minutes, then she gets up and goes to the bathroom, someplace where I couldn't follow. Next couple of weeks, she doesn't talk to me. If I come into the room, she leaves, or, if the family's having a meal, she'll wait until I sit down and then she'll sit at the far end of the table from me. Finally I guess she either forgave me or forgot. Probably forgot.

EMILY: So what conclusion do you derive from this? That it would have been better for you to do nothing?

NEAL: Hey, I'm not Aesop. I don't do, "And the moral of the story is—"

EMILY: Bullshit. You tell a story at a particular moment and then you try to disclaim any responsibility for what it's about. If you have something to say, say it.

GEORGIA: Emily—

EMILY: Why else would you tell this story now? You think it relates somehow. Like my mother is Aunt Agnes?

[NEAL *laughs.*]

What? What are you laughing at?

NEAL: You're saying what he said.

EMILY: Who?

NEAL: Gene. When he made that comment about you saying something but not saying it so you could deny saying it.

EMILY: I'm not saying what he said. I could never say anything he said.

NEAL: No, it's the same thing. It *is*.

EMILY: You think you're being funny.

GEORGIA [*appreciating the humor*]: I hope I meet you one of these days, young man.

[*She exits.*]

EMILY: You're trying to suggest that I'm anything like Gene—if I thought I was capable of saying anything he would say, I'd cut out my tongue.

NEAL: Would you make up your mind? First you tell me you like him OK; now you're pissed off at the idea that I might like him. Which is it?

[*A beat.*]

Look, we don't have to see him if you don't want. If he annoys you so much. We can make an excuse.

EMILY: He'd know it was an excuse.

NEAL: You're worried about his feelings.

EMILY: I can put up with him in small doses. It's not like he's here all the time. If we think of it as missionary work—

NEAL: What? Because he's exposed to the example of our higher moral tone, he'll renounce Satan and all his works?

EMILY: Shit, if he met Satan, he'd probably buy him a beer and sell him a drill.

NEAL: Hey.

EMILY: What?

NEAL: This.

[*He kisses her.*]

Yes?

[*She smiles, kisses him back.* GENE *enters.*]

GENE [*to audience*]: Here's the setup: the hotel where I'm staying. Fifty-fifth Street. There's a bar downstairs.

[EMILY *rolls out a set piece suggesting a bar.*]

They're supposed to meet me, and then I'm going to take them to dinner.

NEAL [*to audience*]: Only Emily and I are coming from different places—

GENE: No kidding.

NEAL: So I get here first.

[EMILY *moves to the side.* NEAL *brings over drinks.*]

GENE: You should have let me take that. I could have put it on my expense thing.

NEAL: Hey, I'm flush. I robbed some widows and orphans today. How's the trip going?

GENE: Oh, fine. Everybody goes to the dentist, you know. I heard about how you two met. Pretty gutsy, going to bat for some fag.

NEAL: You know, there's a possibility we could get along.

GENE: If I didn't use words like "fag"?

NEAL: It would help.

GENE: I'm just—

NEAL: You're fucking with me.

GENE: Yes, you're right. I am. I am fucking with you. Or as the Germans would say, "I am with you fucking." Did you know they put their verbs at the ends of their sentences? The Germans?

NEAL: That's new information to me.

GENE: So I've been given to understand. "I am with you fucking."

NEAL: Is it that you want to find out what pisses me off?

GENE: Will you my apology accept?

NEAL: Will you up your ass it shove?

GENE: You want some totally unsolicited advice? Neal?

NEAL: What?

GENE: Don't do it.

NEAL: Don't—

GENE: Get married. No, let me revise that: don't get married to *her.*

NEAL: I'm not good enough for her? She's not good enough for me?

GENE: "Good enough" has nothing to do with it. You're both—if you'll pardon my salesman's angle—you're both quality goods. Smart, not bad-looking and other items of value. But you don't want to do this. My opinion.

NEAL: Unsolicited.

GENE: Unsolicited.

NEAL: I don't think she's interested in marriage anyway. Not right now.

GENE: Then it's—what is that word you lawyers like to use? "Moot"?

NEAL: Probably.

GENE: I just thought, if this idea were floating around in the realm of the possible—

NEAL: OK, I don't get it. Before, you were talking—you were giving her grief about us living together without benefit of clergy.

GENE: No, that wasn't me. That was me speaking on behalf of Emily's mother. Her mother isn't happy about this, and part of my job is to transmit these feelings to her. Her mother's feelings.

NEAL: I see.

GENE: So I did that. I communicated this to Emily. I can report back that I delivered the message. That I discharged my duty in good conscience.

NEAL: And this advice you're offering me, this is also in good conscience?

GENE: This is me speaking for me. I don't have to agree with her mother. And also, you've got a mouth and you think I'm a jerk, but I kind of like you.

NEAL: So what you're saying is in my interest?

GENE: She's very angry.

NEAL: We're talking about Emily again?

GENE: You've got eyes. This is news to you? Angry. Always has been. Long as I've known her anyway. I mean, I understand. Her father gets stolen from her when she's a kid, the guy her mother remembers as this mythical person—his perfect, handsome photo on the wall, a shrine. She thinks the life—Emily thinks, but her mother, too—the perfect life she could have had, perfect family, maybe her mother wouldn't have started drinking if it hadn't been for the grief, if it hadn't been for the accident of some truck driver falling asleep at the wheel on the same highway as her father. It's not fair. Emily and her mother lose this golden guy and get—me. You ever see a picture of her father?

NEAL: No.

GENE: I look *nothing* like him. His photo, like the picture of a promising rookie on a baseball card. I am no compensation at all. I am a joke. And I come into their home and I don't go away. I tried to get her mother to move somewhere else, we could start in a new place, a house that didn't still smell of him, she wouldn't do it. Wouldn't leave. I pressed as hard as I could, but I could tell it was a deal breaker. And I didn't want that deal to break. I wanted to marry her. Every bit and piece of me wanted to marry her mother. It may be hard for you to believe, given the way she is now—

NEAL: I've never met her.

GENE: That's right, of course.

NEAL: Maybe a word or two on the phone when she calls—

GENE: Well, she really was something. She was drinking too much when I met her, but I could understand that. The loss of this guy she was so nuts about. I thought that that would pass. And I seemed to have a good effect on her. She cut way back. In the early days with me, hardly touched the stuff. That's some feeling, you know.

NEAL: A compliment?

GENE: To think you're having a good effect on someone. You can see that someone's better because you're there. You could fall in love with someone for being better because you're there.

[*A beat.*]

Well, that didn't last. But what does? Oh shit, listen to me. I'm sorry. I *am* a jerk. All right, I've said it. I've given you my very valuable opinion. It's up to you to make the choice for yourself. I mean, far be it for me to—

NEAL: Do you give this pep talk to all of Emily's boyfriends?

GENE: I only met a couple of the others.

NEAL: And did you say this to them?

GENE: No. But they weren't in any danger.

NEAL: Danger?

GENE: They weren't living with her. There wasn't any serious chance of anything happening beyond, how do I say it—

NEAL: Screwing without a license?

GENE: You know how on a carton of milk, they stamp the expiration date? December 12 or whatever. These guys, you could see the expiration date. I didn't feel I had to do anything. Time would take care of it.

NEAL: But me, you feel you have to do something.

GENE: I'm not even really saying not do it.

NEAL: No?

GENE: Just make sure you know what you're getting into first.

[*He laughs.*]

There's a nice specific piece of advice, right? You can really put that plan into action. But you're going to do what you feel like, so fuck me anyway—

[FRED, *played by* DOUBLING ACTOR, *enters during the previous lines.*]

FRED [*overlapping*]: Gene! Good!

GENE: What?

FRED: We've got a problem. [*To* NEAL] I'm sorry—

GENE: Neal, this hedgehog is Fred. He's repping with me at the convention.

FRED: Sorry.

NEAL: No, if you have a problem—

GENE: What?

FRED: Matteo.

GENE: No, that's all set.

FRED: No, well, it isn't.

GENE: I arranged all that before I got on the plane. I called the service from LAX.

FRED: Except, when you called, the girl in question didn't have appendicitis.

GENE: No.

FRED: Swear to God. Got a message, I called in, they told me.

GENE: Is she OK?

FRED: Is that my business?

GENE: That shit can be serious.

FRED: Gene, focus. Matteo.

GENE: They can't come up with a substitute?

FRED: It's short notice and, you know, there's a convention in town.

GENE: So what do you expect me to do? Put on a wig and dress, get Matteo so drunk he can't tell the difference?

FRED: Yeah, that's exactly my plan.

GENE: He's not exactly my type.

FRED: The question is could you be his?

GENE: You know, you have the makings of a good-looking redhead yourself.

FRED: I'm on the rag.

GENE: Wouldn't surprise me.

FRED [*to* NEAL]: What about you? Easy money.

GENE: Neal here is a lawyer.

FRED: Oh, so it's just a question of how much.

[*He laughs at his own joke.* NEAL *musters a smile.*]

GENE: OK, hold on.

[GENE *pulls out an organizer.*]

You got a pen?

[FRED *hands him a pen and* GENE, *consulting the organizer, writes a number on a cocktail napkin.*]

FRED [*taking the napkin*]: Is that a two or a seven?

GENE: A seven.

FRED: Do I ask for anybody specific?

GENE: Rhonda.

FRED: I mention your name?

GENE: Oh sure, Rhonda keeps a light burning in the window for me.

FRED: What if this Rhonda can't help us?

GENE: Fred, this is New York fucking City—there's got to be something worth doing here besides eating and getting laid.

FRED: I'll take him to the Philharmonic.

GENE: That should do it.

[FRED *exits.*]

He forgot his pen.

NEAL: Matteo—he's a client?

GENE: It's like a tradition—every year.

NEAL: Every year you make Mr. Matteo happy.

GENE: Please, *Doctor* Matteo!

NEAL: Respect, yes, of course. *Doctor.*

GENE: What were we talking about?

NEAL: You were giving me nonmatrimonial advice.

GENE: I think I said what I had to say.

NEAL: Did it ever occur to you that you're what she's angry at?

GENE: I'm sorry?

NEAL: You said she's angry—Emily. I'm suggesting—

GENE: Me? I'm why? The reason?

NEAL: That maybe it's not that she's generally angry.

GENE: Oh, I get you. I bring out her anger and you—'cause you're so different from me—you'll bring out a something else? The Emily with a song in her heart and a smile on her lips and a cheerful "good morning" for the milkman?

NEAL: Different people bring out different sides. That's just true.

GENE: Does she talk about the ex-boyfriends at all?

NEAL: Talk about—

GENE: The guys before you she didn't have a license with? Does she talk about them?

NEAL: About as much as I talk about my ex-girlfriends.

GENE: When she does talk about them, your predecessors, what is her tone? Nostalgic? Sentimental? No, huh? But, so what, they were jerks so you can understand why she was angry at them. They *made* her angry. That's it. She couldn't help but be angry. It was completely appropriate that she be angry at them. That was what they deserved. But, because you're a better guy, a nice guy, a more sensitive guy—

NEAL: I don't think we want to pursue this any further, do we?

[*A beat.*]

GENE: What's keeping her?

NEAL: Traffic.

GENE: But maybe there's another question.

NEAL: More?

GENE: A question. What do *you* want? If I've made assumptions and, instead, all you're here for is—all that the two of you are doing is something for the time being, then I apologize. But do you know what you want?

NEAL: Look, all due respect and so forth, but you aren't my dad.

GENE: No. I'm the stepfather of the girl you're shacking up with and that confers upon me no privileges to advise you or otherwise utter this shit. Very true. Besides, knowing how relationships go these days, the next time I come into town, you may not be in the picture. You may be in some entirely other picture.

NEAL: You are with me fucking again.

GENE: And you are with me pissed?

NEAL [*overlapping*]: Here's Emily.

[EMILY *enters, joins them.*]

EMILY: Hiya.

GENE: Welcome.

EMILY: You two amusing each other?

GENE: Sure, I'm a raconteur, didn't you know that?

EMILY: That's French for bullshit artist, isn't it?

NEAL: Traffic?

EMILY: Traffic.

GENE: You want a drink?

NEAL: Do you mind if maybe we go someplace else?

EMILY: I just got here.

GENE: She just got here.

NEAL: OK.

EMILY: Do you have a particular reason—

NEAL: I guess I've exhausted the charm of the place.

EMILY: Charm? What are you—

NEAL: Nothing. Sure.

EMILY: I need a breather before I plunge out into that again.

NEAL: "That"?

EMILY: Traffic.

NEAL: Traffic, right.

GENE: She just got here, Neal. A minute to catch her breath.

NEAL: What's the story with the reservations?

GENE: We're fine.

NEAL: Good. I'll get you that drink. [*To audience, as he picks up a drink for her*] OK, probably if Emily had arrived five minutes later, we would have gotten into some other subject, I'd be over it, and probably I wouldn't say what I'm gonna say. [*Handing* EMILY *her drink*] Actually, Gene's got a problem.

EMILY: Problem?

NEAL: Maybe we could help him with it. Maybe we could give him some assistance.

GENE [*sensing what's coming*]: I don't think so.

EMILY: What kind of problem?

GENE: Nothing for you to worry about.

NEAL: Maybe you have a friend who could use some extra cash.

EMILY: A friend?

NEAL: 'Cause Gene has a friend, too. A friend and a customer. A guy who regularly places large orders. This friend is visiting New York without his wife. This guy, back home in—where? Omaha?

GENE [*resigned*]: Close enough.

NEAL: Back home in Omaha this man and his wife go to the country club. The band plays. Show tunes, Bacharach, a little Glenn Miller. They dance. He tries, but he's not very good—this man, this friend, this customer. He'd like to be.

EMILY: Like to be?

NEAL: A good dancer. See, other men sometimes dance with his wife. At the club. He watches them and they move well together. He'd like to look as good dancing with his wife as they do. It's a matter of pride.

EMILY: Sure. You want to hold your head up.

NEAL: And what does it look like if other men dance better with your wife than you do? What conclusions, however false, might small minds on their third or fourth drink leap to?

EMILY: These small minds—maybe they should stop drinking.

NEAL: What are you going to do, Emily, change human nature? Can't keep people from drinking.

EMILY: Can't keep people from dancing.

NEAL: So he comes to New York—

EMILY: Gene's friend?

NEAL [*nodding confirmation*]: He's by himself, he's got a night free, and it occurs to him that he could brush up a little on his footwork. After all, New York is full of music and full of people who know how to move gracefully to the beat. All he has to do is find one of these people and get a little instruction. Then, next time he's back at the club, when the band starts to play, he'll sweep her to her feet—his wife—

EMILY: Of course.

NEAL: *Sweep* his wife to her feet and dazzle her with his nimbleness, his newly acquired facility with the waltz, the rumba, the fox-trot.

EMILY: The tango?

NEAL: He doesn't want to set his sights *too* high.

EMILY: Still, you know—

NEAL: Yes? What?

EMILY: She's gonna wonder where he learned that, where he picked up these new moves. She may ask him.

NEAL: He'll just smile and twirl her about again. So, what do you think? Think we can be helpful to Gene's friend? Or am I guilty of what you were talking about before?

GENE: Which?

NEAL: About the stereotyping of dentists. As one might be about the stereotyping of lawyers. As you would probably be if you embraced the common belief that people who attend conventions and conferences without their spouses, that these people really are interested mostly in getting drunk and getting laid.

[*A beat.*]

GENE: Did you know that my company puts out a particularly fine set of acrylic burrs? Quick, what's an acrylic burr? Well, my job is to put as many of our fine acrylic burrs into the hands of as many dentists as possible. Other guys have other missions. This is mine. And if I didn't do it, I'm not kidding myself, somebody else would. I am not the absolutely greatest salesman of acrylic burrs. Probably there are guys out there get more and bigger orders than I do. Though probably not that many. I *am* good. My company is happy with me. Now, motivating the people who should buy my acrylic burrs entirely on merit—well, this doesn't always happen. Sometimes people place orders with me for reasons other than solely the quality of the goods I represent. I have a talent for relationships. Most of my regulars, I have the pleasure—when they see my face—the pleasure not only of they remember me, but that they smile recognizing me. Who are we kidding? This is New York. They can probably walk into any of a number of bars if they want dancing lessons. Or instruction or assistance in any other activity they have in mind. They don't need me. This bar—probably here now is someone who would be more than willing. Maybe even, ten years ago, Emily would.

EMILY: I never would.

GENE: No?

EMILY: That wasn't the same. Not at all.

GENE: If you say so.

NEAL: What isn't the same?

EMILY: Can we make a deal?

GENE [*extending his hand*]: Shake.

[EMILY *shakes his hand.*]

NEAL: What?

EMILY: We're going to dinner.

NEAL: We are?

EMILY: What the hell do you think we met him for?

NEAL: You just shook hands.

EMILY: Yes, we did. We are in accord. In agreement.

NEAL: About?

GENE: Going to dinner.

EMILY: Going to dinner. I'm hungry.

GENE: I'm hungry. What about you, Neal? Are you hungry?

EMILY: He's hungry.

GENE: Good. We have a table waiting for us.

[GENE *makes an "after you" gesture.* NEAL *exchanges a look with* EMILY. NEAL *follows* EMILY *to an area to the side of the stage, and* GENE *turns to audience.*]

And the evening probably would have gone into the thumbs-up column if it weren't for the fact that I got arrested. But that's later.

[GENE *exits. Focus now on* EMILY *and* NEAL.]

NEAL: You don't have to tell me.

EMILY: If I had to tell you, I wouldn't.

NEAL: Then don't.

[*A beat.*]

EMILY: Do you remember a place called Mr. Hopper's?

NEAL: No.

EMILY: You must have gone to some places when you were a student.

NEAL: I went to a lot of places.

EMILY: When you were going to college and you came into New York on break. To blow off steam.

NEAL: Wait—you're talking about, like a topless bar—

[*A beat.*]

EMILY: I was nineteen. I wanted to change schools, change my field. Gene wasn't happy with the switch I wanted to make.

NEAL: Something impractical?

EMILY: How many philosophers you know make six figures? That was the gist of his objection. He said, "You switch to that, I'm not paying for college." Never mind that most of the money for school was put aside for me when I was a kid, a thing my dad and his folks set up.

NEAL: So he disagreed with philosophy, threatened to cut you off. And you said—

EMILY: "Do it. Go ahead, cut me off."

NEAL: Of course.

EMILY: "I can make my own money."

NEAL: So you did, at Mr. Hopper's—

EMILY: It was pretty sedate actually. Just my top. Though I can't pretend that what I wore below covered much. So, I did that for a few weeks, and my mother heard about it—

NEAL: Somebody told her?

EMILY: Word got back. I saw to that.

NEAL: And she saw to it that Gene started writing checks again—

EMILY: —to save what was left of my virtue.

NEAL: Can I ask you something?

EMILY: Sure, I'll take questions.

NEAL: Why didn't you just tell him that's what you were going to do?

EMILY: Make the threat? "If you don't send the money, I'm going to do Mr. Hopper's"?

NEAL: Why not?

EMILY: Say I make the threat and he calls my bluff. I don't want to threaten that I'm going to do this and have him say, "OK, go ahead, do it," which he probably would have said. Then I have to choose whether to do it or not. See? *Then* if I don't do it—

NEAL: —he thinks you've chickened out.

EMILY: And if I do, he thinks it's only 'cause he dared me. If you're going to make a threat, you have to be prepared to make good on it.

NEAL: So rather than have him call your bluff—

EMILY: So he doesn't think that anything he says has much to do with what I choose to do.

NEAL: But it does. It did. You got a job at Mr. Hopper's 'cause he said no to philosophy.

EMILY: Yes, but there were any of a number of responses I could have made. It wasn't that Mr. Hopper's was my only choice. I could have gotten on the phone and begged and pleaded—

NEAL: Yes, I can really see you begging and pleading—

EMILY: Well, exactly. Look, I'm not saying it was the most mature reaction. But I wanted to study what I wanted to study.

NEAL: So, looking back on that, you're what? Proud?

EMILY: Yeah. Sure. What's not to be proud of shaking your boobs at strangers? I was a kid. Anyway, that's what that crack Gene made was about. That's what he was referring to. About how I might have once been the kind of person he could have called to entertain his client.

NEAL: He wasn't serious.

EMILY: But, Jesus, are you proud of everything you did when *you* were a kid? You're young so you *can* do dumb stuff. While you're still resilient enough to bounce back. But, at a certain point, there's no excuse— well, not *no* excuse but less excuse.

NEAL: Where is that point?

EMILY: Wherever I say.

NEAL: That's fair.

EMILY: Let's go home.

[*They kiss and exit. A phone rings.* EMILY *returns, addressing the audience.*]

This phone call comes later that night. Much later that night. I am asleep when it begins to ring, and, of course, I'm wearing pajamas, which you will please imagine.

[*Phone rings again. She mimes picking up the phone.*]

Yeah, hello?

GENE: Hiya, kiddo. Can I talk to, what's-his-name, your boyfriend—

EMILY: Neal?

GENE: Can I talk to him?

EMILY: You're calling in the middle of the night to talk to Neal?

GENE: He's there, isn't he?

EMILY: Yes, he's here, asleep.

GENE: Wake him up. I need to talk to him.

EMILY: "Need"?

GENE: I don't have all the time in the world. Please put him on.

EMILY [*calling to him offstage*]: Neal?

[NEAL *enters with a stocking cap on. She looks at it.*]

What the hell is that?

NEAL: It's meant to represent bedclothes.

[EMILY *yanks it off his head wryly. She offers him the mimed phone.*]

EMILY: It's Gene. He wants you.

NEAL [*miming talking on the phone*]: Gene?

GENE: Neal? You're a lawyer, right?

NEAL: That's what it says on a piece of paper on my wall.

GENE: I've got a problem.

[*A beat.*]

NEAL: Yes?

GENE [*to audience*]: OK, here's how it happened—

[MARTA, *played by the* DOUBLING ACTRESS, *wheels on a piece representing a bar. She pulls up a stool and sits at it.*]

I don't want you to think that's all I do, hang around bars. But it just so happens that's where this takes place. A different bar from where I saw the kids. This is after I had dinner with them, which went pretty much OK, by the way. I mean, if we'd had another fight, we would have done it for you, but what's the point of putting up something that shows you people getting along, right? That's not what you came to see.

MARTA [*to* GENE]: I'm ready when you are. [*To audience*] See, I'm sitting over here, and he comes in. This is a neighborhood place, where usually everybody knows each other, so him not being a regular, I notice him right away.

GENE [*to audience*]: The notice is mutual. [*To* MARTA] There's a salesman's technique—

MARTA: Is that what you are? A salesman?

GENE: Let's say I am wise to the ways of salesmen.

MARTA: All right.

GENE: Now the technique—maybe you'll notice this when someone's trying to sell you something—the technique is that they ask you a series
of questions you're certain to say yes to. Like you're on the phone—

MARTA: You mean, if it's a phone salesman?

GENE: They call you up and say, "Are you"—what's your name, anyway?

MARTA: Marta.

GENE: OK, they've got you on the phone and they say, "Are you Marta
Cunningham?"

MARTA: Dershel, actually.

GENE: "Are you Marta Dershel?" And you say, "Yes."

MARTA: Uh-huh?

GENE: And they say, "You live in apartment 3J of 893 West Forty-eighth
Street?" Or whatever your street address is. And you'll say yes, again.

MARTA: Except that 893 West Forty-eighth Street is probably in the
Hudson.

GENE: Not the point.

MARTA: Please tell me the point.

GENE: That they ask you another question that you'll answer yes to.

MARTA: Oh, like you said.

GENE: That's the technique. They get you into the habit of saying yes, so
that when, after ten or twelve yeses, they get around to saying, "I can
give you a great deal on genuine rust-resistant Danish duck blinds?"
maybe just out of habit you'll—

MARTA [*overlapping*]: I'll say yes.

GENE: That's the idea; that's the principle.

MARTA: They try to get me into a yes frame of mind?

GENE: Yes.

MARTA: So they can sell me something?

GENE: Yes.

MARTA: Ha. Sounds like I've got *you* in a yes frame of mind.

GENE: This could be a great opportunity for you.

MARTA: If there was something I was trying to sell.

GENE: Maybe you could think of something. Or something you would
like me to do.

MARTA: Buy a lady a drink?

GENE: Yes.

MARTA: It works; it works.

GENE: I am in your power, Marta Dershel.

MARTA: I believe that. I absolutely do.

GENE [*to* NEAL]: Want to be the bartender?

NEAL: What for?

GENE: To bring the drinks.

NEAL: If we could do pretend telephones, why can't you do pretend drinks?

GENE: It'll make it easier. Cut me a break, will you?

[NEAL *shrugs. He brings* GENE *and* MARTA *drinks.*]

NEAL: That's twelve fifty.

[GENE *mimes counting out money.*]

GENE: Keep the change. [*To* MARTA] You mind if I join you?

NEAL [*to* GENE]: Just a second here.

GENE: What?

NEAL: Correct me if I'm—this is a pickup scene, right?

GENE: You figured that out, huh?

NEAL: So what does this have to do with you needing a lawyer?

GENE: Well, a lawyer is helpful if you've been arrested and want to get out of jail.

NEAL: And why have you been arrested?

GENE [*to* MARTA]: You want to—

MARTA: Well, I'm married.

NEAL: Oh?

MARTA: And about twenty minutes after what we just did, my husband, Terry, comes in and finds me a couple of steps past this point with— what's your name again?

GENE: Gene.

MARTA: With Gene here.

NEAL: I see. And your husband Terry, he's a jealous guy? He has a temper?

MARTA: My husband Terry has a temper. My husband Terry also has a badge.

NEAL: I think I've just connected the dots.

MARTA: Look, I don't want you to get the wrong impression about me. It's not like Terry is this wonderful human being and I'm out every night looking to do the dirty on him. I've tried to get him to go to a marriage counselor. But, like I told you, he's a cop, and if you know cops—

GENE: Excuse me—

MARTA: Yeah, what?

GENE: I'm sure nobody thinks that this is the whole story of who Marta is as a human being.

[*The* DOUBLING ACTRESS *shifts out of* MARTA's *voice into her own.*]

DOUBLING ACTRESS: It really isn't. I've got this all figured out. [*To audience*] This person, all you're going to see of her, of Marta, is this section here. She's not coming back to the story. But, if you take your work seriously, when you play a part, you can't help but think, uh, imagine, figure out, what else there is. So there are more colors, resonances. So you bring to the stage *more*.

GENE: Well, that would be swell if this were *about* Marta.

[*A beat.*]

DOUBLING ACTRESS: All right.

GENE: Thank you.

DOUBLING ACTRESS: But there are things about Marta, things that would be worth hearing, worth knowing. Like that she once saved somebody's life. It's true. I did the research on her. There is a boy—probably he's a teenager by now—a boy who is walking around, who is alive *to* be walking around, because of her. Because of her quick thinking and the fact that she happened to take that Red Cross course. There are other dimensions, aside from someone who does the bar thing.

[DOUBLING ACTOR *enters.*]

DOUBLING ACTOR: Kristine? [*Or whatever the real name of the actress is.*]

DOUBLING ACTRESS: What?

DOUBLING ACTOR: Not appropriate.

DOUBLING ACTRESS: Like that's your call to make.

DOUBLING ACTOR: Kristine—

DOUBLING ACTRESS: I just don't think it's fair. I have two bits in this: the bimbo that Neal picks up at the beginning—Bonnie?—and now

Marta, who, surprise, is someone Gene nearly picks up. I have more range than just playing pickups. I do.

DOUBLING ACTOR: I've got small parts, too.

DOUBLING ACTRESS: You get to play the sensitive gay guy and the jerky businessman; you get a chance to show some versatility. Why didn't anybody think of letting me have a crack at Emily's mother? I could have handled her. And it would have saved a salary.

DOUBLING ACTOR: Come on, Kristine.

[*A beat.*]

DOUBLING ACTRESS: Fine. Fine.

[*She stomps off.* DOUBLING ACTOR *looks apologetically at the others, then follows her, striking the bar.* GENE *turns to* NEAL *and nods, as if it's OK to go ahead. Behind* GENE, EMILY *enters.*]

EMILY: So what, exactly, is the charge?

NEAL: There is no charge. The charge was dropped.

EMILY: What was it before it was dropped?

NEAL: Assault.

GENE: If anybody assaulted anybody—

EMILY: Oh?

GENE: Well, he started pushing the lady around, and I kind of thought that was out of line—

EMILY: You moved in to defend her?

GENE: He misread my defending her for taking him on. That pissed him off. That's when I found out he was a cop.

EMILY: When he arrested you.

GENE: He wasn't in uniform. The whole thing was more or less a misunderstanding.

EMILY: You didn't get around to sleeping with this woman, did you?

GENE: No.

EMILY: But not for lack of trying.

GENE: No.

EMILY: Getting arrested by her husband got in the way.

GENE: I didn't know she was married.

EMILY: Has it escaped your attention that you are?

GENE: Be careful.

EMILY: You've just been caught trying to lay someone else's wife, and you're telling *me* to be careful?

GENE: I didn't know she was somebody else's wife. I think I made that clear.

EMILY: So by you it's OK. You really don't see how I could find anything wrong with this?

GENE: Let's put this into the express lane: I'm a—what?—a liar, a cheat?

EMILY: The language is milder than I'd choose, but—

GENE [*overlapping*]: No, I want to hear the language. Give it to me full strength. I want to hear those nasty words come out of your pretty mouth. An asshole? A dickhead? A worthless piece of shit?

EMILY: What I call you isn't important.

GENE: Actually, "worthless piece of shit," if you think about it, suggests the possibility of the opposite—

NEAL: Shit with value?

GENE: I mean, if you establish the possibility that shit can have some value, then the next thing is to start ranking the quality—good shit, better shit, best. Shit with potential. Shit that has *realized* its potential.

EMILY: Is that what you aspire to?

GENE: Oh yes, I'm filled with hope. I wake up each day just dazzled by the world and its possibilities. It's what sustains me.

EMILY: In your darker hours.

GENE: You betcha.

EMILY: That and the prospect of getting laid.

GENE: You're a fine one to criticize. I don't see you going without.

EMILY: That's none of your fucking business.

GENE: I see: your fucking business is your fucking business.

EMILY: It is.

GENE: But my fucking business is also yours? Why isn't mine just mine? Don't I get the same—what is the legal phrase—rights and protections?

EMILY: No.

GENE: I don't?

EMILY: You put yourself under a different set of obligations—

GENE: When I married your mother. No, I'm familiar with the theory. I just don't see you as being empowered to police my perimeters.

EMILY: I wouldn't give a damn about your perimeters if my mother weren't involved.

GENE: So she sent you a badge?

EMILY: If just from a health point of view.

GENE: The fear that I might pass something on to her.

EMILY: Neal, they still have community property in California?

NEAL: I think so.

EMILY: In case of divorce, wife gets fifty percent of marital assets?

NEAL: That's really not my area of the law.

GENE: No, I think you've got it right.

EMILY: And adultery is still grounds for divorce, right? Even in California?

NEAL: I don't know whether it's a no-fault state or what.

GENE: So that's what you're—excuse me—threatening? You're *threatening* me with what—

EMILY: You think if I tell her, she won't boot you out on your ass?

GENE: No question. And you're right: the community property laws kick in, I'll be in financial doo-doo. No, you tell her, and my lifestyle takes a deep dive south.

EMILY: So?

GENE: Yes, what? I'm sorry, are you proposing something here?

EMILY: Show some self-restraint. Dignity.

GENE: I have to tell you it's been my life's dream to have your good opinion.

EMILY: What about your own good opinion?

GENE [*cheerfully*]: Oh, I gave up on that a long time ago. Lot easier.

EMILY: Gene, I'm not making an idle threat.

GENE: So, what you want—let me guess. I'm supposed to, to knock it off. Is that it? I'm supposed to knock it off and promise you that I won't ever stray again. Right? That from now on I keep my dick in check except in the confines of the marital bed. Or else, right? Or *else*?

EMILY: I'll do it. I'll call her.

GENE: I bet. And she'll thank you for it, too.

EMILY: Maybe she has some pride.

GENE: Yeah, probably some, somewhere.

EMILY: Maybe she doesn't like being humiliated.

GENE: Hard to be humiliated if you don't know why you should be.

EMILY: Oh, so you're saying I shouldn't tell her for *her* sake, to protect her feelings.

GENE: No, not just for *her* sake—

EMILY: I sure won't hesitate for yours.

GENE: Big surprise.

EMILY: Then for whose sake shouldn't I?

NEAL [*seeing where this is going*]: Oh, Jesus—

GENE [*to* EMILY]: Let's take this step-by-step. You call her, you tell her what?

EMILY: About you. About the way you—

GENE: Yeah, yeah, and she does what?

[GEORGIA *appears.*]

GEORGIA: I toss you out. Call my lawyer.

GENE: Community property, et cetera. I go live in a studio apartment somewhere, and she—maybe she's able to afford holding on to the house, though I have my doubts.

GEORGIA: I'd manage.

GENE: But there she is, wherever she is. You've liberated her from me. And what is she doing?

EMILY: Doing?

GEORGIA: Doing?

GENE: Tell me what you see happening from here.

[*Addressing the following lines in* GEORGIA'*s direction, though he continues talking to* EMILY.]

Is she enrolling at the local college for a class in how to write a sonnet? Is she volunteering at the Friends of the Zoo, nursing a baby penguin? Or could she be strolling into the kitchen? Could she be opening the cabinet over the sink and pulling out a glass?

[*Turning back to* EMILY.]

And who's gonna tell her not to? Me? I'm decorating my new studio apartment. So who? You? You gonna find a sublet for this apartment, take a leave of absence from work, fly back to California? Monitor her vitamins? Or—no, I've got it—drag her out from L.A. and move her in with you?

EMILY [*on the defensive*]: She deserves better.

GENE: Well, she's not going to get it!

[*A beat.*]

And neither am I.

[*A beat.*]

You think because *you're* young enough to have choices—because, if you want to, you can change boyfriends with the seasons or move to Seattle tomorrow. Or you can decide you've done your bit for that charity outfit; now you want to switch careers, maybe make some real money. Or you want to work for yourself, start a catering business or some damn thing, make a few other changes you think for the better. But you live long enough, sweetheart, you go past the point where you can make those kinds of changes. And all that's left for you is to keep things going. Or try to.

EMILY: That's all that's left? Maintaining?

GENE: What do you think I've been doing with your mom? Sometimes coming home to scrape her up off the floor. Once in a while I get a call, from Noli or whoever—drop everything and run to the hospital. Stand by her bedside, look in her eyes and know that I'm not who she really wishes was there. Even after all this time. And only now and then do I see a little of what I thought I was marrying. You call what I do cheating. Jesus, what do you call what she's done? Who do you think left who? You worry about my passing the clap on to her. Last I heard, there are certain conditions for doing so, and those conditions haven't been a part of our life together for years. Or do you imagine there's much of anything left for me to share a bed with? But no, go ahead, kiddo, you make that call and punish me good. Get me tossed out of paradise. And once you've had that self-righteous thrill, put on your cap and figure out what you're gonna do next. 'Cause if you think she can hack it by herself—odds are next trip you'd make back wouldn't be for Christmas but for a funeral.

[*A beat.*]

GEORGIA [*to* GENE]: I don't want to be a part of this scene. I don't want to hear any of this.

GENE: That's not up to me. Is it, Emily?

[GEORGIA *looks at* EMILY. *A long pause, then* EMILY *looks at* GENE *and turns away in resignation.* GEORGIA *exits.* GENE *turns to* NEAL.]

Thanks for your help tonight.

[GENE *exits.*]

EMILY: Well, I sure stood up to him, didn't I? Showed him what I'm made of.
NEAL: You don't have to look at it like—
EMILY: Please. I caved. I tried to make a little girlie fist, and he just went—

[*She motions as if flicking an insect off her arm.*]

NEAL: You think you did the wrong thing?
EMILY: Neal—
NEAL: You could still blow the whistle on him if you think that's what you should do.
EMILY: And what about my mom?
NEAL: There are other options beside what he said. You could hire a companion for her.
EMILY: A companion.
NEAL: Somebody to live with her, keep an eye out—
EMILY: With what money?
NEAL: Or, if she really can't handle things by herself—
EMILY: Sell the house, put her someplace?
NEAL: If the question is what would be best for her—
EMILY: And that would be best for her—to be packed away somewhere? Alone?
NEAL: So, isn't the right decision what ends up being best for her?
EMILY: Except that isn't why I won't call her. I'm not not calling her for *her* sake—
NEAL: OK, granted. So?
EMILY: It matters.
NEAL: Look, I think you're doing the right thing.
EMILY: But for the wrong reason.
NEAL: Oh, for God's sake. Why is that a wrong reason? Aren't you entitled to make the life you want?

EMILY: I appreciate your moral support.

[*A beat.*]

Richie's got a futon, yes?

NEAL: Richie?

EMILY: Your friend.

NEAL: What has that got to do with—

EMILY: He'd probably let you use it, don't you think?

[*A beat.*]

NEAL: You want me to use Richie's futon.

EMILY: I could use a little time alone.

NEAL: A little time? Tonight?

EMILY: Maybe a couple of nights.

NEAL: A couple?

EMILY: Maybe.

NEAL: There's a crappy idea.

EMILY: And if I want my apartment to myself—

NEAL: *Your* apartment?

EMILY: Well, it *is.*

[*A beat.*]

NEAL: Emily, this doesn't have to make any difference between us.

EMILY: Am I saying that it does?

NEAL: Then why are you trying to send me away?

[*A beat.*]

EMILY: Did I make any promises to you?

NEAL: No.

EMILY: Did you make any promises to me?

NEAL: I was hoping to.

EMILY: Well, the fact of the matter is nobody's in default. Right?

NEAL: Is this because I saw him beat you?

EMILY: Ah, you agree—he beat me.

NEAL: No, I don't agree. I think that's what *you* think. I think you suddenly don't want me around because I was a witness to you—I don't know—you falling short of your own ridiculous standards.

EMILY: You think standards are ridiculous?

NEAL: If they're impossible. If they strangle something good, yes. What we've got is worth holding on to. I believe that. I do. I'm here. I'm willing to do my part.

EMILY: Aren't you noble!

NEAL: OK, is there anything I can say you won't smash back down my throat?

EMILY: Can't think of anything.

[*A beat.*]

NEAL: That is nuts.

EMILY: Look, maybe it's best for you.

NEAL: Excuse me?

EMILY: You say my not calling her, I'm doing what is maybe best for her. So maybe, if I'm going to do what's best for you—

NEAL: What's best for me is you dumping me?

EMILY: Probably would save you a lot of grief. Come on, you've read all the articles. You know what my mother is, and you know what I had as an excuse for a father figure—

NEAL: What is this? You're a cake?

EMILY: Huh?

NEAL: Like some dim-witted, supernatural Betty Crocker threw together the wrong ingredients, the wrong recipe: fucked-up mother, dead father, fucked-up stepfather—put that in the mix and this is who you have to be? Come on, you don't believe that.

EMILY: How do you know what I believe?

NEAL: You're the one who's constantly framing things in moral terms. Good behavior, bad behavior. Are you forgetting how we met? So now you're going to tell me there is no choice? You have no choice? You have to chase me away because the gods have decreed? Bullshit, bullshit, bullshit.

EMILY: OK, fine, I have choice. This is my choice: I want to be alone tonight. I want to be alone tonight. I want this place to myself.

NEAL: Emily—

EMILY: Or am I only exercising free will in your book if I choose what you want me to choose?

[*A beat.* EMILY *exits.* NEAL *is alone onstage. Lights shift.* GENE *enters.*]

GENE: Didn't I tell you she was angry?

NEAL: I'm gonna give her a couple of days and call her.

GENE: I think that's a swell idea.

NEAL: She'll think twice.

GENE: At least.

[*A beat.* NEAL *goes offstage and returns with the ghost light.*]

What do you say I buy you a beer?

NEAL: Gene, I'm afraid you haven't got me in a yes frame of mind.

[GENE *starts to laugh, but* NEAL *continues, purposefully.*]

Listen to me: I'm not saying what just happened is your fault. But if you hadn't shown up, right now I wouldn't be standing out here on the street. OK—maybe you're right about some of it. Maybe, where you are, what's left is just to make peace with where you are. Maybe someday I'll get to the point where I'll be thinking the same way. But here, today, I don't have to make that kind of peace. If I can put Emily and me back together, I'm going to do it. Your blessing is not sought. Your approval is not necessary. Your absence would be welcomed. You've got a plane to catch this afternoon, right? A hotel to check out of? Do it. Leave a nice tip for the maid, tell a joke to the guy at the desk, grab a cab to the airport, and . . . go.

[*He turns on the ghost light and exits.* GENE *stands alone, illuminated by the ghost light. He looks after* NEAL *for a second, then turns to the audience.*]

GENE: I bet you they do—I bet you they do get back together. Frankly, I think they deserve each other. But, you know, if they don't, it'll hurt for a while, then it'll stop hurting, and they'll end up somewhere else, with other people. Make other people miserable, or, yeah, maybe happy. Maybe. I mean, company. It's a great thing. Really. I'm all for it. Who wants to drink alone? Speaking of which, speaking of which—there's a place around the corner. It's got a red awning. Any of you want to join me, I'll be there in, say, ten or fifteen? And if any of you happen to be dentists, I'd like to tell you about some acrylic burrs. It's a line I'm very proud to represent.

[*He exits. Lights fade.*]

THE ACTION AGAINST SOL SCHUMANN

—for Dennis, Marcie, and Sandy, with thanks for a home at the Victory
  Gardens Theater of Chicago

In the mideighties, I saw an article by David van Biema in the *Washington Post* about the Office of Special Investigations case against Jacob Tannenbaum and a documentary film by Steve Brand called *Kaddish.*

Tannenbaum was a Jew who had been a *kapo* in a labor camp and, it was alleged, had been particularly brutal to fellow Jews under his charge. After the war, Tannenbaum had come to New York, married, had children, and become a pillar of the community. He had also written regular checks to Simon Wiesenthal's center. He did indeed have a stroke before the formal hearing could begin and, having been judged not capable of participating in his own defense, settled with the government by giving up his citizenship in return for not being deported. He ended his days in a nursing home.

Brand's documentary concerns a young American Jew named Yossi Klein whose identity is entirely defined by being the son of a man who survived the Holocaust. The bulk of Klein's energies are focused on political action on behalf of Jewish causes, and he works to prevent the recurrence of conditions that led to the nightmare his father endured. Midway through the film, Klein's father, Zoltan, dies, and the viewer can't help but be concerned that the son will have a nervous breakdown. The film ends on a note of hope, offering some evidence that Yossi will find his equilibrium.

The play began with the speculation of what would happen if this sort of son had had that sort of father. It is fiction. This is not the story of Jacob Tannenbaum and Yossi Klein. I have created characters independent of them.

I have, however, tried to ground the play in the world of the real. I researched the procedures and legal language I quote. Also, the scene of the interrogation in the World Trade Center takes place there not to harvest associations with 9/11 (the play premiered several months before 9/11) but because that's where the Office of Special Investigations interrogation of Tannenbaum took place.

Similar to *Bluff*, my favorite staging of *Sol* involved chairs for the ensemble around a central playing area. The actors moved such set pieces as were required, and the doubling actors made costume changes in full sight of the audience. The lights never went to black until the end.

With thanks to the National Foundation of Jewish Culture, the Center Theatre of Chicago, and David Picker for their parts in the development of this play. Thanks also to Kristine Niven, Ellen Schiff, Tandy Cronyn, Mike Nussbaum, David Pasquesi, Marc Vann, and others who have offered valuable support.

Special thanks to David van Biema, whose article for the *Washington Post* was a particularly valuable resource.

The Action Against Sol Schumann premiered at the Victory Gardens Theater of Chicago on March 26, 2001, under the direction of Dennis Zacek, with the following cast:

Doubling Actress (Mrs. Shapiro,
    Rivka Glauer, and Nurse) . . . . Roslyn Alexander
Paul Fontana . . . . Anthony Fleming III
Aaron . . . . Robert K. Johansen
Michael . . . . Eli Goodman
Kate . . . . Melissa Carlson
Sol . . . . Bernie Landis
Doubling Actor (Holgate, Israel Frieder,
    Lipsky, Bernard Reiner, and Felix Glauer) . . . . Richard Henzel
Diane . . . . Kati Brazda
Leah . . . . Amy Ludwig

The Action Against Sol Schumann received its New York premiere at the Hypothetical Theatre on June 18, 2004, under the direction of Amy Feinberg. The play was slightly revised to accommodate a larger cast:

Doubling Actress (Mrs. Shapiro, Nurse) . . Margaret A. Flanagan
Paul Fontana . . . . Postell Pringle

Aaron..Douglas Dickerman
Michael......................................Nathan M. White
Kate ....Kim Donovan
Sol...Herbert Rubens
Doubling Actor (Holgate, Lipsky,
     Bernard Reiner, Felix Glauer)...................Bruce Mohat
Diane................................Catherine Lynn Dowling
Leah...Susan O'Connor
Israel Frieder ....Jerry Rockwood
Rivka Glauer ....Tandy Cronyn

CHARACTERS

Paul Fontana
Aaron
Michael
Kate
Sol
Diane
Leah

The Doubling Actress plays Mrs. Shapiro, Rivka Glauer, Nurse.
The Doubling Actor plays Holgate, Israel Frieder, Lipsky, Bernard
Reiner, Felix Glauer.

All actors are in the ensemble except when playing specific parts.

SCENE 1

[*Two members of the* ENSEMBLE *enter and address the audience.*]

ENSEMBLE: —The smell of cherry blossoms in the air.
  —Washington, DC.
  —Paul Fontana.
  —Mrs. Shapiro.
  —Mrs. Shapiro has been lying in wait for Paul Fontana.

[PAUL *enters from one side of the stage.* MRS. SHAPIRO *approaches her from the other.*]

MRS. SHAPIRO: Mr. Fontana?

PAUL: Mrs.?

MRS. SHAPIRO: Mrs. Shapiro.

PAUL: Ah, yes.

MRS. SHAPIRO: I thought it was you.

PAUL: I have that feeling myself sometimes.

MRS. SHAPIRO: Excuse me?

PAUL: Nothing. You wanted—

MRS. SHAPIRO: Your secretary—Jennifer I think is her name?—I think maybe she hasn't given you all of your messages. I've left messages.

PAUL: Yes, I know.

MRS. SHAPIRO: Oh, you *did* get them?

PAUL: I—yes.

MRS. SHAPIRO: Because, sometimes, you know, secretaries, they decide what gets to the desk. Their own judgment of what's important. I think maybe your secretary thinks I'm not so important.

PAUL: No, I got your messages.

MRS. SHAPIRO: You never called me back. This is what's got me confused. This is why I wait for you here.

PAUL: Oh.

MRS. SHAPIRO: I didn't hear. I thought, like I said, maybe your secretary. And you didn't get back to me.

PAUL: I didn't get back because I didn't have anything more to get back to you with.

MRS. SHAPIRO: But you're working on it?

PAUL: As I asked Jennifer to tell you, our investigation didn't come up with anything we felt we could—

MRS. SHAPIRO: But he's a Nazi. Everybody in the building knows he's a Nazi. Your job—you're *supposed* to be getting rid of these people.

PAUL: Yes, but we have to prove our case in court—

MRS. SHAPIRO: Fine, then put me on the stand; I'll tell them. The things he says, the kind of person he is, his accent, his dogs—

PAUL: Mrs. Shapiro, from what you've said, I'm willing to believe he's not a very nice person. But we cannot throw him out of the country just because he's not nice. The law requires more than that.

MRS. SHAPIRO: For instance?

PAUL: Proof.

[*She turns to* ENSEMBLE *members for support.*]

ENSEMBLE: —Evidence that he obtained his citizenship under false pretenses—
—Or that he was a member of the Nazi Party.
—Or was involved in war crimes.

MRS. SHAPIRO: But you know that already. He's from Germany, isn't he?

PAUL: The fact that he was born there isn't—*lots* of people have been born in Germany.

MRS. SHAPIRO: And lots of them are Nazis.

PAUL: Mrs. Shapiro, I don't have an answer that's going to satisfy you. I'm sorry.

[*A beat.* MRS. SHAPIRO *nods.* PAUL *starts to walk away.*]

MRS. SHAPIRO: What did he do? Pay you off?

[*A beat.* PAUL *sighs and continues.* MRS. SHAPIRO *hollers after him.*]

You, the Nazis! One government and another. No difference.

[MRS. SHAPIRO *exits.* PAUL *turns to the audience.*]

PAUL: I meet a lot of people like Mrs. Shapiro. Some of them louder. And some—almost a whisper. They talk about what they've seen—what happened to parents or maybe a child. They look at me, and I know they're thinking how can it be fair that they have to put their hopes in—deal with somebody who, from their point of view . . . They have *children* older than me, some of them. Most of what they tell me about happened in the 1940s. I was being diapered when many of them first arrived in this country, tried to figure out how to make a life after so much death. Being my age, and living now—

ENSEMBLE: In 1985. This takes place in 1985.

PAUL: I don't pretend; I *can't* claim to understand. But there's work to do, and I'm one of the ones doing it. I asked to be one of the ones doing it.

SCENE 2

ENSEMBLE: Two brothers.

[AARON, MICHAEL, *and* KATE *enter.*]

AARON: Aaron.

MICHAEL: And Michael.

KATE: Michael's wife, Kate.

[ENSEMBLE *members hand* AARON *and* MICHAEL *yarmulkes and offer them chairs to sit at a table.* SOL *enters carrying a box. He puts it on the table, opens it, and pulls out a paroches—a kind of curtain on which is embroidered a design. At the bottom, there is an inscription.*]

ENSEMBLE: There is an inscription. It reads:

MICHAEL: "Donated by Solomon Schumann, in memory of his family."

ENSEMBLE: —This is Sol Schumann's home in Brooklyn.
—An apartment building in Park Slope.
—He and his wife, Esther, raised the boys here. The boys left to attempt adulthood. His wife died some years before.

AARON [*to audience*]: We come over regularly for dinner.

KATE: What—

[*She hesitates.*]

SOL: Yes?

AARON: She wants to know what it is. Isn't that right, Kate?

KATE: Something religious?

SOL: A paroches.

ENSEMBLE [*in unison, spelling*]: P-a-r-o-c-h-e-s.

KATE: Oh.

SOL: All right: in a synagogue, you know there is the ark, and inside the ark—

KATE: The Torah.

SOL: The Torah, good. So, in front of the ark sometimes there is a kind of curtain. That's what this is—that curtain.

KATE: Yes, I see. Sorry if I'm asking a stupid question—

SOL: How else would you find out? You weren't brought up with this. No, ask—

KATE: So you give this as a gift to the synagogue.

SOL: Yes.

KATE: And it's OK to put messages like this on it.

SOL: A personal thing, "in the memory of." But you wouldn't see on one, for instance, "Coca-Cola."

[KATE *smiles*.]

I thought, there are no graves. My mother, my father, my sister. The others. No graves. No place to visit. To leave stones. So this—so they should be remembered. I told the rabbi what I wanted; he recommended someone. On the Lower East Side, a little old man. So old he called me son. Can you believe such a thing is possible? I told him what I wanted—

AARON: He did a beautiful job, Pop.

KATE: And this is called again—

SOL: A paroches.

KATE [*not getting the "ch" sound right*]: Paroches.

AARON: No, Kate. "Ch."

KATE: "Ch."

AARON: Like there's something in your throat you're trying to get out. "Ch."

KATE: Oh, like in *challah*.

AARON: Yes.

KATE [*correctly*]: Paroches.

AARON: Are you *sure* you aren't Jewish?

MICHAEL: Aaron—

AARON: It's a joke. Michael, I am making a joke.

KATE [*to* MICHAEL]: Honey, you don't have to protect me.

SOL: Sometime this week, Aaron, maybe you can come to services with me? It would be good to help. Some days we have trouble making a minyan. [*To* KATE] A minyan is—

KATE: The ten men you need to hold services.

SOL: Very good.

MICHAEL: You still recruiting people on the street? [*To* KATE] If they don't have ten men, sometimes they go out on the street and ask people if they're Jewish.

KATE: They don't have to be Orthodox?

MICHAEL: No, just Jewish.

SOL: People are kind. If they can, they do.

KATE: It's got to be men, though. Not women.

AARON: Tell you what, Pop, I'll see what I can do.

SOL: Besides, my friends ask about my boys. Lipsky thinks I've made you up, that you don't exist.

AARON: Sometime this week, I promise.

SOL: And maybe you'll have some good news for me?

AARON: Such as—

SOL: You've met somebody.

AARON: Oh, Pop, not that again.

SOL: Michael is younger than you, and he's already married.

AARON: Michael has slightly different priorities, all right?

SOL: Having a family, children, this is not important to you?

AARON: Hey, you know what I am? I am hungry. What do you say?

SCENE 3

[HOLGATE *enters. A member of the* ENSEMBLE *wheels on a podium as* HOLGATE *begins to speak to audience.* DIANE, *a reporter, is one of those observing.*]

HOLGATE [*to audience*]: Germany has worked very hard to reenter the community of civilized nations. The Bitburg ceremony is designed to recognize that fact, that achievement.

ENSEMBLE: —A Jewish community center in Queens.
—German Chancellor Helmut Kohl has invited President Ronald Reagan to visit a German cemetery in Bitburg to honor those who died in World War Two. Reagan has accepted.

DIANE: Some people have opinions.

LEAH [*in the audience*]: I'm sorry, Mr. Holgate, but it seems to me there had to be a way to recognize this without honoring members of the SS.

HOLGATE: There is no question of honoring the SS—

LEAH: There are SS members buried in that cemetery. Laying a wreath there will honor their memory.

AARON [*rising, in the audience*]: I have a question. My name's Aaron Schumann. My question, Mr. Holgate is, aren't you angry?

HOLGATE: About what?

AARON [*approaching the stage*]: Probably tonight you would have liked to spend at home with your family, have some pot roast, watch a good cop show on TV. Instead, you're stuck standing up in front of us to defend the indefensible. I think you should ask yourself about the guy who sent you up here—out of the whole office, why did he choose *you* to do this? Because I'm telling you, whoever he is, this man is not your friend.

[*Others at the meeting are vocal in support of* AARON.]

HOLGATE: Mr. Schumann, I don't expect to satisfy you. If I were in your position I doubt if *I'd* be satisfied. There are, however, aspects of this situation I think you haven't given full consideration.

AARON: Such as what?

HOLGATE: For one thing, people keep talking about Bitburg as if it were an SS cemetery. In fact, the vast majority of the people buried at Bitburg were ordinary soldiers, a lot of them teenagers drafted into the war against their will. Of the more than two thousand buried there, only forty-eight were members of the SS.

AARON: So only about two percent are SS, which makes this graveyard nearly ninety-eight percent pure.

[*Others in the room react.* AARON *turns to talk to them.*]

No, maybe he's got a point. Maybe we can do a deal. [*Turning back to* HOLGATE] Tell you what: you tell President Reagan that as far as I'm concerned, he can go to Bitburg, he can stand there and bow his head for ninety-eight seconds provided, after that, he spits for two.

[*Lights shift.* HOLGATE *exits. The* ENSEMBLE *members remove the podium.* AARON *and* LEAH *end up onstage, looking off after* HOLGATE.]

LEAH: He heard what we had to say.

AARON: Oh, come on, Leah, don't be naive. He didn't hear anything he didn't expect to hear.

LEAH: So why would he—

AARON: Well, what do you think?

LEAH: What is this, a pop quiz?

AARON: Think about it. Why would the administration send this guy to talk to us?

DIANE [*appearing off to the side*]: So that you *could* yell at him.

AARON [*nodding*]: Give us a chance to blow off some steam.

DIANE: Maybe you get it out of your system. Yes or no, it gives the appearance they're a little bit responsive to the concerns of the—

AARON [*continuing to* LEAH]: Appearance, yeah. I mean, you don't seriously think that Holgate's gonna fly back to Washington, tell Reagan, "Look, you're gonna have to cancel this Bitburg thing 'cause there's a whole lot of angry Jews in Queens." Like Reagan's really going to go, "Angry Jews? Gee! Get Germany on the phone. Tell them if it's OK by the chancellor we'll meet in Disney World instead. We'll lay a wreath on the tomb of the unknown Goofy."

[DIANE *laughs.* AARON *looks at her.*]

I don't know you.

DIANE: No.

AARON: Do I want to?

DIANE: Diane Abbott.

AARON: You're a writer.

DIANE: Yes.

AARON: *Mother Jones?* The *Village Voice?*

DIANE: Among others I'd tell you about except I'm too modest.

AARON: What's the story here? For you, I mean. You're doing a story, right?

DIANE: Children of survivors and Bitburg. Your dad's a survivor, right?

AARON: Yes.

DIANE [*to* LEAH]: And your parents.

LEAH: You've done your research.

AARON: So you're interested in what?

DIANE: Your reaction to Bitburg, given what your parents went through.

AARON: Are you having any trouble figuring that out?

DIANE: I think I'm beginning to glean it.

AARON: "Glean"?

DIANE: Yes. It's like "infer" only—

AARON: No, I've heard the word. I know the word. Just it's one of those—do you do crossword puzzles?

DIANE: If I did, would you consider me a less credible person?

[AARON *smiles.*]

LEAH [*persisting*]: All right, so if tonight, like you say, meant nothing—

AARON: Worse than nothing.

LEAH: So, according to you, what *would* mean something? What could someone do?

SCENE 4

[*Cross-fade to* MICHAEL, *who is addressing the audience as* AARON, DIANE, *and* LEAH *exit.*]

MICHAEL: I've heard that there are theories about who you're likely to be, what kind of life you're likely to have, on the basis of when you were born. I don't mean astrology. I mean the order of birth. The firstborn boy supposedly has a tendency to do this, the second born has a tendency to do that. If you're a girl and you're the middle child—and so forth. Well, Aaron's my older brother. So maybe that explains something.

SCENE 5

[ENSEMBLE *member appears with airport ground crew signs. Facing the audience, he goes through the signals guiding a jet into a terminal as we get corresponding sounds of a jet engine. The engine turns off.* MICHAEL *is joined by* LEAH *as the* ENSEMBLE *member signals to* AARON *that it's OK for him to enter.* AARON *is pleased to see the welcoming committee.*]

AARON: Leah!

LEAH: How was the flight?

AARON: More fun than a prostate exam. So, what was the coverage like?

LEAH: Some on the networks, but local carried more.

AARON: Sure, big New York angle.

MICHAEL: That's how I found out you went over.

AARON: TV?

MICHAEL: Kate saw you. On the evening news. "Isn't that Aaron?" I said it couldn't be. "What would he be doing in Germany?"

AARON: But you put that one together, right?

MICHAEL: You didn't tell me you were going.

AARON: It was kind of a quick decision.

MICHAEL: You tell Pop?

AARON: I called from the airport. That's how quick it was.

MICHAEL: It's just—to find out something about a member of your own family from the TV.

[DIANE *enters.*]

AARON [*not bitterly but registering with* MICHAEL]: I didn't know that you'd be that interested.

[*He notices* DIANE.]

Look who's here.

DIANE: The gleaning lady.

AARON: What? Oh yeah, I get it. "Gleaning." Cute, yeah.

DIANE: You free to talk?

AARON: You hungry?

DIANE: Is that your way of saying you're hungry?

AARON: Glad you asked.

SCENE 6

[*The* ENSEMBLE *member with the airline signals returns and holds a signal up to have* AARON, MICHAEL, DIANE, *and* LEAH *wait while other* ENSEMBLE *members bring on a restaurant table, some chairs, and glasses of beer and wine. The* ENSEMBLE *member now signals them to their seats.*]

AARON: Oh, sure, there were cops there.

DIANE: To protect you?

AARON: German cops protecting people, a lot of who—their parents were once dragged away by *other* German cops. Part of me wanted to ask them, "So what did your folks do in the war?"

LEAH: You mean you didn't? There was a possibility for a confrontation and you actually restrained yourself?

AARON: Oh yeah, I recognize this—this is irony, right?

LEAH: No, this is wonderment.

AARON: Me, confrontational?

LEAH: Incredible concept, huh?

AARON: Michael, am I confrontational?

MICHAEL: Let me think about that for a second.

AARON [*joking*]: I asked a question: Michael, you asshole, am I confrontational?

DIANE: You were able to just take off like that? From work?

AARON: One of the benefits of being a substitute.

DIANE: Teacher?

LEAH: You got an assignment on Monday?

AARON: In Bed-Stuy.

LEAH: You going to tell the kids you went to Germany?

AARON: I'd be surprised if most of them knew where Germany is.

LEAH: Oh, come on—

AARON: You should come sit in on one of my classes sometime. You think *I'm* confrontational; you should see some of the kids—I feel safer in Germany.

LEAH: Hyperbole alert.

AARON: Yeah? One of the classes I had a couple of weeks back, this kid—a friend of his comes in. Fact I have some vague approximation of a lesson going, this doesn't matter. He's got something to talk about with this guy. Something to settle, something to discuss. I tell him this isn't the place or time. He puts his hand in his pocket, says, "Hey, motherfucker, know what I got here? A time machine."

DIANE: What *did* he have?

AARON: I didn't ask. I strolled down the corridor and got one of the security guards. Kid was gone by the time we got back. But you learn quick—you don't get in their face, unless you want an unauthorized nose job. Or worse. You're more likely to be assaulted as a teacher than as a cop.

LEAH: This is an actual statistic?

AARON: An actual statistic. What's more, it's even true.

DIANE: So, aside from the protest itself, did you look much around the country? See anything besides Bitburg?

AARON: Visit a beer hall? Tour the Schlossendorfenhoff Castle? I wasn't exactly there for cultural enrichment.

DIANE: Granted. But as long as you were there—man does not live by dread alone.

AARON: So to speak.

DIANE: Sorry.

AARON: I almost wanted to visit Bayreuth. You know Bayreuth?

LEAH: The Bayreuth Festival, right? Where they do the *Ring Cycle.*

AARON: Otherwise known as Wagner central. Did you know that when he was a conductor—Wagner, I'm talking about—when he was assigned to conduct a score by a Jewish composer, he wore gloves? Yes. And after the piece was done, was finished, he'd throw the gloves away? But he manages to get this place built—Bayreuth—this huge opera house so they can stage his endless nutcase operas. So, years later: Hitler—big Wagner fan. During the war, Hitler keeps the place going full tilt—even when there are shortages 'cause of the war— he thinks it's the beating heart of the German soul or something. Including in the orchestra, during the war, Jewish musicians. Yes, playing in the pit. Wrap your mind around that one. You're a Jewish oboe player, at the same time your relatives are being carted away, you're playing *Twilight of the Gods* for *der Führer.* How honored they must have been by his applause. So—this is the part I love—when American troops liberate the town, some of the GIs look at this big opera palace and say, "Hey, cool—a vaudeville house!" And they take it over and put up a show. Every comic routine and number they can remember—the Marx Brothers, the Ritz Brothers, Fanny Brice, Jack Benny, Danny Kaye. Wagner's daughter-in-law hears about it; she nearly has a heart attack. This vast, somber temple of high art being desecrated with a bunch of jokes from kike comics. No, if there were any place in Germany I'd actually want to visit, that would be it.

DIANE: In honor of that one performance.

MICHAEL: You know, apart from being an anti-Semitic nutcase, Wagner did write some good stuff.

AARON: And Hitler could sketch. So, OK, what's your point?

MICHAEL: That sometimes you have to separate a person from what they do.

AARON: Why? Why do I have to do that?

MICHAEL: I mean, from what they accomplish.

AARON: And again I say why?

MICHAEL: I'm not saying that it makes him less of a nutcase that he wrote some good stuff. But I'm saying that it's not right not to acknowledge that he did write some good stuff.

AARON: You're accusing me of being unfair to Wagner?

MICHAEL: People are more complex than that. You can't just put them in easy categories—good, bad. Besides, some people are good because it's been easy for them to be good. They've never faced a hard choice. And maybe, if they did face one, maybe they wouldn't have measured up.

AARON: So you want more categories? Subcategories? Good but untested? Bad but with an excuse? Should we get a huge rubber stamp, stamp that on Germany? "Bad, but with an excuse"?

MICHAEL: I never said that.

AARON: Oh, so for Germany you'll let me use the bad stamp?

MICHAEL: Maybe I'm suggesting you shouldn't use stamps at all.

AARON: You said we should separate people from what they do.

MICHAEL [*attempting to amend*]: *Some* of what they—

AARON: And I say people *are* what they do. What you do, that's who you are. You are the person who does that thing. And, you know, I'm not really concerned about the reasons. The reasons are private. That's for shrinks to worry about. The actions—the actions—if a drunk runs down a five-year-old kid with his car, I don't give a shit if the reason he was drinking was his pet turtle died.

DIANE: So, as far as you're concerned, everybody in the Bitburg cemetery, not just the guys who were in the SS—

AARON: Pretty much, yes. My opinion. You don't have to share it. But if you don't, you're wrong.

DIANE: Tell me something—

AARON [*interrupting*]: Maybe—

[DIANE *looks at him, as if to say, "Are you finished?"*]

I'm sorry, yes, OK. Something you want me to tell you?

DIANE: Have you ever forgiven anyone? For anything?

AARON: You aren't seriously asking me to—

DIANE: No, I'm not talking about Germany now. I'm just talking about you, personally. You. Aaron. Forgive. Somebody who did something, something you thought was wrong, something *to* you maybe—not as a political act particularly—but to you.

AARON: Like what?

DIANE: Hurt you, broke your heart maybe—maybe a girlfriend who cheated on you. I don't know—everybody gets disappointed, feels betrayed by someone sometime. I know I have.

AARON [*mocking intense interest*]: Oh yeah? Tell me about it.

DIANE: We're not talking about me.

AARON: What, aren't you interesting enough to talk about?

DIANE: I'm very interesting. And when you're writing a story about me, I'll be glad to share.

AARON: This story isn't about me. You aren't writing about me.

DIANE: You're going to be in it.

AARON: The story you told me about, that you're writing, is about Bitburg.

DIANE: And about the people who went there. Of which you are one.

AARON: So for this you need to know—

DIANE: Did I say *need*? Just interested.

AARON: You're interested in me?

DIANE: I'm interested in this *aspect* of you. Come on, quit horsing around.

AARON: OK. Let me think.

[*A beat.*]

Yes.

DIANE: Yes?

AARON: Yes, I have. In twelfth grade, I lent eight bucks to my friend Harvey. He never paid it back. And you know? It's OK. But you know, forgiveness—

DIANE: Unh-hunh?

AARON: Fine as a kind of abstract principle, I guess. But in moderation. You don't want to let it get out of hand. I mean, for instance, Nixon.

DIANE: Oh, well, Nixon—

AARON: Yeah, well, you see—

DIANE: You've got to draw the line *some*where.

[*They share a laugh. A beat.* LEAH *rises.*]

LEAH: Well, I've got a meeting with a client tomorrow morning. I should look over his brief.

AARON: Anything interesting?

LEAH: Landlord-tenant thing. Landlord A wants to convert apartment to condos. Tenant B doesn't want to move—

AARON: Fill in the blanks.

LEAH: It's a living.

AARON: Whose side are you on?

LEAH: The side of righteousness and justice.

AARON: Just checking.

LEAH [*putting money on the table*]: This should cover it.

AARON: What are you doing?

LEAH: You flew to Germany; least I can do is buy a few drinks.

AARON: OK.

DIANE: Where do you live?

LEAH: Chelsea.

DIANE: I'm heading to the Village. Want to split a cab?

AARON: What, you've got everything you need for your story so it's OK to take off?

DIANE: Absolutely. I never talk to people just to talk to people.

LEAH: Maybe she wants to talk to me, Aaron. Get my perspective.

AARON: Why would she want to do that?

LEAH [*giving* AARON *a kiss*]: Get some sleep, huh?

AARON: Will do. [*To* DIANE] Write a good article.

DIANE: Gee, if just so as not to disappoint you.

LEAH: 'Night, Michael.

MICHAEL: 'Night, Leah.

[LEAH *and* DIANE *exit.*]

She's looking good.

AARON: Leah?

MICHAEL: Is she with someone these days?

AARON: Don't know.

MICHAEL: Might be worth finding out.

AARON: You're married.

MICHAEL: I'm talking about you.

AARON: What are you doing? Are you trying to matchmake?

MICHAEL: You like her; she likes you—

AARON: We're friends, yes.

MICHAEL: OK, I'll shut up.

AARON: In my own good time, OK? When I'm ready.

MICHAEL: At that rate, you'll pay for the honeymoon with your Social Security.

AARON: Who's this talking? Pop? Pop, is that you under a mask?

MICHAEL: All right.

[*A beat.*]

What did he say?

AARON: Pop? When?

MICHAEL: When you told him you were going to Germany? You said you phoned from the airport—

AARON: I phoned, yes.

MICHAEL: And he said?

AARON: "Don't."

MICHAEL: He was afraid that brownshirts would jump out and drag you away?

AARON: Not funny.

MICHAEL: I'm not laughing. But, you know, to worry about something like that—

AARON: Given what he went through, I think it's natural—

MICHAEL: You don't have to remind me what he went—

AARON: Sometimes I wonder.

MICHAEL: You wonder?

AARON: Forget it.

MICHAEL: No. You made that crack before, you didn't think I'd be interested about your going to Germany, and now, as if I don't care about what Pop went—

AARON: I didn't say that.

MICHAEL: I'm not reverent enough or something? *Mindful?*

AARON: You've got to admit you're pretty assimilated.

MICHAEL: Why would that qualify as an admission? You think I should feel guilty I'm assimilated?

AARON: It's a reason why some of this other stuff might not be as important to you.

MICHAEL: Other stuff like the camps and Bitburg—

AARON: Or do I have it wrong?

MICHAEL: You have it wrong.

AARON: Yeah? What if I'd called and said, "Hey, come with me."

MICHAEL: What? To Germany?

AARON: Would you have? OK: It's three days ago. "Michael, I'm going to Germany. I'm going to show Ronny Reagan how I feel about this. Come with."

MICHAEL: It would have been hard to take those particular three days off.

AARON: Oh?

MICHAEL: In case you forget, this is April, and April is a pretty important month in an accountant's life.

AARON: Famous for it.

MICHAEL: All right.

AARON: You wouldn't have gone.

MICHAEL: I *couldn't* have.

AARON: Fine. Wouldn't because you couldn't still comes down to the same—

MICHAEL: Which makes me what?

AARON: Makes us different, that's all. That's what I'm saying. But since when is this news? You haven't set foot inside a synagogue since you were bar mitzvahed. You married a—

MICHAEL: A shiksa?

AARON: Not my word.

MICHAEL: Of course not.

AARON: But when you have kids, you won't raise them Jewish. Probably Unitarian, right? Or Ethical Culture, if anything. When you come to Pop's for Sabbath dinner, you think I don't see that look Kate shoots you when you put on the yarmulke? "Isn't that adorable? Michael's wearing a beanie."

MICHAEL: I think we've just reached the end of the conversation.

[MICHAEL *rises.*]

AARON: Hey. Michael—

[MICHAEL *wheels on him.*]

MICHAEL: I don't know where you get off sitting in judgment on me, my wife. We don't even *have* kids yet, already you're making cracks about them.

AARON: Sorry.

MICHAEL: At least *I've* got a life. It ever occur to you, Aaron, this obsession you've got with the past and camps and memorials maybe is a way of avoiding—

AARON: Not just an accountant, a shrink, too.

MICHAEL: Think about it. What does it tell you about someone your age, your education, after twelve, thirteen years is still running around the city as a substitute teacher?

AARON: Well, you may have a case. Of course, I'm teaching kids to read and you're helping rich people dodge taxes. We might draw some conclusions from that, too.

MICHAEL: OK, fine: you're the righteous Jew and I'm the assimilated sellout. So I'll do you a favor: I'll keep out of the way so I don't embarrass you anymore.

SCENE 7

[KATE *enters, joining* MICHAEL *as* AARON *exits.*]

MICHAEL: As if he were handing out licenses to be Jewish.

KATE: Do you feel Jewish?

MICHAEL: I feel Jewish-*ish.*

KATE: What relationship does that have to being Jewish? Like Cheez Whiz is to cheddar?

[*A beat.*]

MICHAEL: Some people—I don't know how they can. Pop—everything he went through—still, every morning he can he goes to that synagogue.

KATE: Maybe that's what helped him get through it.

MICHAEL: I just can't imagine praying to a God that could let such things happen.

KATE: Did you pick up the dry cleaning?

MICHAEL: Was I supposed to?

KATE: Never mind.

MICHAEL: Sorry.

KATE: We'll cope. It doesn't ever bother you, does it?

MICHAEL: What?

KATE: That I'm not Jewish?

MICHAEL: What kind of question—

KATE: So the answer's no?

MICHAEL: Kate—

KATE: It's such a large part of Aaron's life, and you're brothers—

MICHAEL: I am not my brother.

KATE: I know.

MICHAEL: I am *not* my brother.

[*Cross-fade.*]

SCENE 8

[AARON *appears onstage.* DIANE *approaches him, hands him a copy of a magazine à la* Mother Jones.]

DIANE: Thought you might like to see it.

AARON: Oh?

DIANE: My article. You're in there. It'll be on the stands tomorrow.

AARON: You're welcome.

DIANE: Excuse me?

AARON: No, really, it was my pleasure.

DIANE: OK, don't tell me. I'll figure it out. You have me thanking you because—

AARON: Well, they paid you for the article, didn't they?

DIANE: I see: I was able to make money because you were worth writing about. Well, you know, you're welcome, too.

AARON: Right.

DIANE: Hope it helps.

AARON: Diane, because of your article, genocide will be a thing of the past.

DIANE: I'm happy if you think so.

AARON: Now, if you could do something about male pattern baldness—

[*She smiles and begins to exit.*]

DIANE: See you next time.

AARON: Next time?

DIANE: Or is this it? Are you retiring from the field?

AARON: You've selected yourself to be my chronicler. Ah. And I have nothing to say about this?

DIANE: Well, you could stop being an interesting person.

AARON: Then you'd drop me.

DIANE: I'm a fairly heartless broad.

AARON: Well, that's obvious.

DIANE: Take care.

[*She exits. He opens the magazine, begins to read. He smiles, looks in the direction in which she exited, then exits.*]

SCENE 9

[PAUL *enters, and* ENSEMBLE *members assemble the suggestion of an office.*]

ENSEMBLE: —The World Trade Center.
   —Photo of Ronald Reagan on the wall.

[ISRAEL FRIEDER, *a very intense elderly man, stands looking out of where the window was placed.*]

FRIEDER: I was at a bar mitzvah. A grandson. Donald. Not at the synagogue I usually go to. But there is sometimes in front of the ark a kind of curtain. And I'm standing there and I'm looking at the curtain in this synagogue, and I see a name stitched into it—as part of the dedication in memory of his family. And I ask the rabbi about the man who donated this curtain. And the rabbi tells me that there is an Orthodox congregation that meets in a room downstairs, and that this man is a member of that congregation. So the next morning, I go. I want to see if it's him. I go. The other members of the congregation, they're glad to see me. They sometimes have trouble making a minyan. You need ten men to have services, you know.

PAUL: Yes.

FRIEDER: And I'm there and I'm waiting. I think maybe I'll try to ask them about him. And then I think maybe I should say nothing, just wait. A couple of minutes later, he comes in. Next thing I know, I'm looking at the ceiling. They tell me I've fainted. He doesn't recognize me. I tell them I'll be all right, and I leave.

[*A beat.*]

The bridge, the promenade, Prospect Park. This is some view you've got.

PAUL: It's not really my office. They lend it to me—as a courtesy. When I come up from Washington.

[*A beat.*]

Mr. Frieder, you're sure?

FRIEDER: I'm sure.

PAUL: You understand I have to ask.

FRIEDER: Yes.

PAUL: If I'm going to take this into a courtroom, we have to be certain. After all, to identify someone after so many years. It's been so long since you've seen him.

FRIEDER: Not so long. At least once a week, at night when I close my eyes. He hasn't changed so much. The hair is grayer, but the hands are the same. I remember the hands very well.

[FRIEDER *looks out the window, points.*]

I've been living over there since forty-eight. And all this time, he's been living over there, too. Just a few miles away. Raising a family, praying, pretending.

PAUL: If we do this, it could take a long time.

FRIEDER: Mr. Fontana, I've waited forty years.

[*Cross-fade.*]

SCENE 10

[*Chamber music by Schubert plays.* AARON *is waiting.* MICHAEL *arrives.*]

MICHAEL: She come down yet?

AARON: Do you see her?

MICHAEL: Fancy building she works in.

AARON: Oh yes, let's talk about that. Good idea.

[*A beat.*]

She's late. Maybe we should go upstairs.

MICHAEL: She asked us to meet her in the atrium. So why don't we just stay here? What's that?

AARON: Juilliard students play here sometimes.

MICHAEL: No, I mean the piece. The composer.

AARON: Schubert something, I guess.

MICHAEL: It's nice.

AARON [*ironically*]: Yes, it's very soothing.

MICHAEL: You know, you're not going to do Pop or yourself, *any* of us, any good if you don't calm down a little.

AARON: Calm down?

MICHAEL: Relent. You know what I mean.

AARON: Take it easy? Be cool? Go with the flow?

[MICHAEL *shakes his head, raises his hand as if to say he won't pursue this anymore, and moves away.* LEAH *enters wearing a neatly tailored suit and carrying a briefcase.* AARON *sees her.*]

OK, Leah, what's going on? What's the story?

[LEAH *notices something's just happened between the two of them, but rather than get into it, she dives into business.*]

LEAH: OK, I've made a few phone calls, and from what I understand— they haven't formally accused him of anything. It's a request for an interview.

AARON: A request. That means he could say no.

LEAH: Technically, but I wouldn't advise it. With a little luck, we meet with them; we could put an end to the whole thing.

AARON: A little luck being—

LEAH: They see there isn't sufficient basis to continue the—

AARON: Of course there won't be sufficient basis. This is a joke. A sick joke.

MICHAEL: Pardon me for being dumb, but—who are these people?

AARON: You mean the OSI?

MICHAEL: Yes.

AARON: You really don't know who they are?

MICHAEL: I have a general idea. I'm asking for more specific—

LEAH [*jumping in before* AARON *can reply*]: Aaron—

[AARON *covers his mouth with one hand and raises the other to signal he won't say anything more.* LEAH *turns to* MICHAEL.]

OK: it's 1947, 1948. The war is over but Europe is still a big mess. You've got a lot of people who, for various reasons, want to come to the United States. Maybe where they used to live is now behind the iron curtain and they aren't real eager to go back, or maybe they're Jews and there's nothing much to go back to—

AARON: Except the good neighbors who said nothing when the Nazis dragged you off to the camps.

LEAH: For reasons you can guess, some of the bad guys would also like to get out of Europe—Nazi collaborators and other unpopular types.

MICHAEL: Right.

LEAH: So you have all these people who want to come to America. Which they do. And they apply for citizenship. And when they apply for citizenship, they have to swear that they have not been concentration camp guards and didn't push people into gas chambers. Of course, if you *did* push people into gas chambers, you're not likely to have serious qualms about telling the immigration office lies.

AARON: Which they did.

LEAH: And not just two or three either.

AARON: More like hundreds, maybe thousands.

MICHAEL: So the OSI—the OSI?

AARON [*impatiently*]: The Office of Special Investigations.

MICHAEL: They're supposed to go after them.

LEAH [*nodding*]: Take away their citizenship, deport them.

MICHAEL: So, what are they going after Dad for? He was a *victim*. It doesn't make sense.

AARON: Obviously they've screwed up. They've confused him with someone else. Sol Schumann—it's a common name. Right?

LEAH: It's possible.

AARON: It's a mistake. We'll go to his place, see him, get this straight. It's a mistake.

SCENE 11

[SOL *enters.* AARON, MICHAEL, *and* LEAH *turn to face him.*]

AARON: Pop?

[*A beat.*]

Pop?

[*A beat.*]

SOL: No.

AARON: What?

SOL: It's not. Not a mistake.

[*A beat.*]

AARON: Are you saying it's true?
SOL: It's more complicated.

[*A beat.*]

AARON: What are you *saying*?
LEAH: Aaron—

[*A beat.*]

SOL: I thought it was behind me. Forty years.

[*A beat.*]

AARON: You were a *kapo.*
SOL: Yes.
AARON: And you never said. You never told us.
SOL: You didn't need to know. No point to your knowing.
AARON: Of course not.
SOL: Do you think it was a job I asked for? Something I wanted? They came to me. They said, "Schumann, *you. You* will do this." You didn't refuse them. Not if you wanted to live.

[*A beat.*]

I *had* to live. My sister, mother, my father, *their* mother and fathers—all gone. Only me. The whole family. All gone. Only me.

[*A beat.*]

My *duty* to live.

[*A beat. Then, agitated,* AARON *rises, leaves the room.* MICHAEL *looks at* LEAH *and* SOL, *then follows* AARON.]

SCENE 12

MICHAEL [*to audience*]: I follow him up to the roof.

[MICHAEL *stands next to* AARON.]

ENSEMBLE: From here you can see the lights of the World Trade Center. Right over there.

AARON: You know about *kapos,* don't you? You know who they were? What they did?

MICHAEL: Some of them.

AARON: *Any* of them.

MICHAEL: What they were forced to—

AARON: Where have we heard this before?

MICHAEL: Come on, there's a big difference—

AARON: Right.

MICHAEL: You know there is.

AARON: What a laugh, huh?

MICHAEL: Laugh?

AARON: The paroches he had made in the memory of the family he lost—except it turns out when it comes to memory, his is pretty selective, wouldn't you say?

MICHAEL: It's not something he wanted to remember. Can you blame him?

AARON: That's the question, isn't it?

MICHAEL: Aaron, he needs our help. Come back.

[*A beat.* KATE, *enters,* MICHAEL *turns to her.*]

And I go to the stairs, and he follows me down. When I get to the floor where Pop lives, I open the door from the stairwell to the hallway—

[AARON *hesitates, looks at* MICHAEL, *and exits.*]

And he keeps going down the stairs. I hear the door to the lobby slam.

KATE: What did he think, your father's perfect?

MICHAEL: Aaron grew up with this idea about Pop—this image.

KATE: He didn't grow up with any idea that you didn't grow up with, but are *you* pissing and moaning?

MICHAEL: Well, we're different people.

KATE: Thank God. And what does Aaron think *he'd* do if someone put a gun to *his* head?

MICHAEL: What are you arguing with me for?

KATE: I'm not arguing with you. But if you're going to defend Aaron's behavior—

MICHAEL: I'm not defending. I'm just telling you what it *is* about him.

KATE [*dismissively waving her hand*]: What it is: he's disillusioned, he's hurt. His father isn't pure and perfect. But what gives Aaron the right to expect that? Your dad suffered through something—we can't *begin* to conceive of. But since when does suffering make you a better, more wonderful human being? Except in the case of a few saints, which is why they're so unusual, which is why they're called saints. I mean, child abusers were usually themselves abused as children, right?

MICHAEL: Right: Pop's no worse than a child abuser. That'll really give Aaron comfort.

KATE: Like right now I'm concerned about Aaron's comfort.

MICHAEL: With luck it will all be over after this interview.

SCENE 13

[SOL, MICHAEL, *and* LEAH *enter where* PAUL *is waiting.*]

PAUL: Mr. Schumann?

SOL: Yes. This is my son, Michael.

LEAH: I'm Leah Abelson.

PAUL: Yes, we talked on the phone.

LEAH: I'm here as Mr. Schumann's counsel.

PAUL: You understand I'm recording this.

SOL: Yes.

PAUL: All right, then, why don't we—

[AARON *enters.*]

   Yes?

AARON: I'm Aaron Schumann. I'm his son.

[*He looks at his father.* SOL *nods. Lights shift.* SOL *sits.* PAUL *turns on the tape recorder. We are in the middle of the questioning.*]

SOL: There were eight of us in Ordenhaupt.

PAUL: Eight *kapos?*

SOL: Yes.

PAUL: Ordenhaupt was a camp?

SOL: Yes.

PAUL: What sort of labor was done there?

SOL: Pardon?

PAUL: What was done there? What did the prisoners do?

SOL: Different things. Some—what they did before: carpenters, tin-smiths. Also sorting.

PAUL: Sorting what?

SOL: Eyeglasses, shoes. What had belonged to those who had died.

PAUL: And as a *kapo,* you supervised this work.

SOL: This is what we were told to do.

PAUL: And you did it.

SOL: What I was told to do. Yes.

PAUL: And what did this consist of? What did you do? As a supervisor.

SOL: To see to it that it is done—the work. To solve problems.

PAUL: And if somebody wasn't doing his job, doing his share of the work—

SOL: You try to get him to.

PAUL: How?

SOL: How?

PAUL: How would you get him to?

SOL: You tell him that he must do it. Everybody must do it. We must all work. We have no choice. He doesn't. I don't. We are not there by choice. We are not there *for* choice. But this we all knew. This we lived with knowing.

PAUL: But, still, if he doesn't do it—

SOL: Maybe he's sick, so you try to protect him.

PAUL: Protect?

SOL: Yes. You try. You put him where you think he might not be noticed.

PAUL: By?

SOL: By the Germans. The guards. You tried to hide him.

PAUL: And you did this?

SOL: Yes.

PAUL: Often?

SOL: When I could. It was dangerous to do. If they thought you were trying to—

PAUL: The Germans?

SOL: If they thought you were trying to help, to protect, they would— [*Suddenly agitated*] You know this. I don't have to tell you what they were, what they did. Why do you ask me to tell you what you already know?

PAUL: I'm sorry, Mr. Schumann, it's necessary to our investigation. We need your words. In your own words. How you saw it.

SOL: Yes, I'm sorry. Yes, of course. You ask.

PAUL: If someone still wouldn't work, and he wasn't sick, and you couldn't hide him—how would you deal with that?

SOL: You would try to get him to see. It wasn't just him. It was all of us. If the Germans got angry, it might not be just this one person they might hurt, but maybe four or five others. Just because they were sitting near or because of the way they were looking. So it wasn't just for yourself. You had to think of the others.

PAUL: And if, after you've explained that, someone still doesn't respond, what might you do?

[*A beat.*]

SOL: You're trying to get me to say I hit them.

PAUL: Did you?

SOL: Only when it was required. For the safety of others. But not to *hurt*.

PAUL: To what then?

SOL: Sometimes they were—what is the word?—dazed. To wake them.

PAUL: You would hit them to wake them.

SOL: You tried to avoid this. You're a Jew. They are Jews, many of them. You don't want to.

[*A beat.*]

But you're talking about only a part of what happened. You're not talking at all about the people I helped. It was possible to help, which I did as often as I could.

PAUL: How did you help? We would like to know this.

SOL: Food. Sometimes I was able to get extra. I would share. When I had it, when I could do it. There are people alive today—if it weren't for me, they will tell you—people whose lives—you must ask them.

PAUL: We will. We would like to. Any names you can remember, you give to us.

SOL: You'll find them.

PAUL: We'll try.

SOL: You must be fair.

PAUL: We'll look. We'll ask who we can find.

SOL: People think, a *kapo*. They think only about the things you were made to do. And this was the worst. That sometimes they made you do things that they would do. The Germans.

PAUL: Such as hit people?

SOL: Yes.

PAUL: With what?

SOL: Well, your hands.

PAUL: Anything else?

SOL: Excuse me?

PAUL: You had a whip.

SOL: Yes. They gave me one. I carried it.

PAUL: You used it.

SOL: Rarely.

PAUL: But you did, sometimes.

SOL: You would try to hold back, but they might say, "No, harder. Harder or it will be *your* back." They thought this was—amusing. To make you do what they do. To try to turn you into— [*Forcefully*] Yes, you might be forced to do these things, but inside you hold on to who you are. You know you must not become one of them. You must not lose yourself.

[*Lights shift.* PAUL *turns off the machine.* SOL *looks at* PAUL *wordlessly.* AARON *touches his arm.* SOL *nods.* AARON, SOL, MICHAEL, *and* LEAH *leave the room. In a space separately defined by lighting,* AARON *turns to* SOL.]

AARON [*reassuringly*]: It's over, Pop.

[MICHAEL, AARON, SOL, *and* LEAH *leave the stage.* PAUL *turns to audience.*]

PAUL [*to audience*]: I don't want you to think that's all there is to it. We interview other people, we examine documents, records, cross-check. We don't make a decision casually.

[*He raises a paper and reads from it.*]

"This is an action brought pursuant to section 340(a) of the Immigration and Nationality Act of 1952 to revoke the United States citizenship of Solomon Schumann. It is charged that defendant was at the Ordenhaupt labor camp, located in what was then southern Germany, which was controlled by the forces of Nazi Germany—that

Ordenhaupt labor camp was operated by the Nazi SS and relied on prisoner assistants known as *kapos* in the daily operations of the camp and in disciplining other prisoners—that during the time he served as a supervisory *kapo* at Ordenhaupt, defendant participated in persecution by brutalizing and physically abusing prisoners . . ."

SCENE 14

[SOL *is sitting in a chair, still.* MICHAEL *enters.*]

MICHAEL: Pop? Pop, it's me, Michael. I've been trying to call you, but the phone's been—

SOL: I took it off the hook. Since they released it to the news, the phone calls I've been getting.

MICHAEL: Oh.

SOL: I haven't heard from your brother.

MICHAEL: He's gone climbing.

SOL: That was this week he was doing that?

MICHAEL: Yes.

SOL: I forgot.

MICHAEL: Have you had anything to eat? Do you want me to make you something to eat?

SOL: I'm fine.

[*A beat.*]

I don't understand. I answered their questions. What do they want? Why are they doing this?

[*Lights shift.* SOL *leaves the stage.* MICHAEL *stands on one side of the stage,* KATE *on the other. They are on the phone with each other.*]

KATE: It was on the TV.

MICHAEL: A camera crew rang the bell, but we didn't open the door.

KATE: They interviewed some of your father's neighbors.

MICHAEL: "We've known him for years. Who would have guessed?"

KATE: Basically. How's it going over there?

MICHAEL: I got him to bed. He's asleep now. It's so—

KATE: What?

MICHAEL: I was just thinking, all the years of him looking in on me when I was a kid. You know, to check on how I was sleeping, make sure I hadn't kicked the covers off in the night—

KATE: And now you're looking in on him.

MICHAEL: I mean, as long as I can remember, he's been the one Aaron and I could always turn to. Chase away bullies, come to bat for us when we needed a hand. Tonight, he looks so—

[*A beat.*]

KATE: You get some sleep yourself, OK?

MICHAEL: Will do.

[*Lights shift.* SOL *appears, wearing a yarmulke, dressed to go out.*]

MICHAEL: Pop, what are you doing?

SOL: What I do every morning.

MICHAEL: Pop, I don't know—

SOL: It is what I do every morning.

[SOL *hands* MICHAEL *a yarmulke.*]

ENSEMBLE [*to audience*]: —They walk to the shul.

[LIPSKY *enters.*]

—A friend of his, Lipsky, sees him approaching on the street.

MICHAEL: Lipsky walks up to us.

SOL: Do we have a minyan yet?

LIPSKY: Not yet.

SOL: I brought my son. Michael, you remember my friend, Mr. Lipsky.

LIPSKY: I think you should go home.

SOL: Home? But you need us. You don't have enough without us.

LIPSKY: The others won't stay if you stay.

SOL: Are they telling me I can't daven here?

LIPSKY: Not with us.

SOL: Us?

LIPSKY: I'm sorry.

[LIPSKY *walks away.* SOL *looks at* MICHAEL. MICHAEL *removes his yarmulke and they exit.*]

SCENE 15

[ENSEMBLE *brings in a park bench.* REINER *appears, wearing a scarf.*]

ENSEMBLE: Bernard Reiner.

REINER [*taking off scarf*]: It's warmer out than I thought.

ENSEMBLE: Washington again. The mall.

REINER: National Art Gallery over there. Over there, the building with the rockets and such.

[PAUL *enters.*]

PAUL: We could have met in my office.

REINER: That would have made it formal.

PAUL: Or in a restaurant.

REINER: Then I'd have to make a fuss with the waiter about not putting salt into the food. No, actually I enjoy sitting here, watching the tourists run in and out of the Smithsonian. Dragging their kids. Of course, the kids are mostly teed off. What does all this junky old stuff have to do with them?

PAUL: So.

REINER: The Schumann case.

PAUL: Yes?

REINER: This Schumann—you seek to take away his citizenship and deport him for being a *kapo*.

PAUL: Not for that, exactly. As I'm sure you know, the United States can't prosecute crimes committed on foreign soil.

REINER [*nodding*]: Not within your jurisdiction.

PAUL: But if he lied about his activities during the war on his application for citizenship, his naturalization can be invalidated, and then, yes, we can move to have him deported.

REINER: But surely many people lied on these applications. About their ages, their health, past political affiliations—any number of things.

PAUL: Yes.

REINER: But you don't pursue them. You don't prosecute them.

PAUL: The question is whether the lies were of sufficient gravity.

REINER: So this is what might be called a selective prosecution.

PAUL: You think that we shouldn't be pursuing this?

REINER: I and some of the people I'm associated with, we question whether you've considered all the implications.

PAUL: Implications?

REINER: I'm sure I don't need to tell you that it is very difficult to be a Jew in the Soviet Union.

PAUL: I don't see how this has anything to do with the Schumann case.

REINER: Then you're lucky to be talking to me. Part of our effort to pressure the Soviets to allow Jews to emigrate involves marshaling public opinion.

PAUL: All right.

REINER: The United States did disgracefully little to help Jews get away from Hitler. We didn't allow many into the country. Most of those we didn't let in ended up dying in the camps.

PAUL: Yes, I know this, but I really don't see what this has to do with Schumann or getting Jews out of the Soviet Union.

REINER: The barriers to Jews coming into this country were the product of anti-Semitism. And now, here you have this man Schumann. A Jew.

PAUL: Yes.

REINER: A Jew who did terrible things to other Jews.

PAUL: So we believe, yes.

REINER: There are some who feel that this can only encourage anti-Semites. "Look, you see, those Jews, give them the opportunity, they even turn on each other. Some of them—no better than Nazis."

PAUL: That's ridiculous.

REINER: Yes, but believe me, that's what some will think. And it will only make our job, our work on behalf of other Jews, that much harder. Nobody will *say* anything about this to us, of course, but it will influence the climate. And we're not talking only about the issue of Soviet Jews. Also the Middle East. The political rationale behind Israel is partially based on the idea of reparation. A homeland for people historically persecuted and brutalized. But if you announce to the world—see, some of them *helped* the Nazis do it to their own kind—

PAUL: Schumann is just one man. To generalize from that—

REINER: —is exactly what people do. After all, it isn't the story of the many which captures people's imagination. Four hundred die in an earthquake in Chile. Very sad. By next week, you've forgotten. After all, you can't focus on four hundred people. They're just a mass. Four hundred. Six million. Both big numbers. But *one* person can cast a long shadow in the public's imagination. Schumann has the capacity of casting such a shadow. As far as I'm concerned, what he did puts him beyond the pale. I will not argue that he is anything other than a monster. I talk to you not for his sake, but for the sake of others whose causes may be damaged because of the unhappy fact this man was born a Jew.

PAUL: I'm not prosecuting a Jew; I'm prosecuting a man whose actions demand a response, and that man happens to be a Jew.

REINER: Paul, anti-Semitism isn't something I made up. It's a fact. I am old enough to know firsthand what it can lead to.

PAUL: I'm sorry, I don't think the answer is to back off on this. I understand your concerns. I do. But to not prosecute him *because* he's Jewish, because he violates the accepted image of the camp prisoner as pure victim? Don't you see the implications of that?

REINER: Tell me.

PAUL: It would be as if you were trying to—

REINER: Yes? Trying to?

PAUL: To promote the idea that if you're Jewish—if you're born Jewish, you couldn't be capable of such things. That to be born a Jew carries with it a presumption of moral superiority. To be separate from, *better than*, others by virtue of ethnicity or nationality.

REINER: And you see a danger in this?

PAUL: Seems to me that's not too far from what the Germans believed.

REINER [*slightly smiling*]: I think we both have reason to be glad this is not a formal meeting. How are your parents?

PAUL: Fine.

REINER: You remember me to them, please.

[*After shaking* PAUL's *hand,* REINER *makes his way offstage.* PAUL *looks after him, still upset. A beat. He exits in the other direction.*]

SCENE 16

[KATE *opens a door.* LEAH *is standing there.*]

KATE: Michael?

MICHAEL [*from offstage*]: I'm still on the phone.

KATE: Come in.

[LEAH *enters.*]

LEAH: I was in the building.

KATE: You have friends in the building?

LEAH: The Laschers. You know them?

KATE: No.

LEAH: Eighth floor.

KATE: No.

LEAH: It's a big building.

KATE: Yes.

LEAH: I should have gone downstairs and rung you up from the door-man's intercom, made sure I wasn't interrupting, instead of just coming straight—

KATE: No, it's OK. People do that, in small towns, you know. They see a light on, they know someone's home, they knock, drop in, say hi. Or if you're on the front porch.

LEAH: You're from a small town?

KATE: I used to visit my grandparents in Ohio.

LEAH: I don't think I've ever been in Ohio.

KATE: Then you probably never met my grandparents. Would you like something to drink—

[MICHAEL *enters.*]

MICHAEL: Leah.

LEAH: Michael.

MICHAEL: Did we have—was I expecting you?

LEAH: No, this is spontaneous.

MICHAEL: Something the matter?

LEAH: Something we should talk over.

MICHAEL: Without Aaron?

LEAH: Yes.

KATE: Without me?

LEAH: It's about Sol.

MICHAEL [*to* KATE]: Stay. If you want to.

KATE: Is it my business?

MICHAEL: It's family. It's your business. [*To* LEAH] Some kind of problem?

[*A beat.*]

LEAH: You and Aaron called me, asked me to help your father on this.
MICHAEL: We needed a lawyer. You're a lawyer. You're a friend.
LEAH: And also possibly because my mom's a survivor? Maybe you figured that might help me have a better—appreciation of the situation?
MICHAEL: I don't remember either of us saying anything like that, but maybe.

[*A beat.*]

LEAH: I had dinner at my folks' the other night.
MICHAEL: Oh?
LEAH: My mom and I had a long talk. About my sister, who has three kids. My brother, who has one and a second on the way. About me—
KATE: Your lack of kids?
LEAH: Yeah. And my work.
MICHAEL: And my father?
LEAH: The subject came up.
MICHAEL: She isn't happy about you handling his case.
LEAH: Not excessively.

[*A beat.*]

KATE: She wants you to drop it?
LEAH: That isn't exactly what she said.
MICHAEL: What did she say?
LEAH: "Do what you think is best."
KATE: Your choice.
LEAH: Completely.

[*A beat.*]

You've never come to one of our meetings, have you?
MICHAEL: Meetings?
LEAH: Of our group.
MICHAEL: Kids of survivors?
LEAH: Hasn't Aaron ever invited you?
MICHAEL: Oh, he's asked, but it's not really my kind of thing.
LEAH: Why not?

MICHAEL: I guess I'm arrogant enough to want to believe whatever mess I may or may not make of my life, it's my own mess. And it's got nothing to do with what happened to my father before I was born.

LEAH: So you think that? You think being the son of a survivor has had no—

MICHAEL: Oh, I'm sure it's had some effect—

LEAH: But it's not something you want to look into too closely. Is that it?

MICHAEL: I know it must have had some kind of effect. All I have to do is look at Aaron, see how much a part of him it is. Maybe he gets something out of your group. But I—

LEAH: If it were right for you, you'd do it.

MICHAEL: I couldn't have said it better.

[*A beat.*]

LEAH: I'm worried about him.

MICHAEL: Aaron?

[*She doesn't reply.*]

KATE: Can I ask something?

LEAH: What? About me and Aaron?

KATE: The two of you like each other, you share the political stuff—I mean, it's your own private concern and so forth and so on—

LEAH: But why didn't anything ever happen between us?

KATE: Yes.

LEAH: It did. Sort of. If a couple of nights counts.

KATE: Why only a couple of nights?

LEAH: I know you may find this hard to believe, but there are times when I want to kick back and forget the weight of history and the rest of what you call the political stuff. Times when I want to put Carly Simon on the stereo, wear slippers with bunny ears, and unclench.

MICHAEL: You have slippers with bunny ears?

LEAH: Doesn't everyone?

KATE: I bet Aaron doesn't.

LEAH: Aaron also does not know how to unclench. And therein lies the problem. There's a part of me that for years has been hoping that he would—

KATE: Mellow?

LEAH: Something like that. Not just in the hope that someday we could give it a fair shot but for his own sake.

[*A beat.*]

MICHAEL: So your mother said you should do what you think is best.

LEAH: Yes.

MICHAEL: Leaving little doubt as to what she thinks that would be.

LEAH: Now I do *lots* of things my mom doesn't agree with.

MICHAEL: But this time it's different?

LEAH: The case is getting a lot of attention. And it's going to keep getting attention. I don't mind that for myself. But my mom. To have me plastered on front pages defending your father on these charges, it'll bring her too close to things I'd just as soon—you see what I'm saying?

[*A beat.*]

KATE: Can you do that? What are the rules? Can you bail out now? Ethically?

LEAH [*to* MICHAEL]: It would be a lot easier if you could tell Aaron and your father you think you need someone else.

MICHAEL: Another lawyer?

LEAH: Yes.

MICHAEL: And what reason would I give?

LEAH: It's an immigration case. You could use someone who's more familiar with immigration law than I am. There's some truth in that.

KATE: So that's why you wanted to bring this up without Aaron around. You want Michael to get you off the hook with him.

LEAH: Pretty chicken shit, huh? What do you say?

MICHAEL: And what would we do for a lawyer?

LEAH: I've got someone to recommend.

MICHAEL: That would be good.

LEAH: I wouldn't recommend him if I didn't think he was—

MICHAEL: No, I'm sure.

LEAH: I don't look forward to calling your father.

KATE: You wouldn't have to call very far. He's here.

LEAH: Here?

KATE: Asleep in the second bedroom.

LEAH: Oh.

MICHAEL: We had kind of a problem on Sunday. Aaron was off on a camping trip this last weekend?

LEAH: Yeah.

MICHAEL: On Sunday night, he stops by Pop's place on his way back from—

LEAH: From camping.

MICHAEL: Right. He and I have been taking turns staying with him. Anyway, Aaron comes upstairs and finds this idiot with a can of paint painting a red swastika on the door.

LEAH: Of your father's apartment?

MICHAEL: Yes.

LEAH: I hope this idiot has insurance.

MICHAEL: Yeah, well, I'm inside with Pop, right? And I hear this commotion in the hallway. I open the door, and there's Aaron beating the shit out of this guy. And the paint can's been kicked over, and there's paint all over the hallway. Red paint. And Aaron's given this guy a bloody nose.

LEAH: Great.

MICHAEL: So he grabs the guy by the back of his shirt and drags him over to the door. And he tells him that he's going to clean it off, if necessary with his tongue.

LEAH: That's Aaron.

MICHAEL: Meanwhile, Pop has come out of the apartment. He looks at this guy. He tells Aaron to let him go. And Aaron does.

LEAH: And that's why he's staying with you. Your father.

MICHAEL: Well, he couldn't stay where he was. And Aaron doesn't have enough room in his place.

LEAH: Oh, hell. Never mind.

MICHAEL: What?

LEAH: This conversation didn't happen, OK?

MICHAEL: I'm sorry?

LEAH: Forget what I said about getting someone else. You're stuck with me. If you still want me.

MICHAEL: Hey, that isn't why I told you about this.

LEAH: I know that.

MICHAEL: I wasn't trying to—

LEAH: Michael, it doesn't need to be said. Just do me a favor and don't tell your brother I ever raised the subject.

MICHAEL: OK. But what about you and your mom?

LEAH: I'll figure out some way to make it up to her.

KATE: You could always get pregnant.

SCENE 17

[KATE *exits as* AARON *enters. Lights shift.* LEAH *is in conversation with* AARON *and* MICHAEL.]

LEAH: There's another possibility to consider.

MICHAEL: What is that?

LEAH: Your father might simply take a plane to another country.

AARON: Excuse me?

LEAH: If he were to go to England, for instance—

AARON: And what would that accomplish?

LEAH: If you're stripped of your citizenship and deported, you've got to find some place that's willing to take you. Not real easy to do. But if you go *before* the government can take you through the proceedings, then you have some choice about where you end up.

MICHAEL: And the OSI doesn't pursue any further action?

LEAH: All they're interested in is getting him out of the country. If he's someplace else, he's not within their jurisdiction and the case is over for them.

AARON: But you're talking about giving up.

LEAH: Aaron, it's my responsibility as your father's lawyer to make him aware of the alternatives. That's what I'm doing.

AARON: You seriously advise doing this?

LEAH: The government's going to put a series of witnesses on the stand who will say they saw your father do various things. Your father's case is that these were done under duress. Further, he claims that when the Germans' backs were turned, he used his position to help people when he could.

AARON: So what's wrong with that? Isn't that a viable defense?

LEAH: Yes, if you could find somebody to testify to that. But so far, all these months, we haven't found anybody who will.

AARON: The list of names he gave you, the people he remembers helping—

LEAH: We've advertised; we've gone through the various agencies. Most of them never came to this country. Of those who did, most are dead. Some, frankly, are not in any shape to take the stand. We're talking about some pretty old people. And some we simply haven't found yet, though we're still looking.

AARON: Are you telling me we're going to lose?

LEAH: I'm saying we've got a tough fight ahead, and it would be helpful if we could find someone to back his version of things.

SCENE 18

[*The sound of a school bell, the noise of high school kids.* ENSEMBLE *sets up scene as they move furniture into place.*]

ENSEMBLE: —Dewey High School.
—The teacher's lounge.

[AARON *is correcting papers.* DIANE *enters.*]

DIANE: Aaron?

AARON: Diane.

DIANE: Grading papers?

AARON: Threw a surprise English quiz. Did you know that "tadpole" is the opposite of "fish"?

DIANE: Really?

AARON [*holding up paper*]: That's what young Mr. Kevin Barkham thinks. I asked him to list three antonyms. You know: "good," "bad," "hot," "cold"—

DIANE: "Tadpole," "fish."

AARON: When I sub for history, it's even more illuminating. A lot of them think we fought the Soviet Union in World War II. And a lot of the black kids think that slavery ended sometime in the 1950s.

DIANE: Is that so?

AARON: Jesus, how are people supposed to know who they are if they don't know what's happened before? Whether we like it or not, we live in times that came out of other times, we're part of something. Isn't it better to have some inkling of what?

DIANE: You say that, don't you? To your classes?

AARON: And I inspire them. Yes, I do. Nothing like a white Jewish guy getting up and telling them about A. Philip Randolph to make them want to hit those books.

DIANE: And if they knew about A. Philip Randolph, if they carried this knowledge of him in their hearts—

AARON: Political enlightenment followed by profound social change.

DIANE: Well, that would make it all worth it.

AARON: The thing about history—

[*He stops.*]

This is just us talking.

DIANE: Huh? Oh yes, of course.

AARON: No, I mean, that's all this is.

DIANE: Till you say otherwise. All right. "The thing about history"?

AARON: You tell me.

DIANE: Well, what's the old line about being condemned to repeat it? That if you don't know it, if you don't learn from it, you're in danger of—

AARON: And do you believe that?

DIANE: Well, I must, or why am I doing what I do? I have chosen to do this. I have chosen to write about this stuff.

AARON: And do *I* believe it?

DIANE: You went to Bitburg.

AARON: I went to Bitburg.

DIANE: And it's like you said that night—

AARON: Which night?

DIANE: When you came back from Germany. We were in that restaurant—you and your brother and your girlfriend—

AARON: She's not my girlfriend.

DIANE: My mistake.

AARON: Some reporter you are—

DIANE: Hey, I wasn't doing a story about your private life.

AARON: Well, if you did, it wouldn't be much of a story.

DIANE: Sorry to hear that. But that night, you said that thing about people being what they do. What you do is who you are.

AARON: And so, because I went to Bitburg, that makes me who I am.

DIANE: Some people talked, but you—you got on the plane. You flew across the Atlantic Ocean.

AARON: A Jewish Lindbergh.

DIANE: Absolutely.

AARON: What if I went to Bitburg for crummy reasons?

DIANE: How could you do that? How would it be possible to do that?

AARON: Let's say I didn't really deep down give a shit about Reagan or Kohl or the SS or ethical anything. Let's say I went 'cause I like showing off, or because a girl I was interested in was going and I thought by tagging along I could get into her pants?

DIANE: It still wouldn't take away from the fact that you were there. I mean, yes, take Lindbergh. What if really the only reason *he* flew was to get into someone's pants? The fact is he still flew solo across the Atlantic. He still was the one who did that. Anyway, the meaning of what he did wasn't up to him to decide. He did what he did and people decided what it meant. But the reasons why? Nobody can really know the reasons you do something. Sometimes even you don't know the reasons you do something. I mean, isn't that what people pay money to shrinks to find out?

AARON: Tell me.

DIANE: A shrink says, or may say, "OK, you say you did this, you did that, you did something else. There's a pattern there. And if you saw somebody else do these things, what would you think that person was about?" And so you say what you'd think, and then you see what you said about a person who did that is what *you* are 'cause *you're* the person who did that.

[*A beat.*]

AARON: I assume you're writing an article.

DIANE: Planning to. Yes, I will.

AARON: I won't be part of it. I decline.

DIANE: You didn't like what I wrote about Bitburg?

AARON: I liked it fine.

DIANE: So my writing you like OK.

AARON: Your writing—

DIANE: Content, style, execution—

AARON: You know how to push a pen.

DIANE: I try.

AARON: Don't take it personally. It's not just you I won't do this with.

DIANE: I understand your feelings—

AARON: I'm sure you do. Completely.

DIANE: Well, I don't pretend that.

AARON: No, I'm sure you can read my heart of hearts like the back of a cereal box. Kind of makes talking to me irrelevant, don't you think?

DIANE: I thought you might like the opportunity to present your side.

AARON: And I'm very grateful for the opportunity, but no thank you.

DIANE: I'm going to write this article. If you talk to me or not. I will write it.

AARON: I'm sure you'll find no shortage of people who will say things to you. People you can quote.

DIANE: It must be hard. Given who you are, how active you've been—

AARON: We're back to you reading my soul.

DIANE: People are out there, making assumptions—

AARON: I'm really not all that concerned about what people are assuming—

DIANE: Don't you think it might be worth—

AARON: Excuse me, but I think I gave you a pretty good no. I wasn't hostile—not in an overt way anyhow. You made your case, I considered it, I declined. You're not supposed to be in here, you know. This is a school. Do you want me to call the security guard?

[*A beat.*]

DIANE: I've come across something I thought you should—I saw the list of people you're trying to locate. People your father says he helped. I know where to reach one of them.

AARON: Who?

DIANE: Rivka Glauer.

AARON: Where is she?

DIANE: Canada.

AARON: Could you be more specific?

DIANE: Here's the deal: If I tell you—

AARON: Then I have to talk to you?

DIANE: That's it.

AARON: You're sure it's the right Rivka Glauer?

DIANE: I'm sure.

AARON: But if I don't promise to talk to you, you won't tell me where she is?

DIANE: You've heard my offer.

AARON: This woman could help my father. Are you saying if I don't promise this, you'll stand in the way of that happening?

DIANE: Aaron—let's say you do this, you get your father out of his trouble—

AARON: Yes?

DIANE: And the Soviet Union lets their Jews go wherever the hell they want, and Israel gets complete security, the Arabs disarm and promise to live in peace, and the surviving concentration camp inmates get reparations and apologies and the whole wish list—

AARON: All right.

DIANE: So what would you see as your life then? What would be Aaron Schumann's path to happiness?

AARON: Well, that's easy. I would take up golf.

[*A beat.* DIANE *pulls out a notebook, a pen, and a file card. She writes on the file card and hands it to him.*]

DIANE: Rivka Glauer.

[*A beat.*]

AARON: You're paying your own way. You know that.

DIANE: OK.

AARON: And you don't say anything. I ask the questions.

DIANE: Agreed.

AARON: OK, let's go.

DIANE: Now?

AARON: Why not?

DIANE: All right.

AARON: You want to make a phone call or something?

DIANE: Phone call?

AARON: If there's someone you want to let know you're taking this trip. Maybe a date to cancel.

DIANE: No, it's OK. I'm cool.

AARON: You've got nobody to call?

DIANE: Nobody I have to.

[*A beat.* AARON *looks at her for a second with a small smile.*]

Don't we want to go somewhere?
AARON: Yes.

SCENE 19

ENSEMBLE: —Another plane, this time to Toronto. At the airport.
—Is this trip for business or pleasure?

[AARON *and* DIANE *wait as* FELIX GLAUER *helps his wife,* RIVKA, *into a chair, then stands behind her. They are an aging couple.* AARON *pulls out a cassette recorder.*]

FELIX: I'm Rivka's husband, Felix. She doesn't see so good.
RIVKA: He's my Seeing Eye person.
FELIX [*to* RIVKA]: He's got a tape recorder. [*To* AARON] You're going to tape this?
AARON: If you don't mind.
FELIX: He's going to tape this.
AARON: It could be helpful for our lawyer.
FELIX: You didn't bring him with you, your lawyer.
AARON [*correcting*]: Her.
RIVKA: A lady?
AARON: Yes. I wanted to talk to you first.
FELIX: Maybe we should have our lawyer here.
RIVKA: Felix.
FELIX: Or call him, get his advice.
RIVKA: Felix, we don't need a lawyer. [*To* AARON] Does she know you're here? Your lawyer?
AARON: No.
RIVKA: Shouldn't she?
AARON: When it's time, she will.
RIVKA [*referring to* DIANE]: And this is?
AARON: She came with me.
RIVKA: Yes?
AARON: Diane Abbott.

RIVKA: A friend?

[DIANE *looks at* AARON.]

AARON: Kind of an interested party.
RIVKA: What do you do, darling?
DIANE: I write.
AARON: She helped me find you.
RIVKA: I didn't know I was lost. Well, all right.
AARON: I'll just turn this on—

[*Turns on the tape recorder. A beat.*]

RIVKA: We came from the same town, your father and I. I had an older brother, Theo. They were best friends. My brother, he asked your father, if something were to happen to him—
AARON: Yes.
RIVKA: That your father should promise to keep an eye on me. We were sent to Ordenhaupt, in Germany. A camp. My brother died. An infection. Then the Germans made your father a *kapo*. He kept his promise to Theo. He looked out for me.
AARON: If you could give me some specifics? An example. A time when he did something to help—
RIVKA: I see. Yes. One day, I managed to steal some potatoes. The Germans found out they were gone. They started a search while we were at our jobs. I was afraid they would find them, but I couldn't leave to hide them better. I told your father. He managed to get there first and move them. It was a risk. They would have shot him. They didn't hesitate to make an example of *kapos*.
AARON: If they *had* found out you stole the potatoes—
RIVKA: I would not be here talking to you now.
AARON: He saved your life.
RIVKA: Yes, that's fair to say. And other times when there were selections, people who were going to be sent elsewhere, he protected me. Wouldn't let them take me. "I need her," he'd say. "She's one of my best workers."
AARON: You'll say these things at the trial.

[RIVKA *looks at* FELIX. *A beat.*]

FELIX: Well, that may not be possible.

AARON: Mrs. Glauer, it's very important—

RIVKA: Yes, I know, but there are difficulties—going down there.

AARON: We'll cover your expenses, of course.

RIVKA: No, it's not that.

AARON: Mrs. Glauer, we need you. You tell me he saved your life. Now he needs your help.

FELIX: No, you don't understand.

RIVKA: If I testify for you, then the other side—the prosecution—they can ask me questions?

AARON: Well, yes.

RIVKA: What they ask me, I have to answer. I am under oath. They want to know about what happened in Ordenhaupt; I have to tell.

AARON: Yes.

RIVKA: You don't want me to have to answer those questions. You don't want me to tell what I saw, what I know. [*Gently*] This is why, when I heard about his trouble, I didn't contact you myself.

AARON: But you're talking to me now—

RIVKA: *You* called *me*. I felt I didn't have the right to refuse. And then I thought maybe there was something I could do to help.

AARON: But you just said you can't help him—

RIVKA: Not him. You.

[AARON *doesn't know how to respond. With pain, trying to phrase it correctly,* RIVKA *continues.*]

You're going to hear terrible things at the trial. But what I feel you must know is that it wasn't your father who did these things. Not the same person who brought you up. Not the same boy I knew in the village.

AARON: What are you saying?

[*A beat.*]

RIVKA: Do you remember—was it ten years ago?—the girl with the rich father in California, kidnapped—

FELIX: Patty Hearst?

RIVKA: They put her into a closet, yes? Abused her, kept her blindfolded, cut off from the world. At the end of this, she was somebody else.

They put a gun into her hands, she helped them rob a bank. She was in that closet four weeks, five? Your father, for him it wasn't weeks—it was *months, years.* The things he was forced to see. A mother, murdered in front of his eyes. A father shot. Something broke. That's what I believe. That's what you must believe. Or how could he have done such things?

AARON: But they *made* him—the Germans.

RIVKA: No, he did these things even when the Germans were not there. When there was no reason. But that's what I mean: there was no reason. Where there's no reason, all that's left is madness.

[*Numbly,* AARON *switches off the recorder. He just sits there.*]

I'm sorry.

[RIVKA *looks to* FELIX. *He helps her leave.* AARON *is alone with* DIANE.]

AARON: So, what do you say we head into town, hit some nightspots?

DIANE: I would like—

[*She stops.*]

AARON: What? What would you like?

[*A beat.*]

DIANE: I'm going to write what I think is fair.

AARON: I know that. I don't doubt that.

DIANE: OK.

AARON: But you know I'm going to hate it anyway.

DIANE: Sure.

[*A beat. She laughs.*]

You remind me of the boyfriend in college I didn't have.

AARON: You didn't have a boyfriend in college?

DIANE: A few actually. But none of them were—

AARON: What—my type?

DIANE: No.

AARON: So I remind you of someone who didn't exist.

DIANE: I'm not saying what I want to say.

AARON: No, my hunch is what you want to say is something sympathetic. Something that would signal to me the fact that, even though you're going to write this, how deeply you—that underneath there's this human being. But, you know, Diane, even if you could come up with some really good words, they still wouldn't—

DIANE: —mean shit.

[*A beat. She looks at him for a moment, nods, then exits.*]

SCENE 20

[*A member of the* ENSEMBLE *brings on a bench.* AARON *heads for it, sits.* MICHAEL *enters.*]

AARON: Must be nice to wake up, look out your window, see the Hudson. Jersey. The sunsets.

MICHAEL: Why don't you come up and look at it from the inside? You haven't seen Pop in days.

AARON: What would I say to him?

MICHAEL: I've never known you to be short of things to say.

[*A beat.*]

Go to the top of the building; you can see jets making approaches to all three airports. When it's nice out, we sometimes go up there with a thermos of coffee, watch the show.

AARON: Were you up watching tonight?

MICHAEL: It was kind of chilly out.

AARON: You might have seen me making an approach to Kennedy.

MICHAEL: You flew somewhere?

AARON: And back. It's been a busy day. Toronto.

MICHAEL: What's in Toronto?

AARON: Rivka Glauer.

MICHAEL: You found her? Why didn't you—

AARON: I didn't want to have to wait to talk to her.

MICHAEL: You should have told Leah. What good is it having a lawyer if—

AARON: I'm not going to argue about this. It's done. I went there, I came back.

MICHAEL: And?

[AARON *hands him the cassette.*]

What's on this?

AARON: It ain't good.

[*A beat.* MICHAEL *absorbs this.*]

He did help her, but mostly—

MICHAEL: Oh, God.

AARON: She thinks he went off his rocker and that's why.

MICHAEL: Off his rocker?

AARON: The shock of some of what he saw, went through. You know the routine.

MICHAEL: But that counts.

AARON: It does?

MICHAEL: It has to.

AARON: Where?

MICHAEL: I mean it's a basic. If you're not in your right mind, you can't be held accountable—

AARON: According to whom?

MICHAEL: It's a legal principle. Diminished capacity I think they call it.

AARON: Well then, we don't have a problem, do we? We're off the hook. Wow, I'm relieved.

MICHAEL: Aaron—

AARON: Except, actually, we're not. It isn't.

MICHAEL: Not?

AARON: Relevant. Legally the issue is did he lie to immigration when he came into this country. What his frame of mind was before that— beside the point. And, even if it weren't, what could we do? Put him on the stand? To say what? "I was nuts at the time? I didn't know what I was doing? Have a heart, cut me a break?"

MICHAEL: It doesn't match.

AARON: Match?

MICHAEL: With the man we know. The guy we grew up with. He doesn't act like somebody who could have—

AARON: What? Been the ogre of Ordenhaupt?

MICHAEL: I mean, even assuming he did this stuff, does he even know he did?

AARON: So?

MICHAEL: So how can it be right to go after someone, punish someone for something he doesn't even know he did? Doesn't that render the whole idea of punishment meaningless?

AARON: No, I think you're making excellent points. Why don't you ask Leah if they'll allow you to say this at the hearing?

MICHAEL: You don't think it's worth bringing up, getting them to consider?

AARON: You're talking like something can be said or done to change the way it's going to go. Michael, the tracks have been laid and we're on them. The witnesses will climb into the witness box and say their pieces. Leah will do her best to raise doubts about their memories. The judge will look sober and make notes. And you and me—we'll get dressed up in suits and play the loyal sons, walking in and out of the courtroom with Pop.

[*A beat.*]

Oh, swell.

MICHAEL: What?

AARON: I don't *have* a suit. I'm going to have to buy a goddamn suit for this!

MICHAEL: The last straw, huh?

[*A beat.*]

AARON: You remember when Mengele's son was on the TV? Josef Mengele? Talked about visiting his father in South America. Knowing who his father was and what he did. Not excusing, not explaining. But this was his father, and what was he supposed to do? Expose him? Christ, at very least, if I were him, I would have changed my last name. Even if I *weren't* related and was born with the name Mengele, I would have changed it. I mean, when you look in the phone book, how many Hitlers do you see? But I remember this Mengele kid was on TV—not a kid—a lot older than a kid. But I remember looking at him and thinking, "You poor schmuck." Talk about being stuck with baggage. For all we know, he might have had the talent to be a singer—the German Frank Sinatra. But who would buy a record, *Freddy Mengele—In a Quiet Mood*?

MICHAEL: You aren't comparing, are you?

AARON: Yes, I know: differences, distinctions.

MICHAEL: There are big ones. Mengele and Pop—they're hardly in the same—

AARON: No, you're right. There's consolation—compared to some, Pop wouldn't rate a footnote.

MICHAEL: That's not fair.

AARON: I'm sorry, I don't know what the fairness standard on this is. Where would you even begin to look for such a thing?

[*He stops.*]

You know, flying back down, all I could think—he did these things and he survived. He survived because—crazy or not—he did these things. And here we are. You and I—the two of us—we are alive because he did these things. I owe my existence to the fact that he—

MICHAEL: You can't look at it that way.

AARON: No?

MICHAEL: You can't.

AARON: If you say so.

[AARON *rises.*]

I've got to prepare for a class in the morning. Subbing for geometry. I hate to tell you how little I remember of geometry.

MICHAEL: Aaron—

[AARON *stops, looks at him.*]

Give me a call tomorrow. If you have time between classes.

AARON [*smiling ironically*]: Sure. It'll all look different in the morning.

MICHAEL [*overlapping the previous line; seeing* SOL *offstage*]: It's Pop.

AARON [*turning to look as* SOL *enters*]: What?

SOL [*to* AARON]: I saw you down here with Michael. From the window. Why don't you come up?

AARON: We had a—a few things to talk about.

SOL: Private?

AARON: Stuff there wasn't any point in bothering you with.

SOL: Are you sure you're warm enough?

AARON: I'm fine, Pop.

SOL: It's just, I can see your breath.

AARON: I'm OK.

SOL: Or a hat. You know what you need?

AARON: A wife.

SOL: You laugh. But look at your brother. He doesn't get colds. Look at me. All the time your mother was alive—

AARON: I'll give it real serious thought.

SOL: Come up.

AARON: Can't tonight.

MICHAEL: Aaron's subbing for a class tomorrow. He's got to prepare tonight.

SOL: Of course. But soon?

AARON: Just let me get a little ahead.

[AARON *hugs* SOL.]

Night, Pop.

[*He exchanges a look with* MICHAEL *and exits.* SOL *looks at* MICHAEL. *They exit.*]

SCENE 21

DIANE [*to audience*]: This is the story I got: Aaron Schumann is in the high school cafeteria. Cesar Segura, age seventeen, comes into the cafeteria and begins yelling at a student named Rosie Alvaro, starts to hit her. Aaron runs over. Segura reaches inside his jacket and pulls out a knife. "OK, man, come on," he says to Aaron. "OK, man, try it." And Aaron does.

[*A beat.*]

"I don't understand it," one of the teachers tells me later. "Aaron knew not to do that. He knew better than to challenge that kid. How dangerous it could be. Why did he do it?"

[*A beat.*]

I wanted to go to the service. The funeral. But I figured—well, of course, his father would probably be there. His brother. Friends. Some of them, they know who I am. And if I were to show up—last thing they need. Maybe if I were a better reporter I would have gone, but—

[*She exits.*]

SCENE 22

[LEAH *enters from one side,* MICHAEL *and* KATE *from the other.*]

LEAH: All right, this is the deal: we don't contest the citizenship issue, and they agree not to deport him.

MICHAEL: Don't contest? What does that mean exactly?

LEAH: Your father admits the allegations against him and relinquishes his citizenship. For their part, the government doesn't challenge the assertion that, given your father's recent stroke, deportation would endanger his life. So, they won't take any further action against him.

KATE: So, that's it?

LEAH: That's it.

SCENE 23

[*In the middle of a conversation between* FRIEDER *and* PAUL.]

PAUL: It was the best we could do under the circumstances.

FRIEDER: I don't accept that.

PAUL: Mr. Frieder, what would you have us do?

FRIEDER: What you said you were going to: put him on trial, deport him.

PAUL: He wasn't well enough to stand trial.

FRIEDER: Lies.

PAUL: His son was killed. He had a stroke during the funeral. We had a doctor examine him. He had a stroke, Mr. Frieder. He wouldn't have been able to participate in his own defense. He can barely speak.

FRIEDER: And what about the people he killed? Where are *their* voices? What defense were *they* allowed against him in the camp? I'm telling you, Mr. Fontana—maybe you and your office have closed this case, *I* haven't.

PAUL: Mr. Frieder—

FRIEDER: You think I'm not serious?

PAUL: Don't do anything that would get you into trouble.

FRIEDER: Trouble? Schumann murders dozens, and how do you punish him? Tell him he can't vote anymore. For whatever I may do, I'll make you a bargain—you punish me the same.

[*He exits.*]

SCENE 24

MICHAEL [*to audience*]: The rabbi calls and says that, for reasons we may appreciate, he has had to take down the paroches my father donated. I decide not to tell Pop when we visit him.

[NURSE *wheels* SOL *in.*]

KATE [*to audience*]: There really was no way to keep Sol at our place and give him proper attention. The doctors believe, given time and therapy, he may regain more of his speech.

MICHAEL [*to* SOL]: I thought maybe I could make a list of your records. Then, if we could figure out which are your favorites, I could make cassettes so that you can listen to them here. Next week.

SOL [*with difficulty, whispering*]: Yes.

KATE: Honey, not next week.

MICHAEL: Oh, that's right. I'll be in Seattle on business all next week. But as soon as I get back. And we'll visit regularly. You can count on it.

[MICHAEL *and* KATE *kiss* SOL.]

Get some rest, Pop.

[MICHAEL *and* KATE *exit, leaving* SOL *alone with the* NURSE.]

NURSE: Well, that was a nice visit, wasn't it? You have a very nice son. Why don't we put on the TV now? Would you like that? I think there's a concert on Channel Thirteen.

[*She raises a remote control and the sound of symphonic music is heard.*]

Too loud.

[*She adjusts.*]

That's better. I'll look in on you again in a little while, all right, Mr. Schumann?

[*She exits.* SOL *closes his eyes.* FRIEDER *enters behind* SOL. *He takes hold of the chair.* SOL *opens his eyes.*]

FRIEDER: I feel like some air, don't you?

[*He pulls the chair back and offstage.* MICHAEL *appears.*]

MICHAEL [*to audience*]: When I get to the car, I realize I've left my umbrella. I go back to the room, but Pop isn't there. I ask an attendant. He tells me that he just saw Pop with a friend who said he was taking him for a walk.

SCENE 25

[FRIEDER *has his hands on the wheelchair in which* SOL *sits, close to the edge of the stage. The sound of traffic roaring by below. During the following, the* ENSEMBLE *forms a semicircle around* SOL *and* FRIEDER.]

ENSEMBLE: —The Long Island Expressway.
    —In front of them, an exit off the expressway.
    —Cars leaving the expressway curve right and up a hill.
    —They are at the top of the hill.
    —At the top of the exit.
    —Frieder turns Sol's chair so that it faces down the ramp.
    —The wheels are at the edge of the curb.
FRIEDER: I've never trusted people who drive red cars. I think there's a statistic about that. Insurance companies. Something about people who choose to drive red cars; they get into more accidents. Tend to speed more. Risk their necks to maybe save ten seconds. A lot of flash, a lot of hurry. Speed. Still, some people, they love it. Speed. The blood pumping, the heart pounding faster. I could make you that gift. One push. You'd roll slowly for the first few seconds, but then gravity would take effect and you would accelerate. Until something stopped you.

SOL [*with difficulty, whispering*]: Who?

FRIEDER: What?

SOL: Who are—

FRIEDER: You don't remember me, do you? You don't remember which one I am. I understand. There are so many of us. So many with reason. Maybe I won't tell you. Maybe it's better if I let you guess. Something to occupy you on your way—

[MICHAEL *breaks through the semicircle of the* ENSEMBLE, *grabs* FRIEDER *from behind, and pulls him away from* SOL *and the chair.* FRIEDER *falls to the ground.* MICHAEL *pulls* SOL *back from the edge of the stage.*]

MICHAEL: Pop?

[*Satisfied that his father is indeed all right,* MICHAEL *turns to look at* FRIEDER, *who is lying on the ground.*]

Are you all right?

[FRIEDER *doesn't answer.*]

Mr. Frieder, are you all right?

[*A beat.*]

FRIEDER: You know who I am.

MICHAEL: I know who you are.

[*A beat.*]

Can you stand?

[*He offers his hand.*]

Here.

FRIEDER: I don't want your help.

[FRIEDER *begins to get up, but loses his balance.* MICHAEL *catches him in his arms, holds him.* FRIEDER *holds on to* MICHAEL *and begins to weep.* SOL *sits mute in his chair. The lights intensify on the three of them. The rest of the* ENSEMBLE *stands, witnesses in silhouette. The lights fade.*]

NOTES

Sometime after the run of *Sol* at the Hypothetical Theatre, most of the cast reunited to put up a staged reading for a theater conference. Afterward, the director, a couple of cast members, and I were approached by a man who introduced himself as Tannenbaum's son. As you might imagine, we were apprehensive of his reaction. He laid to rest our concerns. Though he told me he thought I should have written more about how Sol himself had suffered under the Nazis, he said that in the main he liked the play and thought it was fair. (I couldn't quite summon the nerve to ask him how, as Tannenbaum's son, he had viewed the story of Aaron.) He joined a handful of us for dinner, during which we learned that he had gone on to a career as a court officer and that he had worked in the same courtroom where a member of our company's family had often appeared as an attorney. Six degrees indeed.

STAY TILL MORNING

—for Pat Birch

The original title of this play was *Immoral Imperatives*, and it received its first few productions under that name. A few years later, working on a staged reading with director Marshall W. Mason and actors Jill Eikenberry, Michael Tucker, Kevin Geer, and Kristine Niven, someone in the room expressed the opinion that it was a title too clever by half. And then most of the others chimed in agreeing. "Please consider changing it," Mason said. I did and I have. And I do think that *Stay Till Morning* is the better title. You'll find the source of the title in the beginning of the second act.

This is the only time I've written a play that has had its genesis in another play. *Flyovers* (which appears in the Northwestern University Press anthology, *Victory Gardens Theater Presents: Seven New Plays from the Playwrights Ensemble*) includes a woman in her forties named Iris who, at one point in a conversation with a former classmate named Oliver, discusses her father's situation:

> IRIS: He and an old buddy named Hank and Hank's wife share a place down in the Florida Keys. I went down to visit, and I got the feeling that they'd moved a lot of stuff around before I got there, for my sake.
>
> OLIVER: Cleaned up?
>
> IRIS: More hiding the evidence.
>
> OLIVER: Evidence of what? They running drugs or something?
>
> IRIS: I think when it comes to Hank's wife, it's share and share alike.
>
> OLIVER: Hank's wife puts up with this?
>
> IRIS: Actually, I think it was more or less her idea. Apparently Hank has slowed down some.
>
> OLIVER: Oh.
>
> IRIS: And she hasn't.
>
> OLIVER: And your father?

IRIS: Well, he's always tried to make himself useful.

OLIVER: They didn't want you to know this?

IRIS: I guess they thought I might have opinions.

OLIVER: You don't?

IRIS: At this point in their lives, jeez, if they can put together something that works for them, who am I to—

OLIVER: Sure.

IRIS: Kind of a hoot though, when I think back to how hard I tried to hide the stuff I was doing from him—my dad . . . But the same guy, you know—my dad—same guy who gave me grief about what I did back then, now here he is in a seniors threesome. And it seems kind of OK.

Every performance, this passage was received by the audience with hearty laughter. It was an uncharacteristic passage for me to write; I almost never have an extended reference to unseen characters in my work, but this chunk came out as if by dictation from Iris's mouth. She insisted on saying it, so I took it down.

A few years later, I started imagining Hank, Hank's wife, and Iris's dad saying to me, "OK, it's time to tell our story." It was as if I moved out of one room into another, turned on a light, and there they were waiting for me—Hank and Terri and Dale. And again, some of the writing felt as if I were taking dictation. I've heard other writers describe the same sensation—that characters and their stories sometimes announce themselves as if they had independent existences and that they were looking to find a trustworthy author to shepherd them into public.

Much of what I drew on in writing about Florida came from visits I took to the Keys during participation in the Key West Theater Festival. Some of it came out of stories that were told me there. The story about the Cubans came from a friend whose father had owned a small fleet of charter boats that was diminished by one boat because of said Cubans.

The premiere came just after September 11, 2001. Perhaps it was the somber atmosphere that suffused those days, but certainly the audience came to see the show with a heightened awareness of the fragility of our illusions about order, and that subtly shifted the play's meaning and impact.

Incidentally, one of the pleasures of working at the Victory Gardens Theater has been coaxing colleagues from the company onstage. James

Sherman, a fellow member of the playwrights ensemble, played one of the leads in *With and Without* (opposite his real-life wife, Linnea Todd). Another member playwright, Kristine Thatcher, first lent me her talents as an actress in *Bluff*. Kristine appeared again in this play, and I had the good fortune of being able to persuade artistic director Dennis Zacek (who has directed many of my other works) to take on the role of Hank, which he did with aplomb.

The setting should suggest the sun and vegetation of the Florida Keys. Moves to different locations should be suggested by shifts of lighting and a few easily moved props and set pieces. As is usual with my stuff, the simpler the devices, the better. For instance, the scenes in Dale's car don't require anything more than a couple of chairs.

Immoral Imperatives premiered September 24, 2001, at the Victory Gardens Theater in a production directed by Cal Maclean, with the following cast:

Terri	Kristine Thatcher
Dale	Tim Grimm
Hank	Dennis Zacek
Liz	Linda Reiter

Immoral Imperatives was produced by the Wellfleet Harbor Actors Theater in a production that opened on September 9, 2004, directed by James Glossman, with the following cast:

Terri	Laura Esterman
Dale	W. T. Martin
Hank	Malachi Throne
Liz	Tanya Clarke

CHARACTERS

Terri
Dale
Hank
Liz

ACT 1

[*The play takes place in various locations in the Florida Keys at the end of the twentieth century.* TERRI, *a vital and attractive woman in her middle years, enters.*]

TERRI: OK, we're gonna start this with a story. A person who shall remain nameless is hired to give a talk at a theater festival in Florida. He gives this talk in a lecture hall on Key West, at the San Carlos Institute on Duval Street. I offer you this detail to enhance the impression of authenticity: this anecdote is true. So, this guy gives the talk. It goes well. Much applause. After the talk, one of the members of the audience approaches the speaker. A young woman. She is, yes, good-looking, and she is dressed in clothing that calls attention to some aspects of her good-lookingness. She says to him, "I liked your talk very much." This person, the speaker who shall continue to remain nameless, says, "Thank you." "I would like to show you *how* much," she says. "Oh?" he says. And she asks, "Which hotel you staying at?" He says, "Well, I'm very flattered, but actually, I'm in a, you know, committed relationship." "Oh," says the woman, "did your girlfriend come down with you?" "No, she's home." "Home?" "In New York." "Ah," says the young woman. And she smiles. "She's on the mainland. It won't count." Key West. That's where this story begins. A bar.

[DALE *and* HANK *in a bar.* DALE *is roughly* TERRI's *age.* HANK *is ten or fifteen years older.*]

DALE: Up till then, I would've said I was having a good day.

HANK: Till the gun.

DALE: Till the gun.

HANK: The day turned around right about then.

DALE: Just before that moment, I'm at the wheel, a Dos Equis close at hand, sunshine dancing on the water, Tito Puente playing on the speakers, and I'm thinking, OK, life is mostly waiting for one kind of crap or another to blindside you, but damn, every now and then you get a really sweet patch—

HANK: —a good stretch—

DALE: —and you feel the muscles in your back get loose and maybe a breeze brushes through your hair—

HANK: —and then someone has to go and pull a—

DALE: I almost laughed, it was so—I mean, a gun!

HANK: Should be some kind of appeals process. Or someone you could hand a petition to.

DALE: To protest.

HANK: To get satisfaction.

DALE: You figure out who and I'll do it.

[TERRI *enters, carrying a bag, kisses* HANK.]

TERRI: What's he telling you? About how the Cubans stole his boat?

DALE: You know?

TERRI: I was in the liquor store, told them Hank and I were meeting you here; they tell me the story.

DALE: Glad to be the talk of the liquor store.

TERRI: You have entered legend.

DALE: Well, since you've heard—

HANK: *I* haven't.

TERRI: Hank hasn't. You can tell him. They put a gun in your back or something, isn't that the way it—

DALE: That about covers it.

TERRI: Am I spoiling the story?

HANK: They stole the boat? Your boat?

TERRI: The way I heard it—

DALE: Yes? How did you hear it?

TERRI: No, it's your story. Your boat, your story.

HANK: So they sneaked up behind you?

DALE: Behind me, yes. One of them.

HANK: With a gun?

TERRI: You were distracted, weren't you, Dale?

DALE: Now *that* isn't true.

TERRI: OK.

DALE: I don't know how that got started—that story.

TERRI: Not true?

HANK: What isn't true?

DALE: Oh fuck—pardon me.

TERRI: Jeez, I've never heard the word.

HANK: What story?

TERRI: Well, he says it isn't true.

DALE: It isn't—

TERRI: So, I'm not about to be the bearer of false narratives.

HANK: So, if it's not true, whatever it is, why does it have credibility?

TERRI: Well, one could see, knowing Dale, how it *could* be true.

DALE: Not just me. Any guy. Any person period. I think anybody would be tempted to look—

TERRI: Only natural *to* look—

DALE: When there's something to see.

HANK: So this whatever it is that isn't true has something to do with a display of some sort?

DALE: Tell him. I don't care.

TERRI: The story is there were women on the charter, the charter in question. Cuban women.

HANK: Uh-huh.

TERRI: So Dale takes the boat out; they're an hour or so out, and he's standing behind the wheel, and up front—

DALE: That's "fore" if you want the right word—

TERRI: Up fore the ladies, the Cuban ladies, decide to sunbathe. And they don't want any of those nasty tan lines, either fore or—

DALE: Aft.

TERRI: Hence the expression "piece of aft."

DALE: Ho, ho.

HANK: So his mind is elsewhere, which is how one of the Cuban guys can sneak up behind him with the gun. Because he's distracted.

TERRI: That's the story.

DALE: And that's what it is—a story.

TERRI: No truth in it at all.

DALE: Only that a Cuban guy put a gun in my back.

HANK: So, where did this tale come from?

DALE: Not from me. I wouldn't spread something like that about myself.

TERRI: That leaves the Cubans and the Cuban women.

DALE: No.

TERRI: Why not?

DALE: There were no Cuban women. No women and so nobody on board whose lack of clothing would be distracting. So if there were no women to tell the story, and if I didn't tell this story, and if the Cuban guys are in Cuba, who does that leave as being possible to tell this about me being—

HANK: Nobody.

DALE: Unless you think these guys phoned someone *from* Cuba just to embarrass me.

HANK: So, these guys are in Cuba.

DALE: Yes.

HANK: That means your boat is—

DALE: In Cuba. That's my assumption anyway.

HANK: Based on what?

DALE: When this guy put a gun in my back, he asks me a question.

HANK: Yes?

DALE: He asks, "Have you ever seen Havana?" I say no. Then he asks if I want to see Havana—

HANK: And you say no again.

DALE: He tosses me a life jacket and says, "Then you're gonna want to put this on."

TERRI: Considerate.

HANK: So, they put you into a life jacket—

DALE: I get picked up not too long after.

HANK: Too late to do anything about your boat?

DALE: The folks who pick me up don't have a radio or a phone. By the time we get to land, nothing much the coast guard can do.

HANK: Don't you live on that boat?

DALE: I did, yes. Before it went to Cuba.

TERRI: So, it's not just your boat—

DALE: No, this has larger—

HANK: Reverberations?

DALE [*to* TERRI]: Is that what I mean?

TERRI: Ramifications?

DALE: It means more than just the loss of boat.

TERRI: What are the chances of you getting it back?

DALE: Well, I was thinking of writing a letter to Castro.

TERRI: So, it's just a matter of time.

DALE: But if you'll do me a favor, you won't repeat this Cuban women story.

TERRI: If it upsets you—

DALE: It's not a story that puts me in the most flattering—

TERRI: Some hypothetical Cuban women take off their hypothetical clothes. Like you say, who wouldn't look? Straight or gay, who wouldn't look? Particularly if they were attractive. Were they attractive?

DALE: Nice try.

TERRI: Hey, *I'd* look. And I'm a woman and I'm not gay. People look. Hank, you'd look, wouldn't you?

HANK: I've made a career of looking.

TERRI: Ain't that the truth.

HANK: I looked at *you*.

TERRI: Ah, memories.

DALE: But they take my boat; they take where I sleep. So I have to find somewhere else to sleep—

HANK: And have you?

DALE: This woman I used to go with. Liz.

[LIZ, *a plainspoken woman in her late forties or early fifties, enters. In this passage, she interacts only with* DALE.]

TERRI: Used to?

DALE: Complicated, but she hears about my trouble and she says—

LIZ: You can stay at my place for a little bit.

TERRI: She's an ex? Liz?

DALE: Yes, but you know, sometimes it's less ex than others.

LIZ: Your poor boat.

TERRI: So you're getting along—

DALE: Except the other day Liz gets a call—

LIZ: My ex—

DALE: I thought I was your ex.

LIZ: My other ex. *Another* ex—

TERRI: Can't tell the layers without a scorecard.

LIZ: I mean, actually, I'm still technically married to him. Mitch.

HANK: This guy who called.

LIZ: Mitch is coming to town next Tuesday and he's thinking of moving back to Key West and, you know—

TERRI: Liz, she's still interested in him?

LIZ: Well, I have to see.

DALE: This guy left you, dumped you, ran off—

LIZ: I mean, I'm not an idiot, but on the chance—

DALE: It would not be cool for me to be there.

HANK: It would hamper some of her options?

LIZ: Something like that.

TERRI: So does *she* have a boat you can sleep on?

DALE: No.

LIZ: Sorry.

[*She exits.*]

TERRI: So, when do you get your insurance?

DALE: What insurance?

TERRI: You don't have insurance?

DALE: I had insurance in case something happened to a customer.

TERRI: Liability insurance?

DALE: That you have to have. But every now and then we have these noisy things called hurricanes. They tend to do damage to stuff bobbing around in the water. Insurance companies don't like the odds. Not a lot of the boats I know of are insured.

TERRI: What are you going to do?

DALE: Well, I have a couple of bucks salted away. Enough for a down payment if the right boat comes onto the market.

HANK: A used one.

DALE: Can't be buying a new one. But I don't want to be spending that money to live. I spend it, I'll never get another boat.

HANK: Well, this puts a damper on my plan to hire you to take us out fishing.

DALE: Pretty much.

HANK: You have no boat.

DALE: I am currently without boat. I am without boat, I am soon to be without bed—

HANK: You are in a general state of without.

DALE: I mean, as far as your going out, I can recommend someone. Somebody with a boat and also the good luck not to be hired by homesick Cubans.

HANK: But you'd go out with us, wouldn't you?

DALE: Well, it wouldn't be my boat.

HANK: Half the thing I was looking forward to—part of the point of our moving down here—was going out with you.

DALE: Right, that's the reason.

HANK: Going out fishing.

DALE: Lot of places you could go fishing.

HANK: What can I tell you? Retirement looms, we start discussing where to go, Terri says—

TERRI: Happiest I think I've ever seen you, times we've come down on vacation—

DALE: Here?

HANK: Why go somewhere else?

TERRI: He's telling you the truth.

HANK: Fishing with you. Yes, it would be best if your boat were here, but, OK, so I hire you and we go out on someone else's.

DALE: How can I charge for taking you out on a boat I don't have?

HANK: Your time, it's worth something—

DALE: I don't know.

HANK: I don't know whom to ask, do I? Whose boat to turn to next? Without your help, your advice, I could be placing myself into the hands of someone unscrupulous or unskilled. You are wise in matters beyond my ken.

DALE: Sure.

HANK [to audience]: I'm not bullshitting him. Really, he's half the reason we moved down here.

TERRI: And the weather.

HANK: Definitely the weather. February in New England, if I never see another one—

TERRI: Not to mention the prospect of running into faculty in town.

HANK: I spent enough years looking at those faces in committee meetings. And there's another thing I came to escape, thank you—

TERRI: Committees.

HANK: The teaching I liked. The teaching I still enjoyed. The committees—

DALE: So you're here. You've actually moved?

HANK [*back in the scene with* DALE]: Yes.

DALE: Here on Key West?

TERRI: No, a place on Marathon.

DALE: Not far away. Under an hour.

HANK: That was the idea. Easy to get here. Not hard to get to Miami.

DALE: That's what they tell me. Haven't been there in a long time. Miami.

HANK: No?

DALE: Nothing up there for me. So—a condo? A house?

HANK: A house.

TERRI: Something that has some of the characteristics of a house anyway.

HANK: It'll be fine. Just need to fix it up some.

DALE: In what way?

HANK: Electrical stuff. And I've got half a ton of books. Would like to get them out of the boxes and up. You know someone can make shelves?

DALE: I can do that.

HANK: You can?

DALE: Sure. And I probably can handle some of the electrical.

HANK: Tell you what—

TERRI: I know where this is going.

HANK: You think it's a bad idea?

TERRI: Give me a chance *to* think—

HANK: No, you're right, you and I should talk about it. Sorry.

DALE: Talk about what?

TERRI: You. Staying at our house. Building shelves. And I imagine whatever else neither of us is competent enough to handle. Which is to say anything more mechanical than running a microwave. Like, for instance, there's something wrong with our stereo.

[*Transition to house.* DALE *starts to fiddle with the back of a stereo system as he talks. They talk to the audience and one another in the next segment.*]

DALE: It's a pretty good size place.

HANK: There's a spare bedroom at the end of the hall.

DALE: What about that—out back? Could I stay there?

TERRI: The bungalow?

DALE: That would feel—

HANK: Sure, I understand.

DALE: So it's not like I'm underfoot or something.

HANK: Your own four walls.

DALE: It has a john.

HANK: Previous owner used it as an office.

TERRI: That's what Dale moves into.

DALE: Sure, privacy. For them, for me.

[*Shifts away from addressing the audience.*]

TERRI: Well, that's something we have to talk about.

DALE: Excuse me?

TERRI [*teasing*]: If you think we're going to stand for a parade of women—

DALE: Yeah, that's my life all right. You'd be surprised how many women are just knocking down the door of a guy my age with no dough.

TERRI: Maybe some nice widow with money of her own. Florida's full of them, you know. Spent thirty, forty years married to a man who worked long hours at the office, retired, had a heart attack from the stress of not having work. Really, all of those dames, their husbands dead, what are they supposed to do?

HANK: Is that really Dale's problem?

TERRI: No, that's the point. It's not his problem. It's his opportunity.

DALE: Absolutely.

TERRI: You underestimate yourself, Dale. Quite a lot of women, I suspect, would be more than pleased.

DALE: That's me, the love god.

TERRI: He thinks I'm kidding. You think I'm kidding.

HANK: Maybe he's afraid you aren't.

TERRI: Why should I be? What the hell, why not? What's so wrong about bringing comfort and companionship to the lonely and grief stricken, especially if they have a winning combination of gratitude and liquid assets?

DALE: I'm not exactly Richard Gere.

TERRI: Honey, please, you have it all over Richard Gere.

DALE: That would come as news to Richard Gere.

TERRI: Hey, Richard Gere isn't here; you are. But, my opinion, the operative image here isn't Richard Gere. We're more into John Wayne territory.

DALE: John Wayne?

TERRI: You kinda walk like he did.

DALE: What? On two legs?

TERRI: Two legs with the suggestion of a third.

DALE: Terri—

TERRI: Hank, you tell me, am I insulting him?

HANK: She's not insulting you, Dale.

DALE: All right, but—

TERRI: But what?

DALE: Skip it.

TERRI: What? Are you blushing?

DALE: Me?

TERRI: Why? Because I'm imagining your thing? Haven't we got past the point where people are embarrassed by having their things imagined? Isn't that the point of modern fashion? People pay big money to get clothes that play strategic peekaboo with their various whatnots. Modesty is an outmoded concept, baby. You know this. For God's sake, look where we're living. Go to the local beach and see the thongs. You know what the kids call them—call thongs? Butt floss.

DALE [*finishing with the stereo*]: Yeah, but do you see me wearing one?

TERRI: And who would care if you did? You think people don't know what you or I or any one of us has in our pants? Go ahead, imagine what I have in my pants. Guess what? You're right. Who cares? What is so special about what I've got, or you've got?

DALE: Well, mine's kind of important to me.

TERRI: Really? OK, if I were to show you three pictures of three relatively normal specimens, and if I told you one of them was yours, would you be able to pick it out? Would you be able to identify it? I mean, if the other ones weren't tattooed or some hugely endowed porn star's or something that made them obviously distinct so you could do process of elimination. But three normal examples of male equipment at rest—would you really be able to say with any great degree of certainty, "Yes, that one there is mine. I'd know it anywhere"?

HANK: Is there a point to this?

TERRI: So to speak? Yes, I think there's a point.

HANK: I await it breathlessly.

TERRI: I was talking about modesty. About the illogic of modesty in a society that celebrates immodesty. I mean, so you see somebody naked. What can you claim to know about someone from seeing them naked? Can you read anything about, say, their politics?

HANK: Well, if it's a guy, you could tell if he leans to the left.

TERRI: But what is private? Certainly not what they used to call privates anymore. How can privates be called private when they've gone public?

HANK: Are you complaining?

TERRI: I don't think so. Am I?

HANK: I'm not sure. You're saying things, and you're saying them with a certain amount of fervor, which would suggest that you believe you're pressing some kind of a case. Trying to persuade us of something. And, you know, aside from the fact—the very pleasing fact—that I'm married to you, you're a charming lady and so I'm kind of inclined to agree with you. But I do have to understand what I'd be agreeing with, if I did agree. I'm not offering you a blank check of endorsement.

TERRI: I just think we live in a hypocritical society.

HANK: Ah, now there's an original thought.

TERRI: Doesn't make it any less true.

HANK: Doesn't make it any more original.

TERRI: Does a thought have to be original in order to have validity?

HANK: It's nice if it at least hits someone else's brain with some freshness of expression. "We live in a hypocritical society" is a cliché. It's a conclusion that, at the moment, is unsupported by any premises.

TERRI: What I was saying before about an immodest society pretending to be a modest one.

HANK: That isn't quite what you said. You said that modesty was pointless in a society that celebrates immodesty. That's a different statement.

TERRI: You really wish you were back teaching a seminar, don't you? What do you think, Dale?

DALE: I've never been in a seminar, so I don't know what one sounds like.

TERRI: It sounds like this. Some puffed-up somebody pretending to lead a discussion when he's really trying to impose his opinions on everyone else. They call it the Socratic method, but mostly it's old-fashioned bullying.

HANK: What opinion do you imagine I'm trying to impose on you?

TERRI: OK, knock it off.

HANK: Gladly.

[*She puts a tape into the stereo. Sultry music plays.*]

TERRI: Practice.

DALE: Practice what?

TERRI: Hey, if you're gonna take up the trade, got to know the moves.

DALE: Moves?

TERRI: Dance.

DALE: I know how to dance.

TERRI: Let's see. Come on, I'm Ethel Kapinsky, the widow of Arnie Kapinsky, former sturgeon king of Great Neck or wherever the hell—

HANK: Why don't you throw in references to mah-jongg while you're at it?

TERRI: Since when are you deputy for the Anti-Defamation League? Just trying to get Dale here into the mood.

[*Smoothly,* DALE *stands and pulls* TERRI *into a dance.*]

OK there—natural talent.

DALE: I'm not Gene Kelly.

TERRI: Maybe Hank will show you some stuff.

DALE: You dance, Hank?

HANK: Used to. When I was a kid. The Catskills. A job to earn dough for college. I spent a summer or two on staff.

DALE: As a dancer?

HANK: If you were on staff, no matter what you did, you were a dancer. Part of the job, make sure all the guests are kept happy and occupied.

TERRI: So you may have danced with Ethel Kapinsky yourself, back before she met Mr. Kapinsky.

HANK: I danced with a lot of ladies before they met their Kapinskys.

TERRI: You could pass on some of the tricks of the trade to Dale here. Some of what you remember.

[*Phone rings.* TERRI *breaks off.*]

I'll get it.

[*She exits the room.* HANK *turns off the player.*]

DALE: Is everything OK?

HANK: OK?

DALE: I mean, if my being here is going to make things difficult—

HANK: Dale, aren't you used to us by now? All the time on the boat?

DALE: Well, yes, that was on a boat. I worked for you, but it was my boat.

HANK: Your boat and your home.

DALE: Yes.

HANK: And this is different.

DALE: This is *your* home.

HANK: But out back there, that's your bungalow.

DALE: Well, but it's yours, too.

HANK: Yes, but if I come back there, I knock on your door.

DALE: What doors should I knock on here?

HANK: Doors. I don't—well, you need to be able to get to the kitchen whenever, so don't worry about that.

DALE: OK.

HANK: And this area here—

DALE: The den—

HANK: This is pretty much a common room. My office, though—

DALE: Yes, well, of course, your office. And your bedroom and bathroom.

HANK: Stands to reason.

DALE: But I think, to spell out—

HANK: Of course.

DALE: Just to avoid—

HANK: —embarrassment.

DALE: Awkward stuff, sure.

HANK: I'm sure we'll feel our way through the first week or so. I don't think we have to make up a lot of rules ahead of time. More often than not, rules emerge out of practice and custom.

DALE: Practice and custom.

HANK: That's my theory anyway.

DALE: I'll have to chew on that.

HANK: Sorry—

DALE: What?

HANK: I was slipping into lecture mode there. You catch me doing that again, just hit me in the kisser with a cream pie.

DALE: I don't guess you stop being a teacher.

HANK: Yes, but it's appropriate for me to be a teacher with a student, and you aren't a student.

DALE: I don't know it'd hurt me now and then to brush up against an idea, something beyond what bait to use. You were saying, about making up rules and—

HANK: Well, figuring out what the rules are—must be—from what you observe, what you see.

DALE: OK.

HANK: All right, I know. Let's say you go to court.

DALE: Court, OK.

HANK: Let's say you've never been to court before—for the sake of argument—and you've never seen any episodes of *Law and Order*—

DALE: Yes and—

HANK: OK. So you get there and when the judge enters someone says, "All rise for his honor, Judge So-and-So," or whatever the words are. And everybody stands up. And then you have the trial. And somebody objects and everybody looks at the judge, and the judge says whether or not the objection is sustained. Makes a ruling. And sometimes the lawyers argue stuff, trying to persuade the judge to buy the way they see it, whatever the issue is.

DALE: All right.

HANK: OK—if you knew absolutely nothing about law and the rules of procedure and all of that, but you were plunked down in this courtroom and you watched how things transpired, went, you'd know what from what you saw?

DALE: The judge calls the shots.

HANK: So, you would figure out from observing this that the rules in this courtroom are that the judge is the person everybody defers to.

DALE: So I'm figuring out the rules from what I'm seeing.

HANK: Yes.

DALE: All right, but in that case, aren't I figuring out rules that were written down somewhere? Some book of courtroom procedure? So, it's not my figuring out the unwritten rules based on what I'm seeing.

HANK: No, you're right. Hmm. Let me see if I can—a better example.

[TERRI *returns, takes a seat.* HANK *looks at her for a second.*]

OK, I know.

[HANK *goes to* TERRI, *gets down on his knee, removes one of her sandals, and kisses her foot. He replaces the sandal and returns to his seat. He looks at* DALE. DALE *nods. He goes to* TERRI, *gets down on his knee, removes the sandal, and kisses her foot. He replaces the sandal and returns to his seat.* TERRI *just blinks. The two guys sit silently for a second, then start to laugh.*]

TERRI: I'm considering calling both of you assholes.

HANK: After we just paid you homage?

TERRI: Is that what you were doing?

HANK: Don't you feel honored?

TERRI: You want to honor me, I'll tell you what to kiss.

HANK: Who was that on the phone?

TERRI: For me, but I got a call-waiting for you. Guy from the community college, wanted to know if you'd be interested in teaching a course for them. I got his name and number.

DALE: What would you teach?

HANK: Fishing.

DALE: I've seen you fish.

HANK: You suggesting I should teach something I know about? What would be the fun in that?

DALE: Is that the point of teaching—fun?

HANK: It would be the only point if I did it. Haven't you heard? I'm retired. Now that I've worn out my stamina in the service of youth, it's time for me to service myself.

TERRI: And we all know what that's called. [*To audience*] I wouldn't be here right now—*we* wouldn't be here right now—if it hadn't been for a mistake I made in 1972. I was a grad student then, living with this very nice guy who was, natch, another grad student. Anyway, we're coming home from something and—Trevor, his name was—we're at the front door and Trevor can't find his keys. So I say he should reach into my bag—my arms are full—he should reach into my bag and get mine. And as soon as I say it I realize I've made a goof. He finds the case. My diaphragm case. Why would I have carried that out of the house in my bag? He'd taken a course in logic so it isn't too tough for him to arrive at a conclusion. Or, as they say in logic, a valid conclusion. And it doesn't take too much work for him to figure out the reason for the diaphragm leaving the apartment is Hank, who is, yes, on the faculty. Well, Hank was married at the time. Trevor makes enough of a scene that Hank's wife hears about it and pretty soon Hank isn't married anymore. And soon after, to his surprise and mine, we marry. This isn't what I was looking for. But, it just, I don't know—what can I tell you, we're still married. And that surprises a lot of people, including me. But I always thought that how we got together had something to do with why Hank never made full professor. His first wife had lots of friends at the university.

HANK: Not that anybody would actually say that was the reason.

TERRI: You should have filed a grievance. You had a case. They had no right to deprive you just because of what happened between us. Students and professors have been seducing each other for as long as—

HANK: Anyway, I always thought it was kind of a trade. I didn't make full professor, but I got—

TERRI: Me?

HANK: I didn't think it was such a bad deal—

TERRI: At the time?

HANK: I still don't.

[DALE *presses a button on the stereo and music begins again.* TERRI *and* HANK *look at him, laugh, and begin to dance again.* DALE *watches for a second, then leaves them alone together to continue dancing.*]

TERRI: You should take them up on teaching. You miss it.

HANK: It's a community college.

TERRI: So? They're people. An adult-ed class so it'll be grown-ups who actually want to be there. Maybe even some folks who know who you are.

HANK: And show me due reverence.

TERRI: You're due any reverence they can muster, kiddo.

HANK: Is this working for you? Being here?

TERRI: I'll manage.

HANK: I don't want you to just manage.

TERRI: At this point, I think managing puts us ahead of the game. Hell, look at Dale. They stole his boat.

HANK: But at least he'll get another boat.

TERRI: Hank—

HANK: OK.

[*They exit as* DALE *appears.*]

DALE [*to audience*]: As you probably know, Key West has got a pretty large gay population. Recently, Maureen McLeary has added to that population by moving in with a lady who has a house down here. The complication in this part of the story is Maureen's husband Kyle. When Maureen told him that she had a new idea of who she was and she was going to go off and be true to that—or however she put it—Kyle, he just stands there like he's stepped on the wrong end of a rake and the handle jumped up and did to him what handles in that situation do. She packs up, leaves, and comes down to be with her girlfriend down here. A week or two later, one morning Kyle is driving to work, and on the way there's the turnoff to the airport, and instead of going to work he goes to the airport. He puts his car into the parking lot and buys a ticket to Florida. On the flight, in his head, he's working on a speech. Something about the mistakes he figures he must've made, though he's vague about what those are 'cause he really is traveling without a map. But some words that he hopes will put everything into a whole new perspective, point the way to a fresh start. But when he gets face-to-face with Maureen, the speech doesn't come out the way he intends. And she lets him know that the fresh start she's working on is the one she's beginning with her girlfriend, the one who owns the house in Key West where she is now living and that she's making new curtains for. Kyle runs out of things to say. And he goes to a bar.

[TERRI *enters, picks up the story.*]

TERRI [*to audience*]: He goes to a bar. He puts some effort into being cheerful and he's actually pretty funny. Anyway, a lady in the bar thinks he's pretty funny. Funny enough. And when she gathers from what he's saying that he's only in town for the night, she figures that he'll do. He'll suit her purposes. Later that night she makes a phone call from the emergency room.

[TERRI *and* DALE *are on the phone.*]

DALE: Terri? Hank's not here right now.

TERRI: Yes, I know that. [*To audience*] He's taking a kind of field trip on the mainland. His being away is how come I came to Key West tonight. [*To* DALE] I'm calling you. You're the one I need right now.

DALE: Need? You OK?

TERRI: Aside from a fractured rib and some miscellaneous bruises.

DALE: You been in an accident?

TERRI: Look, they've given me some painkillers that are making me—I shouldn't be behind the wheel of a car. Can you come down and get me and bring me home?

[DALE *in driver's seat.* TERRI *sitting next to him. A beat.*]

DALE: We'll have to figure out some way of getting your car back.

TERRI: Maybe the next time two of us are going down to Key West anyway. Hank and I or you and I.

DALE: Or me and Hank.

TERRI: Whatever combination.

DALE: Yeah, that should work.

TERRI: We all can drive. We all have driver's licenses.

DALE: Well, that's solved.

[*A beat.*]

I didn't know you were going down tonight.

TERRI: I didn't tell you.

DALE: That's what I'm saying.

TERRI: Telling you was not something I felt I needed to do.

DALE: You didn't need to. You don't.

TERRI: I can go where I want, when I want.

DALE: Of course. Not saying I should have known.

TERRI: OK, we've established what you're not saying. What *are* you saying?

DALE: Not much, I guess.

TERRI: What are you thinking?

DALE: Not much more.

TERRI: How do you think I got banged up?

DALE: You said something on the phone about an accident.

TERRI: I said I had a rib fractured and bruises. I said I needed you to pick me up. I didn't say anything about an accident. You did.

DALE: Well, I assumed. I mean, a fractured rib—something has to hit you pretty hard to do that to a rib.

TERRI: Something or someone.

DALE: Someone?

TERRI: Someone.

DALE: Someone hit you?

TERRI: Yes, he did.

DALE: He?

TERRI: I believe his name is Kyle.

DALE: Why?

TERRI: I guess he's an angry guy, old Kyle.

DALE: Why you?

TERRI: I was nearby when he got angry.

DALE: So, has he been arrested?

TERRI: I'm not pressing charges.

DALE: But he hit you. He hurt you. This guy just goes nuts and, what, attacks you in a public place?

TERRI: It wasn't a public place.

DALE: Oh.

TERRI: Oh.

DALE: Do I want to know this? What am I supposed to do with knowing this?

TERRI: You could avenge me. How'd you like to do that? Go to his hotel room and bang up one of *his* ribs. A rib for a rib. Has kind of an Old Testament ring to it.

DALE: Jesus.

TERRI: Wrong testament.

[*He looks at her blankly. She explains.*]

Jesus.

DALE: Somebody beats the crap out of you and you make jokes.

TERRI: I'm sorry, I haven't had much practice being a victim. Am I doing it wrong?

DALE: You want some music?

TERRI: You're disappointed in me.

DALE: I'm not in a position to be—it's not my right to be.

TERRI: You're not my husband.

DALE: No.

TERRI: Thank God?

DALE: I didn't say that.

TERRI: No, you're too much of a gentleman.

DALE: Is that something you think I should be ashamed of?

TERRI: Oh, so you admit it.

DALE: That I'm a gentleman?

TERRI: Yes.

DALE: Do I look like a gentleman?

TERRI: Do I look like a lady?

DALE: What else would you be?

TERRI: There are some other words in your mind.

DALE: Why are you pushing this?

TERRI: I'm sorry, Dale; you are a gentleman. That's what you are. Live with it.

DALE: I could show you what kind of a gentleman I am. I could pull over to this side of the road—

TERRI: And push me out?

DALE: You think I couldn't? Maybe leave you in the middle of a bridge. What do you think would happen?

TERRI: I'd be in trouble.

DALE: Why didn't you call a car service or something? Why me?

TERRI: No, you're right.

DALE: Your husband is my friend.

TERRI: Am I your friend?

DALE: I don't know.

TERRI: Dale, I am your friend. You are my friend. You came in the middle of the night and picked me up. That's something that a friend would do. A friend and a gentleman.

DALE: And a schmuck.

TERRI: My, I *have* disappointed you. You really expect women to behave better, don't you? You're one of those guys who secretly believes that men are filth and women have some head start when it comes to pure thoughts and good actions.

DALE: I do expect better.

TERRI: Well, don't. If maybe, in the chronicles of evil, more has been done by men than women, it's only because men have had more opportunities.

DALE: Thanks for opening my eyes.

TERRI: It's the truth I tell you. And frankly, I don't know if I can bear the strain of trying to live up to your expectations. And while I'm at it, I want to say I do not accept the responsibility for representing or speaking for all women. I was not elected. Nor would I allow my name to be put into nomination.

DALE: All right.

[*A beat.*]

TERRI: OK, I'm sorry.

DALE: What for?

TERRI: What do you want me to be sorry for? Name it.

DALE: Didn't you hear me say "all right"? Christ almighty!

[*A beat.*]

TERRI: Moments like this, I wish I still smoked. I'd strike a match, light up, shoot two perfect streams out my nostrils.

[*A beat.*]

Don't worry. It's gonna be fine.

[*Lights dim on them as slides of Celebration, Florida, begin appearing. (Note: it is possible to stage the scene without actually seeing the slides.)* HANK *appears.*]

HANK [*to audience*]: This is the lakefront. This is the town hall. That building, incidentally, was designed by Philip Johnson, for those of you who are architecture groupies. I took these shots. Drove up to the Orlando area, bought one of those one-use cameras in a gas station along the way, went to the town, and took some pictures. That's why

I was away for a couple of days. To go, look around, take pictures of the town. The town in question being Celebration.

Celebration, Florida, was opened in 1997 by Mickey Mouse. All right, by the Disney organization. It's a town, like I say. A lot of us have grown up with images of the small town in our heads. Many of these images are from the movies. *It's a Wonderful Life,* Bedford Falls. Or you go to one of the Disney parks and there's Main Street, USA. This idealized view of the small town main street. You go there and it stimulates in you a nostalgia, except nostalgia is usually for somewhere you've actually been. That's some trick, to make a place where you've never actually lived feel like it's your hometown.

Most cities or towns spring up because of some resource that's already in the neighborhood—a river or a lake, or maybe to be near a railroad to take and deliver goods. People have a reason to live in a place, and the place arises in response to that reason.

But there was no preexistent reason to live on the territory Celebration now occupies. It was a swamp. It came into being for the sake of the town itself. As an experiment. The Disney people built a town, and people came to match the needs of the town. In a sense, the people came to play the parts of townspeople in Celebration. It's like there's an endless civic pageant, and people move there for the right to play pilgrims in the diorama.

[*Slide presentation is over. Lights shift. Turns to* DALE.]

What do you think?

DALE: That's what you're planning on beginning with? The class you're gonna teach?

HANK: Something like.

DALE: What's the course actually going to be about?

HANK: Well, since we've moved here, to Florida, I thought maybe I'd use this as an excuse to explore Florida through its images. There's an old saw that if you want to learn a subject, you should teach it.

DALE: And the subject here is—

HANK: The idea of this state. The state of second chances. This is a place that sells itself as the hope of the next good thing. A place to come to. That's the whole appeal of Celebration. Everybody comes to Celebration from somewhere else. Another chance to get it right. And it's a theme that's in a lot of writing, too. Hemingway, Tennessee Williams, Carl Hiaasen, what's-his-name who wrote Travis Magee.

DALE: John D. MacDonald.

HANK: Right.

DALE: You know Travis Magee?

HANK: Sure.

DALE: Wouldn't have thought that was your kind of reading. Detective stories.

HANK: You like him, too?

DALE: One of the reasons I moved down here. Used to read the Travis Magee stuff. Those stories about him living on his boat—

HANK: The *Busted Flush*.

DALE: When my wife died, after I settled everything . . . I'd hardly set foot out of Ohio all those years. So I thought maybe, before I got too old, I'd see what kind of life I could put together down here. I didn't expect to chase crooks or punch out bad guys or hop into bed with every other blonde, but—

HANK: OK, there, what you're saying is part of what I'm saying. You came down here partially to put yourself into this image you had of your second chance. You came down to be a version of Travis Magee.

DALE: What's wrong with that?

HANK: Nothing. Like I say, I think that's part of the point of the state.

DALE: Who did you come down to be a version of?

[*A beat.*]

HANK: Terri says you're thinking of leaving.

DALE: I haven't said anything.

HANK: No, she didn't say you said, she said you were thinking. Does it have anything to do with you fetching her from Key West while I was gone?

[*A beat.*]

DALE: She told you about that?

HANK: If that's what was making you feel uncomfortable—that you came to know a thing you thought you had to keep secret from me—

DALE: Yes.

HANK: Well, I guess we owe you an apology. Anyway, I hope you'll stay, if that's really all it was.

DALE: All?

HANK: Yes.

DALE: You two have some kind of an arrangement? You both can go off and do whatever?

HANK: Not exactly. Let me show you something—

[HANK *retrieves a vacuum constriction device.*]

Put your finger in there.

DALE: My finger?

HANK: There. Don't worry.

[DALE *sticks a finger into the tube.* HANK *works the pump for a few seconds.*]

DALE: Was that supposed to do something?

HANK: Did your finger get any bigger?

DALE: Uh, no.

HANK: Well, perhaps it's not meant to be for the finger. Maybe it's meant to be for some other body part.

DALE: Are you serious?

HANK: Only when I have to be. Yes, you see, you're supposed to put it in there, and you're supposed to do it so that the chamber is sealed off. Airtight. Then you pump this thing, and you get a vacuum going. So the air pressure drops, and that kind of encourages something else to rise. Then, the way it's supposed to go, you roll on what they call a constriction band.

DALE: Constriction?

HANK: It's a little like tying off a balloon with a rubber band to keep the air in it. This has the desired effect for about thirty minutes. Long enough to get the job done. According to the statistics, this works for the vast majority of the guys who want it to work. And, in a sense, it works for me. It does what it's supposed to do in the physiological respect. But in other aspects, it leaves something to be desired. I acquired this novelty item a little over two years ago. Terri made a good show of enthusiasm. She was game. Oh, what fun. A new way to play. For a while I played along. But—I don't know, call it misplaced pride. I have a goddamn doctorate. What am I doing sticking myself into a plastic tube, coaxing my flesh out of reluctance with a pump?

DALE: There are other ways, aren't there?

HANK: Pills, injections, a variety of ingenious responses. Some go for some kind of implant. Me? I don't think so. I might have been able to deal with the pills, but there were medical reasons that didn't make that advisable. And I came to see that it wasn't so much my own pleasure I was missing as I was . . . concerned about disappointing her. So, once in a while, when I sense it would be appreciated, I find a chore or a project that takes me away for a day or two. If she's in the mood, she takes care of whatever she feels moved to take care of, and life goes on otherwise fairly pleasantly. When we were still at the university, it was never with a colleague, somebody else on the faculty. Or, God help me, a student. She would go to another town, a place where there was little likelihood of encountering someone who might show up in our normal lives.

DALE: OK, it's probably just me seeing it the way I figure I would—

HANK: If it were you.

DALE: Yes.

HANK: You'd be jealous.

DALE: I would be.

HANK: Well, I'm a pure soul, completely removed from such petty things.

DALE: Well, that would do it.

HANK: I also can fly and spin hay into gold.

DALE: I knew that.

HANK: I don't mean to make you uncomfortable. But I thought there were certain things you should know. You're a part of this household. It's not like we sat down and decided all this. It's something we stumbled into. I skipped over a couple of steps in my story. She did leave for a while.

DALE: Terri?

HANK: She got her own apartment. She didn't think it was right to be doing the other stuff and still live under the same roof with me.

[TERRI enters.]

TERRI: I thought it was unfair to him.

HANK: You felt bad.

TERRI: I moved out. Got the apartment. You were angry.

HANK: I was.

TERRI: We met at a restaurant to talk it out. I made an idiot out of myself.

HANK: She did not.

TERRI: I cried.

HANK: Well, hell, so did I.

TERRI: I run out of the restaurant.

HANK: I catch up with her standing by her car.

[*And they're back in the moment.*]

Come back. Come back to me. Please.

TERRI: How can I?

HANK: You switch on the ignition and point your car toward home. Please come back.

TERRI: It doesn't feel right.

HANK: Does it feel right this way?

TERRI: No.

HANK: So what we're left with is what will feel less not right. I like being married to you. I think you like being married to me.

TERRI: Yes.

HANK: Through nobody's fault, certain things have changed. If it were the other way around—

TERRI: If it were the other way around, I'd look for the exit.

HANK: Would you?

[*A beat.*]

TERRI: No.

HANK: We're bright people. We should be able to come up with something that works. We just have to figure out a different way to be married.

TERRI [*to* DALE]: And it seems that we pretty much have.

HANK: I am not happy, though, about what happened in Key West. I don't like her putting herself at that kind of risk. I don't think I'm alone in thinking there are more nuts out there than there used to be. Unstable people capable of—but I don't have to tell you. They took your boat.

[*A beat.*]

> Actually, what we have here is related to what we were talking about
> before.

DALE: What?

HANK: The idea that rules of a society are not imposed from above but
> come out of the needs and resources *of* the society. Among the three
> of us, there are these needs and there are these resources.

[*A beat.*]

DALE: Let me see if I understand you.

TERRI: Yes. Yes, you do.

HANK: We're not going to twist your arm, Dale. If this doesn't sit well
> with you . . . [*To audience*] It helps that I go off on another jaunt with
> a disposable camera.

[HANK *exits.* DALE *is seated.* TERRI *stands, turns down a light. She kisses*
DALE. *She begins to unbutton her blouse.* DALE *sits quietly for a second.*]

DALE: No.

TERRI: What?

DALE: Not in the house.

TERRI: Your bungalow then.

[*She heads off. A beat.* DALE *follows her. Lights shift to morning.* TERRI
returns, wearing a robe, entering from a different direction from that in which
she exited. She hears the sound of a car pulling in. She goes to the door, opens it.
HANK *stands there with a couple of bags.*]

HANK: You heard the car.

TERRI: Morning.

HANK: Hold these?

TERRI: Sure.

[*She takes the bags.* HANK *goes offstage and rolls on a butcher's block on wheels.*
On it are plates, cups and knives, and a carton of juice. She puts the bags down
on it. HANK *pulls out of the bags bagels and a plastic container. He stops in the*
middle of his fiddling to give her an inquiring look. She nods, smiles a little
shyly. She goes over to HANK's *side of the table, gives him a kiss.* DALE *enters,*
sees them standing side by side.]

HANK: I picked up some bagels on the way back.

DALE: Bagels?

HANK: Got an assortment—poppy seed, onion, pumpernickel.

DALE: Great.

HANK: And a few different spreads.

TERRI: What's your pleasure?

DALE: Poppy seed, I guess.

HANK: Poppy seed it is.

[*He begins to prepare the bagel, pulls out a knife, and slathers some spread on it.*]

DALE: What's the red stuff in the cream cheese?

HANK: Pimento.

DALE: Isn't that what's in olives?

HANK: They put it into some olives, yes. After they take out the pit. Somebody must've thought it was a good idea to take the pit out of olives—

DALE: Sure, pits are a hassle.

TERRI: They're the pits.

HANK: But when they tried it, they saw it left a hole, and thought, "What do we put into it?"

DALE: Something that would fit.

TERRI: Pimento.

HANK: But it has an identity apart from olives.

DALE: Well, that's good news for the pimento.

HANK: I think you'll like it.

TERRI: I'll be glad to eat it if you don't want—

DALE: No, I'll give it a try.

[*He takes a bite.*]

HANK: What do you think?

DALE: Not bad.

[HANK *and* TERRI *share the duties of cutting bagels and spreading pimento cream cheese on for each of them.* HANK *pulls out cups and the juice.*]

HANK: Grapefruit juice?

TERRI: Sure.

DALE: Why not?

[HANK *pours and distributes cups for all of them. They stand eating and drinking.*]

HANK: OK?
DALE: Yeah.
TERRI: OK by me.
HANK: OK.

[*Lights fade.*]

ACT 2

[TERRI *and* DALE *in bed.*]

DALE: Mom and I are sitting there in the room with him. The hospital room. There's this one point my mom gets up to go to the bathroom or something. But she leaves the room and he waves me over. I figure he wants to share something. Some word of advice. Wisdom. Or maybe even, "I know I haven't said it to you much, but I love you, son." So I go over to him and what he says is, "The closet in my office. In the back, there's a box where my boots are. Anything happens to me, get rid of what's in there before your mother—" He sees on my face that I don't exactly get what he's saying. "You listening to me?" "Yes, Dad," I say, "you want me to get rid of your boots." Did I tell you this is when I was twelve? I was twelve years old. So he says to me, "I'm not talking about boots. Something else *in* the boot box. OK?" I still don't get it. He looks at me impatiently. "Just promise you'll do it. Don't let her see it." He dies a day or two later, and I go into his office to do what he asks. I go to the closet, open the boot box, and under the boots—

TERRI: Pictures.

DALE: No animals or kids, but just about anything else people could do to each other with whatever they have to do it with. I hear a noise behind me, and I make a move to close the box. It's Mom. "Oh please," she says, "you think I don't know?" I try to stonewall her. Something like, "Know? Know what?" And she says, "As if I care. Hell, if it kept him from poking at me."

TERRI: Nice.

DALE: But here I thought I was going to finally share a moment of father-son closeness, and all he wanted me to do was get rid of his magazines.

TERRI: Well, it showed he trusted you.

DALE: Trusted me? Who else was he going to ask? But this is a guy who taught me nothing, nothing at all, about women.

TERRI: Well, you said he died when you were twelve. Maybe he was waiting.

DALE: He waited too long. And you can imagine, with my mother's attitude, what a big help she was.

TERRI: Did you do better? You've got a kid, don't you?

DALE: A daughter. Iris.

TERRI: Did you tell her anything to prepare her about men?

DALE: She found out on her own.

TERRI: Oh?

DALE: Got pregnant. I didn't handle it very well.

TERRI: You threw her out?

DALE: I didn't make it easy for her to stay. Dumb.

TERRI: And?

DALE: She had the baby. She kept the baby. A girl.

TERRI: She marry the father?

DALE: No, but that was OK by me. If the father is who I think he was. Some asshole who played the drums.

TERRI: Was he an asshole because he played the drums?

DALE: No. I mention the drums strictly for, whaddayacallit, identification purposes.

TERRI: He doesn't have any contact with his daughter? The drummer?

DALE: He doesn't even know he's a father. He left town to go to college, never came back.

TERRI: If he's the one you think he is.

DALE: Iris didn't want him to know. I can imagine what she'd say if she saw where I am now. How things are arranged between you and me and—after all my lecturing.

TERRI: How do things stand with the two of you now?

DALE: Oh, we patched it up mostly after her daughter was born. Hard to stay too stupid when you've got a granddaughter. Thank God, 'cause it turned out my wife only had a few years left.

TERRI: It was a good marriage?

DALE: You know, it was. I like being married.

TERRI: So do I.

[*A beat.*]

DALE: What do you do?

TERRI: Excuse me?

DALE: I have no idea what you do. Did you teach at that college, too?

TERRI: I had what you might call a social service job.

DALE: Tell me about it.

TERRI: I don't know if you'd find it all that interesting.

DALE: Or do you think I wouldn't be able to appreciate—

TERRI: I worked with political refugees. People who come into this country in order to get away from some other country. Maybe you're from the Balkans or South America or Rwanda, and you need to get set up. Somewhere to live where people might understand the language you speak, a start on finding work, a place for your kids to go to school.

DALE: Wow. That's like a real job.

TERRI: Yes, it was.

DALE: You helped people, sounds like.

TERRI: That was the idea.

DALE: You gonna do more of that? I mean, it's a cinch in Florida there's a call for that. If someone had done the job right with those Cuban guys, I might still have my boat.

TERRI: I'm taking a break for a little while. Besides, who says you have to do the same thing your whole life?

[TERRI *moves to leave.*]

DALE: I wish—

TERRI: What?

DALE: That sometime you'd stay till morning.

[*A beat.* TERRI *kisses her hand then puts her hand to his forehead. She puts on her robe and exits.* DALE *puts on appropriate clothes and turns to audience.*]

We're skipping ahead a few months here. There comes a point when Hank doesn't bother leaving the house on made-up trips. Terri visits my bungalow a couple of times a week. She always leaves well before dawn. And in the morning, it's the three of us passing the jam for the toast and figuring out the chores for the day. Oh yes, during this time, my daughter, Iris, visits from Ohio. I think she guesses. I see her smiling at me, kind of laughing. Not in a mean way. But even if she did, she would've had the right. But she visits for a week, goes home, and things go back to normal. Which is how we know that it's become normal. Maybe if you do it regularly enough, anything can become normal.

[*The sound of a doorbell.*]

And one day, I get a surprise visit. I answer the door and she's just standing there. Liz.

[LIZ *enters, carrying a plastic bag, faces* DALE.]

LIZ: You didn't even know they were missing.

DALE: No, not really.

LIZ: Sure. Well, they're yours. I thought you might want them.

DALE: I hope you didn't drive all the way up just to bring me dirty T-shirts—

LIZ: I washed them.

DALE: That was beyond the call.

LIZ: You toss some soap in, press a button, no big.

DALE: Well, thanks.

LIZ: I was coming up anyway.

DALE: Oh?

LIZ: No, I wasn't. I wanted to see you, how you're doing. An impulse.

DALE: I have them sometimes.

LIZ: I should have called, huh?

DALE: You want to come out to the back, have something to drink?

LIZ: Here's my arm, twist it.

[*They move to the patio. The shadows of palm leaves dapple the stage. He gives her a beer.*]

Nice patio.

DALE: Thank you.

LIZ: Oh, is it a compliment that belongs to you?

DALE: Actually, yes, I rebuilt a lot of it. It was in bad shape.

LIZ: You cleaned it up good. It's very—

DALE: The bungalow over there, that's where I bunk.

LIZ: Cozy.

DALE: A little more space than I had on the boat.

LIZ: What are you doing about that?

DALE: The boat? Hoping to find another one. Something I can buy. If you hear of anything—

LIZ: I'll keep my ears open.

DALE: Sometimes I take Hank out on someone else's boat, but it's not the same.

LIZ: No, I can see.

DALE: A lot of the charter guys, they're friends. They sometimes let me take the wheel, and that's good. But I never forget it's not my wheel.

LIZ: But otherwise, you're OK.

DALE: I'm here. I fix stuff.

LIZ: The patio—

DALE: I run a few errands.

LIZ: You make yourself useful.

[DALE *nods, shrugs.*]

Doesn't it sometimes get boring?

DALE: What makes you think?

LIZ: He's a professor; she's from that kind of thing, too. Probably sit around all day reading books and talking about classical Greek shit. Journals. Footnotes.

DALE: Yeah, that's pretty much all they do. Though every now and then, just to keep me amused, they break out some Legos and we build stuff on the living room floor.

LIZ: Nuclear reactors?

DALE: Actually, they can barely set an alarm clock without a seminar.

LIZ: A seminar?

DALE: You know, like in a college.

LIZ [*overlapping*]: I know what a seminar is. You're picking up their lingo.

[HANK *enters.*]

HANK: I hope we're not doing him too much damage. Hello.

LIZ: I didn't realize—

HANK: You must be Liz.

LIZ: You know about me.

HANK: Dale has mentioned your name.

LIZ: I can imagine.

HANK: No, fondly, I assure you.

LIZ: Fondly, after I booted you out on your ear?

DALE [*to* HANK]: How'd it go? [*To* LIZ] Hank started teaching a course at the community college today.

HANK: My first class. A nice surprise—

DALE: What?

HANK: A guy I went to grad school with at Columbia, he was there. Signed up for my course. But you know, he's gotten kind of old.

LIZ: Isn't it amazing how old other people can get?

DALE: Has Mitch gotten old?

LIZ: Huh?

DALE: Mitch. Mitch is his name, right?

LIZ: Yes.

DALE: Your husband.

LIZ: Yes, Mitch is his name. It isn't what I call him, though.

HANK: Something affectionate?

LIZ: Dickhead.

HANK: Well.

DALE: So, it's not—

LIZ: No.

DALE: I'm sorry.

LIZ: It's my own stupid fault.

DALE: How could you know?

LIZ: From being married to him. [*Explaining to* HANK] Which I was and still am technically.

HANK: Yes, I heard.

LIZ: I should have picked up a few clues from that. But, you know, you hope. Anyway, I do. I did. I did hope.

DALE: That he'd changed.

LIZ: And you know, he didn't even *say* he'd changed. The phone call. When he said he was coming back. He didn't say, "Liz, honey, I see what a jerk-off I was. Dawn has broken. I'm a changed man."

DALE: You have to give him that—he didn't lie to you.

LIZ: Which I guess is something.

DALE: But then he didn't call and say, "I *haven't* changed" either.

LIZ: Which would have been honest.

DALE: If he'd said "I haven't changed—"

LIZ: "Hello, Liz, I'm still the jerk-off I was when I left. What do you say?" Like I would've gone, "God, so *that's* what's been missing from life! Sure, come on back." [*To* HANK] I'm sorry. This can't be interesting to you.

HANK: At least as interesting as the Greek shit I read.

[*He smiles at* LIZ. *At first she's startled, then she smiles back.*]

DALE: So the story is what?

LIZ: The story is he's there and he won't go. In my home.

DALE: You could wait until he's out of the house and change the locks.

LIZ: I tried that. He broke back in.

DALE: You call the cops?

LIZ: Well, that would be kind of hard.

DALE: It's your home.

LIZ: Sure, it's my home. But it's his place.

DALE: How's that?

LIZ: When we got married, I moved in with him. Into his house. When he took off a couple years ago, I stayed. In the meantime, I paid the bills. The electric, the gas, the taxes. But if you're gonna look at the actual legality of the situation—

HANK: Doesn't your having married him mean that the house becomes your property, too?

LIZ: But you see, even if it's mine, too, it still means he can stay there if he wants.

DALE: And he wants?

LIZ: He's got what he wants. He's staying. At least until it gets warmer up north.

HANK: And you? What about you?

LIZ: Well, we were on friendly terms for a few nights, and then he starts coming home late, and one night I'm tired of waiting and I go to sleep. And when I wake up, he's just getting in. I ask him where he's been, and he says he doesn't feel like saying. I tell him that if he doesn't, he can sleep on the couch. And he says that's fine by him. And that's pretty much where he's been ever since.

DALE: On the couch.

LIZ: A lot of good he does me there. I suppose I should be grateful he doesn't bring home any of his lady friends.

DALE: He's messing around?

LIZ: Big surprise.

HANK [*with genuine sympathy*]: That must be difficult for you.

LIZ: It sure isn't what I had in mind when I married him. As if I knew what I was doing. As if I know what I'm doing now. You find yourself someplace and you know you must have got there because you made these choices—like you're driving and you think it would be a good

idea to turn left at the gas station. But maybe I only turned there
'cause the sun was in my eyes at that moment, and if I hadn't made a
left right there—

DALE: At the gas station?

LIZ: But it could be that stuff I did for reasons as important as the sun
was in my eyes one day is why I'm sitting here with you now drinking
this beer.

[*A beat.*]

HANK: I hope at least you're enjoying the beer.

LIZ [*smiling and shrugging*]: This is not who I was intending to be, in case
you were wondering. This is not—

[*She stops as* TERRI *enters, with a bag.*]

TERRI: Hello.

HANK: Terri, Liz. Liz, Terri.

TERRI: Hi?

HANK: Friend of Dale's.

TERRI [*getting it*]: Oh. Yes. Hi.

LIZ: Hello.

HANK: What have you got there?

TERRI: I couldn't help it. A garage sale—

HANK: OK, let's see.

[*She hands over the bag. He pulls books out.*]

TERRI: Only a buck apiece.

HANK: Great, except you know this is one of the ones we had that we
said we didn't need. That we gave away.

TERRI: Yes, I know.

HANK [*to* LIZ]: We go through this long negotiation over what books we
should take and what we should donate to the local library. We knew
we couldn't take everything.

LIZ: Not practical.

HANK: And actually an opportunity, to prune out the nonessential. [*To*
TERRI] And this fell into that category. This was one of the nones-
sentials. *The Guns of August.*

TERRI: Barbara Tuchman. It was good.

HANK: But, realistically, will either of us read it again?

TERRI: Probably not. But it was sitting in a cardboard box, mixed in with Dr. Atkins diet books and manuals for Wordstar Version 3.1 and I can't explain it, I—

HANK: It looked lost.

TERRI: It did.

HANK: You rescued it.

TERRI: Go ahead, mock me.

[*He smiles; they kiss.*]

There was a baby at the garage sale. Little girl.

HANK: I'm surprised you didn't buy that, too.

TERRI: They were asking too much. Anyway, she's playing in one of those rubber wading pools. Her mother's sitting nearby, drinking a Coke, talking to someone. But the baby—the little girl—she's splashing, making baby sounds. Then she looks up and sees me. I smile at her and she reaches for Mommy and starts to cry.

HANK: Did you scare her?

TERRI: No, she just saw me and I guess she didn't like my looks.

HANK: Ouch.

DALE: Babies can be that way.

TERRI: Babies *are* that way. Anything they're feeling, it registers on their face.

DALE: Oh yeah.

TERRI: But it got me started wondering—when does that change?

HANK: When does what change?

TERRI: When they're real young, you watch kids attempting to—they try to tell you that they don't know where the ice-cream sandwich in the freezer went, honest, though you can see some of the chocolate cookieish part on their fingers, and you look at them and say, "No?" and they can't keep their face. The one they've put on—the glue holding it on begins to melt and it slides off and their real face pops out. And maybe their nose begins to run. It's really a terrible moment, but you can't help smiling.

LIZ: They're not good at it.

TERRI: Then at some point kids do get good at it. Good at hiding, good at lying. That's the change I mean. Has anyone documented when that happens?

HANK: Piaget probably had something to say about it. [*To* DALE *and* LIZ]
Piaget was this Swiss guy who came up with theories about the stages
of child development. When kids develop what kinds of skills.

LIZ: Like lying?

HANK: Actually, I think more cognitive things. When they begin to
appreciate what sorts of concepts. Concrete ideas. Like if you put a
small block on top of a big block, it probably will work better than if
you try to balance a big block on top of, say, a Ping-Pong ball.

LIZ: I've noticed that.

TERRI: But lying—it's a necessary skill, don't you think? How long
would any of us survive if we didn't lie? Or at least know how to with-
hold information? Where would we have been in World War II if we
hadn't been able to lie? If we hadn't made Hitler think we were going
to land in Calais instead of Normandy?

DALE: Yeah, that's a good one.

HANK: You know who talks about this sort of thing? Lawrence Kohlberg.

DALE: What does he say?

HANK: Not a lot these days, he's dead. But he had this idea that was a
little like Piaget.

LIZ [*proving she's been listening*]: The Swiss guy.

HANK: Piaget, like I said, was into trying to figure out the steps of when
kids understand what kinds of ideas and concepts. Kohlberg's idea—
he was American, not Swiss by the way—

TERRI: One for our side.

HANK: Thank you for that constructive contribution. Anyway, his idea
was that there are steps to how you learn or come to believe what's
good and bad, right and wrong. You start off—when you're a baby—
thinking something's good if it makes you feel good. Or something
you do isn't bad if you don't get punished for it. So the idea of good is
something that exists entirely in terms of how it affects you.

LIZ: So that's the first step?

HANK: According to him, yes.

LIZ: How many steps are there?

HANK: Three.

LIZ: So the second is—

HANK: You absorb, accept the ideas of the people around you, your society. On a local level, your family, your neighbors, your friends, the

kids in fifth grade with you. On a larger level, say if you're Lithuanian, other Lithuanians. Nationality. Or ethnicity or race. If you're gonna get along with the other people you deal with, you've got to be sensitive to their values.

DALE: But wouldn't that fall apart if you were brought up with the wrong people?

LIZ: Sure, you've got to be lucky. You've got to grow up in the right group. You don't always get to choose that.

HANK: No, you don't.

LIZ: You get raised in Nazi Germany in the thirties, and everybody's saying this shit, you've got to get your ideas about what's good from somewhere else.

HANK: Yes.

DALE: Where?

HANK: That's a good question.

LIZ: OK, number three. The third step.

HANK: That's when you get your moral ideas or values from some larger source.

LIZ: God?

[HANK *smiles.*]

Did I say something funny?

HANK: Not at all.

[*And he turns the smile on full strength.* LIZ *blushes and laughs.*]

TERRI [*to audience*]: I could be pissed about what he's doing—

HANK: What am I doing?

TERRI [*still to audience*]: Have you ever seen such an innocent face?

HANK: What am I doing?

TERRI: You think I don't recognize it? You think I don't remember what it was like to have you focus all that high-cholesterol charm at me?

HANK: I have no idea—

TERRI: Just second nature, I'm sure. But what if you *did* charm the pants off her? What good would she be to you without her pants?

HANK: Ah now, is that called for?

TERRI: Listen, kiddo, if I thought an outside dish would help in that department, I'd set the table for you myself.

[*Back into the scene.*]

DALE [*rising*]: I'm going into the kitchen. Can I get anybody a drink or something?

LIZ: Sure, I'll go for another one.

DALE: You guys?

TERRI: An orange juice.

HANK: Nothing for me, thanks.

[DALE *heads offstage.*]

LIZ: He's a good guy.

TERRI: Yes, we're very fond of him.

[TERRI *and* LIZ *head upstage as* DALE *returns. He hands the orange juice to* TERRI, *then picks up the middle of a conversation with* HANK *downstage.*]

DALE: You invited her to stay?

HANK: For the night. She's here, we're going to have dinner, it's getting late. Sounds like what she has waiting at home is pretty depressing. We have the spare room.

DALE: This is a woman I had a relationship with.

HANK: Yes.

DALE: A relationship she ended in order to—

HANK: Yes, her husband.

DALE: Did it maybe occur to you that maybe I have a few feelings about this?

HANK: You ask her in for a drink. I figured that things were OK between you.

DALE: OK enough to ask in for a drink.

HANK: Do you want me to come up with a reason we can't do this tonight?

[*A beat. Transition to the four of them laughing together, seated in the living room. The laughter subsides.* HANK *rises.*]

Well, I've got some reading I should do before I pass out.

LIZ: Dinner was great.

HANK: Our pleasure. See you all in the morning.

LIZ: Good night.

HANK: 'Night.

[DALE *is left alone onstage with* TERRI *and* LIZ.]

LIZ: Actually, now that I think of it, I should make a phone call.

TERRI: Oh?

LIZ: See if someone can take my shift at brunch tomorrow. I do the hostess thing, you know. At Captain Conch's. OK, it's a stupid name, but it's a good brunch. You should come sometime.

TERRI: There's a phone in the kitchen.

LIZ: Back in a moment.

[LIZ *leaves the stage. A beat.*]

DALE: Don't worry.

TERRI: What shouldn't I worry about?

DALE: I won't let anything happen.

TERRI: Wow, you're one hard-hearted cookie.

DALE: What?

TERRI: She looked after you when you had trouble, didn't she? When they took your boat, you must have been pretty nuts. Didn't she offer shelter, comfort?

DALE: She was great.

TERRI: So now she's the one who's having a rough time of it.

DALE: I know that. I can tell that.

TERRI: You don't give a shit?

DALE: Of course I do.

TERRI: Or do you think it's her own damn fault? The way she sent you packing?

DALE: I think she had every right to decide what she did.

TERRI: Then why are you pissed at her?

DALE: I'm not pissed at her.

TERRI: I can tell.

DALE: I'm not.

TERRI: So what's this about? This I-won't-let-anything-happen routine? Wait, are you being—wait a second—are you being faithful to me? Oh Jesus, you are, aren't you?

DALE: What is so funny about that?

TERRI: It's not funny. It's sweet. Very. Really.

DALE: Go to hell.

TERRI: But, Dale, if you're not doing anything for my sake, don't.

[*A beat.*]

DALE: Don't do it, or don't not do it?

TERRI: Don't be concerned, whatever.

DALE: I get it—you're being generous with me.

TERRI: Generous?

DALE: Lending me out. Sharing the goodies. It gets even nobler because she wouldn't even know you were doing it.

TERRI: Like I'm really in the nobility business.

DALE: You can only lend out something that's yours.

TERRI: I know that.

DALE: I'm not yours.

TERRI: And I'm not yours.

DALE: No.

TERRI: So how can you be faithful to me? How can it even be an issue?

[*A beat.* DALE *exits.* TERRI *stays standing as* LIZ *returns.*]

LIZ: Where's Dale?

TERRI: He went out on an errand, I think. Let me show you your room.

[LIZ *and* TERRI *clear the stage as* DALE *takes some chairs and puts them together to suggest a car during the following speech.*]

DALE: Where I've gone is to sit in my car, which is sitting in the driveway.

HANK: I see him out the window.

[DALE *is now sitting in the driver's seat.* HANK *approaches what would be the window.*]

Thinking of going somewhere?

DALE: Thinking of it.

HANK: Where?

DALE: If I knew, I'd be on my way.

HANK: You want to do a beer somewhere?

DALE: No, thanks.

HANK: You and I could go to Angler's.

DALE: If I wanted to go to Angler's, I'd be there by now.

HANK [*referring to the front seat of the car*]: You mind if I join you?

DALE: So you can talk at me?

HANK: Is that what I do?

DALE: Pretty much.

[*A beat.* HANK *doesn't move.*]

HANK: Is this about Liz? Because of our invitation?

DALE: She's lonely and hurt and on her third beer. She's staying over. Middle of the night, whose door do you think she's going to be tapping on?

HANK: If that doesn't interest you, nothing says you have to let her in.

DALE: Well, of course it would interest me.

HANK: Nothing says you *can't* let her in.

DALE: That's basically Terri's attitude.

HANK: That's what's pissed you off?

DALE: Is that all anybody thinks I'm good for?

HANK: You fix the stereo, too. That makes two things you do I can't. But what if Terri or I had told you that you couldn't go anywhere near Liz?

DALE: Where would you get the right?

HANK: Absolutely. So you're pissed if we say it's OK as much as if we said it wasn't.

DALE: Maybe your saying either thing—maybe that you think you have the right to say either thing—

HANK [*revealing a flash of irritation*]: Of course, it *is* our house.

[*A beat.*]

Sorry, I don't mean that.

DALE: Yes, you do, and you're right. It is your house. I don't have a house. I used to have a boat, but right now somebody else is probably cruising it off the coast of Cuba. All that I have now is this car. Right now this is the only place on earth where I get to call the shots.

HANK: But then, it's parked in our driveway.

DALE: Fine, I'll move it.

HANK: Don't. Please don't. I didn't say that because I want you to move it.

DALE: No, you said it because it's another smart thing to say. You and Terri both—a smart remark pops into your head, you've got to say it. What does it do for you? How does it help, Hank? How does it make things better?

[*A beat.*]

HANK: I don't guess it does always. Except every time you think you know something, understand the way this idea relates to that one, you get—*I* get, anyway—it's like you're not totally at the mercy of what's going on. Even if it just means being in on the joke. And sometimes being some kind of smart is helpful. Maybe someday, someone will understand how the right this idea relates to the right that one, and they'll cure cancer, or solve the Middle East.

DALE: Are you working on cancer and the Middle East?

HANK: Well, I'm not working on the Middle East, but you could say cancer is working on me.

[*A beat.*]

DALE: Well, there's another smart remark. Is it true?

HANK: Yes.

[*A beat.*]

DALE: Shit.

HANK: Pretty much my feeling.

[*A beat.*]

DALE: Have a seat.

HANK: Sure, now that you think I'm dying you invite me.

DALE: Just sit the fuck down. I'm getting a crick in my neck.

[HANK *takes the seat next to* DALE.]

Is this why you left the college, came down to Florida?

HANK: It made me less eager to use whatever time I have left in commit-tee meetings. But I wasn't kidding when I said you're half the reason I moved here. Going out on the boat with you has always been pretty much my idea of as good as it gets.

DALE: So how long do they figure—

HANK: It isn't time to order the lilies. The doctors say I'm responding well to the treatments. I wasn't going to tell you this yet.

DALE: You didn't want it to be part of the—

HANK: No. Anyway, the kind I've got, there's a pretty good chance that something else will finish me off first.

DALE: So there's hope.

HANK: Better watch out—some people might think that's a smart remark.

DALE: You've told Terri.

HANK: Sure. You know, as I was talking about Kohlberg before—you remember what I was saying about Kohlberg's first stage of moral development?

DALE: I wasn't taking notes.

HANK: Kohlberg said that the first stage was the baby who thinks that what's good is what gives him pleasure or takes away pain. And as I was telling that to your friend Liz, I thought, wait a second, is that very far from where I am now? This idea that you develop morally as you get older, OK, that's a good theory as far as it goes. Maybe, though, you get to an age where you start slipping. You regress to earlier stages.

DALE: Doing what feels good to you, avoiding what hurts.

HANK: Maybe your morality is based on what kind of options you think you have. The more you can do, the more opportunities you have to make choices—

DALE: No, I follow you. I just don't think that this is what I'd be thinking about—

HANK: If you found out you were sick?

DALE: Talking, thinking this way. Getting all up in your head. It wouldn't be my first reaction.

HANK: It's not my first reaction. You're not seeing my first reaction. My first reaction was back in Massachusetts.

DALE: Oh?

HANK: Nothing philosophical about my first reaction. Drank a lot of vodka. Broke things. Fractured a bone in my hand slamming something. That was smart. The anger comes back now and again, but mostly now I'm in a—well, I don't know how I would describe it.

DALE: Do you have to describe it?

HANK: I'm going to break the habit of a lifetime?

DALE: Please.

[*A beat.*]

HANK: I'm surprised she hasn't told you about it. She's furious, you know. At me for being sick.

DALE: Like that was something you decided to do.

HANK: So then she gets angry at herself because she catches herself being angry at me. So she visits you and she works some of that out, and then she joins me and I put my arms around her and sometimes she cries.

DALE: I've never seen her cry.

HANK: And you never will. Not if she can help it.

DALE: She's not married to me.

HANK: No.

DALE: There's no way in the world that I'm somebody she would ever marry. Ever *consider*—

HANK: If I thought there were, what we've got going here couldn't work.

DALE: You'd be jealous.

HANK: More jealous. But really, would you *want* to be married to her?

[DALE *addresses the audience as the elements of the set are shifted.*]

DALE: The night goes pretty much as I figured it would. Liz knocks on my door. And I open it. The next morning . . .

[HANK *pulls on the butcher block on wheels with plates and bagels and spreads similar to before.* TERRI *stands beside* HANK, *who is playing host. On the other side of the block,* LIZ *joins* DALE *onstage, taking his hand.* TERRI *spreads cream cheese on a bagel and hands it on a plate to* LIZ.]

DALE: That's pimento.

LIZ: Yes, I know.

HANK: You like?

LIZ: Oh, sure.

[LIZ *takes a bite.* TERRI *and* DALE *take downstage while* HANK *and* LIZ *wander off together.* TERRI *just looks at* DALE *for a second, smiling.* DALE *looks at her with a guarded smile. She approaches him, still smiling, shaking her head. Then she punches him in the arm.*]

DALE: Ow.

TERRI: That's the sound I want to hear.

DALE: Aren't you the person who said something last night about being faithful not being an issue—

TERRI: Yes, I said it.

DALE: I believed you.

TERRI: I believed me, too. Thanks for making me a liar.

DALE: I made you a liar.

TERRI: Sure.

DALE: You didn't have anything to do with it.

TERRI: You want me to punch the other arm?

DALE: What's the matter? Run out of words?

TERRI: Never.

[*A beat. She punches the same arm.*]

DALE: I thought you were going to punch the other arm.

TERRI: Can't trust me, can you?

DALE: You finished punching?

TERRI: Yeah.

DALE: I mean, really?

TERRI: Yes.

DALE: 'Cause you've used up your allowance.

TERRI: It was just a mercy fuck, right?

DALE: Do you think I would talk like that about you?

TERRI: I hope not.

DALE: Then why would I say something like that to you about Liz?

TERRI: There you are, acting the gentleman again.

DALE: Or do you think there's something different about you that you deserve to be talked about nicer than her? Because you went to college and she didn't—

TERRI: OK.

DALE: If you're smart, the rules are different? Or it's less trampy?

TERRI: You think I'm trampy?

DALE: I think you think Liz is trampy and I'm trying to see how you're different.

[*A beat.*]

TERRI: All right, you've done it. You've proved I'm full of shit.

DALE: I did? You are?

TERRI: I don't hear you disagreeing with me.

[*A beat.*]

DALE: Hank told me about his situation.

TERRI: He wasn't going to do that.

DALE: So he said.

TERRI: I don't think he wanted it to have anything to do with how you two get along.

DALE: That's what I figured.

TERRI: So will it?

DALE: I think now I understand better what's been going on. How it happened. Why. From his point of view anyway.

TERRI: Do you want to say?

DALE: No. If I say, you'll just tell me I've got my head up my butt and what's the point of my hearing you tell me that again?

TERRI: Oh?

DALE: I don't hear you disagreeing with me.

[*A beat.*]

TERRI: Dale, is there anything about being with her, with Liz, that's— Just curious.

DALE: Well, I'll tell you one thing—she stays till the morning.

[*A beat.* TERRI *nods and takes a seat.* HANK *and* LIZ *return.*]

Liz, if I come back with you to your place, stay with you, you think that might make your husband uncomfortable enough to leave?

TERRI: Back to her place?

DALE: For a while.

LIZ: That could work. Yeah, it probably would.

TERRI: And assuming it does work and he leaves, what then?

DALE: Maybe by then I'd have my new boat.

HANK: Well, that would be great. We could all go out on it.

DALE: That could be a lot of fun. Don't you think?

TERRI: Sounds swell.

DALE: What do you think, Liz?

LIZ: You mean it's my choice? You'd do this if I wanted?

DALE: Your choice. Do you think you could put up with having me around the place again for a while?

LIZ: I think so. Sure.

DALE: What do you say?

LIZ: Now? Today?

DALE: Whenever you want.

LIZ: I should probably drive back first. Get the place straightened up a little.

DALE: Yeah, and I guess I should put some stuff together.

LIZ: And then you'll—

DALE: I'll be there.

HANK: Sure I can't interest you in another bagel before you go?

LIZ: No, no thanks. I'm full. It was great. You guys have been great.

[*She kisses* HANK.]

TERRI: Our pleasure.

[LIZ *goes to where* TERRI *is sitting and gives her a kiss which* TERRI *receives with some grace.*]

LIZ [*to* DALE]: So I'll see you at the place in a little while?

DALE: Pretty soon.

[LIZ *heads for the exit.*]

LIZ: Let me get my house into shape and you'll come visit us?

HANK: We'd be delighted.

LIZ: OK then. Great. Soon.

[LIZ *waves and exits.*]

DALE: Guess I'll pack.

[*A beat. He exits in another direction.* HANK *moves behind where* TERRI *is seated.*]

HANK: Well, mother, our chicks are leaving the nest.

TERRI: Ha. Shall we wrap this up?

HANK: OK. [*To audience*] We won't see Liz again. And, after he takes off in a few minutes, I won't see Dale again. I will take a turn for the worse, bow out of the course I'm teaching here, and, for reasons I can't begin to fathom, decide to go back to Massachusetts for the end.

TERRI: I'll go back up with him, of course.

HANK: After I die, some of my old students from the college will set up a scholarship in my name.

TERRI: That'll piss off a few people.

HANK: I'm sorry I'll miss it.

TERRI: And then I will come back down to Marathon to sell the house. I'll make a nice profit. I'll drive down to Key West with a check for Dale.

[DALE *enters, carrying his bag.*]

DALE: And I'll ask her what the check's for.

TERRI: One of the reasons I got so much for the house is the work you put into it. The deck, the repairs. Only fair you get a piece of it. I think Hank would have agreed.

HANK [*to audience*]: She's right, I would.

DALE: I was sorry to hear the news.

TERRI: I miss the hell out of him.

DALE: I was hoping to take him out again on my boat.

TERRI: Do you have a boat again?

DALE: I have my eye on one. The check will help a lot. So what's doing with you?

TERRI: I'll be going back to work soon. I'm not ready to become a Mrs. Kapinsky. You and Liz?

DALE: We're getting along for now.

TERRI: And after you get your new boat? What do you figure?

DALE: I'll tell you when I know. If, when the time comes, it matters enough to you to ask. [*To audience*] But that conversation happens seven or eight months down the road. Right now I'm still standing for the last time in their house in Marathon, holding my bag.

[*He turns to* HANK *and* TERRI.]

HANK: You'll keep us posted how it works with the husband and the rest of that.

DALE: Sure.

HANK: Well, all right then.

DALE: All right.

[DALE *stands silently for a second. Then he puts down his bag, kneels down in front of* TERRI, *removes a sandal, and kisses her foot. He gets up, picks up his bag, and exits. A beat.*]

TERRI: Asshole.
HANK: That's not fair.
TERRI [*intensely*]: Tell me about fair. You just try and tell me about fair.

[HANK *leans over and puts his arms around her.*]

HANK [*comforting*]: Hush now.
TERRI: Just try.

[*She reaches up and holds the arms he has about her. She seems to be on the verge of weeping as the lights fade.*]

BERLIN '45

—for T.

Years ago, sitting in a Greenwich Village bar, an older friend told me about being drafted by the army and sent to Europe in 1945. World War II was over, and he recalled standing on the deck of a ship seeing a wall slide by with WELCOME HOME, SOLDIERS! painted on it as he was, in fact, leaving home. He spent the next few years as part of the American occupation forces in Germany. While a few films dealing with the occupation were released in the wake of the war—notably Fred Zinnemann's *The Search* and Billy Wilder's *A Foreign Affair*—I couldn't recall a script that dealt substantively with the experience of American soldiers during the years between the fall of Berlin and the Berlin airlift. I started research.

And I got sidetracked. Twice. While looking up an article in a *New York Herald Tribune* from March 1945, I stumbled on the story of the court-martial of some black WACs near Boston. That became the basis of my play *Court-Martial at Fort Devens*. And then, reading Douglas Botting's *From the Ruins of the Reich*, I became intrigued by the experience of German civilians after the Russians' defeat of Berlin. That started this play.

I was particularly lucky to happen upon a book Heidi Scriba Vance wrote with Janet Barton Speer called *Shadows over My Berlin* about Vance's experiences during those days. Vance had been a dancer, and part of her story involved trying to maintain some continuity with civilization through her art as the world was going to hell around her. I contacted the authors, telling them I was hoping to tell a fictional story that was informed by some of this material. They graciously gave me permission to draw on their book as long as I didn't dramatize Vance's specific story. I decided to make my leading character, Ilse Kammer, a woman who had maintained her job as an administrator with a dance company even as the city was destroyed around her.

Of course, it was necessary to know about the occupiers as well as the occupied, which led to a lot of reading about the Soviet Union at the time, particularly about the troops that took Berlin. It occurred to me that Ilse was likely to meet one of the Soviet engineers sent into the city to dismantle and spirit away as much German technology as possible before the Soviets opened Berlin to four-power control. Sometimes I think that, just by becoming interested in a subject, one becomes a magnet and attracts the materials necessary. In any case, in a secondhand bookstore, my hand happened to rest on *The Ghost of the Executed Engineer* by Loren R. Graham. Concerning the life, execution, and legend of Peter Palchinsky, a towering figure in Soviet engineering circles who ran afoul of Stalin, Graham's account was exactly what I needed. I decided that my second leading character, Gregor Akimovich, had met Palchinsky and that his political doubts had been triggered by this contact.

The presidency of George W. Bush had not begun when I started work on this piece, but it's probably no accident that a play about two people who loathe the leaders they believe have betrayed their countries opened during Bush's tenure.

Maybe someday I'll get around to writing about the American occupation. I still think it's an intriguing idea.

Most of the action of the play takes place in Dietrich's house in a suburb of Berlin amid a landscape of ruined buildings. The environment should suggest this destruction. The different locations for the various scenes should be suggested by sparing but differing arrangements of furniture and lighting. The props—such as the Victrola—should be realistic and persuasive. And there is no way of doing this play without a choreographer who can research the Dance of Death in Kurt Josss's *The Green Table*.

Berlin '45 premiered on March 28, 2005, at the Victory Gardens Theater in Chicago. It was directed by Calvin MacLean, with set design by Jack Magaw, costume design by Judith Lundberg, lighting design by Julie Mack, sound design by Andre Pluess and Ben Sussman, and choreography by Mark Goldweber. It featured the following cast:

Ilse Kammer . . . . Tandy Cronyn
Doubling Actress
    (Berthe, Female Soviet Soldier) . . . . Deborah Leydig
First Doubling Actor
    (Dietrich Fleischer and Petrov) . . . . Gary Houston

Ursula Muller .... Melissa Carlson
Second Doubling Actor
    (Emil von Kammer, American Officer) .... Chris Cantelmi
First and Second
    Russian Soldiers.............. Gary Houston, Chris Cantelmi
Gregor Akimovich .... Roderick Peeples

Special thanks to members of the Blueberry Pond Theatre for contributions to the development of this play.

CHARACTERS

Ilse Kammer
Ursula Muller
Russian Soldiers (First and Second)
Gregor Akimovich

The Doubling Actress plays Berthe and Female Soviet Soldier.
The Doubling Actors play Dietrich Fleischer, Petrov, Emil von Kammer, and American Officer.

ACT 1

[ILSE *has just arrived on* DIETRICH's *doorstep. Her clothes are dirty and show hard wear.*]

ILSE: Where are the others? Your sister, her husband?

DIETRICH: On a road heading west.

ILSE: You didn't go with them.

DIETRICH: Some choice—being stuck on the road in mud or risk having your home brought down around your ears.

ILSE: So?

DIETRICH: At least here I can still get a phone call, have some chance of knowing what's going on. Besides, when they come in, their officers are going to need somewhere to stay. Maybe they'll keep this place standing just so they have one decent roof over their heads. If they even have a concept of what a decent roof is. And I might persuade them it would be useful to keep me around, keep it running. My housekeeper—

ILSE: Berthe?

DIETRICH: She's staying, too. I can't tell if it's for my sake or the house's. But you aren't leaving?

ILSE: Like you.

DIETRICH: Yes, but I'm not a woman. I don't run the same risks.

ILSE [*to audience*]: Not twelve hours ago, I was hiding in an underground station with a couple of hundred others as bombs explode above us. When the all clear sounds, I climb up to the street to go home. And it's not there. I've made my way through miles of ruins to the western suburbs. By some miracle, most of his house is still standing.

DIETRICH [*to audience*]: Most of me is still standing, too. That's another miracle.

[*Back into scene.*]

Come in, my little refugee.

[*She enters his house.*]

ILSE: Maybe we should be thinking about what to present?

DIETRICH: You're optimistic.

ILSE: However this plays out, it will be over soon. Why shouldn't we do what we're supposed to?

DIETRICH: Without a theater, without scenery—

ILSE: There are pieces we can do that don't require much. There should still be spaces somewhere. We've been putting up programs in hospitals, so we know we can adapt—put up *something.*

DIETRICH: We should do one of the Tchaikovskys, don't you think? That should be popular with our visitors.

ILSE: At least excerpts. What about the music? The orchestral parts? The piano scores?

DIETRICH: I have a very big cellar. You might be surprised what can be found there. I suppose we can present something that won't disgrace us. I do wish you would leave the city.

ILSE: If I could think of somewhere better to go.

DIETRICH: Ilse—

ILSE: I'll be all right. What would they want with a scrawny old bird like me?

[DIETRICH *exits.*]

DOUBLING ACTRESS [*to audience*]: April 1945. Berlin.

FIRST DOUBLING ACTOR: The Russians surround the city in preparation for the final assault.

[URSULA *enters. She and* ILSE *see each other.*]

URSULA: Frau Kammer.

ILSE: Ursula. I didn't realize you were here, too.

URSULA: Herr Fleischer said I could stay.

ILSE: He's a kind man.

URSULA: He's a very kind man.

[BERTHE *enters.*]

BERTHE [*to* ILSE]: Your room is ready.

ILSE: Thank you.

BERTHE: You two know each other, yes?

ILSE: From the company . . .

BERTHE: Oh, of course.

URSULA: Frau Kammer is surprised to find me here. "Surprised" is the word, isn't it?

ILSE: It's just I suppose I assumed with your connections, your friend would have seen to it that you'd be—

URSULA: My friend?

ILSE: The gentleman I've seen you with, the one with the impressive uniform.

URSULA: My gentleman friend made arrangements I didn't agree with. We were going to stay in the Hotel Eden, drink a great deal of champagne, fuck a lot, and when the Russians showed up, pop one of these—

[*She digs in a pocket and pulls out a little box that she opens. It contains a capsule.*]

He actually gave me my own personal pillbox. Thoughtful, huh?

ILSE: Is that what I think it is?

URSULA: I haven't tested it. If you want to check it out, though, be my guest . . .

[ILSE *demurs.*]

The drinking and fucking I could go for, but I wasn't keen for the rest of the program. When I heard him snoring, I tiptoed out of the room.

BERTHE: Well, if you two will pardon me . . .

[*She exits.*]

URSULA: Do you think I offended her?

ILSE: Possibly.

URSULA: What about you?

ILSE: I'm scandalized beyond recovery.

URSULA [*to audience*]: Frau Kammer doesn't approve of me. She thinks, How can someone wear a tutu and play a swan and be a tramp?

ILSE [*to audience*]: I've never called her that.

URSULA: It's only coincidence her nostrils contract in my presence.

ILSE [*to* URSULA]: What about your family?

URSULA: After I got away from the hotel, I went back to our building. There was one wall left standing, and I couldn't find a message marked there that says where they've gone. My sister has a head on her shoulders. If they're alive, she'll see our folks through. That's all we can do right now anyway, right? Get through this and pick up the pieces on the other side.

[*A beat.* URSULA *moves to another area of the stage. Transition to* ILSE *and* BERTHE *in the middle of a conversation.*]

ILSE: When?
BERTHE: This morning, while you were out.
ILSE: They arrested him?
BERTHE: No—
ILSE [*overlapping*]: For what?
BERTHE: Not arrested, conscripted.

[URSULA *joins the scene.*]

ILSE: Conscripted?
BERTHE: Drafted. The home guard.
ILSE: Dietrich, a soldier?
BERTHE: Can you believe it?
ILSE: But do they have any idea how old he is? How unsuitable—
BERTHE: They don't care. They took the boy next door, too, and he's only twelve.
ILSE: This what is supposed to defend us?
URSULA: I don't know about you, but I feel safer already.
ILSE [*to audience*]: Things stop dropping from the sky. Now they come sideways, from tanks, blasting holes in what's in the way. We're fortunate—apparently they don't consider the house we're in too much in the way.
BERTHE: The phone has stopped working and the electricity is mostly off.
ILSE: There is nothing to do but to stay inside and wait for history to happen to us.

[*Transition to a new scene.* ILSE *is reading a book.* BERTHE *is involved in a chore.* URSULA *is practicing barre.*]

BERTHE: What's that?
ILSE: I'm sorry, Berthe?

BERTHE: The book you're reading.

ILSE: A novel. I found it in the library.

BERTHE: Which?

ILSE [*slightly embarrassed*]: *War and Peace.*

URSULA: Sure, a little something to take your mind off things.

BERTHE: Russian, isn't it?

ILSE: One of the reasons I picked it up.

BERTHE: Oh?

URSULA: You think you're going to find something useful in there?

ILSE: I read it before, when I was in my teens, There's a passage toward the end. You remember, it's about Napoleon.

URSULA: Actually, I don't.

ILSE: What?

URSULA: Remember. I've never read it.

ILSE: Well, as I say, it's about Napoleon invading Russia and how he loses there. There's a general, a Russian general named Kutuzov—this old man. It's mostly his strategy that's beaten the French. So, he's surrounded by his troops as they're lowering the flags of the French into the dust. Everybody's out on a frozen field, and his troops are cold. But it's even worse for the prisoners. The French. There are thousands of them, they're starving, they're frostbitten.

URSULA: And?

ILSE: Kutuzov—the general—gets up and makes a speech. Here: [*reading*] "Brothers, I know it's hard for you"—he's talking to his troops.

URSULA: The soldiers, yes.

ILSE: "'Bear up; it won't be for long now! We'll see our visitors off and then we'll rest. It is hard for you, but still you are at home while they—you see what they have come to,' said he, pointing to the prisoners. 'Worse off than our poorest beggars. While they were strong we didn't spare ourselves, but now we may even pity them. They are human beings too. Isn't it so, lads?'"

URSULA: Somehow I doubt this guy is riding a tank into Berlin.

ILSE: You're missing my point.

BERTHE: I'm afraid I am, too, Frau Kammer.

URSULA: Oh, I'll tell you her point. She's thinking that this book, this old book, has something to say about how the Russians will—she's thinking, she's *hoping*—

ILSE: I'm not naive, but—

URSULA: That the Russians who are coming in will have read that thing, will think, "OK, I'm in Berlin, how do I do this?" That they'll think this is some guide how to act, how to treat us?

ILSE: But if this is at all accurate about Russians, the way they think or see the world—

[*A beat.*]

No, you're probably right. I'm sorry.

URSULA: Hey, you know someday they'll probably write a book about what's happening now. *That* one I may read. Maybe find out what's been going on outside.

BERTHE [*to audience*]: Oh, we have a piece of luck—

[*A projection or sound effect of a horse.*]

She comes galloping into the street. Maybe from a riding stable. Poor thing looks terrified. Along with our neighbors, we come running out with whatever we can grab.

ILSE: A poker.

URSULA: A hoe.

ILSE: We surround it. It rears up on its legs but we manage to subdue it.

URSULA: Subdue it. That's a nice ladylike way to put it. For a day or two at least, we will have meat.

BERTHE: Too bad we don't have ice for our icebox.

ILSE: The first visit from Ivan.

[*Light shift.* FIRST AND SECOND DOUBLING ACTORS *play* RUSSIAN SOLDIERS. *We see them only in silhouette.*]

FIRST RUSSIAN SOLDIER: You, down in the cellar, come up!

[*A beat.*]

Come up! We don't want to have to come down. You don't want us to come down.

[*The women move to where they can be seen.*]

Any others down there? Any men?

ILSE: No, no others. Just us. [*To audience*] I speak some Russian. This seems to make an impression.

FIRST RUSSIAN SOLDIER: No men, no guns in this house?

ILSE: No, just us.

SECOND RUSSIAN SOLDIER [*reporting*]: Nobody else in the rest of the house, comrade.

FIRST RUSSIAN SOLDIER: Be smart. Stay inside the rest of the day. Tell your friends.

URSULA: We go to the window and look out. The two Ivans call to others in their unit. They make gestures, pointing at the house, then, pointing farther up the street, they move on.

[*The shadows of the soldiers fade.*]

BERTHE: Well, that wasn't as bad as I expected.

URSULA: We settle down to a quick meal of horse.

ILSE: The second visit from Ivan. Nighttime. I have come into the parlor, returning from the latrine we've improvised in the backyard since our plumbing has stopped working. Suddenly, I am grabbed from behind. There are three of them.

[*The shadows of three men.*]

They shove a bottle into my mouth. "Drink!" they order. Vodka. I begin to choke. They drag me now to a sofa. Hands grab at my clothing. Then, from behind them, comes a voice. They look.

[URSULA *enters a light.*]

She stands in a doorway.

URSULA: I tell her to translate.

ILSE: She says, "Why are you wasting your time with that old bat when I'm here?"

URSULA: Ilse doesn't say anything. I tell her again to translate.

ILSE: I do. The soldiers look at her and they look at me. They drop me. They move toward her.

URSULA [*putting her hand up, affecting a smile for the Russians' consumption*]: Tell them they are to wait their turn. Tell them it will be worth it.

ILSE: Ursula—

URSULA: Oh, just say it.

ILSE: And I do.

URSULA [*to* ILSE *as she continues smiling at the Russians*]: Now get out of this room as soon as you can.

[*Turning to a Russian (he should be placed by her focus, not a real actor on the stage)*] You first.

[*She exits. The shadows disappear.*]

ILSE: I go to the backyard, I make a fire. I haul a tub to a space between the shed and a wall—a place that cannot be seen from the street. I pump the water, I heat it, I pour it into the tub. I return to the house. The Russians are gone. I get a robe for her from Dietrich's closet.

[URSULA *enters in robe.*]

URSULA [*referring to the tub*]: Thank you.

ILSE: Well—thank you, too. I'm sorry, that sounds stupid.

URSULA [*overlapping*]: Look, just so you understand, it looked to me like you were going to get worked over, and I knew that I could take care of myself. I usually can. I mean, they could tell you were afraid.

ILSE: Yes.

URSULA: If they think you're afraid, it's worse. I know this much. I had the choice of not being afraid.

ILSE: You can choose that?

URSULA: All right, I had the advantage of not being panicked. Also, not to go into too much detail, I know a few tricks to make them shoot before they can put it in. I had to go all the way with only one of them. I was scared you were going to get yourself killed, and I have reasons for not wanting that to happen.

ILSE: Oh?

URSULA: But don't you get the impression this has anything to do with my usual tastes. When I do the military, I don't look at anything less than a captain.

[*A beat.*]

I owe you an apology.

ILSE: You do? Whatever for?

URSULA: Calling you an old bat.

ILSE: No offense taken.

URSULA: OK, I think that settles things. Now, if you'll excuse me—

ILSE: I could wash you.

URSULA: I've had enough of other people's hands on me for one day.

[URSULA *heads for the tub as the scene shifts.*]

SECOND DOUBLING ACTOR [*perhaps through a megaphone*]: Anyone who falls for Berlin dies in vain.

ILSE [*to audience*]: We hear this from loudspeakers mounted on trucks. It's the voice of Weidling, the highest-ranking officer now that Hitler's dead.

SECOND DOUBLING ACTOR: On agreement with the high command of the Soviet forces, I demand that the fighting cease immediately.

BERTHE [*entering, to audience*]: With the surrender of the city, we hope the worst will be over.

ILSE: Our hopes are misplaced. More Russians visit. They're in a mood to celebrate. They bring vodka. They are too drunk for Ursula's strategy to work a second time.

URSULA: They do what they please with us. Including Berthe.

[*A beat.*]

They also steal the damn Victrola. And they come back again. And again. And again.

ILSE [*to audience*]: Berthe, the housekeeper, cannot stop weeping. She apologizes. She tries to hold it in, but then she chokes and weeps some more.

BERTHE [*exiting*]: I go to my room.

ILSE: That night, when the Ivans return—

SECOND DOUBLING ACTOR: Where's the other one?

ILSE [*to audience*]: He goes upstairs, forces open the door to her room. When he emerges, his face is changed. Berthe lies still on her bed. Ursula sees something on the table next to the bed.

URSULA: My pill case. It's empty.

ILSE: The Russians decide to be helpful. They bury her in the backyard. They sing.

[*Music.*]

The sons of bitches sing beautifully. Out of some sense of—uh, etiquette?—they refrain from . . .

URSULA [*finishing the phrase* ILSE *can't say*]: Jumping us that night. A lot of people are being buried in their yards.

ILSE: I will not let that happen to me.

[*Light shift.* PETROV *appears.* URSULA *sits to the side and watches.*]

PETROV: You're Frau Kammer? That was the name of the lady they said who came by the office.

ILSE: Yes, that's me.

PETROV: You visited headquarters with a complaint. A German lady who speaks Russian, they told me. Interesting. Your house?

ILSE: A friend's. I came to stay with him after I was bombed out.

PETROV: And he is where?

ILSE: They conscripted him in the last days.

PETROV: You've heard from him?

ILSE: No.

PETROV: He might be dead or a prisoner.

ILSE: Yes.

PETROV: It's quite a house. You're lucky to have such a friend. I don't think I've ever been in such a large house owned by one person.

ILSE: I think it was his family's. But, the reason I stopped by the office—

PETROV: Some of our troops?

ILSE: It's happening almost every night. They show up; they take our watches. They reset them to Moscow time.

PETROV: It has been decreed that Berlin will run on Moscow time.

ILSE: I have no problem with that. But the soldiers—they break in; they force us. You understand?

[*A beat.*]

A friend has died. She took her own life, after one of these—visits.

PETROV: You have my condolences.

ILSE: You're an officer. You have some authority over them?

PETROV: Well, that's a little complicated. I'm a *political* officer.

ILSE: Does that mean you don't have authority?

PETROV: I will make a report of your complaint.

URSULA: What are you doing?

ILSE: I'm trying to get us some protection.

URSULA: The way he's looking at you. You have an opportunity here.

ILSE: An opportunity?

URSULA: If you take it. But don't expect him to do all the work. It's a buyer's market.

PETROV [*referring to* URSULA]: What is that one saying?

ILSE: Something about electricity. When it might be working again.

PETROV: We hope to have that in hand soon.

ILSE [*more warmly*]: I'm sorry, I didn't mean to be so sharp. What I said before.

[*A beat.*]

PETROV: You've been living with fear. That can affect your tone.

ILSE: Yes. I'm sorry.

[*A beat.*]

It must be a strain for you as well.

PETROV: Well, yes.

ILSE: You must be tired.

PETROV: I cannot remember not being tired.

ILSE: Why don't you sit down? Or do you have duties that call you elsewhere?

PETROV: I have some time.

ILSE: You were explaining something to me.

PETROV: I was?

ILSE: About being a political officer. I'm not certain I understand the concept.

PETROV: This war has been fought for certain reasons, true? It's not only that your country attacked ours, although this is a substantial reason in itself, of course. But our country—what makes our country unique—our government, our system . . .

ILSE: You have a philosophy.

PETROV [*delighted she's getting it*]: Yes! Most countries come into being because of certain geographic factors, or perhaps there is a concentration of certain racial stock that creates an identity, a national coherence. People who feel that they belong together and have a shared interest? And then the task is coming up with a rationale for why their dominance on a given piece of land supersedes someone else's. The justice of it. Your country, for instance—

ILSE: Please, I would like for you to understand—

PETROV: You're uncomfortable when I say "your country."

ILSE: It's my country in the sense that I was born here—

PETROV: And it gave you your primary language.

ILSE: Yes. But that doesn't mean I endorse what has been done by the people who claimed to be our leaders. I don't. I'm not just saying this.

[PETROV *takes out a knife, puts it on the table.*]

PETROV: You're hungry.

ILSE: I'm sorry?

PETROV: You look hungry.

[*Out of his pack he takes a loaf of bread. He begins to cut the bread.*]

You speak Russian very well, by the way.

ILSE: Thank you.

PETROV: Why?

[*A beat.*]

ILSE: I have a lot of friends in the Russian community here. We share cultural interests. So, in order to learn from them, to understand them . . . And I've always had a gift for languages. I speak some French, too.

PETROV: These are white Russians, the friends you speak of in what you call the Russian community.

ILSE: I suppose.

PETROV: People who left their country and chose to come to this one.

ILSE: From what they've told me, I don't think they had many choices. They mostly accepted where the wind blew them.

PETROV: They would see it that way, yes.

[*He offers her bread. She reaches for it.*]

Wouldn't you like sausage with that? Really, it's more of a meal with sausage.

[*She hesitates as he pulls out sausage and begins to slice it.*]

Your friend here, she doesn't understand Russian.

ILSE: No.

PETROV: It wouldn't hurt for her to learn.

URSULA: What's he saying about me?

ILSE: That you should learn Russian.

URSULA: As fast as I can.

[PETROV *looks at* ILSE.]

PETROV: What?

ILSE: She enjoys new tongues.

[PETROV *smiles at* URSULA, *returns to* ILSE.]

PETROV: As I was saying, my country, we have little ethnic cohesion. There are so many strains, so many racial mixes, dialects, cultures. So the rationale has to come from somewhere else.

[*He finishes cutting the sausage, puts it onto the bread, and passes it to her. She looks at him.*]

ILSE: You?

PETROV: I ate earlier. No, you go ahead, enjoy.

ILSE: And my friend?

PETROV: Oh, of course.

[*During the following, as* ILSE *starts to eat,* PETROV *slices some bread and sausage and passes it along to* URSULA, *who nods.*]

So, my country—national identity comes from certain political ideas, a philosophy.

ILSE: Philosophy.

PETROV: One that has been tested in the laboratory of history. We know where we are supposed to go, and so everything can be evaluated in terms of how it relates to that direction and destination. But I don't imagine these ideas are entirely new to you.

ILSE: No.

PETROV: Perhaps you even have friends who are Communists. Secretly so, of course, given the realities—

ILSE: Yes, in particular, a couple I know.

PETROV: A married couple?

ILSE: Yes.

PETROV: So this must be a vindication for them. Our being here.

ILSE: Well, theoretically, yes—

PETROV: Why only theoretically?

ILSE: Well, the soldiers visited them, too. She tried to tell them she's a Communist. A comrade. That didn't seem to count for much.

[*A beat.*]

PETROV: Ukrainians? The soldiers who visited them?

ILSE: I don't know. She didn't go into details.

PETROV: Of course, it doesn't make any difference.

ILSE: Excuse me?

PETROV: I mean, whether they were Ukrainians or not. Although the Ukrainians feel they have a special license. I'm sorry. Your friend, will she be all right?

ILSE: Hard to say. But it's . . . had an effect on their political convictions.

PETROV: But, you see, that would compound the tragedy.

ILSE: Oh?

PETROV: Not to minimize what she has suffered. Or he. But this was not the product of our ideas, our values. This was pure hooliganism. This is what we are firmly against.

ILSE: I'm glad to hear that.

PETROV: No, this sickens me. Did I hear you're a dancer?

ILSE: Was. A long time ago. A lifetime. But, as I had a talent for languages, and the company used to travel, it was a natural move to the business side.

PETROV: So you must have seen a fair amount of other countries.

ILSE: Yes. Actually, I visited Russia while I was still a dancer.

PETROV: You performed in our country?

ILSE: Petrograd. When I was a member of the Kurt Jooss company.

PETROV: I can't say I know who that is. I know little of dance.

ILSE: But you were saying—

PETROV: Was I? I am very easily distracted. That is a failing.

ILSE: Oh, I don't know.

PETROV: *You* distract me.

[*A beat.*]

You really should have something to wash that down with.

[*He takes out a flask and offers it to her. She hesitates.*]

ILSE: Vodka?

PETROV: Drink.

[ILSE *pulls out a glass. A beat. Then she pulls out a second glass. She puts them on the table.*]

Ah.

[URSULA *clears her throat. Apologetically,* ILSE *pulls out a third glass.* PETROV *smiles and pours. He salutes her and drinks.*]

At any rate, I'm supposed to remind people—the soldiers—of what the larger perspective is. In the heat of the moment, particularly in the middle of military actions, people can so concentrate on immediate appetite that they can be—

ILSE: Distracted?

PETROV: My job is to provide a reminder of larger purposes. From the start, our leadership has said that our enemy is not your people. Our enemy is a criminal gang that betrayed you. We want to build a new Germany. We want to share with you what we have learned. If you are happy, you won't feel the need to start another war. But how can we win your hearts if we behave like animals?

ILSE: You say this, do you? To the soldiers?

PETROV: Yes, I do. But for some of the troops—the war is not about building a better world based on science. It's about comrades who have been slaughtered. It's hard to keep the appropriate sense of purpose if such memories are fresh.

ILSE: I can't blame your people for hating us.

PETROV: Science and logic can't entirely overcome the human impulses. Sometimes, though it is to be regretted, certain impulses must be allowed to run their course. Sometimes you must let steam escape or a pipe may burst. Your friends. The couple. Dreadful. All the more reason to put society on a scientific, rational basis so such things never happen again.

ILSE: And this is your job?

PETROV: I can't prevent all of the inevitable excesses, but I can some-times provide a context that will discourage further excesses.

[*He is about to pour more vodka into her glass.*]

ILSE: No, thank you.

PETROV: I'm in a position to be helpful to you.

ILSE: Yes?

PETROV: Most of the women are being sent to clear rubble. To sort brick that might be used for rebuilding. It's necessary work, but it's hard on the hands. I look at your hands, and I think this would be inap-propriate. And also the fact that you speak Russian, so you might be useful to me.

ILSE: You don't have an interpreter?

PETROV: Useful for informal situations.

[*A beat.* PETROV *smiles, rises, puts his hand on the back of* ILSE's *neck, and exits.*]

URSULA: I couldn't have done it better.

[ILSE *looks at her.*]

Please, I mean it as a compliment. It's what you wanted, isn't it?

ILSE: A dream come true.

[*A beat.*]

URSULA: There was once this tailor.

ILSE: Tailor?

URSULA: Gentlemen's suits. He had a good clientele, a good reputation. He lived in a roomy apartment in Berlin with his wife and their two daughters.

ILSE [*beginning to get it*]: All right.

URSULA: One day, Mutti says she thinks the girls should have some culture. Concerts, theater, ballet. One of the girls—the younger one—she goes crazy over the ballet. Dances around the apartment, practices dying gracefully a lot. But she has talent. She begs for les-sons. Papa says yes.

But then something happens in America. Of course, the younger daughter has no idea what Wall Street is or why what happens over there should have anything to do with her family. But, at this point, she's sixteen, so she hardly notices anything outside herself anyway. For a while, Papa tries to hold on, to shield the family from the truth, but it's no use. His clientele don't need new suits in the middle of a depression. The savings dribble away.

One night, the older girl, Veronika, comes home late. Mutti says, "Do you know what time it is? Where have you been?" Veronika pulls out some bills and says, "Will this cover the rent?" "Where did you get that money?" Mutti wants to know. "A friend." "A friend? Who?" And Veronika says she thinks he comes from Hanover. Papa and Mutti send the younger girl to her room, but the conversation gets loud enough that she can hear what's going on. At one point, Papa cries out, "Have you no shame, no sense of decency?" Veronika says, "Yes, but I have a stomach, too."

It takes three or four days, but eventually Papa and Mutti discover they also have stomachs. They start looking at Veronika's contributions to the family in a different light. Not too long after, Mutti says to Papa that she gets very nervous about Veronika putting herself at risk like this. If she has trouble with one of the gentlemen, she should be where somebody can come to her aid. So Veronika starts working out of the home. And Papa? Well, to spare her the awkwardness of dealing with money matters, he becomes what you might call an agent. As for Mama, she starts to pull in a little extra by serving schnapps.

ILSE: God in heaven.

URSULA: Oh, don't think that any of this is done without misgivings. Sometimes—especially when Papa and Mutti have had schnapps themselves—tears trickle down their faces. "How could we allow this to happen? God will surely punish us." Sometimes Veronika comforts them. "No, Mutti, Papa, you mustn't blame yourselves. It's just the times." Sometimes she simply doesn't have the patience. Tells them the racket they're making is bad for business.

Meanwhile, the younger daughter is not happy. The dance lessons stopped shortly after the trouble in America. She wants to go back to class. Papa and Mutti say there isn't enough money. At this point, she's seventeen. And she notices that the house pretty much revolves around Veronika. So she makes a choice.

Of course, Papa and Mutti object. "You're so young," they say. But the girl sees this as a marketing advantage. Veronika is OK with it, though, as long as there's no poaching of her regulars.

The years pass and they manage to hold on. They don't lose their apartment. And then a new government takes over and money is easier to come by.

ILSE: And the tailor—did he go back to tailoring?

URSULA: Not suits. But there were a lot of uniforms to be made, and he had managerial experience. It made Mutti happy to see him go off to work in the morning again.

ILSE: And Veronika?

URSULA: She actually married one of her regulars. He went into the army. Last year she started getting a widow's pension. You're not going to ask me what happened to the younger daughter?

ILSE: You have a reason for telling me this story.

URSULA: Just returning the favor.

ILSE: Favor?

URSULA: You read to me from *War and Peace*. The thing is the younger daughter found out how much she wanted to dance. Needed to dance. You never can tell how you'll learn where your priorities lie.

[ILSE *accepts this. Light shift.* PETROV *enters with another younger Russian, who carries a Victrola.* PETROV *displays it to* ILSE *and* URSULA.]

PETROV: Look what we have found!

ILSE: Found?

PETROV: Liberated.

[URSULA *looks to* ILSE *for a translation.*]

ILSE: Liberated.

URSULA: Oh good, that will replace the one that was liberated from *us*.

PETROV: Have you any records?

ILSE: We can look.

PETROV: Another time. We can make our own music.

[*The younger Russian plays a folk song on the guitar and sings with* PETROV. ILSE *and* URSULA *listen.*]

Now, you—your turn.

ILSE: I don't play an instrument. I don't sing.

PETROV: You dance.

ILSE: I used to dance.

PETROV: You can no longer move your arms, your legs?

ILSE: I can no longer do what I would describe as dance.

PETROV [*referring to the Russian with guitar*]: He doesn't play in an orchestra, that doesn't keep him from picking up a guitar. I don't perform opera, still I sing. This idea that you must have a certificate, a license—

URSULA: What's he saying?

ILSE: He wants me to dance.

URSULA: You dance?

ILSE: I used to. I wasn't always an administrator.

URSULA: I'd like to see you dance.

PETROV: What's that one saying?

ILSE: I'm being bullied in two languages. All right, you want to see me dance. I'll show you something. You—you just play chords in a rhythm. Ba-ba-ba-ba! Harsh chords. Yes, like that. Just keep playing that.

[ILSE *gets up and is about to begin dancing when* GREGOR *enters.* ILSE *stops.*]

PETROV: Comrade. Good.

GREGOR: Am I interrupting—

PETROV: The lady is a dancer.

ILSE: Was a dancer.

GREGOR: You speak Russian.

ILSE: I speak—yes.

GREGOR: Ah. I apologize for interrupting.

PETROV: Gregor Akimovich, colonel in the engineers corps. I invited him to join us. Ilse Kammer.

GREGOR: A pleasure.

PETROV: She was about to dance for us. [*To the other Russian*] You were playing chords in rhythm.

[*The other Russian plays the sharp, rhythmic chords again and* ILSE *dances some steps from Death's first dance in Kurt Jooss's* The Green Table.]

What is that?

ILSE: That's a dance.

PETROV: That?

ILSE: Yes.

PETROV: People dance that? For what?

ILSE: People don't. Dancers do. It's from a ballet.

PETROV: You danced this? Audiences paid to see you dance this?

ILSE: Well, no, I didn't. It's for a man.

PETROV: What you just did?

ILSE: Yes.

PETROV: I ask you to dance and this is what you choose to dance?

ILSE: It's a famous dance. It's part of a ballet.

PETROV: You said that.

ILSE: I thought you might find it of interest.

PETROV: Is this considered beautiful?

ILSE: Pardon?

PETROV: Maybe it's a difference in taste, in culture. But to me—music, dance—they're supposed to be beautiful. They're supposed to inspire. But you do this—this stamping and making faces—

GREGOR: It's representational, yes?

ILSE [*to* GREGOR, *of his evident comprehension of what she means*]: You guess that?

PETROV: Do it again. Never mind the guitar—

[*She does it again.*]

Well, you're stamping around. You're stamping around and this is done by a man.

ILSE: Well, by a male dancer. It doesn't necessarily mean that this is a man, a human being.

PETROV: All right, enough riddles.

ILSE: I'm sorry, I don't mean to make such a fuss about it.

PETROV: So?

ILSE: Well, death.

PETROV: That's death?

ILSE: Yes. That's what it's supposed to be, to—

PETROV: That's your idea of death?

ILSE: That's the way death is depicted in the ballet.

PETROV: Sweetheart, I've seen my share of death. That's not—comrade colonel, does that look like death to you?

GREGOR: This is from a ballet?

ILSE: I'm sorry, it was foolish of me to—forgive me.

GREGOR: Tell me about it.

ILSE: Maybe Ursula would like to dance something. A folk dance or something—

URSULA: You want me to do something?

GREGOR [*overlapping*]: I'm curious. I would like to know.

URSULA: I could do something.

PETROV [*shutting up* URSULA *with a signal*]: Frau Kammer, the comrade colonel is curious.

GREGOR: A ballet, you say—

ILSE: It's called *The Green Table*. It's by a German choreographer named Kurt Jooss. I worked with his company years ago. In fact, I covered one of the roles. An old woman. Death dances with an old woman.

[*She laughs.*]

Now I'm too old to play the old woman.

GREGOR: Why the title? Is there a green table in it?

ILSE: At the beginning and end of the ballet. And all of these grotesque figures are around it, arguing, bargaining.

PETROV: And these figures represent something, too, I suppose.

ILSE: Different people see different things. The Nazis thought it exposed how Germany was betrayed at the end of the last war. They thought it was about the Treaty of Versailles.

GREGOR: But they were wrong? It means something else?

ILSE: As I understand it, the figures are meant to represent war profiteers.

PETROV: People who promote war for gain?

ILSE: Yes.

PETROV: So this man who made the ballet—

ILSE: Kurt Jooss, the choreographer—

PETROV: He's a Communist.

ILSE: I wouldn't say that exactly.

PETROV: War profiteers. War profiteers are capitalists, aren't they?

ILSE: Yes, but it's not that simple.

PETROV: Anyway, if the Nazis thought this could be about Versailles—it sounds like this could be confusing. It isn't clear.

ILSE: It's ambiguous.

PETROV: A fancy way of saying it isn't clear. If you're going to say something, say it. If I get up to make a speech, I want people to understand what I mean. I'm clear. I phrase things so they can be understood. I don't go for horseshit, pansy symbolism. If you're a man, if you're not ashamed of what you believe, you say it.

GREGOR: And then you get arrested.

PETROV: Comrade?

GREGOR: If you're lucky, you get sent somewhere for—what is the phrase—reeducation?

PETROV: Well, I suppose you would know.

GREGOR: Yes, I suppose I would.

PETROV: Those teachers seem to have done a fine job with you.

GREGOR: Oh, I learned a great deal, Comrade Petrov.

PETROV: Feeling a twinge of nostalgia for old school days? Your classmates? A reunion can be arranged.

GREGOR: Were you thinking of being helpful along that line?

PETROV: Me? No. I don't believe in misplacing valuable talent.

GREGOR: Am I valuable?

PETROV: What a question!

GREGOR: Am I valuable to you?

PETROV: Would you like another drink?

GREGOR: It seems you are not as opposed to ambiguity as you say.

PETROV: Would I offer you a drink if I didn't value you?

GREGOR: You have offered these ladies drinks.

PETROV: Yes. I have; I share. I am plagued with a generous nature. Look, you have a friend in me. You know that. Did I not invite you here? Are you not having an evening to remember? Food, drink, company—

ILSE [*completing* PETROV'*s line*]: Ballet.

[PETROV *looks at her, a little surprised that she's interrupted, but he affects amusement.*]

GREGOR: Yes, you were telling us about this dance. About the man who made it. Kurt—

ILSE: Jooss.

GREGOR: The Nazis liked it? They liked his work?

ILSE: They misunderstood it.

GREGOR: As you say.

ILSE: But they made him an offer. They wanted to be associated with his prestige. They summon him to a meeting. The resources of the state will be at his disposal. But there's a problem with his composer. The man who did the music—

GREGOR: Jewish?

ILSE: The name was Cohen. The Nazis want Jooss to get rid of him, choose a nice Aryan composer to work with.

GREGOR: And he says?

ILSE: Things it would be safer he didn't say. Two days after Jooss says no to the Nazis, the Gestapo arrive at his front door.

PETROV: And?

ILSE: The Gestapo find an empty house. He took a train out of the country the night before. He and most of the company.

PETROV: You say you were a member of that company?

ILSE: Yes.

PETROV: But you weren't on that train.

ILSE: I tore a ligament. A few weeks before. During a rehearsal. I was on a leave of absence while I healed.

PETROV: They left without you.

ILSE: I knew about the plan, but my injury was fresh and I was afraid to travel. Dietrich—the man whose house this is—he offered me an administrative job with the opera ballet, to give me something to do, while I was healing, for the meantime.

GREGOR: And meantime became permanent.

ILSE: Yes.

GREGOR: And what became of your friends, the members of that troupe?

ILSE: Last I heard, some of them are on an estate in England. Before the war, I got letters from there. I could tell I wasn't the first person to read these letters. Fingerprints, coffee stains. The authorities didn't even care I knew they were reading them.

GREGOR: No, they want you to know. They enjoy that you know.

[*A beat.*]

PETROV: Music!

[*The Russian with the guitar plays the chords again and* PETROV *does a burlesque of Death's dance. He laughs and he and the guitar player wander off, taking* URSULA *with them.* ILSE *is alone with* GREGOR.]

ILSE: Should you do that? Is it safe?

GREGOR: What?

ILSE: The way you were just talking to him.

GREGOR: To Petrov.

ILSE: Do I misunderstand? He's a political officer. He makes reports.

GREGOR: Reports are among the things he makes.

ILSE: He talks about people being sent away. Am I wrong in thinking he's one of the people who sends people away?

GREGOR: I've been brought back from away. They've brought me back. I know how to do things they need to have done. I'm safe.

ILSE: For now?

GREGOR: For now.

ILSE: And when now is over?

[*He makes a face.*]

Am I being troublesome, asking you such things?

GREGOR: You have your own difficulties to deal with. Don't let the mosquitoes who bother me distract you.

ILSE: You're an engineer. That's what Petrov said.

GREGOR: Me? I am a thief.

ILSE: Are you a thief pretending to be an engineer?

GREGOR: I am a better thief for *being* an engineer. Sometimes in order to steal something, you have to dismantle it. It helps if you understand how it was put together. It also will help if you know how to put it back together again after you transport the parts to their new home.

ILSE: Transport?

GREGOR: Go to the train station, you'll see a lot of railroad cars being loaded with—shall we call them souvenirs? Industrial souvenirs. And toot-toot goes the whistle and off to the east goes the train. I'm helping collect these souvenirs. Engines, laboratories, printing presses, machines that make tools. I'm working against time, though. Comrade Stalin has an arrangement with the people he's been calling allies. At a certain moment still to be determined—but fast approaching—we're obliged to turn over half the city to their control. I'm supposed to make that half as empty of useful technology as possible. Of course, the approved word for my activity isn't "theft." It's "reparations." This doesn't weigh too heavily on my conscience, given what was done to much of our industry in the past few years. But, you know, even in theft you can make moral distinctions. Well, you can try.

ILSE: How so?

[*A beat.*]

GREGOR: It's getting late. I should be on my way. May I visit again?

[*A beat and the lights go down.*]

ACT 2

[*Music from slow movement of Haydn's String Quartet, op. 76, no. 3—the tune we know as "Deutschland, Deutschland, über Alles"—begins to play. It is playing on the Victrola that* PETROV *brought in the first act. A small stack of records sits nearby.* ILSE *appears.*]

ILSE: "Über Alles." "Germany, Germany, Above Everything." Shortly after the war, we sing that tune with different words. "Deutschland, Deutschland, *Ohne* Alles." *Ohne* meaning "without." And we are indeed without many things—bread, butter, honor, self-respect.

[ILSE *stops the recording of Haydn.*]

Some of the less sophisticated Russian troops are intrigued by bicycles. The peasants have never seen bicycles. Berliners are riding them; they want to give them a try. The problem is that the bicycles tend to fall over when the Russians get on them. Bicycles that seem to work perfectly well when Germans ride them. The Russians smell sabotage. They suspect that when they liberate the bicycles, the Germans do something to the gears—remove the secret stabilizing mechanism. Why else would they fall over? So some of these Russians go from bicycle to bicycle, trying to find one that hasn't been tampered with. So much is happening around us, and mostly we don't know what. Sometimes we hear gunfire, sometimes we see smoke, sometimes the sound of crying or an accordion, sometimes a shout, "*Frau, komm!*" *Frau, komm* means, "Come here, lady, I've got something for you."

One Russian officer gives the women in his sector inkwells. He tells them that if they are attacked, they should toss this ink onto their attackers. When he lines his men up for inspection, he sees which tunics are stained with ink. A few of these he shoots. Many of the others he ships back home to prison sentences. Behavior in this sector improves speedily.

But after a few weeks, what was at first taken now is bartered. When you have to eat and the rations are insufficient and you have no valuables left to trade, you trade what you have left.

[ILSE *turns to the task of sorting records. One catches her eye. She puts it on the Victrola. As it begins to play, we see her succumb to the impulse to dance a few steps. She is facing away from the door when* GREGOR *appears there. He looks*] *at her for a second, then steps back. A beat. Then he begins to make conspicuous noise. She stops dancing.* GREGOR *reenters.*]

GREGOR: Records.

ILSE: I found some in one of Dietrich's cubbyholes in the basement. I'm sorting them. Something to do.

[*He nods. She takes the record off and puts it into its sleeve.*]

GREGOR: Frau Kammer, you know—I hope you appreciate how much I have enjoyed our conversations.

ILSE: I, too.

GREGOR: Comrade Petrov has also noticed that we enjoy these conversations.

ILSE: Comrade Petrov has his perceptive moments.

GREGOR: You spend—you have spent a lot of time with him.

ILSE: Spent time?

GREGOR: I do not mean to offend.

ILSE: You are attempting delicacy in a world that has little use for it. You are trying not to mention the fact that Comrade Petrov makes himself welcome in my bed.

GREGOR: Does he in fact make himself welcome?

ILSE: He believes himself to be welcome.

GREGOR: Is he not?

ILSE: His attentions are not rejected. We both know why.

GREGOR: Yes.

ILSE: I get food; I get protection. It's an arrangement. It's what's available to me.

GREGOR: As I say, Comrade Petrov has noticed that you and I enjoy speaking with each other.

ILSE: Is he proposing to facilitate further conversations?

GREGOR: He has suggested to me . . .

[*A beat.*]

ILSE: I meant that as a joke. Are you telling me that you and he . . . ?

GREGOR: As I say, he's made a suggestion—

ILSE: Which you're relaying to me. How gallant. What does he expect you to put up?

GREGOR: Put up?

ILSE: Surely he expects something in return. I am curious. It would be nice to know what is my current . . . valuation.

GREGOR: I would like you to understand something: if I tell him I agree to the new arrangement—

ILSE: Accept delivery of me?

[*A beat.*]

GREGOR: I'm not conveying my meaning.

ILSE: You're presenting me with a deal—a deal between the two of you of which I am the subject. It's as if you were talking about one of the bicycles that so fascinate your soldiers. Of course, a bicycle has no say. A bicycle doesn't care who rides it. And even if it did, it wouldn't matter.

GREGOR: I don't think this comparison is appropriate.

ILSE: I am not a bicycle?

GREGOR: He can think he's handing you to me, but that will just be what he thinks.

[*A beat.*]

ILSE: You wouldn't ride me?

GREGOR: Excuse me?

ILSE: I won't be obliged to sleep with you.

GREGOR: No.

[*A beat.*]

ILSE: I would do so voluntarily?

[*A beat.*]

GREGOR: I do not wish you to be in a situation in which you'd feel . . . pressure to make the offer.

ILSE: If I made the offer, it would be refused?

GREGOR: I don't want you to entertain the possibility of making an offer.

ILSE: Is it because you're noble or I'm unappealing?

GREGOR: Oh, I'm very noble. I am beyond compromise, corruption, or temptation.

ILSE: But will I be under your protection? Will you keep me from going hungry? Will you give the others the impression that I am yours so that nobody else appropriates me?

GREGOR: If you like.

ILSE: So you will do these things for me, but I will owe you . . . what?

GREGOR: I will expect nothing in return.

ILSE: Then what are you getting out of this? People do things for reasons. You are making this gesture for a reason. If there is nothing I can offer you—

GREGOR: Are you trying to persuade me not to say yes to Petrov?

ILSE: Excuse me?

GREGOR: As you say, people do things for reasons. So you must be arguing with me for a reason.

ILSE: Am I arguing with you?

GREGOR: No?

[*A beat.*]

ILSE: I am, aren't I? Why?

GREGOR: I'm not giving *you* explanations. I don't think you owe me one.

[*A beat.*]

All right, I expect that from time to time, he'll ask the odd, idle question about what I've been talking about. What's on my mind.

ILSE: He expects me to spy on you?

GREGOR: He expects everybody to spy on everybody.

ILSE: I can't say it's a big change from how we've been living for the past dozen years.

GREGOR: I only mention this so you aren't caught unawares.

ILSE: Is there anything you'd like me to say?

GREGOR: Tell him I kiss Comrade Stalin's picture every morning.

ILSE: I should tell you, whatever terms you're offering Petrov, it's not a good deal. He's lost interest in me. I used to amuse him because I can speak Russian. Now I annoy him; I speak too much Russian. He'll be a lot happier with Ursula. She speaks little Russian, but she has a good eye for what's necessary. Do I assume right, that my successor will be Ursula? He seems to be fond of this house, and she's attached to it at the moment.

GREGOR: I think it's likely.

ILSE: But you should appreciate that he'll be trading away nothing he values.

GREGOR: I don't look to Comrade Petrov for guidance on what is of value.

[*A beat.* GREGOR *exits. Now lights shift to daylight.* URSULA *enters wearing the costume of a villager. She carries another dress.*]

ILSE: Good God.

URSULA: You recognize it?

ILSE: Yes, but where from?

[URSULA *dances a step or two from the villagers' waltz in* Meistersinger's *third act.*]

Meistersinger. Where did you—

URSULA: I found what's left of one of the costume storage rooms. Here.

ILSE: Me? That?

URSULA: How much longer do you think what you've got on will last?

ILSE: I really feel like dressing up as a merry villager.

URSULA: Nothing says you have to wear it as is. We can always cut stuff off. Try it on.

[ILSE *laughs and she indeed takes the dress and steps where she won't be seen from the street and starts to change.*]

There's more.

ILSE: More?

URSULA: Costumes. If we can get our hands on a truck or a car, we can get the rest. We could trade them for things. I don't guess our currency will be worth anything.

ILSE: But the opera company will need them when it reopens—

URSULA [*laughing*]: We're staggering around with our butts hanging out, and you're worried about whether the company will have costumes at some vague time in the—

ILSE: What do you expect from me? I'm an administrator. But yes, I take your point. Besides, who knows how long before anybody will be allowed to do *Meistersinger* again?

URSULA: Why should that be a problem?

ILSE: Has it occurred to you what it's about? The story?

URSULA: *Meistersinger?* As the title says—a singing contest. A contest to compose a song.

ILSE: And who is the villain?

URSULA: I forget his name, the town clerk.

ILSE: And he loses the competition, yes?

URSULA: So?

ILSE: So why does he lose the competition?

URSULA: He's not as good as the hero.

ILSE: And why is he not as good?

URSULA: All right, just say it. I feel like I'm back in school, for God's—

ILSE [*overlapping*]: Because he can't sing a true German song. Because he doesn't have a true German soul. He doesn't belong. He gets laughed offstage, laughed out of town probably.

URSULA: So?

ILSE: Maybe into a nice waiting railroad car.

URSULA: Uh-huh.

[*A beat.*]

Let me ask you something.

ILSE: Yes?

URSULA: What did you do?

ILSE: I beg your pardon?

URSULA [*swiftly and with a nasty edge*]: You're so brave and so full of opinions, you must have done something, yes? I can't imagine having all these insights without taking action. So how many Jews did you hide? Couple of dozen? In your closet? Your basement? And in your spare time, I'm sure you made counterfeit documents for the underground. Don't be modest. It's just us here, and I'd like to know.

[*A beat.*]

ILSE: Well, at least I didn't fuck Nazis.

URSULA: No, you're choosy. You held out for Russians.

[*They have actually managed to shock each other. For a second they look stonily at each other, and then* ILSE *starts to laugh.* URSULA *is a little startled, then she begins to laugh, too. And it is at this moment that the barrier between them melts. A beat.*]

URSULA: You were with the Kurt Jooss troupe?

ILSE: When I was young. Younger.

URSULA: I heard about *The Green Table,* of course. I mean, I know the title.

ILSE: Maybe someday you'll get to see it for yourself. The premiere was one of those nights—

URSULA: You were in the premiere?

ILSE: Not the premiere. But I was part of building it. In the studio. There was a competition. An international competition for new choreography. And our company was invited to submit something. So we begin to work. A group of us in the room for six weeks. Jooss pulls it out of us. *Wills* it out of us. "Try this. At that moment, hesitate then turn. Look at him, *look at him*!" And maybe one of us does something and he cries out, "Yes!" and that goes in, that becomes part of it. A few moments I did first—almost accidentally, out of . . . momentum— they're still in there. Transformed, heightened by him. And our composer, Cohen, at the piano, sometimes almost like a dog at our heels, sometimes racing ahead with a rhythm or a figure that pulls out a gesture, an expression. Things we didn't know we could do. Things we didn't know we knew. There is a green table, of course, and these figures around it—masked, elderly men—two opposing camps. They disagree; they debate. The debate turns into an argument. They pull out revolvers. But they don't shoot each other. They fire into the air, and this releases death.

URSULA: Death?

ILSE: The spirit of death. His figure.

URSULA: That's what you were dancing the night the colonel first came.

ILSE: And most of the rest of the ballet is of how death dances with various people. How he takes them. Some he takes brutally. But he's almost gentle with others. There is an old woman. Ultimately he cradles her in his arms. He brings her relief. The premiere is in Paris. The audience starts applauding in the middle of the performance. In the middle. It takes first prize. Everybody wants to see it. We take it on tour. We bring it home to Germany. I am covering the role of the old woman and I get to dance it a couple of times here. One perfor-mance, I have a feeling that I've never felt before—that I am not just performing but that somehow I . . . I am the physical expression, the realization of something that exists in the audience. Something in the shared experience, memory, *dream,* of the people. The people in the room with us. That I have become the instrument for that. The great war is still with them. It's still with me. We all know what the dance means. Jooss lost a brother. And I lost someone.

URSULA: Oh?

[ILSE *doesn't elaborate.*]

ILSE: But, as I say, it wasn't my part. I didn't create it. I covered it. But I did get to play her a handful of times.

URSULA: You were good.

ILSE: I can't even tell you that. But it was something else entirely. The sense of being used the way you're supposed to be . . . I don't call myself religious, but for those moments . . .

[*A beat.*]

But I don't supposed I have to describe this to you.

URSULA [*with a touch of doubt*]: No.

[*A beat.*]

ILSE: Listen, about Petrov: you want him?

URSULA: Are you offering?

ILSE: The arrangement he and I have is coming to an end, and . . . If that would suit you.

URSULA: As long as he continues to bring food. What about you?

ILSE: I'm accounted for.

[*A beat. Lights shift.* EMIL—*played by* SECOND DOUBLING ACTOR—*enters. His arm is in a sling.*]

EMIL: Finding you. It took some doing.

ILSE: What doesn't these days? Your arm.

EMIL: Please, I'm lucky.

URSULA [*to audience*]: The Russians have been in Berlin for five weeks now.

ILSE: Ursula, this is Emil von Kammer. Emil is my nephew. Fräulein Muller. Ursula is a dancer with the opera's resident ballet company.

EMIL: The company you work with, isn't it?

ILSE: Yes. This house belongs to one of the company directors. He was kind enough to invite us to stay here.

URSULA: Do you attend the opera, the ballet?

EMIL: Not regularly, no. But then, the last few years . . .

URSULA: Of course.

EMIL: But it will be good when these things start again.

URSULA: Opera, ballet?

EMIL: The theater, concerts, all these. A sign that civilized life is resuming, don't you think?

ILSE: Yes.

EMIL: And the two of you will be part of that. How exciting that should be.

ILSE: How's the family?

EMIL: Grandpapa is—well, physically he's managing, he and Grandmother. Before everything fell apart, they went to the house in the West. They have some Americans staying with them now. In the house.

ILSE: And how is that?

EMIL: Not as bad as it could be. He is working with the Americans to get the factories in their area going again.

ILSE: They weren't too badly damaged? The factories?

EMIL: It will be months before they return to full production, but the important thing is to start.

ILSE: Yes.

EMIL: But that is part of the reason I'm here. And to see you, of course. Naturally the family was concerned about you.

ILSE: You will relay to them my thanks. When you see them next.

URSULA [*sensing it's time to leave*]: A pleasure to meet you.

EMIL: And you.

[URSULA *exits.*]

ILSE: Your father?

EMIL: Missing. We don't hold out much hope.

ILSE: I'm sorry.

EMIL: If he were around, it would probably be him here. Instead of me.

ILSE: You're on some kind of an errand?

EMIL: The word is that one of the senior Russian engineers spends many of his evenings in this house. A Colonel Gregor Akimovich.

ILSE: Yes.

EMIL: I was told he might be helpful. You are friendly with the colonel?

ILSE [*with some edge*]: If you're thinking I have influence over him—

EMIL: You understand I'm not here for myself.

ILSE: The family.

EMIL: Yes.

ILSE: The Berlin plant.

[GREGOR *enters.* ILSE *plays scenes simultaneously with* EMIL *and* GREGOR.]

GREGOR: The Berlin plant?

ILSE: It belongs to the family. The von Kammers.

GREGOR: You say "the family." Is it your family?

ILSE: My late husband's. I maintain a distant but courteous relationship with them.

GREGOR: You call yourself Kammer, not von Kammer.

ILSE: *Von* is a name for aristocrats. I can't pretend to be one.

EMIL: We were hoping—

GREGOR: What were they hoping?

ILSE: Presumably, because of what they imagine is our relationship—

GREGOR: I see.

ILSE: That I am such good company that you won't take away their Berlin holdings.

EMIL: I wouldn't put it like that.

GREGOR: You say this is your nephew?

ILSE: My late husband's brother's son.

GREGOR: And?

ILSE: I feel some obligation to bring this to your attention for the sake of my husband. His memory.

GREGOR: You haven't spoken before of your husband.

ILSE: What should I tell Emil?

GREGOR: The matter isn't under my control. The plant was on the list to be transported from the beginning. But the von Kammers have other plants in the West.

ILSE: Yes.

GREGOR: They should consider themselves fortunate to come out of this with those.

ILSE: I'll tell him.

GREGOR: And something else you should tell him.

ILSE: Yes?

GREGOR: But you can't let him know this comes from me. He must get the idea that this is your advice.

ILSE [*to* EMIL]: Get back out of Berlin as quickly as possible. Go back west to the Americans.

[GREGOR *nods to her and exits.*]

EMIL: But I have obligations here.

ILSE: They're not just shipping factories east. If they think you might be valuable to them running the plant when it's put back together in Russia—

EMIL: They would take me?

ILSE: Without a second thought.

EMIL: How do you know this?

ILSE: I overhear things. What does it matter? Take care of yourself. That's all any of us can do right now.

EMIL: Yes, so I see.

[*A beat.*]

ILSE: This is not a conversation you want to have with me.

EMIL: It was foolish to come to you for help.

ILSE: I haven't got the influence you think I have.

EMIL: If you did, would you use it?

ILSE: Emil, I have just given you the best advice I can give you. I urge you to take it.

EMIL: You were never one of us.

ILSE: The mistake you make is thinking I wanted to be.

EMIL: You married into our family.

ILSE: I married in spite of your family.

[*A beat.* EMIL *nods and exits.* ILSE *removes the dress and, standing in her slip, pulls out the tools to remove the froufrou from the costume.* GREGOR *enters.*]

GREGOR [*seeing she's undressed*]: I'm sorry.

[*He begins to leave.*]

ILSE: Oh, please, it's all right. I'm just going to alter this so I can wear it without cringing.

[*She begins to work on the dress.*]

GREGOR: I didn't know you were married.

ILSE: A long time ago. A whole different war. Lord, to be old enough to have lived through two of these. When he met me, I was a dancer. And I intended to continue dancing. He agreed to that. His family was horrified.

GREGOR: Aristocrats, you said.

ILSE: He was killed in France. His family did the correct thing regarding me. There was a settlement. But I couldn't bear to be a widow for the rest of my life, and so I went back to dancing. The family made their feelings clear. It was not hard to say good-bye.

GREGOR: You really don't know how to sew, do you?

ILSE: Pardon?

GREGOR: You take out the wrong stitches, the whole dress will—let me have it.

ILSE: You know how to sew?

GREGOR: Knowing how things are put together is part of my job. And I've had to repair more than my share of uniforms in the field. Allow me.

[*Bemused,* ILSE *passes the dress and needles to* GREGOR *who proceeds to go to work with confidence.*]

You were never tempted to marry again?

ILSE: I suppose you could say I married dance. And then, when I got too old to dance myself, I decided to do what I could to be useful to dance. So I became an administrator.

GREGOR: But that still wasn't appropriate for your husband's family?

ILSE: I was past caring. But the family and I finally cut off ties because of politics.

GREGOR: They liked Hitler?

ILSE: Hitler. They thought he was vulgar and crude. Most of the aristocrats thought that. But they believed he would be useful to do what was needed to get the economy going again. Disagreeable things, maybe, but necessary. A lot of practical people felt that way. That he was a tool to be employed for the moment, then cast away. They thought he was too extreme, too ridiculous to be able to hold on. Even a couple of my Jewish friends voted for him.

GREGOR: I expect they regret that vote.

ILSE: None of them are left *to* regret.

GREGOR: Here, try this on.

[ILSE *puts on the dress and* GREGOR *stands back to take a look.* EMIL *appears on the other side of the stage. He holds a folded piece of paper and reads it.*]

EMIL: Dear Aunt Ilse: I am writing to apologize for the manner in which I conducted myself during our last meeting. I am writing, also, to thank you for your advice about leaving the Russian-controlled area while I was still able. I have since learned of several who have indeed disappeared on transports heading to Russia along with their factories. I am safely away and consider that I owe you a debt of gratitude.

[EMIL *now puts the paper into an envelope. The* DOUBLING ACTRESS *enters, takes the letter, and begins to cross the stage with it.* PETROV *appears and stops her.*]

PETROV: I'll take that.

DOUBLING ACTRESS: But it's addressed to—

PETROV: I'll see she gets it.

[*The* DOUBLING ACTRESS *hands over the letter.* PETROV *opens it and reads it. He goes to* ILSE *and hands it to her.*]

You'll appreciate this. It's an apology.

ILSE: I would appreciate your apology for reading it.

PETROV: Be glad it was I who read it. I warn when others might have acted. Any further interference with our plans could be viewed as sabotage. And it wouldn't stop with just you. Anyone who put such ideas into your head would be at risk.

[*A beat.*]

Comrade colonel, I will have the pleasure of your company later this evening?

GREGOR: Later.

[PETROV *exits.*]

Let me see that dress again.

[ILSE *takes off the dress, hands it to him. As he goes back to work, she reads the letter.*]

ILSE: I didn't tell anyone it was your advice.

GREGOR: It wasn't too hard for Petrov to figure that out. Oh well.

ILSE: Petrov threatens you and that's your reaction? Oh well?

GREGOR: I know what his job is and he's doing it. I can't be surprised by him doing his job.

ILSE [*understanding*]: He's your watchdog.

GREGOR: Yes

ILSE: Then why do you choose to spend time with him?

GREGOR: If I didn't, he'd have to put some effort into keeping track of me. That might put him into a bad humor. Besides, there isn't a great deal else in this city at the moment to keep the mind alive. In this house, at least, there is conversation, music, as you say, ballet.

[*The lights go out.*]

ILSE: There goes the power again.

[*She pulls out candles and begins to light them.*]

What is he afraid you might do? Petrov.

GREGOR: Afraid?

ILSE: You say he's watching you. I assume he's watching you in case you do something.

GREGOR: Well, you heard the word he used—"sabotage." If I were caught trying to sabotage a project under my authority.

ILSE: Why would you do that?

GREGOR: Because I'm secretly an agent of the imperialists.

ILSE: Are you?

GREGOR: Lots of people I knew before the war were convicted of being agents of the imperialists. Many of them even confessed.

ILSE: They were guilty?

GREGOR: I said they confessed.

ILSE: I see.

GREGOR: I don't suppose you've ever heard of a man named Peter Palchinsky.

ILSE: No.

GREGOR: There's no particular reason you should have. It has been convenient to forget him in my country. Prudent.

ILSE: He was a friend?

GREGOR: I wouldn't presume to claim that. But when I was a younger man, I had the honor of spending some time with him.

ILSE: Who was he? "Was"?

GREGOR [*confirming*]: Was. An engineer.

ILSE: Like you.

GREGOR: You can't imagine what it was like in the early years to be an engineer. The Russia we took from the czar was a backward nation. Some corners, almost medieval. But after the revolution, here we were—building a new state. A state founded on scientific principles. We had no use for religion anymore. Religion demands faith. But now, thanks to Marx, we had reason, and reason creates its own faith. But I'm being unfair. I was one of the believers.

ILSE: Was.

GREGOR: Pardon?

ILSE: You said "was" again.

GREGOR: Yes. I know a lot about "was." I'm an authority on "was."

ILSE: Does the *was*ness of your friend Palchinsky have anything to do with—

GREGOR: *My* wasness?

[*A beat.*]

As I say, he was an engineer.

ILSE: Palchinsky?

GREGOR: Maybe *the* great engineer. He was brought in to consult on all sorts of projects. Stalin fell in love with one particular project. A hydroelectric plant. A dam. It was going to be the biggest dam ever. Not just in Russia. Anywhere. A clear proclamation to the world of what the Soviet Union could accomplish. In itself, the idea of a dam is neither good nor bad. But you have to look at where it's going to be built. You have to look, also, at what it will displace. And you have to look at people. Human beings. Anyway, Palchinsky thought you had to. What the project will probably cost in human terms. Humanitarian engineering, he called it. The authorities thought this was sentimental bullshit. There is a saying—"When forests are cut, the chips will fly." Well. They asked Palchinsky for his observations on the project. He answered candidly. He paid no attention to the frown lines growing on the official foreheads. I was one of the people assigned to help organize the logistics. I met with him. I went to him as a believer in the dam. He shared with me some of his thoughts. I left with doubts.

ILSE: And you did what?

GREGOR: What I was ordered to do by the officials. Ten thousand farmers were in the way. I helped persuade them to move. Their villages and farms disappeared underwater. Some of the most productive land in the country. If you took the hay harvested from these farms and burned it as fuel, it would produce more energy than the plant. But you had all of these farmers and their farms were gone. Many of them ended up working on the construction of the dam. The living conditions—the barracks, the tents—between the cold and the hunger and disease—God knows how many thousands of chips flew.

ILSE: And Palchinsky said?

GREGOR: At that point, he was beyond saying anything. They came for him before the dam was finished. The secret police. Unlike your friend the dancer, he was home when they knocked on his door. They took him away. They shot him.

ILSE: For what?

GREGOR: For being the head of a plot by engineers to overthrow the government.

ILSE: Were you part of the plot, too?

GREGOR: From the questions they asked me during interrogation, I got the idea they thought I would blow up the dam. So they put me into a camp. And then they got me out—to blow up the dam.

ILSE: I'm sorry, I don't understand.

GREGOR: Oh, it was on orders. One day I'm a prisoner in the camp, the next, they decide I can be useful. The enemy was advancing, Stalin didn't want the dam to fall into German hands, so they figured— since I knew something about how it was built—I might be helpful in taking it down. I expect, one of these days, they'll ask me to help put it back up again. I'm getting kind of sick of that dam.

[*A beat.*]

Here's the big difference between Palchinsky and your friend the dancer—

ILSE: Kurt.

GREGOR: Your friend saw the writing on the wall and he got away. But like me, Palchinsky was a believer. He believed all this rhetoric about a state based on science and truth. What he didn't realize is that the truth is decided by whoever has the power. And Stalin had the power. Mere facts didn't have a chance when stacked up against the truth of Stalin. And now, Stalin has more power than ever. And I have helped him.

ILSE: But you didn't fight for Stalin.

GREGOR: I haven't been fighting *for* anything. I have been fighting against a man who murdered Russians, in order to secure the regime of another man who has murdered Russians. Possibly *more* Russians. And I expect he's going to murder still more. Talk about satisfaction. Yes, Peter Palchinsky "was." He got to be a was by dying. I get to be a was by living. [*Referring to the dress*] I think this should be all right.

[*He hands the dress to her. She puts it on.*]

It's hard to tell in the dark.

ILSE: No, I think it's . . . it's very good. Thank you.

[*He shrugs, a little embarrassed. The lights come on again.*]

They fixed the electricity faster than usual. That wasn't long at—

[*When she turns around,* GREGOR *is gone.*]

Colonel?

[*A beat, then* ILSE *exits.* DOUBLING ACTRESS *enters as* FEMALE SOVIET SOLDIER. *She carries a rifle.*]

FEMALE SOVIET SOLDIER: My first sight of Germany: I'm with my unit. We've just crossed over from Poland. It's a town. I look around at this, the place where the enemy lives. Even with what has happened because of the war, you can't help but notice what a comfortable, beautiful little town it is. Yes, beautiful. I know the others are thinking what I'm thinking. Look at this. How clean, how neat, how pretty. How *charming*. They live like this, what did they need to come bother us for? What could they have thought they could take from us that was better? I mean, do they know how we live?

I'm supervising in Berlin now. Cleaning up. Moving mounds of rubble, sorting bricks. Every day, I go out and persuade the women of Berlin to do this work. They stand in long lines, passing garbage from hand to hand. I take particular pleasure in persuading those who look like they could profit from the experience of using their hands for once in their lives. There was this one woman. I see her wearing this dress. It looks like something out of a drawing you would see in a children's book. I assign her to scrape shit off the bricks.

[*Lights up on* URSULA *in her villagers' costume, now tattered and filthy, holding one shoe, a toe wrapped in a makeshift bandage. She looks bedraggled and miserable.* ILSE *enters.* URSULA *moves toward her, in pain.*]

ILSE: You're limping.

URSULA: You'd limp, too, if someone dropped a goddamn brick on your toe.

[ILSE *fetches a chair and* URSULA *sits.* ILSE *looks at the foot.*]

What do you think?

ILSE: I'm not an expert, but it doesn't appear to be broken.

URSULA: If that Bolshie cow ruined me for dancing, I swear—

ILSE: I don't think you could stand on it if it were broken.

[PETROV *and* GREGOR *enter.* PETROV *sees* URSULA *looking bedraggled and begins to laugh.*]

URSULA: What's Russian for "go fuck yourself"?

[URSULA *throws a shoe at him, and* PETROV *continues to laugh.* URSULA *hobbles out of the room.*]

ILSE [*to* PETROV]: It doesn't matter much to me, but if you ever want her in your bed again willingly, you'll apologize.

PETROV: No, all I'll have to do is wait till she gets hungry.

GREGOR: Why don't you go talk to her anyway? Go on.

PETROV: How do I know where she is?

ILSE: She's probably on the roof. That's where she likes to go to be by herself.

PETROV: I'm supposed to go climbing around up there?

GREGOR: Now, now, comrade, I seem to remember some of your political talks. Something about how we can only truly win the battle of Berlin if we win the people's hearts?

PETROV: I don't really give a crap about her heart.

GREGOR [*reproachfully*]: Comrade . . .

[*A beat.*]

PETROV: Oh, all right. The roof you say?

ILSE: That's where I'd look.

[PETROV *shrugs, goes to a cabinet, pulls out a bottle, and exits.* ILSE *turns to audience.*]

Not long after, we hear—

[*The sound of* PETROV's *scream and a thump.* ILSE *and* GREGOR *run and look down.*]

GREGOR: He must have slipped.

[*He kneels, looking down at where he and* ILSE *place* PETROV *with their attention.*]

He's breathing. He's alive. If we can get him into my car—

ILSE: Wait.

GREGOR: What?

ILSE [*carefully*]: What if we find him later? In the morning. It would be better for you, wouldn't it? He wouldn't be around to make inconvenient reports.

[*A beat.*]

It's not as if we pushed him. He got drunk; he had an accident. We must have been asleep in bed at the time. I'll confirm that.

[*A beat.*]

GREGOR: I'll pull the car around.

ILSE: He's probably going to die anyway.

[*A beat.*]

GREGOR [*firmly*]: I will pull the car around. You go get some blankets to wrap him in.

[PETROV *is wheeled in by the* SECOND DOUBLING ACTOR, *bandaged and in a wheelchair.* ILSE *and* GREGOR *are visiting.*]

PETROV: It may have been my fault.

GREGOR: Oh?

PETROV: I went up to the roof. Ursula's sitting there. She's crying. I show her the vodka. She turns away. I show her the vodka again and make noises she can believe are an apology. She grants me the favor of taking the bottle. She drinks, passes it back to me. We pass it back and forth a few times. I see what I think is the beginning of a smile. I think I may have reached for her. I mean, that would be the logical immediate move, yes? And the next thing, I'm looking up at the night sky, watching her face get smaller and smaller. And then the entire earth hits me.

[*A beat.*]

You brought me here.

GREGOR: We did. Frau Kammer and I.

PETROV: You saved my life. This is what I'm told.

GREGOR: You fell off the roof. We couldn't just leave you there.

PETROV: I am in your debt.

GREGOR: I don't—

PETROV [*overlapping, waving him aside*]: Here is how I settle it between us: I give you advice.

GREGOR: Advice?

PETROV: You follow it. You be smart.

GREGOR: What advice?

PETROV: You can visit the American zone. Say that it is to coordinate one of your damn technical things. But you go to the American zone, and you don't come back.

GREGOR: You don't know what you're saying.

PETROV: I know what I'm saying. It is up to you to *hear* what I'm saying. You are going to be denounced again. Not by me. You may not believe it, but I have never meant you harm. But I know what is happening. They will say you've had too much contact with the West. And you will be accused of bourgeois humanism.

ILSE: Bourgeois humanism?

PETROV: Nice phrase, huh?

ILSE: What does it mean?

PETROV: What it really means? He's been caught not treating the Germans working under him like shit.

ILSE: And that's a crime?

PETROV: Serious enough to get him sent back to a camp. Akimovich, are you listening?

GREGOR: Yes.

PETROV: This makes us even.

[GREGOR *nods. The* SECOND DOUBLING ACTOR *wheels* PETROV *off the stage, leaving the stage to* ILSE *and* GREGOR.]

GREGOR: Well, I must say that surprises me.

ILSE: The fact that he warned you?

GREGOR: Perhaps I underestimated him.

ILSE: I think you estimated him correctly. If you hadn't driven him to the hospital, he would have kept his mouth shut and let you be arrested.

GREGOR: If we hadn't driven him to the hospital, he wouldn't have been able to *open* his mouth.

ILSE [*shrugging this off*]: You're going to do something about this.

GREGOR: The Americans?

ILSE [*with fervor*]: You have the chance your hero Palchinsky didn't. For God's sake, take it.

[*A beat.* GREGOR *exits. A beat.* ILSE *exits. Time shift. Morning.* URSULA *enters.* ILSE *returns with cards and pencil.*]

URSULA: Is it safe for me to come back into the house?

ILSE: Yes.

[*A beat.*]

He's going to recover. Petrov. They're going to send him back to Russia in a week or so.

URSULA: I didn't push him.

ILSE: Oh?

URSULA: I thought you might like to know that. It did occur to me, but—I may not have your scruples, but I do have *some* limits.

[ILSE *nods. A beat.*]

He shouldn't have teased me though. Rape is bad enough, but *teasing* . . .

[*A beat.*]

Should I go to the hospital, visit him?

ILSE: I'd have to go with you to translate, and I really don't want to be a party to that.

URSULA: Oh.

ILSE: If you don't mind.

URSULA: You're probably right. So where'd your Russian disappear to? Akimovich?

ILSE: Something having to do with industry. He went two days ago. A liaison meeting in the West.

URSULA: The British, the Americans?

ILSE: The Americans, I believe. Do you think Ingrid could do the *pas de deux* from—

URSULA [*overlapping*]: Do we know if Ingrid's still alive?

ILSE: That would be useful information. She used to live near the Ku'damm.

URSULA: If we organize the cards by who lives in which districts—

ILSE: We can divide the districts, go out, and see who is where.

URSULA: Start with who is on what side of the river.

[*She points, suggesting two proposed piles. They split the cards and start sorting into piles.*]

I was thinking, there's enough room in the house to put up a dozen or so dancers from the company. They'd have to share rooms, but it would make calling rehearsals easier.

ILSE: Yes, I think Dietrich would approve. If Dietrich were around to approve. Have you heard anything about your family?

[URSULA *shakes her head.* ILSE *has the impulse to reach out in reassurance, but can't quite do it. A beat.*]

When the Americans take over this sector, I'm told the rations for artists will be pretty good.

URSULA: Why do I think Berlin's going to suddenly be home to a shitload of artists? There will be some kind of certification process? Who's an approved artist, who isn't? Some sort of committee or panel?

ILSE: There'll probably have to be.

URSULA: My bet is that you'll end up on one of those panels. You're an administrator; you don't have any inconvenient political associations.

ILSE: All right. If that happens, if I have any kind of a say—that's what you're asking me, isn't it?

URSULA: That's what I'm asking you.

ILSE [*very directly, with real assurance*]: I will do my genuine best.

[*They continue working. Lights shift and* ILSE *gets up to turn on a lamp.* GREGOR *enters.* ILSE *sees* GREGOR, *becomes quiet.* URSULA *notices the quiet, looks up from her work, then wordlessly excuses herself.*]

GREGOR: I'm here to say good-bye.

ILSE: You've made an arrangement? You talked to them—the British, the Americans?

GREGOR: An American. Not a successful meeting.

ILSE: What happened? Why did they say no?

GREGOR: They didn't. *I* did.

[*A beat.*]

ILSE: I gave you credit for some intelligence.

GREGOR: Well—

ILSE [*interrupting*]: No! You have a chance, and you throw it away? It's an insult to everyone who *hasn't* had a chance! It's an insult to *me* for being stupid enough to care!

GREGOR: I'm flattered.

ILSE: You're flattered I call you a moron?

GREGOR: I tried to go. I wanted to.

ILSE: Then why?

GREGOR: The American I spoke with—

[*The* SECOND DOUBLING ACTOR *enters as an* AMERICAN OFFICER. GREGOR *plays scenes with him and* ILSE *simultaneously.*]

AMERICAN OFFICER: Understand I'm not talking to you officially here, and I'm not making any commitments. This is an exploratory conversation.

GREGOR: Very well.

AMERICAN OFFICER: At the moment, a lot of people want to come over to our side. Much as we'd like to, we can't open our arms to everyone. How would we accommodate all of you? And then we signed a treaty at Yalta—we and the British—we signed a treaty with your country, agreeing to repatriate Russian nationals.

GREGOR: Repatriate.

AMERICAN OFFICER: See to it that the Russians we encounter do indeed return to Russia. The Soviet Union.

GREGOR: Even against their will.

AMERICAN OFFICER: One doesn't have to agree with a country's policy to be bound by it.

GREGOR: Yes, that's a situation I've encountered.

ILSE: It has a familiar ring.

AMERICAN OFFICER: On the other hand, we're likely to give extra consideration to the cases of people with special talents. You're an engineer.

GREGOR: I am.

AMERICAN OFFICER: This could put you into that category.

GREGOR: You have use for engineers in the States.

AMERICAN OFFICER: With the war over, the relationship between us and Stalin is liable to evolve. We might have particular use for an engineer who knows where and how certain projects in the Soviet Union were built.

[*A beat.*]

GREGOR: Pardon me?

AMERICAN OFFICER: Such information could be of value.

ILSE: Value?

AMERICAN OFFICER: Strategic value.

GREGOR [*to* ILSE]: Maybe I was hearing in this things that weren't intended, but the idea that they would want to use what I know against my people—

AMERICAN OFFICER: As I mentioned, I'm not saying anything official. Just suggesting some parameters. If you wish to pursue the conversation with an appropriate contact, I would be happy to arrange that. It's up to you. You know how to reach me.

[AMERICAN OFFICER *exits. A beat.*]

ILSE: There's another alternative. You could stay.

GREGOR: Stay?

ILSE: There must be a thousand passports floating around Berlin now. We get our hands on one—a German one—and you become that person.

GREGOR: And how do I explain the fact that I don't speak German?

ILSE: You don't speak at all. A war wound. Or you've been traumatized. You *can't* speak.

GREGOR: Frau Kammer—

ILSE: I can get you a job, something technical, at the opera house. No, it could work.

GREGOR: Too many people in Berlin have seen me, know my face.

ILSE: So we change your face. You shave, you dye your hair. Or maybe you don't stay in Berlin.

GREGOR: So I will be a mute, alone in a country where I don't understand the language.

[*A beat.*]

ILSE: I'm being ridiculous.

GREGOR: No. Never.

ILSE: But still, there must be some other alternative.

GREGOR: You're overlooking the possibility there might be reasons *to* go back.

[*She looks at him questioningly.*]

I told you about the dam. I told you about the land I had to help clear for the dam.

ILSE: Yes.

GREGOR: A few days before we're going to throw the levers and drown all these fields, all these towns, I'm driving with a few soldiers. A token inspection that what needs to be cleared has been cleared. It's getting dark. I see a light in a window. I say to the driver, drive over there. That house. I look for the light. I walk into a room. The light is coming from a candle on a table. A man, perhaps in his sixties, asleep on a sofa. I go over to him. I put my hand on his shoulder to wake him. I say to him, "Little father, you shouldn't be here. Soon the water comes. You must leave with us." He looks up for a second, then he starts flailing away at me, hitting with everything he has. I fall onto the floor. He runs for the door. I call out, "Stop!" He runs outside. I follow. My men are there, and I shout to them, "Stop him!" And the sons of bitches shoot him.

[*A beat.*]

I tell myself that if I hadn't found him he would have drowned a few days later anyway. This is a great comfort. From then on, I do what I can so as not to be part of it. To step away. To not be complicit. As much as possible. This is how I get arrested. I don't give them a confession, but I don't protest being sent away to a camp. On the outside, I sensed there was worse to come. By not being out there, I wouldn't have to be part of it. And then, on some level, I thought it appropriate I be sent away.

ILSE: How is it appropriate?

GREGOR: Not for the reasons they trumped up. But I owed something. I trained to be an engineer. To build things. To be of use. Instead, I've spent most of my life putting up things that shouldn't have been built, or, since they let me out to be part of this war, to destroy more efficiently. At least in the camp I built things to shelter people. So I'll probably end up doing more of that.

[*A beat.*]

He's older than I am. Stalin. If I can hold on, he'll die a decade or two before it's my turn. If I can outlive the bastard, maybe I can be useful. Maybe finally be a real engineer.

[*A beat.*]

ILSE: All these weeks I've been trying to figure out what you really got out of our arrangement. But this is it, isn't it? I'm your little proof that you haven't surrendered. A little carefully tended patch of honor, suitable for display.

[*A beat.*]

[*Less severely*] Look, I can say this because I've cultivated my own patch. I found a place where I could dig in without too much contamination. I had an office. I spent my days figuring out rehearsal schedules and double-checking budgets. From time to time, I would accidentally lose a file behind a cabinet.

GREGOR: Something that might cause someone trouble.

ILSE: That was the extent of my bravery—pretending to be inept. Every now and then, usually after a performance, there'd be a reception, and I'd be obliged to be in the same room with these . . . art lovers. Standing around in their uniforms, talking about the immortal Beethoven and Goethe. And they served good wines, hired string quartets to play in the background, and filled their walls with paintings of heroic subjects. A nice collection of persuasive props. As much as I walked through those rooms filled with what I assure you was sincere loathing, I knew that I had allowed myself to become one of those props. And here I am again. It's becoming a career.

[*A beat.*]

Do you know, in the last months, before you and Petrov and the others came here, there was a saying.

GREGOR: Yes?

ILSE: "Enjoy the war. The peace will be worse." Part of me wanted it to be true.

GREGOR: You felt you deserved to be punished?

[*A beat.*]

ILSE: Yes.

GREGOR: So, have you been punished sufficiently?

[*A beat.*]

ILSE: In a few days the Americans will take over this sector of Berlin.

GREGOR: The reports I've heard so far have been encouraging.

[*A beat.*]

ILSE: So really there's nothing more you can do for me. I mean, if I invited you . . . to stay tonight . . . if you wanted to . . . it would be my choice. You see?

GREGOR: Frau Kammer—

ILSE: Not because I feel obligated. But because I . . . I wanted you to?

GREGOR [*slightly embarrassed*]: Ilse—

ILSE: I mean, Jesus, *some*thing. There has to be *some*thing. I can't just see you leave like this.

GREGOR: You were ready to dispose of Petrov for my sake. That was very flattering.

[ILSE *covers her face, embarrassed.*]

All right, yes. I know what.

[GREGOR *moves to the Victrola.*]

ILSE: What are you—

[GREGOR *holds up a hand, asking for patience. He puts the needle onto the record she danced to before. It begins to play.*]

You realize it's been years.

[*The music begins. He sits facing her. A beat. She begins to dance. At a moment in the dance, she approaches him and draws him into the dance. He doesn't move gracefully, but she accommodates herself to this. They stop for a second in something that is half dance position, half embrace.* DIETRICH *enters behind* GREGOR. ILSE *sees him and she stops. Her face fills with joy, and she runs to* DIETRICH *and embraces him with a physical investment we haven't seen from her before.* GREGOR *moves to the Victrola, lifts the needle off of the record, and turns off the machine.*]

Colonel Akimovich, this is Herr Fleischer. This is his house.

DIETRICH: Hello.

GREGOR: Herr Fleischer.

ILSE: I had stopped hoping.

DIETRICH: Where's Berthe?

ILSE: I'm sorry. She didn't . . .

[DIETRICH *understands, lowers his head. A beat.*]

DIETRICH: But you, you've come through all right?
ILSE: Let's talk of that another time. Where have you been all these weeks?
DIETRICH: I'll make you a deal: when you're ready to talk, I'll be—
ILSE: Agreed.

[*A beat.*]

GREGOR: I was just leaving.

[ILSE *approaches him.*]

ILSE: Please survive.

[*He kisses her hand, leaves.* ILSE *sits down and resumes her work. After a second,* DIETRICH *joins her. Lights fade to black.*]

COURT-MARTIAL
AT FORT DEVENS

—for Richard Christiansen

This is how this play began: as I said earlier in this book, I was researching a project about the American occupation of Germany (a project I still haven't written). Reading a story about U.S. troops in the city of Aachen in a microfilm of a 1945 *New York Herald Tribune,* I came to the end of the column and saw the story was continued on page 14. I cranked the microfilm to that page, and toward the bottom I spotted a headline that said, "Four Colored Girls to Be Tried for Mutiny." Two short paragraphs. Naturally, I wanted to know what happened to them.

So I kept cranking the microfilm for follow-up information. Subsequent short entries filled in a few stray details but not enough for me to feel I had the meat of the story. And I thought, "Well, of course, this is the white press. At that time they wouldn't make a big deal out of what was happening in the black community." So I went to the Schomberg Center in Harlem, which houses a collection that focuses on black history and culture, and I discovered that indeed this case was front-page news in the black press of the time. And what I read made me want to read more.

I felt like a detective following leads. One of those leads led me to the Library of Congress, where I looked at long-unopened boxes dating from the forties donated by the Boston branch of the National Association for the Advancement of Colored People. There were official releases and private notes, a stirring sermon, and a letter about legal strategy from Thurgood Marshall (many years before *Brown vs. Board of Education* and Marshall's tenure on the Supreme Court). Another of those leads prompted me to call a military history archive in Falls River, Virginia. The woman who answered the phone there said a copy of the court-martial transcript would probably come to about seventy-five dollars. I sent a check. A couple of weeks later, I got the transcript and

I was hooked. The testimony of Lieutenant Tenola Stoney in response to lawyer Julian Rainey's questions was dialogue that demanded to seize a stage.

Whenever you deal with material derived from history, inevitably you discover one or two things that distinguish then from now. In 1945, calling an African American "black" was considered offensive. It was only in the sixties that linguistic politics shifted and "black" became a term used with pride. To enter into the world of this story, you have to reset your mental clock to a time when the accepted terms were "colored" or "Negro." (The historian Henry Louis Gates Jr. says that in his college application essay he wrote, "My grandfather was colored, my father was Negro, and I am black.") Of course, what's important when Colonel Kimball uses the word in his confrontation with the female privates is the *intent* to offend. And offend he does.

A word about the style of the play. Because filling the stage with the fifty young women to play the platoon who confronted the colonel that day is impractical, I thought it advisable to embrace a nonrealistic mode. A raised platform offers a generous playing area at center stage. The cast stays onstage throughout the action, seated in chairs bordering the central playing area when they aren't actively engaged in a scene. Handy to them, on pegs or racks or in military-style lockers, are costume elements and props that relate to the characters they play. When actors are called to simply supply a line or two, the director may choose to have them play standing in front of their chairs without entering the main playing area. For instance, the white woman might play the white trainee from her chair in scene 16, then, in a quick transition, put on the cap associated with Lieutenant Lawson and enter the playing area a few lines later in scene 17. I have not always indicated when players exit. But generally they should return to their seats when scenes are over and they don't go straight into the next scene. The point is to celebrate the transformational gifts of actors, not camouflage them. Along this line, I occasionally employ some of the conventions of story theater. For instance, the actress playing Ginny Boyd initially speaks of her character in the third person before stepping into the role. The point is to embrace the artifice of the stage, not to hide it. I have seen a production that used more elaborate sets and, truth to tell, it was well received by critics and audience, but I do think it works better in this simpler, less naturalistic mode.

This script is designed to be played by eight actors, but it may also be done with a larger cast. Those interested in seeing a version that accommodates more players should contact Playscripts Inc. (at www .playscripts.com).

I would like to thank Joe Coyne, Laura Gherardi, Rosalie Muskatt, Murray Schisgal, and Frank Von Zernick for their parts in the development of this script.

Court-Martial at Fort Devens opened February 12, 2007, at the Victory Gardens Theater at the Biograph, Chicago (Dennis Zacek, artistic director; Marcelle McVey, managing director; Sandy Shinner, associate artistic director). It was directed by Andrea J. Dymond, the set was by Mary Griswold, lights by Charles Cooper, sound design by Victoria Delorio, and costumes by Birgit Rattenborg Wise. It featured the following cast:

Sherman Miles; Evan Kimball;
    Edwards; Leon McCarthy . . . . James Krag
Virginia Boyd. . . . . Ericka Ratcliff
Johnnie Mae Malone . . . . Samantha D. Tanner
Ruby; Gertrude Hale . . . . Lili-Anne Brown
Curtis; J. D. Steele; Kenneth Hughes . . . . Morocco Omari
Tenola Stoney . . . . Velma Austin
Victoria Lawson, White Trainee,
    Eleanor Roosevelt . . . . Cameron Feagin
Virginia Boyd's Father;
    Julian Rainey . . . . Phillip Edward Van Lear

CHARACTERS

Virginia Boyd
Johnnie Mae Malone
Tenola Stoney

The following roles are divided up among the ensemble members: General Sherman Miles, Ruby, Lieutenant Victoria Lawson, Curtis, Virginia Boyd's Father, Gertrude Hale, Colonel Evan Kimball, White Trainee, White Woman, Captain Edwards, Julian Rainey, J. D. Steele, Major Leon McCarthy, Kenneth Hughes, Eleanor Roosevelt

SCENE 1

[*Sounds of military drumming, then lights up on* GENERAL MILES *facing the audience.*]

MILES: You know where I should be right now? In my office. I should be figuring out the fastest and safest way to send troops over for our final push against Germany. *That's* what should be occupying my attention. Instead, I am here. Your actions have brought me here. Your actions, ladies, have required me to turn my focus away from Mr. Hitler.

[*Lights up on* GINNY BOYD, *facing the audience, standing at attention in a line with* JOHNNIE MAE, RUBY, STONEY, *and* LAWSON.]

GINNY: This is the first time Private Virginia Boyd has seen a general up close. His name is Miles. General Sherman Miles. He has a chestful of ribbons. Ginny is standing with forty-eight other young Negro women.

JOHNNIE MAE: They are all privates.

RUBY: They are all at attention.

GINNY: And General Miles is not happy with any of them.

MILES [*reading from a paper*]: "Any person subject to military law who, on any pretense whatsoever, willingly disobeys any lawful command of his superior officer shall suffer death or such other punishment as a court-martial may direct."

JOHNNIE MAE: Death? Did he say "death"?

MILES: That passage is from the Articles of War. The articles are rules— rules that apply when we're fighting a war. And ladies, we *are* fighting a war. There are men in the hospital who have been wounded in this war. The hospital where you are supposed to be working. These men have been wounded doing their duty. And that is what you also are expected to do: your duty. You may not be doing the jobs in the hospital you want to do, but they are necessary jobs. They have to be done by someone. Now, out of consideration for your inexperience and my belief that you have been misled by elements among you, I make the following offer: those who do return to their posts will not be punished for their actions of yesterday or today. However, should any of you refuse to obey this order, you will be removed from this detachment and placed in restricted quarters, and you will be court-martialed.

[*He pauses.*]

GINNY: Permission to speak, sir.
MILES: Permission denied.

[*A beat.*]

> As commanding general, I give each and every one of you the following direct order—you will immediately fall in ranks in front of this building and be marched to your assignments at the hospital, and you will continue thereafter to do your duty.

[*A beat. He exits.*]

SCENE 2

[*Light shift as* GINNY *and the other women march to another section of the stage representing an area in Lovell Hospital.*]

JOHNNIE MAE: Before we only had a colonel mad at us. Now it's a general. Hey, if we try really hard, maybe we can get chewed out by Eisenhower himself.
RUBY: Do you think he'd do it? That general? Have us arrested?
JOHNNIE MAE: He'd *have* to do it. After standing up in front of us like that? Making that big a deal? Matter of pride for him.
RUBY [*turning to* GINNY]: So what are we gonna do?
GINNY: Why you asking me that? Looking at me that way.
RUBY: Something wrong in my looking? I can't look if I like?
GINNY: You look all you want, but if you think I came here—if you think I'm back in this hospital to do anything but fill a bucket . . .
RUBY: Oh.
GINNY: What, Ruby, you expect more?
RUBY: I didn't say that.
GINNY: You don't have to say.
RUBY: Just that you, you always seem to know what to do.
GINNY: Well, not anymore.
RUBY: If you say so.
GINNY: Why is it up to me anyhow?
JOHNNIE MAE [*trying to make peace*]: Nobody says it is.
GINNY: I didn't ask for you to look *at* me or *to* me.

RUBY: All right.

GINNY: I did what I did, and now I'm doing what I'm doing. It's for you to decide for your own self what you're going to do now.

RUBY: OK. Yes. Sorry.

[RUBY *exits, leaving* GINNY *with* JOHNNIE MAE.]

JOHNNIE MAE: I don't guess you want company.

[GINNY *doesn't reply.*]

It's not an insult, you know.

GINNY: What?

JOHNNIE MAE: People looking *to* you. There's respect in that.

GINNY: I don't need that kind of respect. I'm not looking to carry that weight.

[JOHNNIE MAE *nods and exits.* GINNY *grabs a mop and begins to work with a fury.*]

SCENE 3

[CURTIS *appears. His leg is wrapped and he is leaning on a cane.*]

CURTIS: You getting your revenge on that floor?

GINNY: You heard?

CURTIS: Saw you through the window by my bed, being marched over to the hospital here.

GINNY: Curtis, now, don't you start on me, too.

CURTIS: Am I starting on you?

GINNY: Aren't you?

CURTIS: Just standing here.

GINNY: Standing there thinking.

CURTIS: I hope so.

GINNY: Well, stop thinking so loud.

[*A beat.*]

How's your leg?

CURTIS: Mending. Be able to go dancing soon.

GINNY: I tried to talk to him. Asked permission.

CURTIS: The general.

GINNY: "Permission to speak, sir." Shut me off like I was a switch. Flick. Lights out.

CURTIS: What about the colonel? He have anything to say?

GINNY: No, he wasn't there.

CURTIS: Kimball wasn't there?

GINNY: Didn't I just say?

CURTIS: Doesn't that tell you something?

GINNY: So he wasn't there.

CURTIS: Think it out. Why do you figure?

GINNY: Curtis—

CURTIS: How it must be for him—a colonel—needing the general to come in, try to get you to do what he couldn't. One day, he's bossing the whole hospital—thousands of people—the next day he can't get a bunch of colored girls to do what he says. Has to bring someone else in to make you do what he can't. How do you figure he's going to look when he walks into the officers' club? What he knows people must be saying about him behind his back.

GINNY: End of the day, Kimball is still a colonel and I'm still pushing a mop.

CURTIS: Well, you've got the knowledge you did your best.

[*He moves off.*]

GINNY: Yeah.

[*A beat.*]

My best.

[*Impulsively, she tosses aside the mop and crosses into the next scene.*]

SCENE 4

[GINNY *approaches* LAWSON *and* STONEY. STONEY *sees her, addresses her.*]

STONEY: Private Boyd?

[GINNY *exchanges a look with* STONEY, *then decides to bypass her and turns instead to* LAWSON.]

GINNY: Lieutenant Lawson, ma'am . . .

LAWSON: Private?

GINNY: Lieutenant, I will take a court-martial.

LAWSON: Excuse me?

GINNY: I've decided to take the court-martial.

[*A beat.*]

LAWSON: Do you understand what you're doing?

GINNY: Yes, ma'am.

LAWSON: Do you know what a court-martial is?

GINNY: Yes, ma'am.

LAWSON: Tell me, then. What is a court-martial?

GINNY: Ma'am?

LAWSON: Tell me. You say you know what a court-martial is. What is it?

GINNY: A trial. A trial that the army—the army puts you on trial if they think you've done something wrong.

[*A beat.*]

LAWSON: Private Boyd, I ask you to reconsider. For your own sake.

[*A beat.*]

Have you nothing to say?

GINNY: What if the army does something wrong?

LAWSON: The army?

GINNY: Yes, ma'am. I do something wrong, like you say, I get a court-martial. If the army does something wrong—

LAWSON: You can't court-martial the army.

GINNY: No, ma'am.

LAWSON: It doesn't make any sense.

GINNY: Ma'am.

LAWSON: It's not the way the army works. There are ranks, chains of command, duties. Somebody above you, with higher rank—a colonel, a general—gives you an order: you're a private; there is no question. You had basic training. You know this. There is no question. An order, there is no doubt what your response should be, must be.

[*A beat.*]

Please, I wish you would—

[*A beat.*]

Private Boyd. Ginny.
GINNY: I'm sorry, ma'am. Meaning no disrespect to you, ma'am.

[*A beat.*]

LAWSON: You know what happens if they find you guilty.
GINNY: They punish you.
LAWSON: You heard the general say what that punishment can be. Is that what you want?
GINNY: No, ma'am, I don't want it. I'm not doing this because I *want* to. I just can't seem to do different.
LAWSON [*to* STONEY]: Lieutenant Stoney, she's one of yours. Is there anything *you* can say to her?
GINNY: No.

[*A beat.*]

LAWSON: Lieutenant Stoney, take down Private Boyd's name and serial number.
STONEY: Yes, ma'am.
LAWSON: And when that is done, have her go to the barracks, collect her things, and go to restriction. Is that clear?
STONEY: Yes, ma'am.

[LAWSON *exits.* STONEY *turns to* GINNY.]

You realize that they may ask me to testify against you.
GINNY: Ask?
STONEY: Order.
GINNY: An order's an order.
STONEY: If you believed that, we wouldn't be having this conversation.
GINNY: You think I'm wrong? What I'm doing?
STONEY: It doesn't matter what I think anymore. You're doing it. Unless you want to go back in there right now, tell Lawson different—

GINNY [*interrupting*]: No.

[*A beat.*]

No.

STONEY: All right, let's go.

[*Somebody tosses* GINNY *her duffel. She follows* STONEY *to another area—an area defined by a bench and a square of light. Perhaps the sound of a heavy door being closed.* STONEY *leaves her there and exits.*]

SCENE 5

[*The white actress who plays* LAWSON *moves downstage and is joined during the following by the black actress playing* JOHNNIE MAE.]

LAWSON [*to audience*]: In a way you could say it was Eleanor Roosevelt's fault.

JOHNNIE MAE: Eleanor Roosevelt has opinions, and, as the wife of the president of the United States, she can get her opinions heard. One of these opinions—

LAWSON: Women should be allowed to serve their country in the armed forces.

JOHNNIE MAE: And so the Women's Army Corps—called the WACs for short—is organized. But Mrs. Roosevelt has another opinion.

LAWSON: Negro women should be allowed the opportunity to serve, too.

JOHNNIE MAE: And that is how, back in the summer of 1944, Ginny Boyd came to have this conversation with her father.

SCENE 6

[*Pick up a scene between* GINNY *and her* FATHER.]

GINNY'S FATHER: But you've got a good job at the Treasury Department. You're going to give that up?

GINNY: Pop—

GINNY'S FATHER: They won't pay you in the WACs like your job at the Treasury.

GINNY: They're gonna train me.

GINNY'S FATHER: Train you?

GINNY: As a medical technician. Learn to work in the lab. While the war is still on, I get experience in army hospitals. After the war, something I can do. A career. Something I can do, you see? Something better.

GINNY'S FATHER: Who's saying this?

GINNY: The army.

GINNY'S FATHER: The whole army? All together?

GINNY: The recruiting officer.

GINNY'S FATHER: Well, then it's got to be so. A recruiting officer isn't gonna lie, is he?

GINNY: She.

GINNY'S FATHER: She?

GINNY: She was a woman, the officer.

GINNY'S FATHER: Even better.

GINNY: What are you being like that?

GINNY'S FATHER: Like?

GINNY: Like you wouldn't believe a dog was a dog unless it barked.

GINNY'S FATHER: Does a dog bark?

GINNY: So the proof is in the barking.

GINNY'S FATHER: Or the biting.

GINNY: Nobody's gonna bite me, Pop.

GINNY'S FATHER: Huh. Who runs the army?

GINNY: Commander in chief is the president.

GINNY'S FATHER: You're not gonna see him. Who you gonna see? Who's gonna be in front of you giving orders? I want you to picture those faces. Any of them belong to people, if you ran into them on the street here, you would trust them to treat you right? So why do you think putting them in uniforms will make a difference?

GINNY: Because the army is about rules. Because everybody's supposed to follow those rules.

GINNY'S FATHER: There's a big gap between "supposed to" and "is."

GINNY: The war has to change *some*thing. Too much is different.

GINNY'S FATHER: You're counting on change being for the better. It's a two-headed coin. At least.

GINNY: So you think I should just sit quiet and wait to see what side comes up?

[*A beat.*]

GINNY'S FATHER: No, I don't guess that's something you'd do.
GINNY: I'll take care. Promise.
GINNY'S FATHER: I'll be expecting you to write.

[*A final gesture between them and* GINNY'S FATHER *exits.*]

SCENE 7

[GINNY *picks up a duffel, leans against something, and begins to write.*]

GINNY: November 1, 1944. Dear Pop: I've survived military processing, orientation, and paper cuts from filling out more forms than you can imagine. As I write this, I'm with a lot of other girls who just got off a train out of Boston. In a couple of minutes, a bus should come along to take us to Fort Devens. I hear it's as big as a city.

[JOHNNIE MAE *and* GERTRUDE *approach.* JOHNNIE MAE, *eating an apple, is boisterous and outgoing.* GERTRUDE *is shy, a little awkward, and wears glasses.*]

JOHNNIE MAE: Who you writing? Mom?
GINNY: My dad.
JOHNNIE MAE: Letting him know you're still alive.
GINNY: He worries.
JOHNNIE MAE: You're lucky.
GINNY: That he worries?
JOHNNIE MAE: That you've got someone *to* worry. Buried the last of my folks last spring. Nothing to keep me in Pittsburgh. I heard rumor there were places where the air isn't made of smoke. Thought I'd like to see that. I'm Johnnie Mae Malone.
GINNY: Virginia Boyd. Ginny.
GERTRUDE: Gertrude Hale.
JOHNNIE MAE: You're from where?
GINNY: D.C. Washington.
JOHNNIE MAE: This one here's from someplace called Broken Toe.
GERTRUDE: Broken Creek.
GINNY: Where's that?
GERTRUDE: Texas. You never heard of it.

GINNY: That doesn't mean it isn't a great place to be from.

GERTRUDE: It's better to be *from* there than to stay. Why I joined up—a way to get out of there.

JOHNNIE MAE: Got crackers in the North, too.

GERTRUDE: But if you look the wrong way at them here, they probably won't kill you.

JOHNNIE MAE: Guess you're not homesick, huh?

[*The sound of the bus horn.* JOHNNIE MAE *tosses the apple core aside and she,* GINNY, *and* GERTRUDE *grab their duffels and hustle on their way. Light shift.*]

SCENE 8

[LAWSON *enters a spotlight and speaks as if addressing a group.*]

LAWSON: A lot of medicine is detective work. Mostly patients can't tell you very much except where it hurts. Before a doctor can come up with a treatment, he has to know what's wrong. And usually this means tests. And that, mostly, is what we will be training you to do—administer tests. Some of them simple ones like—yes, reading a thermometer. And some, more complex—tests involving blood, saliva, urine, tissue of various sorts. The quality of the work a doctor does can only be as good as the quality of the work we do. We will train you to do very good work. We have a hospital on the base. Lovell General and Convalescent Hospital, that's its full name. Lovell is going to be your second home. I'm Lieutenant Lawson. I am very pleased to welcome you here.

[*A rack is rolled on, on which are hung white uniforms.*]

Your hospital uniforms. The white uniforms of trainees.

[GINNY, JOHNNIE MAE, *and* GERTRUDE *enter from behind the rack, finishing putting on their uniforms.*]

GINNY: And Ginny and the others throw themselves into the training.

[LAWSON *and* JOHNNIE MAE *exit in different directions.*]

SCENE 9

[CURTIS *enters on crutches, his leg bandaged. Because this takes place earlier, he looks to be in worse condition than when we met him in scene 3.*]

GINNY: A couple of weeks later . . .

GERTRUDE: Excuse me, sir.

CURTIS: You don't have to "sir" me. I'm a private. Private Curtis.

GINNY: We're privates, too. Ginny Boyd, Gertrude Hale.

CURTIS: What did you want to have excused? You said, "Excuse me."

GERTRUDE [*overlapping*]: Just I noticed your bandage; it's not wrapped right.

CURTIS [*to* GINNY]: Does she know what she's talking about?

GINNY: Pretty much a hundred percent.

[GERTRUDE *pulls a chair on and indicates he should sit.*]

CURTIS: And what are you going to do?

GERTRUDE: Do it right.

[CURTIS *looks at* GINNY.]

CURTIS: Pretty much a hundred percent?

GINNY: Pretty much.

[CURTIS *takes a seat, and* GERTRUDE *begins to unwrap and then rewrap the bandage over the following.*]

CURTIS: You ladies floating around, looking to do good works?

GERTRUDE: Some corners of the hospital we haven't seen before.

CURTIS: Goes both ways. Some corners of the hospital haven't seen you.

GERTRUDE: This area is what?

CURTIS: This here, this is the colored ward. Want to know how you can tell?

GINNY: How?

CURTIS: Look at the patients.

GINNY: Not a lot of you here.

CURTIS: Hard to be wounded if they don't let you fight. You're not wearing blue.

GERTRUDE: Blue's for orderlies, people who scrub floors and do the cleaning up.

CURTIS: What's white for? You nurses?

GERTRUDE: Maybe someday. Right now we're medical technicians. In training. Drawing blood, taking temperatures—

CURTIS: Bandaging. Got you. Medical technicians.

GINNY: You give me fluids; they tell me what put you in here.

CURTIS: I don't think any fluid's gonna tell you what put me in here.

GINNY: Your leg?

CURTIS: Got smashed up pretty bad in France.

GINNY: I thought you said they didn't let you fight.

CURTIS: Not the Germans. If you treat my fluids right, I'll tell you sometime. Listen, when I can put weight on this leg again, maybe you ladies would care to join me in Boston for some dancing.

GERTRUDE: We're not supposed to do that.

CURTIS: Do what?

GERTRUDE: Go out with other soldiers. They made a big thing about that in orientation. Trying to discourage the idea that WACs are for, you know, the entertainment of the men.

CURTIS: People are saying that?

GERTRUDE: They're trying to *keep* people from saying that.

CURTIS: No, I can see how that would be important. Sure. So I promise not to ask you out. But, you know, if on leave you happen to show up at the same place I do in Back Bay. Someplace where they play music and the lights are low.

[GERTRUDE *finishes the rewrapping.*]

GERTRUDE: There, finished.

CURTIS: Yes, I'd call that a first-class job. You've got me all wrapped up.

GINNY: Private Hale, we have other places we should get to.

CURTIS: You better listen to Private . . . ?

GINNY: Boyd.

CURTIS: Private Boyd. She strikes me as a very sensible type.

GINNY: We'll check in on you some other time, Private Curtis.

CURTIS: I'll look forward to that.

[*He begins to head off.*]

[*Over his shoulder*] Good to see a colored girl in this place not holding a mop.

[CURTIS *exits.* GINNY *and* GERTRUDE *exchange a look.* GERTRUDE *can't suppress a giggle.*]

GINNY: Am I going to have to watch you?

[GERTRUDE *smiles and exits.*]

SCENE 10

[GINNY *moves to another area of the stage, pulling out a thermometer and shaking it out.* COLONEL KIMBALL *enters, sees her, goes to* LAWSON.]

KIMBALL: Lieutenant?

LAWSON: Yes, sir.

KIMBALL: That colored girl—

LAWSON: Sir?

KIMBALL: What is her name?

LAWSON: That's Private Boyd, sir. Private Virginia Boyd.

KIMBALL: And what is that in Private Virginia Boyd's hand?

LAWSON: A thermometer, sir.

KIMBALL: Would you like to explain this?

LAWSON: Explain, sir?

KIMBALL: What she is doing with that thermometer?

LAWSON: She's going to be taking a temperature, sir.

KIMBALL: Whose?

LAWSON: I assume a patient's, sir. Would you like me to get his name?

KIMBALL: Is he white?

LAWSON: Well, yes, sir. I believe so.

KIMBALL: The patient is white.

LAWSON: Yes, sir.

KIMBALL: A colored girl is going to stick a thermometer into the mouth of a white soldier. A white boy.

LAWSON: To take his temperature, sir.

KIMBALL: Why?

LAWSON: He has a fever, sir.

KIMBALL: I am not asking you why he is having his temperature taken. I am asking you why he is having his temperature taken by a colored girl.

LAWSON: She's training to be a medical technician. She and the other girls in the detachment, sir.

KIMBALL: A detachment of colored girls?

LAWSON: Yes, sir.

KIMBALL: And are all these colored girls sticking thermometers into the mouths of white boys?

LAWSON: It's a standard part of the training, sir.

KIMBALL: Then wouldn't you say an error has been made?

LAWSON: Sir?

KIMBALL: I do not have colored WACs as medical technicians. They are here to scrub and wash floors, wash dishes. That is where their capabilities lie.

LAWSON: But sir—

KIMBALL: Lieutenant?

LAWSON: Scrubbing and washing—those are the duties of hospital orderlies.

KIMBALL: Scrubbing and washing are not appropriate tasks for their classification. Is that your point?

LAWSON: Yes, sir.

KIMBALL: Well, we certainly don't want them to be assigned to tasks not appropriate for their classification.

LAWSON: No, sir.

KIMBALL [*as if this is a bright idea*]: We'll change their classification.

[KIMBALL *exits*.]

SCENE 11

[LAWSON *turns, speaks as if addressing a group*.]

LAWSON: Ladies, by order of Colonel Kimball . . .

[*A rack is rolled in. On it are blue uniforms.* GINNY, GERTRUDE, *and* JOHNNIE MAE *are visibly dismayed*.]

GERTRUDE: Blue? He's putting us into blue?

JOHNNIE MAE: Blue's for orderlies.

LAWSON: Yes, Private Malone.

JOHNNIE MAE: He's making us orderlies?

GERTRUDE: Ma'am, he can do that?

LAWSON: He's the colonel.

GINNY: How do we appeal this?

LAWSON: We don't.

GERTRUDE [*bitterly echoing* LAWSON]: He's the colonel.

LAWSON: As of today, you have new duties.

[GINNY, JOHNNIE MAE, *and* GERTRUDE *quietly change out of the white uniforms and into the blue. A beat.*]

JOHNNIE MAE [*to* GINNY]: Don't ask me how you look.

[*Without a word,* GERTRUDE *exits.* GINNY *and* JOHNNIE MAE *exchange a look.*]

SCENE 12

[GINNY *gets a mop and a bucket and starts to work.* CURTIS, *hobbling on a crutch, appears.*]

CURTIS: The colonel? He put you into blue?

[*She doesn't reply.*]

I was in France, driving a supply truck. This is a few months back. I'm thirsty, and I'm ahead of schedule on a delivery, so I stop in one of the towns we've secured. I go to this café. There's a waitress in Frenchy getup—the skirt, the apron, the lace. She tries her English out on me. She makes mistakes, I correct, she tries again, we're laughing. As we're laughing, three or four white boys, from the Twenty-ninth, come in. I mean, the Twenty-ninth—lot of southern gentlemen with a reputation. They see us; they go outside. I ask if there's a back way out. Some of them are waiting for me. "What's so funny?" they ask. "You and the mademoiselle, you were laughing. We like a good joke. Tell us." And then they pile on, and here I am. It's the only combat I've seen. Joined to get a piece of one war, end up fighting in another. Welcome to the front, Private Boyd.

[*A beat, then* GINNY *turns away.*]

SCENE 13

[GINNY *discovers* GERTRUDE *crying in a closet defined by a square of light.*]

GINNY: Gertrude?

GERTRUDE: Close the door. I don't want anybody to—

[GINNY *enters the square.*]

GINNY: OK, it's closed.

GERTRUDE: Don't tell anybody how you see me.

GINNY: You just look the way the rest of us feel. I just know what my father's going to say. He warned me.

GERTRUDE: Against joining?

GINNY: Practically predicted this.

GERTRUDE: My folks *wanted* me to join. My dad showed me this article in the newspaper, what Mrs. Roosevelt said, how it was her idea. I figured if it was Mrs. Roosevelt's idea . . . Too bad Mrs. Roosevelt isn't here to see the promises kept.

GINNY: Can you imagine the colonel's face if she *did* show up? [*Imitating* ELEANOR ROOSEVELT] "Colonel Kimball, I'm here to visit my brave colored girls. Where, sir, are you keeping them?"

GERTRUDE: One of them's hiding in a closet with mops.

GINNY: And she's got to get out of here.

GERTRUDE: A minute. You think that would be OK?

GINNY: I don't suppose anyone will miss us that long.

GERTRUDE: It's just, you know, if I wanted to clean toilets, I didn't have to join the army to do it.

GINNY: They've got toilets in Broken Creek?

GERTRUDE: Broken Creek *is* a toilet.

GINNY: Gertrude, there are things we can do about this.

GERTRUDE: Such as?

GINNY: We all know how to write letters.

GERTRUDE: Like the army is gonna pay attention to letters from us.

GINNY: And we know how to write letters to people who *know* how to write letters. Army may not pay attention from the inside, but they care about what people say on the outside.

GERTRUDE: You know this, or you think this, or you want to believe this?

GINNY: It's worth trying. What do you say you team up with me the rest of the day?

GERTRUDE: How's my face?

GINNY: Just a second.

[GINNY *pulls out a handkerchief and cleans* GERTRUDE's *face.*]

Better.

GERTRUDE: All right.

[GERTRUDE *exits.* GINNY *turns to audience.*]

GINNY: Nobody can exactly prove that this campaign of letter writing has anything to do with it, but a month or so later there is a new arrival at Fort Devens.

SCENE 14

[*A light comes up on* TENOLA STONEY *standing alone.* LAWSON *enters and joins her as if in midconversation.*]

LAWSON: Lovell Hospital is home to a number of WAC detachments. I am in charge of them. One of them is colored. The thinking is that it might be good for the colored girls to have their own officer. You are going to be that officer. You will report to me.

STONEY: Yes, ma'am.

LAWSON [*overlapping, as she sees* KIMBALL]: The colonel—

[KIMBALL *enters. They salute him.* KIMBALL *looks at* STONEY.]

KIMBALL: This girl—she's wearing a lieutenant's uniform.

LAWSON: Sir, this is Lieutenant Tenola Stoney.

KIMBALL: Is that so?

STONEY: Sir.

LAWSON: She's new to the hospital.

KIMBALL: And what is Lieutenant Tenola—Tenola?

STONEY: Yes, sir.

[KIMBALL *is obviously amused by her name.*]

KIMBALL: What is the lieutenant supposed to do in her uniform?

LAWSON: Supervise the colored WACs, sir.

KIMBALL: She's to report to you, yes, Lieutenant Lawson?

LAWSON: Yes, sir.

KIMBALL: Then I'm sure you will inform me if she comes up with anything I need to be bothered with.

[KIMBALL *exits.*]

LAWSON: That was Colonel Kimball.

STONEY: Yes, ma'am.

LAWSON: He's the CO of the hospital. You been told much about Lovell?

STONEY: Just that it's big, but I can see that for myself.

LAWSON: It started off as one building, then a second went up, then we absorbed some more buildings dedicated to rehabilitation, and now we've got more construction planned. We expect to have something like sixty-five hundred patients here soon. Add to this doctors, nurses, orderlies, secretarial, kitchen, supply staff. It's larger than most forts. The colonel's in charge of all of this.

STONEY: Must be a busy man.

LAWSON: He knows how to keep the place going. You have to give him that.

STONEY: Ma'am?

[*A beat.*]

LAWSON [*deciding not to say anything more on the topic*]: We, uh, try not to attract too much of the colonel's attention.

[LAWSON *exits.*]

SCENE 15

[GINNY *and* JOHNNIE MAE *approach* STONEY. *We pick up in midconversation.*]

JOHNNIE MAE: I've never seen one of you before.

STONEY: What am I one of?

GINNY: Colored woman officer.

STONEY: There are a few others.

GINNY: Don't think you'll find any others in this fort.

JOHNNIE MAE: But then, if it were up to Colonel Kimball—

[*She stops herself from continuing.*]

STONEY: If it were up to Colonel Kimball, what?
JOHNNIE MAE: Maybe it'd be better I don't finish that sentence.
STONEY: Oh? Why not?
JOHNNIE MAE: Maybe it'd be better I don't start the next one.
GINNY: We're glad you're here, ma'am.
STONEY: Yes?
GINNY: Somebody who can understand.

[STONEY *considers this for a second.*]

STONEY: Carry on, privates.
GINNY: Yes, ma'am.

[STONEY *exits.* JOHNNIE MAE *turns to* GINNY.]

JOHNNIE MAE: We should have told her about what's going on.
GINNY: It's better she find out some for herself and then she ask us. No way she's not gonna find out.

[GINNY *exits.*]

SCENE 16

[JOHNNIE MAE *turns to audience.*]

JOHNNIE MAE [*to audience*]: It happens pretty soon. Gertrude is sweeping up in a ward when she sees a white girl—one of the trainees in the medical technician program—doing something that makes her speak up.
GERTRUDE [*facing downstage*]: Excuse me—
JOHNNIE MAE: And the white trainee says—
WHITE TRAINEE [*played by* WHITE WOMAN *facing upstage, wearing white*]: Yes?
GERTRUDE: You're fixing to draw blood for this soldier?
WHITE TRAINEE: What about it?
GERTRUDE: Well, you're doing it wrong.
WHITE TRAINEE: Thanks for your opinion.
GERTRUDE: No, really, you are. That's the wrong—
WHITE TRAINEE: You think you know better?

GERTRUDE: I've been through this part of the training.

WHITE TRAINEE: Then why am I here and you there?

GERTRUDE: All right, don't believe me, ask Lieutenant Lawson.

[*A beat.*]

WHITE TRAINEE: Nigger, you just made yourself a whole lot of trouble.

[JOHNNIE MAE *exits.*]

SCENE 17

[GERTRUDE *turns to* STONEY *in* LAWSON's *office. In the meantime, in view of the audience.* WHITE WOMAN *switches costumes from* WHITE TRAINEE *to* LAWSON.]

GERTRUDE: What was I supposed to do? Stand by and see her do it wrong?

STONEY: It would have been better if you'd come to me.

GERTRUDE: But by the time I get to you, she's done it wrong. Maybe hurt that boy.

[*A beat.*]

STONEY: Look, I know it seems unfair—

GERTRUDE: Yes, ma'am.

[*She hesitates.*]

STONEY: No, if you have something you want to say—

[*A beat.*]

GERTRUDE [*emotionally*]: I want to know, what'd I do? Me and the others?

[LAWSON *enters.*]

STONEY: Private Hale was about to—

LAWSON: I heard. Please continue, Private Hale.

[*A beat.*]

Please.

GERTRUDE: You tell me we did something, something I can see, why, then all right. But I don't see we did anything. And I do know that that white girl—she didn't know what she was doing. You taught me how to do it. You taught me and you tried to teach her, and I'm the one who knows, but I'm the one stuck in the blue.

[LAWSON *doesn't know what to reply.*]

LAWSON: Why don't you take a few minutes, go to the commissary, get a soft drink, collect yourself?

[*A beat.*]

GERTRUDE [*saluting*]: Yes, ma'am. Thank you, ma'am.

[GERTRUDE *exits.* LAWSON *turns to* STONEY.]

LAWSON: This isn't my choice. You know that.

STONEY: Maybe if you talk to the colonel, find a new way to explain it—

LAWSON: Last summer, there was supposed to be a dance here at the fort. So the camp entertainment director, Captain Costello, he hires a band. The Buster Fenton Ensemble. A swing band out of Boston. Scheduled to play in the recreation hall. I go to the hall to supervise putting up decorations. Bunting, that sort of thing. Fenton and his musicians come in to set up. They've got a new arrangement to rehearse so they start playing. Some of the girls begin to dance. All right with me. It's hard enough in this war to grab something you can call pleasure. I see Kimball enter the hall. He's smiling, tapping his toe. Then he stops smiling. He walks closer to the bandstand, looks at the musicians. Most of the band is white.

STONEY: But some aren't?

LAWSON: The bass player and one of the guys on trombone. Kimball waits till the number is done, then he waves over Buster Fenton, says something to him. Fenton goes back to the bandstand, tells his men what the colonel told him.

STONEY: Kimball told him to get rid of the colored musicians?

LAWSON: Told him he could only use white players. The band decides they don't want the job that bad. They leave, and that night there is no dance. You want to talk to Kimball? I give you full and free permission to talk to him.

STONEY: Doesn't sound like he'd hear anything I'd say.

LAWSON: You under the impression he takes me any *more* seriously? You under the illusion he thinks of me as a soldier either?

SCENE 18

[*Shift focus to* GINNY *and* JOHNNIE MAE *crossing the stage in one direction,* GERTRUDE *in the other.*]

JOHNNIE MAE: Gertrude, you're going the wrong way! Lunch is this way!

GERTRUDE: I know.

GINNY: Come on, girl, you've got to eat.

GERTRUDE: Not hungry.

GINNY: Then just come and keep us company.

GERTRUDE: Didn't you hear what I said?

[GERTRUDE *exits.* GINNY *and* JOHNNIE MAE *exchange a look. Light shift.* JOHNNIE MAE *exits.*]

SCENE 19

[*A tire comes rolling onstage.* GINNY *catches it.* CAPTAIN EDWARDS *enters.*]

EDWARDS: You know how to drive?

GINNY: Yes, sir.

EDWARDS: Know how to change a tire?

GINNY: Yes, sir.

EDWARDS: And if the thing stops dead in the rain and won't get started again, you know how to cuss?

GINNY: Figure I could study up on that, sir.

EDWARDS: You'd have to go through training first. Motor school. Motor school, then motor pool.

GINNY: Yes, sir.

EDWARDS: Well, if you want to volunteer for grease and frustration. Tell them to send me the paperwork; it's all right with me.

[EDWARDS *takes control of the tire and exits.* GINNY *moves into midconversation with* STONEY *and* LAWSON.]

LAWSON: What's all right with who?

STONEY: Captain over at the motor pool. Private Boyd asked him if she could transfer there, he said yes.

GINNY: The colonel won't trust me with white soldiers. Maybe he won't mind if I handle green machines.

LAWSON: I don't have the authority to approve your moving over there myself. But I'll give it my recommendation—

[JOHNNIE MAE *runs across the stage.* LAWSON *sees her, calling out.*]

Private?

JOHNNIE MAE: It's Gertrude!

[*They rush to follow* JOHNNIE MAE *off. Shift of scene.*]

SCENE 20

[GERTRUDE, *wearing a hospital gown, with bandages around her wrists, is wheeled on in a wheelchair.* LAWSON *and* STONEY *enter.* GERTRUDE *begins to make a move to stand.*]

GERTRUDE: Lieutenant—

LAWSON: No, don't get up.

[*She nods to* STONEY *to continue.*]

STONEY: I need to ask you—is this something you've been planning on doing or was it . . . ?

GERTRUDE: I was organizing the supply closet, and the razor blades were there. And that moment, it just seemed, given how things are—lieutenant, what's gonna happen to me?

STONEY: First, you've got to get better. Then I expect you'll be evaluated by a doctor and discharged.

GERTRUDE: What kind?

STONEY: Kind?

GERTRUDE: Of discharge?

STONEY: Maybe medical.

GERTRUDE: You mean, if they think I was crazy?

LAWSON: If they think that there were . . . factors.

STONEY: But my guess is you'll be out of here.

GERTRUDE: Back to Broken Creek.

[GERTRUDE *is wheeled away.* (*During the scene that follows, the actress who plays* GERTRUDE *will take off her glasses and change wigs to become* RUBY *within view of the audience.*) STONEY *turns to* LAWSON. *A beat.*]

LAWSON: No, you're right. It's time I talk to him.

[*Shift of scene.*]

SCENE 21

[KIMBALL *is facing downstage, looking up at where the wall would be, shuffling filing cards as* LAWSON *appears behind him. They pick up in the middle of the conversation.*]

KIMBALL: You like baseball, Lieutenant?

LAWSON: I've attended a few games, sir.

KIMBALL: Won't get a chance to see a real game until this war's over. Every player worth a damn is in the service. Maybe if we can get Europe cleaned up by the end of the summer, put Tojo out of business, we'll have some shot at a real season in forty-six.

LAWSON: I'm sure we're all hoping for that, sir.

KIMBALL: I don't mind telling you it's been instructive to have different . . . elements in uniform. Necessary, I suppose, given the scope of the war, but part of the point of fighting is to defend our values. To reaffirm them. When the war is over, things can get back to normal. The way they're supposed to be.

[*A beat.*]

You're awfully quiet, lieutenant. Which part do you take issue with— that the point is to get back to normal, or that normal is the way it's supposed to be?

LAWSON: I can't say I've given it much thought, sir.

KIMBALL: Can't say or refuse to say?

LAWSON: That's just not where my mind goes. I've got enough to handle focusing on the here and now, sir.

KIMBALL: Well, right now you're here. You been in this office before, lieutenant?

LAWSON: No, sir.

KIMBALL: It's all up there on the wall. The whole hospital. Color coded. Who's arriving, the operating theaters, which specialists are coming in or transferring, who's recuperating, who's shipping out. That bloc over there are the German POWs we've got on work details. These are the Red Cross volunteers. Thousands of people to feed, organize, schedule, transfer, take care of. Can you guess where you and your girls are?

LAWSON: Little box down in the corner, sir?

KIMBALL: A little speck next to a little box down in the corner. But you think this is important.

LAWSON: One of the girls cut her wrists.

KIMBALL: Cut her wrists?

LAWSON: Razor blades. Now, she's going to be OK, but—

KIMBALL: One of the black girls?

LAWSON: One of the colored girls, sir.

KIMBALL: Isn't her color black?

LAWSON: We don't use that word.

KIMBALL: "Black"? It's considered, what? Insensitive?

LAWSON: It's a word that causes offense, sir.

KIMBALL: You offended if I call you white?

LAWSON: I suppose it doesn't have the same connotation, sir.

KIMBALL: At any given time, this fort has got thirty thousand people. It's not just that they're different sexes or different colors or from different racial stock, it's also that they're from different places. Different areas of the country. Where do you hail from?

LAWSON: Hail, sir?

KIMBALL: What you call home.

LAWSON: Tulsa, sir.

KIMBALL: Oklahoma?

LAWSON: Yes, sir.

KIMBALL: Me, I'm from a little town on the coast of Maine. My bet is on this base we've got people here from just about every corner of every state in the country. Now, one of the reasons we've got all these different states—back when this country was founded the people in each of these places thought of themselves as distinct. And they wanted to keep it that way. Robert E. Lee, for instance. The Civil War was approaching, Lincoln offered him the command of the Union army. Did you know that? He could have commanded the Union army. Lee turned it down. He thought of himself as a Virginian more than as an American. And that's what he fought for, Virginia. Most of the men in this camp—before they joined the army—most of them had never been more than twenty-five miles from the place of their birth. That's been their world. They're like Lee—they're Virginians, or Minnesotans or Texans. They don't have the *experience* of being Americans. Who they are is mostly what their home is. Whatever state, whatever town. And for a lot of the boys here, those towns are in the South. They come here to Massachusetts, they bring the South with them. This base is filled with boys, what they know of the colored and how to deal with them is how they've been brought up. And I don't have time to reeducate them to see things as Mrs. Roosevelt does. And that's leaving aside whether *I* see things as Mrs. Roosevelt does. I'm not going to put together folks who have a historical dislike and mistrust of each other any more than I have to. I have a hospital to run, and I'm going to avoid disruption and upset as much as I can.

LAWSON: Begging your pardon, sir, that's what I'm here about. There *is* disruption; there *is* upset.

KIMBALL: Among those girls of yours.

LAWSON: Yes, sir.

KIMBALL: So you want what? For me to visit them? Talk to them?

LAWSON: They don't understand your reasons for the shift in assignment. It has them disturbed, confused, unhappy—

KIMBALL: Unhappy. Well.

[*A beat.*]

Friday. Eleven hundred hours. Don't you worry, lieutenant, we'll get this whole thing cleared up.

SCENE 22

LAWSON [*to audience*]: Friday, March 9, 1945.

[*Sounds of the women gathering.* GINNY, JOHNNIE MAE, *and* RUBY *stand with* STONEY. *They face upstage so that the audience has to imagine the expressions on their faces during the following scene.* LAWSON *turns to them and the hubbub dies down.*]

As I'm sure you can all appreciate, the colonel is a busy man. Let's do our best to make wise and appropriate use of his time.

[KIMBALL *enters.*]

KIMBALL: At ease.

[*A beat.*]

I hear that you girls are unhappy. I think that was the word—"unhappy." I thought today I would talk with you, try to explain a few things. It is my task, as commanding officer of this facility, to look at the jobs that need to be done here and look at the people under my command and match them up. I have decided, on the basis of my experience with members of your race, what I think is appropriate for you to do. You may think I'm wrong. There's an answer to this: one of you become a general and then you can order me to do different. And I will follow that order, because general outranks colonel. In the meantime, here are the facts:

[*A beat.*]

I am a colonel, you are privates. I am a man, you are girls. I am white—

[*A beat.*]

Wait a second, do I see a tear? What do I have here? A crying soldier? I have a hankie. How many of you would like to borrow my hankie?

[*A beat.*]

Now, I understand that someone here wishes to transfer to the motor pool. Which one of you—?

GINNY: Me, sir.

[*A beat.*]

KIMBALL: I know you.

GINNY: Yes, sir.

KIMBALL: The girl with the thermometer. I'm right, aren't I?

GINNY: Yes, sir.

KIMBALL: You again.

GINNY: Yes, sir.

[*A beat.*]

KIMBALL: I understand you spoke to Captain Edwards?

GINNY: Yes, sir.

KIMBALL: And Captain Edwards said what?

GINNY: Yes, that it would be all right, sir.

KIMBALL: For you to transfer?

GINNY: That's what he said, sir.

KIMBALL: I'm going to have to speak to Captain Edwards about this. He shouldn't be leading you on in this way.

GINNY: Sir?

KIMBALL: Didn't he tell you that they don't want any of you blacks in the motor pool?

[*This registers strongly on all the women present.* GINNY, JOHNNIE MAE, *and* RUBY *bolt to another corner of the stage.*]

Where are they going? Where do they think they're going?

LAWSON: Ladies, you have not been dismissed!

STONEY: Soldiers!

KIMBALL: They can't just run out on me like that.

LAWSON: Ladies!

KIMBALL: I'm a colonel!

STONEY [*stepping in front of* KIMBALL, *to an unseen WAC*]: Don't you do it, soldier!

LAWSON: Ladies?

STONEY: You put that fist down.

LAWSON: You will assemble at attention at once!

[*They leave the central playing area to* KIMBALL, LAWSON, *and* STONEY.]

KIMBALL [*to* STONEY]: Well, you've done a fine job with your . . . soldiers, lieutenant. What have you to say?

STONEY: To you, sir? Not a word . . . sir.

[KIMBALL *exits in one direction, and after the exchange of a look between them,* LAWSON *and* STONEY *exit in another.*]

SCENE 23

[GINNY, JOHNNIE MAE, *and* RUBY *gather in another area. From the sound, the audience gets the impression the room is filled with the other WACs.* JOHNNIE MAE *climbs onto a chair to address the WACs and the audience.*]

JOHNNIE MAE: I don't know about the rest of you, but I ain't going back to that hospital. They can find somebody else to clean their damn toilets. Far as I care, can clean them with the colonel's hankie.

[*Vocal support from most in the room.*]

RUBY: You know what you're talking about?

JOHNNIE MAE: Talking about?

RUBY: Not going back to work. It's called a strike.

JOHNNIE MAE: OK.

RUBY: Yeah, except you don't do that. Not in the army. Look at what happened last year in San Francisco.

JOHNNIE MAE: What?

RUBY: Don't you read?

JOHNNIE MAE: Don't talk to me like that, Ruby. If you're gonna tell me, tell me. There was a strike?

[GINNY *hasn't said anything all during this, but now she speaks up.*]

GINNY [*quietly*]: A mutiny. A mutiny's what they called it in the newspapers. A bunch of colored soldiers, loading munitions on the docks.

JOHNNIE MAE: Munitions?

GINNY: Bombs, explosives. Nobody trained them how to do it, no special equipment. And there was a lot of hurry up and somebody did something wrong. And there was an explosion. Two ships—blown to kingdom come. And the dock. And something like three hundred guys. Just wiped off the face of the earth like that. Most of them colored.

[*A beat.*]

So a few weeks later, there's more munitions to load and they tell a bunch more colored soldiers to do it.

RUBY: And nothing's changed.

GINNY: Still no training, no equipment. It was like the brass didn't care. And the colored soldiers say no. Navy calls it a mutiny. A batch of them were court-martialed. They were convicted. They're serving sentences now.

JOHNNIE MAE: What kind of sentences?

RUBY: Dishonorable discharges. All of them. And some of them have been sentenced to fifteen years' hard labor.

GINNY: They're serving time now. As we talk. Just so you know. Just so you appreciate. This is what we're up against.

SCENE 24

[*A shift in scene.* STONEY *waves* GINNY *over as the others exit.*]

GINNY: You asked to see me, ma'am.

STONEY: All right, it's just you and me talking. OK?

GINNY: OK.

STONEY: Believe me, I understand. I was there. I understand.

GINNY: Yes, ma'am, I expect you do.

STONEY: But you can't do it this way. Just walking out? That's what you and the others are planning in there, isn't it? A strike?

GINNY: We're talking.

STONEY: Tell them it won't work.

GINNY: It's not up to me to tell the others anything. It's not like I'm the leader. They didn't all walk out on him because of me, that I gave some kind of signal.

STONEY: I know that.

GINNY: What surprises me, though . . .

STONEY [*prompting*]: What?

GINNY: *You* didn't walk out. The crap he was saying—calling us black—it wasn't just to us, it was at you, too.

STONEY: I'm an officer.

GINNY: That means you've got to put up with being insulted?

STONEY: Means I put aside feelings and do my duty. If I tangle with Kimball, that's it, it's over. You imagine that man wants me in this army? You think he wants Lieutenant Lawson? And don't you believe that all of you disobeying our orders to reassemble helped either of us one bit.

GINNY: Sorry if we hurt your chances for promotion.

STONEY [*sharply*]: Private!

GINNY: I thought it was just you and me talking.

[*A beat.* STONEY *tries another tack.*]

STONEY: Look, we both want the same thing.

GINNY: Do we? Do we really?

STONEY: You doubt that?

GINNY: Like I say, *you* didn't walk out.

STONEY: Don't confuse goals with methods.

GINNY: Meaning?

STONEY: You're looking at the short term. And no, I can't tell you anything you can do that will change things overnight.

GINNY: So you're looking at—what?—the long term?

STONEY: I am.

GINNY: Well, maybe long term makes sense to you because you're an officer and you intend to make the army your life. But the other girls and I—we joined because Mrs. Roosevelt, the newspapers, and the recruiter all said that we'd learn things that would open a door for us when this war is over. They said nothing about that door leading to being a maid.

STONEY: I do appreciate your position—

GINNY: Well, appreciate further that when I make a bargain, whether it's with a person or the army, I keep up my end, and I expect—

STONEY: You expect the other side to keep up theirs.

GINNY: I do.

STONEY: And if they don't—

GINNY: I will do something about it.

STONEY: You'll fight.

GINNY: If I have to.

STONEY: If you're going to fight something, you've got to understand the *nature* of what you're fighting. And I'm telling you, you *don't* understand the army. First and foremost, it's a machine. A big machine built to fight a war. As long as it's doing that job, the brass really don't give a damn how it works on our level. So you get officers like Colonel Kimball. OK, so you don't like him—

GINNY: Do you?

STONEY [*fervently*]: Doesn't matter. Army doesn't care what you or I feel about him. You know what the army cares about? This hospital's as big as a town, and he knows how to keep the place going. Now I don't have to agree with all the orders he gives, but as long as they're legal, I do have to follow them. Tell you something else: I intend to survive him. Yes, I'm looking to get promoted, so maybe someday I can be part of running things differently.

GINNY: Long term.

STONEY: Nothing this size changes overnight. The day you met me, you were surprised that a colored woman was a lieutenant. I'm looking to when nobody will turn a hair about that. It'll just be, "Yes, ma'am" to me or anybody else with the rank. But that's not going to happen if I can't command respect.

GINNY: It's not you and Lieutenant Lawson who don't command respect. It wasn't you that we all walked out on.

STONEY: Tell that to the army.

GINNY: That's just what I hope to do.

[*A beat.*]

Must be awfully lonely for you.

STONEY: Excuse me?

GINNY: We privates—we've got one another to talk to. But I don't guess there are a lot of people around for *you* to talk to.

[*This surprises* STONEY. *She tries to suppress a reaction, nods, and walks away.*]

SCENE 25

LAWSON: It isn't until the next day, when General Miles shows up and reads out the Articles of War, that the strike that almost was is over. Most of the women return to their posts and do their jobs.

STONEY: But not Virginia Boyd.

[*Reprise of the scene between* GINNY, LAWSON, *and* STONEY.]

GINNY: I've decided to take a court-martial.

LAWSON [*to* STONEY]: Take down Private Boyd's name and serial number, have her collect her things, and go to restriction.

STONEY: Yes, ma'am.

[GINNY *gets her duffel and moves where* STONEY *directs. Back to the square of light and bench representing restriction.* GINNY *sits.*]

SCENE 26

[JOHNNIE MAE *enters, carrying her duffel. The sound of the door being closed again.*]

GINNY: What are you doing here?

JOHNNIE MAE: You know, you're usually so smart . . .

GINNY: You aren't doing this because of me, are you?

JOHNNIE MAE: You think I can't make a mess of my life without your example? I've been getting myself into trouble for years without your help. Anyway, I want a piece of this.

GINNY: You sound like you're scrapping for a fight.

JOHNNIE MAE: I'm not afraid of one.

GINNY: Well, don't you go speaking for me. I've never been more scared in my life. I'm only here because when I joined up, they made a promise to me. Now they're trying to go back on it, and . . . it's just not in my power to let it go.

JOHNNIE MAE: Well, the way I feel, at least I'm finally doing *some*thing worth doing in this damn army. You should have seen Lawson's face. I march into her office and the look she gives me. And Stoney!

GINNY: I don't think she's having a good day.

JOHNNIE MAE: Name me someone who is.

GINNY: She doesn't like Kimball any more than we do. Stoney.

JOHNNIE MAE: Great. So what's she gonna do about it?

GINNY: She's an officer. There are things she can't do, can't say.

JOHNNIE MAE: If she can't do anything, can't say anything, what's left? She gonna *think* real hard? It's like that officer sends his troops out into battle, saying, "I'm behind you boys." Yeah, way behind. Thanks for nothing. So now they put us on trial?

GINNY: I guess that's how it goes.

JOHNNIE MAE: What about a lawyer. Do we get a lawyer?

GINNY: Either we get one or they assign us one.

JOHNNIE MAE: Hey, if we're lucky, maybe they'll send us whoever defended those sailors in San Francisco. Sounds like he did a bang-up job for those boys.

GINNY: Well, we're gonna need someone . . .

SCENE 27

[RAINEY, *dressed in a suit, takes the platform, holding a newspaper.*]

RAINEY [*reading from paper*]: "J. D. Steele, president of the Boston chapter of the NAACP, has stated that he—quote—'deplores the action of the colored WACs,' referring to them as—quote—'misguided.'"

[STEELE, *also dressed in a suit, enters.*]

STEELE: You know, Julian, I was looking forward to a quiet morning.

RAINEY: "Deplores the action"? "Misguided"?

STEELE: I was speaking for myself.

RAINEY: They ask your opinion because you head this office. They think that means you speak for all the Negroes of Boston. Like you were elected to make pronouncements on our behalf. Someone wants to know what colored people think about this or that, they don't have to bother actually talking to a bunch of different, real, live colored people, people who might actually have a bunch of different, real, live opinions. Why go to all that effort when you have the honorable J. D. Steele happy and eager to speak for everyone.

STEELE: I don't represent myself speaking for everyone.

RAINEY: Not a question of how you represent yourself. It's about you being smart enough to know how you're being used and watching out for it.

STEELE: Nobody's using me.

RAINEY [*overlapping*]: You open your mouth and they think you've got the franchise to speak for every Negro within thirty miles of Bunker Hill. Well, you don't represent me. You don't represent this man. And you surely don't represent me when you tell a white reporter you think these girls brought this down on their own heads. That they're guilty before the officers on the panel put their seats on those chairs. And you know what the readers of the *Boston Globe* are going to think. "Hell, if one of their own big cats thinks they're wrong—"

STEELE: I was reacting to what I thought—and still think—is a dangerous situation.

RAINEY: Dangerous?

STEELE: If we come in on their side—if the NAACP comes out in support of them—it'll attract a lot of attention in the newspapers.

RAINEY: Yes. So?

STEELE: If we're going to attract press, I want it to be in support of a stronger case. We have to choose our battles carefully.

RAINEY: And why is this a battle we don't want to choose? Wait. Wait. Because—are you saying because they're just a couple of girls?

STEELE: We're trying to get this country to believe that our people have what it takes to make it in the military. But here you have these girls—privates, no less—refusing to obey first a colonel, then a general. How can that ever be right in the army? You can just hear white folks out there thinking—"Good God, if their girls are such a handful in uniform, what are we going to face with their men?" I say the less attention paid to them, the better.

RAINEY: They're in this trouble *because* of their color. If our job isn't to defend them, then what the hell is? Steele, I'm telling you this: if you do not assign me to take this case on behalf of this office, I will resign as legal counsel *to* this office—

STEELE: Oh now—

RAINEY: No, I *will* do it. I will resign and I will drive out to Fort Devens and I will defend them on my own. And when that smart reporter you're so friendly with asks me why I've quit, I will tell him, and I will make sure he knows how to spell your name. So, what's it going to be?

STEELE [*to audience*]: And that's how Boston lawyer Julian Rainey comes to defend Ginny Boyd and Johnnie Mae Malone.

SCENE 28

[STEELE *leaves the platform and* RAINEY *visits* GINNY *and* JOHNNIE MAE *in restriction.*]

RAINEY: To tell you the truth, I mostly do corporate law in Boston. I've never tried a court-martial before.

GINNY: Who's gonna pay you?

RAINEY: Money isn't an issue.

JOHNNIE MAE: So it won't cost us anything to go to the stockade. Good deal.

GINNY: You get to call witnesses, right? Ask them questions? So the judge and jury understand?

RAINEY: Well, there won't be a judge and jury. Not like you see in the movies. A court-martial works differently. Instead of a jury, there's a panel.

JOHNNIE MAE: A panel?

RAINEY: A bunch of officers sitting behind a long table, all in a line. And one of the officers will act kind of like a judge. We tell our story to them. And at the end of the proceedings, these men will confer and they'll decide what happens.

JOHNNIE MAE: What happens to us.

RAINEY: Yes. The verdict.

JOHNNIE MAE: And the sentence?

RAINEY: If there *is* one.

GINNY: But it's still like a trial, right? You still get to call witnesses, so they understand—the panel—they understand what happened?

RAINEY: Oh, yes.

GINNY: So, you know how you're gonna handle the colonel? Colonel Kimball?

RAINEY: Well, about that—we've got a problem.

GINNY: Let's hear it.

RAINEY: He won't be there for me to call.

[*A beat.*]

JOHNNIE MAE: Not gonna be there?

RAINEY: No. In fact, they gave him temporary reassignment to another part of the country.

GINNY: But what about—it's in the Constitution—the right to face your accusers.

RAINEY: Technically you aren't charged with disobeying Kimball's orders.

GINNY: Yes, but Kimball was the reason.

JOHNNIE MAE: Damn army can't even bother to court-martial us fair.

RAINEY: Just because Kimball isn't going to be there physically doesn't mean he isn't going to be there. This is our job: you have to help me make that panel see him. Make that panel see him. Make the country see him in their newspapers. That's our strategy. They see him, they hear the words that come out of his mouth; that's how we have a chance.

SCENE 29

[*The court-martial setup is assembled.* MCCARTHY *approaches* LAWSON *as she sits in the witness chair.*]

MCCARTHY: State your name, rank, organization, and station.

LAWSON: Victoria A. Lawson, First Lieutenant, WAC, Detachment Commander, Lovell General and Convalescent Hospital, Fort Devens, Massachusetts.

RUBY [*as narrator, to audience*]: Leading the prosecution is Major Leon E. McCarthy. March 19, 1945.

MCCARTHY: Do you know the accused in this case?

LAWSON: I do.

MCCARTHY: Is there any question in your mind, lieutenant, that these girls misunderstood any of the conversations that they had with you with reference to doing their duty?

LAWSON: No, sir.

MCCARTHY: Is there any question in your mind as to whether or not they refused to go back as ordered?

LAWSON: No, sir.

[RAINEY *cross-examining* LAWSON.]

RAINEY: All right, you've testified that Private Boyd came to you and said she wouldn't go on.

LAWSON: Words to that effect, yes, sir.

RAINEY: And at that point you did what?

LAWSON: Tried to make her understand the seriousness of what she was doing.

RAINEY: Tried to get her to change her mind?

LAWSON: Yes, sir.

RAINEY: But you weren't able to.

LAWSON: No, sir

RAINEY: And what did you do then?

LAWSON: I ordered her to collect her bag and go into restriction.

RAINEY: And did she pack her bag and go into restriction?

LAWSON: Yes, sir.

RAINEY: She didn't refuse to obey the order?

LAWSON: She packed her bag and went into restriction.

RAINEY: Private Boyd did not refuse to obey the order that you gave her that day? That or any order?

LAWSON: None that I can recall, sir.

RAINEY: Is it your experience that people who are of a mutinous nature obey orders?

MCCARTHY [*rising*]: I will be happy to stipulate that Private Boyd obeyed Lieutenant Lawson's orders. But I will remind counsel that this is not the issue. Private Boyd is not charged with disobeying Lieutenant Lawson.

RUBY [*as narrator, to audience*]: McCarthy establishes what he wants to—

MCCARTHY [*to audience*]: That the general gave an order to go back to work but that Privates Ginny Boyd and Johnnie Mae Malone decided they would rather take a court-martial.

RAINEY [*to audience*]: That much I expected. What I am looking to get into the record is *why* they prefer to be court-martialed.

[GINNY *takes the stand.*]

GINNY: Virginia Boyd, Private, WAC Detachment, Lovell General Hospital, Fort Devens, Massachusetts.

RAINEY: When you enlisted in the army, what did you expect to do?

GINNY: I expected to work on the ward in a hospital. I expected to take the place of the nurses, as they told me many times. When I was recruited, they told me I was qualified for medical technician.

RAINEY: What did you do before you came into the army?

GINNY: I had a year of college at Howard University, then I took a job in the Treasury Department in Washington, D.C., running an adding machine.

RAINEY: Treasury of the United States?

GINNY: Yes, sir.

RAINEY: What salary were you getting?

GINNY: About one hundred and twenty dollars a month.

RAINEY: That's a good deal more than you're making as a WAC.

GINNY: Yes, sir.

RAINEY: What were you doing at Lovell General?

GINNY: When I first came here, they started to train me as a technician. Learning how to take tests, take on some of what the nurses do.

RAINEY: You say that was when you first came here. You're no longer doing that?

GINNY: No, sir. I was changed to ward orderly. Me and the other girls in the unit. All of us changed. Put us into different uniforms, started us mopping floors, cleaning latrines.

RAINEY: Like that?

GINNY: Like that, sir.

RAINEY: Did you have any feeling that there was a reason that happened?

GINNY: I thought that people thought that because we were colored we couldn't do the work of medical technicians.

MCCARTHY [rising]: Private Boyd is merely voicing a personal opinion. This does not constitute evidence.

RAINEY [to GINNY]: Can you tell us an incident, something that you witnessed, that would support the idea that the treatment that you received was because of color?

GINNY: Yes, sir. The reason we were taken out of white uniforms and put into blue. Because the colonel saw me put a thermometer in a white soldier's mouth. And what he said when he saw me.

RAINEY: Which was what?

GINNY: "I do not have colored WACs as medical technicians. They are here to scrub and wash floors, wash dishes."

RAINEY: Colonel Kimball said a lot of things in front of you. Referring to the meeting that caused these problems, when he spoke to a number of you girls. How many were there present? How many WACs?

GINNY: There were at least fifty girls there.

RAINEY: You spoke to the colonel at that meeting, didn't you?

GINNY: I told him that if I wasn't gonna be trained as a medical technician as I was promised, I would like to take a transfer to the motor pool. I told him the captain of the motor pool said he would take me if the colonel said yes.

RAINEY: And what did he say? The colonel?

GINNY: He said, "Didn't he tell you that they didn't want any of you blacks in the motor pool?"

RAINEY: He called you that to your faces? "You blacks"?

GINNY: Yes, sir. We all heard him.

RAINEY: As a result of that fact was there any noise at that time?

GINNY: Crying. Everybody in the room.

RAINEY: Everybody?

GINNY: Yes, sir.

[RAINEY *steps back;* MCCARTHY *steps forward.*]

MCCARTHY: You took basic training courses, didn't you?

GINNY: Yes, sir.

MCCARTHY: For how long a period of time?

GINNY: Five weeks.

MCCARTHY: Where?

GINNY: At Fort Des Moines.

MCCARTHY: You were acquainted with the fact that you were in the army and expected to do your duty in the army as a soldier, whatever the assignment was?

GINNY: Yes, sir.

MCCARTHY: You remember General Miles addressing you?

GINNY: Yes, sir.

MCCARTHY: You heard him read to you from the Articles of War?

GINNY: Yes, sir.

MCCARTHY: You heard him give an order to the girls in that room to return to work?

GINNY: Yes, sir.

MCCARTHY: And you did go back to your ward?

GINNY: Yes, sir.

MCCARTHY: What time did you get there?

GINNY: Sir, I have no idea of what time.

MCCARTHY: Did you stay on duty all afternoon?

GINNY: No, sir. I didn't. But I did go back with the intention of staying.

MCCARTHY: You reported back to the ward.

GINNY: Like I was ordered, yes, sir.

MCCARTHY: How long a time elapsed between the time you reported until you left your duty?

GINNY: I am not sure.

MCCARTHY: But you left your post of duty to go over to see Lieutenant Lawson?

GINNY: Yes, sir.

MCCARTHY: And why did you do that? Why did you not continue with your duties at the ward after you had reported there?

GINNY: Sir, I was upset.

MCCARTHY: Do you want to tell this court the reason you didn't continue with your duties was because you were upset?

GINNY: Yes, sir. I do. I was.

[GINNY *steps down and* JOHNNIE MAE *takes the stand.*]

JOHNNIE MAE: Johnnie Mae Malone, Private, WAC Detachment, Lovell General Hospital, Fort Devens, Massachusetts.

RAINEY: When you asked for a court-martial, what did you believe you were doing?

JOHNNIE MAE: I believed that I was doing the right thing. To better the way we were treated.

RAINEY: Were there white WACs present in the hospital when you were working there?

JOHNNIE MAE: Yes, sir.

RAINEY: Having that in mind, seeing the white WACs working in the hospital, how did you feel that you were being treated in the hospital?

JOHNNIE MAE: The way I felt, I saw the white WACs, and what they were doing and what we were doing—it seemed like there's a difference between us because of race.

RAINEY: A difference in duties because of race?

JOHNNIE MAE: Yes, sir.

RAINEY: When did you start thinking that?

JOHNNIE MAE: Ever since they put us into blue uniforms and gave the whites to the whites.

RAINEY: Was that in your mind when you said to Lieutenant Lawson that you would be willing to take a court-martial?

JOHNNIE MAE: Yes, sir.

[RAINEY *steps back;* MCCARTHY *steps forward.*]

MCCARTHY: Lieutenant Lawson said to you, "I don't believe you realize the seriousness of what you are doing in refusing to go to work this morning," didn't she?

JOHNNIE MAE: Yes, sir.

MCCARTHY: And she said, "I am going to give you a direct order to report to your ward duty," and you stated, "No, ma'am," didn't you?

JOHNNIE MAE: Yes, sir.

MCCARTHY: She said, "I direct and order you to report back to your ward for duty," and you said to her—what? "I would die before I go back to work"?

JOHNNIE MAE: No, sir. That isn't what I said.

MCCARTHY: That's what she testified to you saying.

JOHNNIE MAE: She misremembers a little.

MCCARTHY: Misremembers? She was under oath.

JOHNNIE MAE: Yes, sir.

MCCARTHY: As I remind you, *you* are.

JOHNNIE MAE: Not saying the lieutenant lied—

MCCARTHY: She misremembered.

JOHNNIE MAE: Yes, sir.

MCCARTHY: You think your memory's better?

JOHNNIE MAE: I do remember what I said.

MCCARTHY: All right, let's hear it. Let's hear your version. When she ordered you to go back to work, what response did you make to your superior officer?

JOHNNIE MAE: I said, "If it will advance the cause of my people, I will take death." That's what I said, sir. That's why I'm here.

[JOHNNIE MAE *steps down.*]

SCENE 30

[*Scene shifts to a conference among* RAINEY, GINNY, *and* JOHNNIE MAE.]

JOHNNIE MAE: So what do you figure, they gonna shoot us or hang us?

GINNY: Or both?

RAINEY: I've got another witness to call—Lieutenant Stoney.

JOHNNIE MAE: How's that gonna help? She's an officer.

RAINEY: She's sworn to tell the truth.

GINNY: She's gonna have to testify like an officer. She's gonna have to say how we disobeyed her and Lawson and the others.

RAINEY: I have a hunch there's more truth there.

GINNY: More?

RAINEY: Something you said about her in the room that day with Kimball . . .

SCENE 31

[MCCARTHY *approaches* RAINEY *informally.*]

MCCARTHY: You're calling the colored lieutenant?

RAINEY: I'm calling Lieutenant Stoney, yes.

MCCARTHY: If anything, she'd be a witness for the prosecution. The girls disobeyed her, too.

RAINEY: Is there a reason you're telling me this?

MCCARTHY: You haven't tried many cases of this sort, have you?

RAINEY: Approximately none.

MCCARTHY: Whether you realize it or not, I've been going easy in here.

RAINEY: Oh?

MCCARTHY: I can't tell you how many things I could have objected to, but I let them slide.

RAINEY: Why are you being so kind to us?

MCCARTHY: I don't believe in overkill. I'm going to win this case in a walk. I'm sorry, I know that sounds arrogant, but I *have* tried quite a few of these. I know this territory. Whether you realize it or not, I'm trying to *contain* this damage. But if you put Stoney on the stand, you will force me to cross-examine her. I promise you, this is not in the interests of your clients.

SCENE 32

[STONEY *takes the stand.*]

RAINEY: I want you to recall when Colonel Kimball addressed your WACs. Do you recall that?

STONEY: Yes, sir.

RAINEY: More specifically I want you to recall the statement that Private Boyd made to the colonel about going to the motor pool. Now, did the colonel answer her when she made the statement about that?

STONEY: Yes, sir.

RAINEY: What did he say?

STONEY: "Didn't the company commander tell you that he didn't want any of you blacks in the motor pool?"

RAINEY: "You blacks"? The colonel used those actual words in front of your detachment?

STONEY: Yes, sir.

RAINEY: Do you think he was aware of the offense such a phrase might cause?

[MCCARTHY *rises.*]

MCCARTHY: The lieutenant is hardly in a position to speculate on what the colonel was or was not aware of.

RAINEY: All right, let me put it this way: the phrase "you blacks" or "black girls"—in your experience would the use of such a phrase cause offense?

STONEY: Yes, sir.

RAINEY: In fact, it did cause offense, didn't it?

STONEY: Yes, sir.

RAINEY: To the point that some of your girls broke into tears, began to cry?

STONEY: Yes, sir.

RAINEY: How many were crying?

STONEY: I am unable to answer that. I don't know the number that were crying.

RAINEY: Did you cry?

[*A beat.*]

STONEY: Not that day.

RAINEY: Not that day.

[*A beat.*]

STONEY: No, sir.

RAINEY: What day *did* you cry?

[*A beat.* STONEY *looks at him.*]

You say you didn't cry that day.

STONEY: I didn't.

RAINEY: That suggests that you cried another day. What day *did* you cry?

[*A beat.*]

STONEY: The next day. Saturday.

RAINEY: Where was that?

STONEY: In my quarters.

RAINEY: You were alone.

STONEY: I was in my quarters.

RAINEY: Well, it has been stated in other evidence that everybody in the room was crying after Colonel Kimball made that remark. You were in that room.

STONEY: I don't think I cried there.

RAINEY: There was great excitement at that time?

STONEY: Yes, sir.

RAINEY: Everybody was hysterical?

STONEY: That is right.

RAINEY: The girls were emotionally upset and apparently very overcome?

STONEY: Yes, sir.

RAINEY: You were overcome yourself.

STONEY: I wouldn't say "overcome," sir.

RAINEY: Might there have been tears in your eyes?

STONEY: If there were tears in my eyes, I don't remember it.

RAINEY: Might there not have been?

[*A beat.*]

STONEY: There might have been tears in my eyes, but I didn't cry.

RAINEY: You didn't cry out. There might have been tears, but you made no outcry?

STONEY: No. There might have been tears, but I didn't let them go down my face.

[*A beat.*]

RAINEY: Didn't you feel a reaction after Colonel Kimball's remarks?

STONEY: I did.

RAINEY: You were not in a normal state of mind, were you?

STONEY: I held myself together.

RAINEY: Were you in a normal state of emotion?

STONEY: Not a normal state of emotion.

[MCCARTHY, *on redirect.*]

MCCARTHY: You felt keenly embarrassed to think your detachment would act that way, isn't that correct? You felt keenly embarrassed to think your detachment would act that way before your commanding officer?

STONEY: I did, sir.

MCCARTHY: I want you to be specific. What did your detachment do up there in front of the colonel that you were embarrassed about?

STONEY: The way they ran out on him, cursing him, and me trying to keep them off him.

[*A beat.*]

MCCARTHY: You doing what?

STONEY: Trying to keep them off him.

MCCARTHY [*genuinely surprised*]: Keep them off him?

STONEY: Keep them from striking him.

MCCARTHY: Physically?

STONEY: I had to stand in front of him. In front of the colonel. Between him and them. They were that kind of angry.

[RAINEY, *on recross.*]

RAINEY: Let's talk more about embarrassment. You said just now that you were embarrassed by the behavior of your troops. You felt keenly embarrassed about the reaction of those girls to being distinguished—because they were colored—from the rest of the American soldiers who were fighting for their country. You felt extremely embarrassed because there was emotional reaction to it. Is that right?

STONEY: I felt they could have handled their emotions a little better than that.

RAINEY: What about the colonel? The things he did and said. Didn't you feel embarrassed when he said that about "you blacks"?

[*A beat.*]

STONEY: I most certainly did.

RAINEY: He did embarrass you, as a colonel in the army?

STONEY: Yes, sir.

RAINEY: You were particularly embarrassed when he made that remark?
He embarrassed you?

STONEY: Not personally, not for myself, but for the girls.

RAINEY: When the commanding officer made the remark about "you
blacks," that didn't faze you at all?

STONEY: Yes, sir, it did.

RAINEY: How did you feel? How? You are a commissioned officer, an
educated lady. You should be able to describe the feelings you had.
See if you can't describe your feelings. You are a colored lady, and an
officer, and a remark was made about "you blacks." What was your
reaction? How did you feel about that?

[*A beat.*]

STONEY: First I got mad, and then I got right.

[STONEY *steps down.*]

RUBY [*as narrator, to audience*]: The evidence having been presented, it is
time for final arguments.

[RAINEY *holds up a newspaper.*]

RAINEY: I would like to read something that appeared in the paper under
the headline: "Negroes, Whites Fight Side by Side for U.S." This is
dated Paris, March 19. "Negroes and whites are now fighting shoulder
to shoulder in the same outfits in both the First and Seventh armies,
marking a break in the U.S. Army's traditional policy of segregation.
So reported the army newspaper *Stars and Stripes* today from the First
Army Front. Negro platoons have been assigned to rifle companies
of infantry divisions in both armies in response to repeated requests
from the Negroes themselves for a chance to fight for their country."

America, of course, is the only country among the Allied forces
that segregates soldiers because of color. England doesn't, and in the
colonies the colored soldiers go in with the rest. In Canada they go in
with the rest, and in all the other countries there is no distinction.

These young women chose to come into the army. They chose on
the basis of the promise that was made as to the training that they
would get. They came in on that promise, and that promise was simply

taken away from them by an officer who did not like to see them in white uniforms. We are fighting for the unconditional surrender of those who discriminate against men and women because of color or creed. That is what we are fighting for. That is what *they* enlisted to fight for. They had every right to expect that someone who embraces racism would wear the uniform of the *enemy.*

Now, I put Lieutenant Stoney on the stand. I did so mindful of the discomfort of her situation. She is a conscientious, disciplined officer with a genuine respect for the chain of command. The questions I asked her were not intended to cause her distress, but to convey to you the dismay she felt on that day. Why is this relevant? An officer is supposed to *inspire* those who serve under him. To inspire, not to visit upon them humiliation and insult. The lieutenant testified she allowed no tears to go down her face. If that is so, then I confess she has more fortitude than *I* would have been able to manage had I been in her place. Tears of rage are *appropriate* when a colonel in this army says, "We don't want any of you blacks taking temperatures. We don't want any of you blacks drawing blood. We don't want any of you blacks in the motor pool."

When an officer puts on a uniform, he no longer has the luxury of representing just himself. He has the responsibility of embodying the ideals of the country that lends him the *privilege* of that uniform. Keeping in mind what you have heard in sworn testimony, are you prepared to affirm that Colonel Kimball embodies this country's values? Is he *fit* to be seen as representative of the United States of America? For *that* is the conclusion the world will draw, *must* draw, if you punish these young women for their courage in standing up to him.

[RAINEY *sits.* MCCARTHY *rises for a response.*]

MCCARTHY: As my friend here says, these girls enlisted. They volunteered for the army. They had five or six weeks of basic training and, like every other soldier in this army, they were classified.

They were assigned to be hospital orderlies. They may have had other hopes and expectations, but we leave it to our officers to use their discretion, expertise, and experience to make assignments as they see fit. Colonel Kimball, an officer universally admired for the way he has run an enormously complex facility during this war, determined their classification. These soldiers didn't like their classification. They thought it beneath them, beneath their dignity. They are members of the army. The women's army. Some women of the Army Nurse Corps have to go into battle, and actually accompany the troops in establishing beachheads, but these young women believe it is beneath their dignity to scrub a floor or to carry out garbage. Isn't that just too bad?

The essential fact is this: these people are members of the armed forces who don't care for their job. They don't want to do their job, because they don't like it. We can't run an army that way. There are lot of things everyone in this room does that they don't like. I have to do things that I don't like. I can't say that I very much like being here right now. I don't get any pleasure out of saying unpleasant things about these defendants. They're obviously young, and, yes, probably they shouldn't have come into this army in the first place. But that's a separate issue. The issue is was there a legal order given and did they obey it? That is all you members of the panel are required to determine.

My friend here has brought up other issues. Racial issues. And I will agree with him in saying yes, there should be no discrimination between the races, as far as their treatment is concerned. Just because people are colored from an accident of birth—I might have been— you might have been—and we hold nothing against them, and we appreciate that some of them, some of their race, are the best scholars, orators, lawyers, and so forth of our time. But there also should be no discrimination in their punishment.

We submit to the court that we have sustained the burden of proof by not a preponderance of evidence but *beyond* a reasonable doubt. I say that it is within the province of this court to give punishment to these people without discrimination, as to race, color, or creed. Now, in time of war, the maximum punishment for this offense is a sentence of death. Of course, we do not ask for any death penalty. But if the court finds them guilty, the punishment should be adequate for the crime.

[*All onstage stand at attention and face downstage.*]

RUBY [*as narrator, to audience*]: Privates Virginia Boyd and Johnnie Mae Malone are convicted. They are sentenced to be dishonorably discharged and to serve a year at hard labor.

[*All exit.*]

SCENE 33

[*Organ music appropriate to an Episcopal service.* KENNETH HUGHES *appears behind a pulpit.*]

HUGHES: This morning we make a radical departure from custom in the choice of a text. You will not find it in the Bible. God speaks not only through priests and prophets but also, as the phrase goes, through "the mouths of babes and sucklings." God spoke at Fort Devens, Massachusetts, through a Negro private. It is she who supplies us with our morning's text: "If it will advance the cause of my people, I will take death."

RUBY [*as narrator, to audience*]: Easter Sunday, 1945. Father Kenneth Hughes of Saint Bartholomew's Episcopal Church in Cambridge, Massachusetts, addresses his congregation.

HUGHES: When they enlisted, these young women were told that they would be assigned duties commensurate with their training and experience. But, having been sworn into the army, they were assigned the traditional, stereotyped occupation of the Negro as a carrier of slops and a scrubber of floors. As ethical beings they rebelled. They refused to go back to work.

Now, I will grant you that these young women had a fair trial according to the rules. You cannot strike in the army. It is illegal. On the purely technical and legal grounds on which the case was tried, they had no case. The court was concerned only with the legality, not the morality of the case.

But we here—*we* look beyond the technically legal. We examine the *ethics* of the case. We search for the grievances which produced this insubordination. And the answer is that the army of the United States is honeycombed with prejudice, and no moral being can tolerate that. No army can ignore morals and keep up morale. So it was with reason that these young women broke the rules. Their action was a refusal to further countenance an insult. If they are rebels against law and order—or what passes for law and order—so were Washington and Jefferson and Madison and the members of the Boston Tea Party.

"I will take death," said Private Johnnie Mae Malone. Is this not what every American boy, Negro or white, who faces a German bullet is saying today? "We will take death rather than acknowledge that Nazis are the masters and we are the slaves." The days of white supremacy—which is no different from the Nazi race doctrine which we now fight—are numbered.

Now the rest of us must do our part. We have been too afraid heretofore. We play safe; we give in to segregation, and sometimes even segregate ourselves because we do not want to be insulted. But somebody must make the test. These young women—hardly out of their teens—were willing to die. What are *we* prepared to do? The world belongs to men and women of pioneer spirit; men and women not afraid to risk something to advance the cause of their people. Only *they* know the joy of rising again with a great resurrection.

SCENE 34

[ELEANOR ROOSEVELT *enters the scene with* RAINEY. *She hands him a cup. This should not be a flat-out impersonation. Some theatrical device should suggest that the actress represents Mrs. Roosevelt short of a full physical transformation.*]

ROOSEVELT: Mr. Rainey, you're from Boston, and I'm serving you tea. That seems appropriate.

RAINEY: Thank you, Mrs. Roosevelt.

ROOSEVELT: I suppose, in some sense, this is my fault.

RAINEY: Ma'am?

ROOSEVELT: I pushed for the WACs to be created. And then I pushed the WACs to recruit Negroes.

RAINEY: Do you regret doing either?

ROOSEVELT: I regret that those young women are behind bars.

RAINEY: We hope you might be able to do something about that.

[*A beat.*]

ROOSEVELT: I am looking forward to the time when I will be irrelevant in these matters.

RAINEY: I don't think you will *ever* be irrelevant, Mrs. Roosevelt.

ROOSEVELT: I appreciate that I am in a position to be helpful, but nobody should have to appeal to someone like me to get what should be theirs by right. You and your young ladies have made quite a splash in the newspapers. That was quite a picture you painted of Colonel Kimball.

RAINEY: In the Negro press.

ROOSEVELT: There have been stories in the white press, too. Perhaps not as large or as sympathetic, but I suspect enough to worry the top brass.

RAINEY: They don't seem to be worried enough to take any action.

ROOSEVELT: My sense of it is that just a little more pressure applied in the right place might break the back of this particular camel. Let's see—whose day can I make a little brighter with a phone call? Ah, yes, I know.

[*She picks up a phone.*]

Would you please connect me to the secretary of war.

SCENE 35

[GINNY *and* JOHNNIE MAE *in restriction.* RAINEY *enters carrying briefcase.*]

RAINEY: The secretary of war has reviewed the case. He's discovered that you were court-martialed under the authority of General Miles.

GINNY: Yes?

RAINEY: Well, since you were being tried for disobeying the general's order, he was technically on the side of the prosecution. Rules are, you can't have authority over a case when you're on one side or the other.

GINNY: And?

RAINEY [*taking a paper out of his briefcase and reading*]: "It is the opinion of this office that the record of trial is legally insufficient and it is recommended that the findings and sentence as to the accused be vacated, set aside, and declared to be null and void and of no effect." They've tossed out your conviction.

JOHNNIE MAE: Are we gonna have to go through another trial?

RAINEY: No, that's it. It's over. They don't want another one.

GINNY [*the light dawning*]: They don't want the publicity.

RAINEY: Let's say they're aware that Mrs. Roosevelt took an interest.

JOHNNIE MAE: She really knows who we are?

RAINEY: She asked me to tell you she admires your gumption.

JOHNNIE MAE: Gumption?

RAINEY: That was the word.

GINNY: Let me understand something. If we had been tried under somebody else's authority—under a different general, say—we probably would still have been convicted.

RAINEY: Probably.

GINNY: But since that would have been according to the rules, we'd have to serve out a year.

RAINEY: Yes.

GINNY: So we're being freed because the army goofed. Because of a technicality.

RAINEY: Yes.

GINNY: Not because we're right.

RAINEY: Maybe they looked for the technicality *because* you're right. You know, you might try to be a *little* happy you're not going to stay in jail.

GINNY: I am. I *think* I am. No, I am. Thank you, Mr. Rainey.

SCENE 36

[GINNY *and* JOHNNIE MAE *pick up their duffels and walk out into daylight.*]

JOHNNIE MAE: I'm really looking forward to meeting up with the colonel again. Can you imagine what he has in store for us?

[GINNY *and* JOHNNIE MAE *report to* STONEY *and* LAWSON.]

LAWSON: Something you two might be interested in knowing.

[KIMBALL *steps downstage into a solo light, facing downstage.*]

You remember the colonel saying that if he was given an order by a superior officer, he would obey it?

GINNY: Yes.

LAWSON: He had a meeting with a superior officer. That superior officer says, "Colonel Kimball?"

[*It should be clear that* LAWSON *is playing a general speaking the lines in* quotation marks.]

KIMBALL: General?

LAWSON: "What do you think about fishing?"

KIMBALL: Fishing?

LAWSON: "You know—bait, hook, water. Hours spent in contemplation of nature. You're from Maine, aren't you?"

KIMBALL: Yes.

LAWSON: "Some good fishing in Maine. Might be a nice hobby to take up."

KIMBALL: Well, maybe when the war is over.

LAWSON: "The war is over. Anyway, *your* war is over. I'm sure your staff will throw you one helluva retirement party."

KIMBALL: Retirement?

LAWSON: "Retirement. I hope you'll take satisfaction in how much good work you did at Devens. First-rate organizational skills. Be proud."

KIMBALL: Wait a second. Is this because—because of those girls?

[LAWSON *doesn't reply.* KIMBALL *starts to bluster.*]

Do you know what a small part of the fort they are?

LAWSON [*in her own voice*]: Barely a speck on your wall.

KIMBALL: And I'm out because of them?

LAWSON [*back imitating a general*]: "Ain't that a kick in the ass?" [*To* GINNY, *in her own voice*] Anyhow, that's the way I was told. I'd like to think it's true.

GINNY: Well, ma'am, I guess sometimes the army gets it right.

[*A beat.* KIMBALL *exits.* LAWSON *salutes and exits, leaving* GINNY *and* JOHNNIE MAE *with* STONEY.]

STONEY: You will return to your old barracks.

GINNY AND JOHNNIE MAE: Yes, ma'am.

STONEY: Something you might consider. A number of new opportunities have opened up here at Fort Devens.

GINNY: New opportunities, ma'am?

STONEY: In the hospital, in the motor pool, and in several other departments. Training programs not previously open to our unit.

JOHNNIE MAE [*with attitude*]: To us black girls?

[STONEY *decides not to respond to* JOHNNIE MAE's *sarcasm.*]

STONEY: After you've settled back in, we'll review the options.

[STONEY *salutes.* GINNY *and* JOHNNIE MAE *begin to move off.*]

Private Boyd, if I can have a minute—

[GINNY *and* JOHNNIE MAE *exchange looks.* GINNY *nods and* JOHNNIE MAE *leaves* GINNY *alone with* STONEY.]

GINNY: Ma'am?

STONEY: Something I want to . . .

GINNY: Ma'am?

STONEY: I still don't think you should have walked out. I still can't agree with that.

GINNY: I know, ma'am.

STONEY: But I can't deny . . . what's happened. How it's turned out. That if it weren't for you and Johnnie Mae, what the two of you did . . .

GINNY: Ma'am, nobody could know it would turn out like this. I sure didn't. And Johnnie Mae? I'd be surprised if she checks there's water in a pool before she dives.

[*A beat.*]

STONEY [*with difficulty*]: Mr. Rainey trying to make me say I lost control in uniform. Here I'm an officer, and it all comes down to is did I have tears in my eyes.

GINNY: Honestly, I think it was more about the colonel than anything reflecting on you. I can't see how anybody watching you in that room could have any doubt about what you're made of. And I do know that if you hadn't testified the way you did—said what you said about the colonel in front of all those people, the newspapers—I wouldn't be standing here right now.

[*A beat.*]

STONEY: Thank you.

GINNY: So what do we do now . . . ma'am?

[*A beat and the lights dim.*]

NOTES

The main events in this play are true. I have altered and condensed a few things both for dramatic purposes and out of regard for the limitations of the records.

In reality, there were four defendants. Virginia Boyd is based on Alice Young. Johnnie Mae Malone is based on Johnnie Mae Murphy. The other two defendants were Mary E. Green and Anna G. (Collins) Morrison. I would have very much liked to use their real names in this script by way of paying tribute to them, but, despite research (including hiring a private investigator), I could find out almost nothing of their lives before or after the court-martial. I don't know, for instance, if Alice Young's parents were alive when she joined the army. Rather than represent real people as something other than who they may have been, I give them new names so as to have license to embellish a little. In this, I am following the example of Jerome Lawrence and Robert E. Lee when they fashioned *Inherit the Wind* out of a well-known case but turned Clarence Darrow and William Jennings Bryant into Henry Drummond and Matthew Harrison Brady. (Truth to tell, I hew to the record more closely than Lawrence and Lee did in their classic.)

Tenola Stoney is the real name of the black lieutenant who served over the four WACs who were court-martialed. Again, despite best efforts, I haven't been able to find information about her other than her actions at Fort Devens. Since I deal with nothing of her background in this play, I feel a bit more comfortable using her real name and writing dialogue that falls within the range of the plausible (given what I learned of her character through her testimony).

Julian Rainey was indeed the Boston attorney who defended the WACs, and my research of the records of the NAACP in the Library of Congress revealed the conflict between him and J. D. Steele about taking the case. Kenneth Hughes was who I represent him to be, and the sermon in the script is a condensation of the sermon he actually gave. (During a trip to Boston, I found the church in which he gave the sermon quoted and the home in Cambridge in which he lived. I happened to run into a neighbor who remembered meeting Hughes when he was a child. From what I gather, Hughes was a heroic figure in the Boston area for decades.) Incidentally, Steele did not run again for the presidency of the Boston chapter of the NAACP; he was succeeded to that office by Hughes.

Colonel Evan Kimball is based on the colonel who was commanding officer at the Fort Devens hospital at the time. Most of the things I have Kimball doing and saying come out of the record. Since I don't have any notes on the way the army actually "retired" him, I decided to change his name for this. But the story of him refusing to allow a "mixed" band to play on the base is true, as is the substance of his confrontation with the WACs that started the strike. General Miles, Captain Edwards, and Major Leon McCarthy said and did what I depict them doing in this script. I don't know if Eleanor Roosevelt had a face-to-face meeting with Rainey, but she did know him and she did contact the secretary of war with the results I relate.

Regarding the court-martial: I have assumed the dramatist's prerogative to condense and shape some of the transcript, but the facts and testimony are accurate to the record. Some of the passages in Stoney's testimony (including, "First I got mad, and then I got right" and the remark that she allowed no tears to roll down her face) are straight from the record. The summations by Rainey and McCarthy again have been shaped a little, but in substance are accurate representations of what those men said.

Part of the pleasure of undertaking this project is to make known the story of some remarkable women who, despite their lack of power, had the stuff to stand up to and prevail a good ten years before Rosa Parks made her stand. People are accustomed to referring to Rosa Parks as someone who was the "first." One of the reasons I tell this story is to draw attention to the fact that sometimes there are people who come before the first.